Liang-Jie Zhang
Jia Zhang
Hong Cai

Services Computing

Liang-Jie Zhang
Jia Zhang
Hong Cai

Services Computing

With 218 figures

TSINGHUA UNIVERSITY PRESS

Springer

Liang-Jie Zhang
Ph.D., Research Staff Member
IBM T.J. Watson Research Center
19 Skyline Drive, Hawthorne,
NY 10532, USA
Email: zhanglj@us.ibm.com
http://www.research.ibm.com/people/z/zhanglj8

Jia Zhang
Ph.D., Assistant Professor
Department of Computer Science
Northern Illinois University
DeKalb, IL 60115, USA
Email: jiazhang@cs.niu.edu
http://www.cs.niu.edu/~jiazhang

Hong Cai
Ph.D., Research Staff Member
Services Research
IBM China Research Lab
Zhongguancun Software Park
Haidian District
Beijing 100094, P.R. China
Email: caihong@cn.ibm.com

ISBN 978-7-302-15075-6 **Tsinghua University Press, Beijing**
ISBN 978-3-540-38281-2 **Springer Berlin Heidelberg New York**

Library of Congress Control Number: 2007930066

Co-published by Tsinghua University Press, Beijing and Springer-Verlag GmbH Berlin Heidelberg

Springer is a part of Springer Science+Business Media
springer.com

Cover design: Frido Steinen-Broo, EStudio Calamar, Spain
Printed on acid-free paper

Preface

Services Computing has become a cross-discipline subject that covers the science and technology of bridging the gap between Business Services and IT Services. Its most recent enabling technology is Web services centered on Service-Oriented Architecture (SOA). This book depicts an overall picture of the state-of-the-art of the field. A comprehensive set of innovative research results and solution methods is described and discussed, including business componentization, services modeling, services creation, services realization, services annotation, services deployment, services discovery, services composition, services delivery, service-to-service collaboration, services monitoring, services optimization, services management, business consulting methodology and utilities, business process modeling, transformation, integration, and management.

What Is the Uniqueness of This Book?

This book introduces innovative ideas and solutions based on existing key techniques and industry standards in the field of Services Computing. In particular, this book illustrates Services Computing as an emerging interdisciplinary science and engineering subject bridging the gap between business/application services and IT services. It presents a lifecycle view of modern services industry, discusses up-to-date innovative research directions and industry solutions in the domain of Services Computing. It explains how to effectively and efficiently establish, operate, and manage business and application services using Services Computing, and it also guides research directions of Services Computing.

There have been numerous publications in the market regarding Web services and Service-Oriented Architecture from specifications and standards perspectives. To our knowledge, however, this book is the first that provides a systematic view of SOA solutions and SOA services to enable the lifecycle of modernized services businesses and applications. In our view, Services Computing is not merely a technical direction;

instead, it is an interdisciplinary area aiming to bridge the gap between IT and business. Therefore, it is not only necessary, but also critical to consider Services Computing from strategic point of view. Moreover, Service-Oriented Computing is just a pure technology fraction of Services Computing that also includes services consulting methodologies, services design and service delivery, as well as services maintenance and management.

As for implementation, there have emerged a number of industry standards and specifications for Web services, such as Web Services Description Language (WSDL), Simple Object Access Protocol (SOAP), Universal Description, Discovery, and Integration (UDDI), Business Process Execution Language for Web Services (BPEL4WS). However, from our point of view, these existing specifications are just examples of infrastructure enabling technologies for Services Computing environment. With the development of Services Computing, these specifications and technologies will continuously be evolving into their next generation or be replaced by new technologies and standards.

Throughout this book, instead of repeating the existing specifications, we concentrate on introducing innovative frameworks and methods on how to leverage related technologies to address real business challenges. The existing technologies are used as examples to study the state-of-the-art of the field and can be used as starting points for further innovations. Along with the newly introduced ideas in this book, the present enabling technologies provide a comprehensive framework that can be used to construct domain-specific SOA solutions. It should be noted that the existing technologies may have to be adjusted, extended, and customized in accordance with particular execution contexts and business requirements.

Finally, this is a foresighted book intended to spur researchers, practitioners, and students into further explorations and investigations in the field of Services Computing. As SOA and services engineering become mainstream, there are numerous efforts underway in both academia and industry, all of which deliver concepts and technologies in the same or similar fashion. This book aims to guide readers to grasp the foundations and state-of-the-art developments in the field of Services Computing.

Who Should Read This Book?

Researchers and students

The audience first includes researchers, graduate students, and senior undergraduates who seek a systemic introduction to the key technologies and research innovations in the field of Services Computing. This book can be used as an introductory textbook, advanced undergraduate textbook, graduate textbook, continuing education textbook (e.g., for executive MBA), or supplemental reading materials in classrooms.

In addition, this book can be used as a reference book on advanced technologies for a set of existing courses such as Modern Software Engineering, Web Engineering,

Web Technologies, Advanced Software Engineering Methodologies, Advanced Software Architecture, and so on. Targeting departments include Department of Computer Science, Department of Industrial Engineering, Department of Business Management, Department of Automation, and Department of Management of Information System.

This book is organized in a way that is suitable for students to learn the Services Computing concepts and technologies step by step. It is written in a way that it can be used as a classroom textbook, as well as a self-study reference book.

Engineers and managers

As Services Computing is being widely accepted by the business world, practitioners who are interested in building value-added services or solutions based on SOA will become suitable audiences. Companies that either develop software using SOA or intend to introduce SOA and Web services in business could use this book as a reference book for their software engineers, IT managers, business managers, salesmen, and IT and business executives.

Outline of This Book

Part 1: Foundations of Services Computing

This part introduces core techniques of Web services modeling, registry, and discovery. SOA paradigm is discussed, along with SOA solution architecture based on industry best practices. Current SOA and Web services standard stack is also presented. Advanced techniques are introduced including multi-dimensional services modeling, dynamic services invocation, federated services discovery, services relationship modeling, and solution-level Quality of Service (QoS) in SOA.

Part 2: Realization of Services Computing

This part introduces services realization technologies from four perspectives: requirements-driven services composition, services value chain collaboration, business process management and integration, as well as business grid.

Part 3: Services Delivery and Services Engineering

This part introduces technologies and methodologies for services delivery and engineering from four perspectives: project-based business performance management, service-oriented business consulting methodology, end-to-end services delivery platform and methodology, as well as software as services and services as software.

Acknowledgements

All the authors would like to acknowledge the invaluable cooperation of many collaborators who have been involved in the research projects in the past years. Those projects served as a basis for some research findings that underlie several of the ideas discussed in this book.

Liang-Jie (LJ) Zhang would like to send his sincere appreciation to Fausto Bernardini for his sturdy support and insightful directions. Special thanks also go to his management team: Robert Morris, Alain Azagury, Manoj Kumar, and David Cohn.

LJ would like to send special thanks to his previous collaborators in the past years: Henry Chang, Tian Chao, Jen-Yao Chung, Bing Li, Haifei Li, Yu Long, John Y. Sayah, Jing Min Xu, Shun Xiang Yang, Qun Zhou, and Ying Nan Zuo.

LJ would also like to appreciate his IBM SOA Solution Stack core team members for their insightful discussions: Ali Arsanjani, Abdul Allam, Kishore Channabasavaiah, and Michael Ellis. He would like to acknowledge the technical advice from Kerrie Holley, Ray Harishankar, George Galambos, and Shankar Kalyana during the past SOA projects, as well as valuable technical discussions with Sridhar Iyengar and Ed Kahan.

Finally, LJ would like to send his special thanks to Cesar A. Gonzales, Maria Azua, and Daniel Sturman for their invaluable encouragement and advice over the years.

Jia Zhang would like to send special thanks to Dr. Raimund K. Ege for his invaluable support.

The authors would also like to thank Annie Wang for helping proofreading the book.

Of course, our most profound thanks go to our families for their continuous love and encouragement.

To my wife, Qun, and my two daughters, Lan and Anna, with all my love.

Liang-Jie Zhang

To my dearest parents for their constant love and inspiration in my life.

Jia Zhang

I would like to express my sincere thanks to my dear wife Yi for her love and patience over the many evenings and weekends when I was completing this book and was unable to spend time with her and little daughter LuYi.

Hong Cai

Contents

Part 1 Foundations of Services Computing

Part 2 Realization of Services Computing

Part 1 Foundations of Services Computing

1 The Principle of Services and Services Computing

1.1 Introduction of Services

1.1.1 Definition of Services

The term "service" has existed for thousands of years along human history. When a person or a group performs some work to benefit another, it becomes a service. Many versions of definitions exist for the term "service". For example, James Fitzimmons[1] defines a service as follows:

> *"A service is a time-perishable, intangible experience performed for a customer acting in the role of co-producer."*

Christian Gronroos defines a service from the perspective of management and marketing as follows[2]:

> *"A service is an activity or series of activities of more or less intangible nature that normally, but not necessarily, take place in interactions between customer and service employees and/or physical resources or goods and/or systems of the service provider, which are provided as solutions to customer problems."*

Although these definitions look different, they all indicate a fact that each service involves two inevitable sides: service provider and service consumer. A service provider offers the service, and a service consumer utilizes the service. The interaction between a service consumer and a service provider may happen in real-time or off-line. Focusing on IT-enabled business services, this book defines the term "*services*" as follows:

> *Services represent a type of relationships-based interactions (activities) between at least one service provider and one service consumer to achieve a certain business goal or solution objective.*

A service provider commits to complete the tasks and provide values to a service consumer during the service's lifecycle. Both sides share a common goal of keeping a healthy, long-term trust with efficient and valuable services.

An IT-enabled business service is typically characterized by two features: its service operation model and its service charge model. A service operation model defines how the service is to be delivered; a service charge model specifies how the delivered service is to be charged.

Services can be realized in different ways, represented by corresponding service operation models. Traditionally, services are typically provided in an end-to-end service operation model, meaning that service providers deliver services directly to their end users (i.e., service consumers). Leveraging the recent Information Technologies, services can now be delivered in several novel approaches, such as hosted service model, business process outsourcing, data-centered outsourcing, and services through online broker agency. These approaches intend to enhance customers' service experiences and enhance service providers' productivity.

Based on different business models, services can be charged in different ways. In general, there are three categories of service charge model: free-of-charge models, fee-based models, and government service models. Adopting a free-of-charge model, a service provider offers free services. Nowadays, free services are common, such as free email services, free Voice over IP (VoIP) services, and free instant message services. Adopting a fee-based model, a service consumer needs to pay a pre-announced fee to use the service. For example, an online payment service charges transaction-based service fee. Between free services and fee-based services, there are public services provided by governments. They are free-of-charge to use; however, they are actually "paid" (funded) by citizens' tax money.

One service may be further divided into different service levels, each being associated with different service fees. A service consumer may choose to pay higher service fees to obtain higher-quality services with advanced capabilities, or pay lower fees to obtain services with less functionality. For example, a Web hosting service provider may provide three levels of services: gold Web plan, silver Web plan, and bronze Web plan. Each plan offers different storage space sizes and file transfer rates with different monthly charges.

1.1.2 Definition of Services System

Business services are realized by IT software systems, called services systems. This section defines a services system hosted by a service provider. As shown in Fig. 1.1, a services system can be viewed as a self-contained encapsulated system providing some services to the outside world. Such a services system shows as a feedback system, meaning that it possesses internal controls and reacts to surrounding environments. Therefore, a services system *SS* can be informally defined as a 6-tuple:

SS = *<Inputs, Outputs, Goals, Transformation, Components, Sensors>*, where: *Inputs* denote input information sent from service consumers, so that the services system can provide customized and personalized services. *Outputs* denote the output of the services system, i.e., the services to be offered. *Goals* denote the objectives of the system as a set of predefined system requirements. These goals

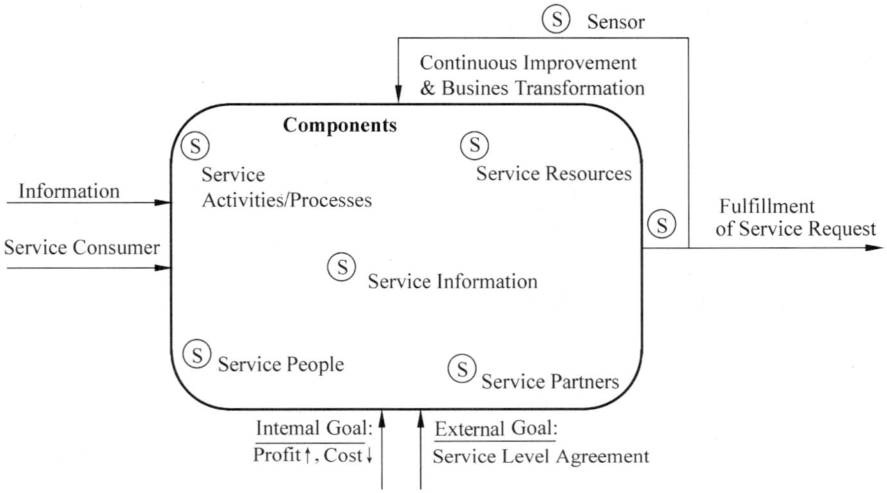

Figure 1.1 Feedback Control-based Services System

can be further divided into internal goals and external goals. Internal goals come from service providers who intend to increase their profits or decrease cost, for example. External goals come from service consumers who request certain levels of service quality. *Transformation* denotes the control or tuning activities applied to the system and its linkage with its interconnected services systems. A services system typically requires support from other services system; therefore, it needs to collaborate with other systems to fulfill the business goal. *Components* denote major elements of the services system, which will be discussed in detail later. *Sensors* denote the system elements that monitor and detect changes from surrounding environments (contexts), so that the services system can react accordingly to provide better services.

Same as a traditional software system, each services system has its proprietary lifecycle, from the time it is created until the time it is destroyed or discarded. During its lifecycle, the services system typically includes the following five major components:

Components = <*service people, service partners, service information, service activities, service infrastructure resources*>, where:

Service people denote the people involved in the lifecycle of the services system. These people typically act in different roles, such as system designer, system developer, and system tester. One person may act in different roles at different times or simultaneously. *Service partners* denote the business partners involved in the lifecycle of the system. *Service information* denotes the information exchanged and required in the lifecycle of the system. *Service activities* denote the activities or business processes conducted in the lifecycle of the system. *Service infrastructure resources* denote all non-people resources required for the system. Three categories can be identified: physical resources such as building offices, IT resources comprising hardware resources (e.g., servers and networks) and software resources (e.g., application servers and operating systems), and abstract resources (e.g., time).

In order to support such a comprehensive services system, innovative technologies and methodologies from cross-disciplinary subjects are required, such as computer science, management science, Information Technology (IT), organizational science, economics, and operational research.

1.2 Perspectives of Services Systems

With the definition of the services system, this section will discuss the essential perspectives internal of the services system. Figure 1.2 illustrates a coherent logical view of a services system, which comprises four major perspectives: model, technology, architecture, and optimization.

1.2.1 Model

Enablement of a services system should be guided by modeling and model-driven methodologies that help developers manage complexity at various levels of abstraction. A model is a "philosophy" of how to design a services system and its development process. Based on different phases during the lifecycle of a services system, various models may need to be adopted to guide the transformations between models (e.g., operational-level models, platform- independent models, and platform-specific models), codes, and other artifacts (e.g., business objects). These models typically define proprietary patterns, which formalize repeatable scenarios and provide tested solutions, to improve developer's productivity.

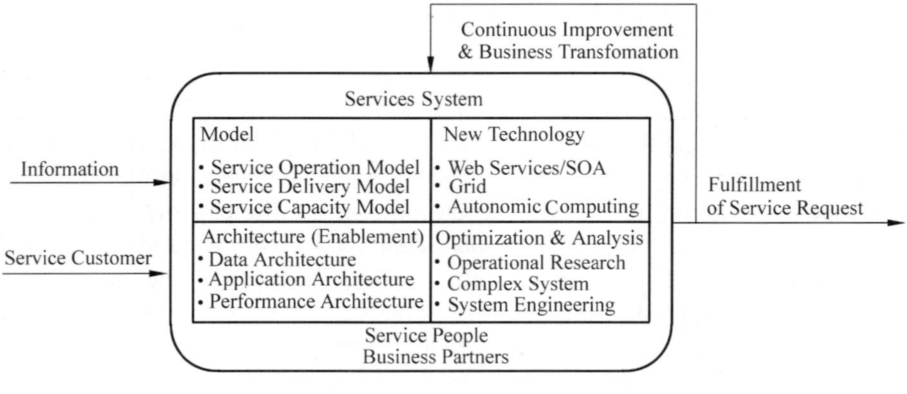

Figure 1.2 Enablement of services systems

1.2.2 Technology

The unique features of services and services systems demand corresponding IT support. The advancement of IT brings more opportunities for innovations. To date, several service-oriented technologies have emerged, such as Service-Oriented Architecture (SOA), Web services, Grid Computing, and Autonomic Computing. These technologies facilitate the construction of the services systems with higher reusability, flexibility, extensibility, and robustness.

1.2.3 Architecture

It has been well accepted that software architecture plays a key role in the design and development of a software system. A sound architectural model allows a software system to be adaptive to future changes. Similarly, software architecture is a critical aspect of a services system. It provides a guidance of designing and constructing a services system, by identifying system components along with the connections and interactions between them. It should be noted that the term "architecture" in Services Computing is not limited to IT architecture. Instead, since the tenet of Services Computing is to align IT with business in a service-oriented framework, the definition of the "architecture" becomes a manifold architectural model, including business architecture, IT architecture, data architecture, and performance architecture.

1.2.4 Optimization

In order to provide optimal services, a services system needs to be adaptive to ever-changing environments and business requirements. Optimization intends to select the best solution when facing multiple choices. This process may be needed during the entire lifecycle of a services system, and includes not only local optimization but also global optimization. Various related disciplines, such as operational research, complex system modeling, and system engineering, can be applied under different scenarios to facilitate the analysis and design of a services system.

1.3 Services Lifecycle

A typical service's lifecycle often consists of six key phases as shown in Fig. 1.3: consulting and strategic planning, services engagement, services delivery, services operation, services billing, and services management. Using a bookstore service as an example, this section briefly summarizes the activities within each phase.

In this example, a customer *C* invites a consulting service provider (*CSP*) and an IT service provider (*ITP*) to construct a set of bookstore branches locating at different places.

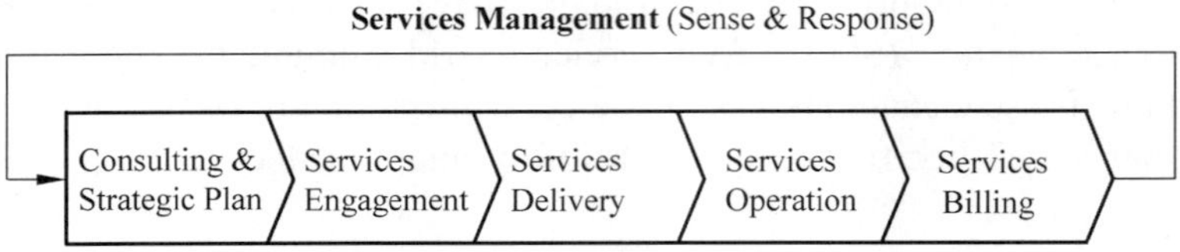

Figure 1.3 A services lifecycle

1.3.1 Phase 1: Consulting and Strategic Planning

The key activity in this phase is to invite third-party consulting companies to perform strategic planning. Using the bookstore example, in this phase, customer *C* invites *CSP* to analyze its potential position in the market together with an IT strategic plan for the next five years. At the end of the consulting phase, *CSP* helps *C* build a Request For Proposal (RFP).

1.3.2 Phase 2: Services Engagement

The key activities in this phase include: opportunity identification, RFP, negotiating service demands, forming the Statement of Work (SoW), and contracting. Using the bookstore example, in this phase, *C* distributes RFPs to multiple service providers to bid for the project; then *C* decides one service provider, say *ITP*.

1.3.3 Phase 3: Services Delivery

The key activities in this phase include: establishing service delivery teams and governing project management, solution creation, work breakdown, macro design, micro design, development and implementation, testing, and deployment. Using the bookstore example, in this phase, *ITP* establishes a project team and selects sub-service providers *ITP*1 and *ITP*2. *ITP*'s project team comprises a project executive, an IT architect, and some senior IT experts with rich knowledge in SOA solution creation. Based on the results from the consulting company and RFP, they decide to adopt the SOA infrastructure. Part of the work is decided to be outsourced to *ITP*1 and *ITP*2; the testing work is decided to be outsourced to *ITP*1.

1.3.4 Phase 4: Services Operation

The key activities in this phase include: call center (contact center) management, selecting tools for service operation, business and IT performance monitoring, change management and problem management, configuration management, and other IT service management functions. Using the bookstore example, in this phase, customer *C* decides to build a call center to improve customer experience. *C* may also decide to run the call center by himself/herself, and outsource other IT service management work to *ITP*.

1.3.5 Phase 5: Services Billing

In this phase, the service provider gathers payment based on the contracts with the customer. Using the bookstore example, in the service delivery case, *ITP* successfully completes the project for *C* by collaborating with *ITP*1 and *ITP*2. The contract will be closed, and *C* will pay *ITP* according to the contract. Besides the transaction-based payment for the completed project, *C* may sign a new outsourcing contract with *ITP* and decide to pay *ITP* the IT maintenance fee annually.

1.3.6 Phase 6: Services Management

Using the bookstore example, in this phase, since *ITP* is in charge of the solution creation and IT service management tasks, *ITP*1 could predict the traffic knowing that customer *C* wants to add a new service, and recommends that *C* increase IT resources for the new service.

1.4 Key Factors in a Services Lifecycle

Seven key factors need to be considered in a services lifecycle: data and information, processes, people, resources, finance factors, knowledge and skills, and innovation and technology.

1.4.1 Data/Information

The output of a business company is typically one of two things: either physical products/goods or business services, which can be fulfilled by manufacturing systems and services systems, respectively. The difference between a services system and a manufacturing system is that, a services system is a "soft" system in that it may not produce "hard" products/goods as a manufacturing system typically does; instead, it generates valuable information or manipulates information and service resources to benefit service consumers. When a customer requests a service, a business object (e.g., an order) is usually submitted; when a service provider wants to charge the customer, a bill is presented containing detailed billing information.

1.4.2 Processes

A services system is typically comprised of business processes to fulfill business objectives. A process usually contains a series of organized activities with regulated inputs and outputs, while chaining different roles together. The efficiency of a business process highly depends on core competency of related service providers. A process can also be further decomposed into sub-processes.

1.4.3 People

Business services typically require people involvement to leverage services, software, or other assets to deliver services to customers. Therefore, people are considered as one individual key factor in a services system. Two types of actors are identified: service customers and service consultants.

Service customers refer to the end users of a services system, whose demands need to be fully understood by corresponding service providers. They are logically considered as an integral part of a services system in that they may influence the status and operations of the system through interactions.

Service consultants refer to human beings from a service provider side who perform certain tasks. Compared with the role of human beings in a manufacturing system, service consultants are oftentimes called "human capital" because their knowledge and skills are critical to system efficiency in a services system.

1.4.4 Resources

Service execution typically needs to consume various types of resources: physical resources, IT resources, information resources, and abstract resources. Examples of physical resources are estates and offices; examples of IT resources are servers and storages; examples of information resources are databases; examples of abstract resources are time and knowledge.

1.4.5 Finance Factors

For both service consumers and service providers, cost and value are two dual factors which should always be taken into consideration. The objective is to best leverage resources available to service providers and generate the most return.

1.4.6 Knowledge and Skills

The degree of the ownership of knowledge and mastering of unique skills (e.g., IT operation) often differentiate a service provider from its competitors. In a service business unit, the employees should continuously be trained to master up-to-date knowledge.

1.4.7 Innovation and Technology

In the present fierce service competition, innovation and technology often decide the time to market. Those having the advanced technologies may have higher opportunity to win the service market by introducing new service products / packages or improving the operations of their services systems.

1.5 Comparisons Between Services and Manufacturing Models

The major differences between a services model and a manufacturing model root in their different outputs: services vs. goods, as described by Sasser[3]:

> *"A precise definition of goods and services should distinguish them on the basis of their attributes. A good is a tangible physical object or product that can be created and transferred; it has an existence over time and thus can be created and used later. A service is tangible and perishable. It is an occurrence or process that is created and used simultaneously or nearly simultaneously. While the consumer cannot retain the actual service after it is produced, the effort of service can be retained."*

A typical manufacturing model is shown in Fig. 1.4. In this model, the goal of manufacturing activities is to produce goods that fulfill common purposes. The products (goods) should satisfy some predefined specifications; however, goods themselves may not directly solve an end user's problem. As shown in Fig. 1.4, goods act as connections between the product provider and end users.

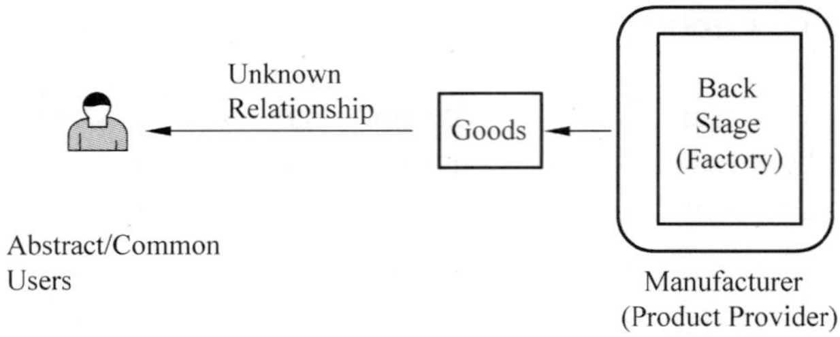

Figure 1.4 Manufacturing model

On the contrary, in the services field, a service provider and a service consumer have closer relationships in a services environment as shown in Fig. 1.5. A service provider's environment can often be divided into two parts: service front stage and service back stage. Interactions between the service provider and the service consumer often happen at the service front stage. The service provider intends to provide good service experiences to consumers to improve customer satisfaction and attract more customers, while keeping current customers' loyalty. Service front stage uses service desks to collect service requirements or other contents captured in pre-designed service forms to serve service consumers. Some key performance indicators include service execution time, efficiency, accuracy, and customer satisfaction.

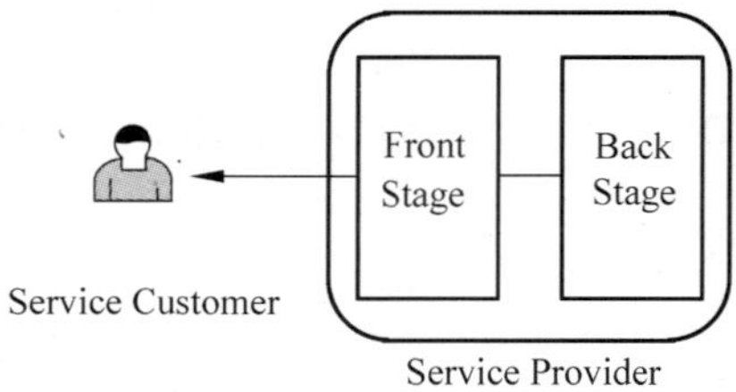

Figure 1.5 Model of services

At the back stage, the service provider uses factory models to seamlessly integrate sub-services to pursue high productivity. Typical activities happened at the service back stage include: making ready the service operation environment, allocating resource to fulfill service consumer requirements and avoid fraud, billing customers, running business intelligent analysis to further improve the service, and so on.

Meanwhile, from product lifecycle point of view, a service consumer may involve in all phases (pre-production, in-production, after-production), while a consumer of manufactured goods is mainly involved in the after-production phase only. In other words, a consumer of goods has little interaction with a goods provider in the goods' overall lifecycle, while a service consumer is usually fully involved in the service fulfillment process. This difference leads to highly different approaches when one tries to improve a manufacturing or services system.

Beyond those components mentioned above, new technologies could play important roles in enhancing a services system. Among other technologies, Service-Oriented Architecture (SOA), Business Process Integration and Management (BPIM) play critical roles for business transformation in recent years.

1.6 Business Services Lifecycle in Telecommunication Industry

Each company typically has many business function units: some provide direct services to customers; others provide back-office support. In an enhanced Telecommunication Operations Map (eTOM)[4] shown in Fig. 1.6 (with some changes based on services industry), key service components are highlighted in the dashed rectangle.

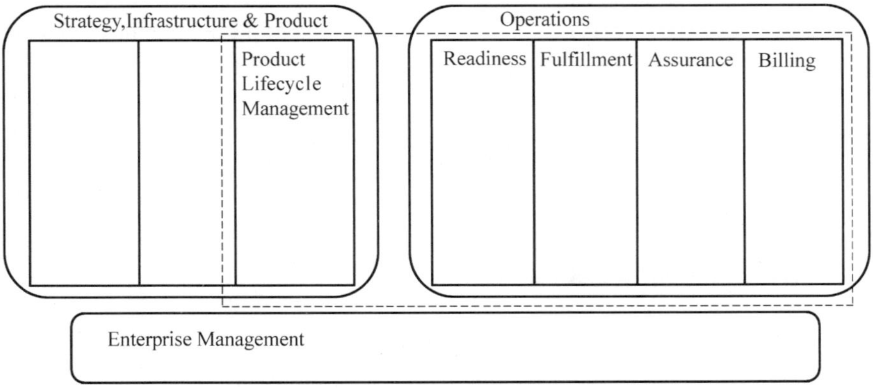

Figure 1.6 Typical service operation model in an enterprise

Figure 1.6 illustrates a typical view of the businesses units in a service-oriented company. As shown in Fig. 1.6, the components in an enterprise can be divided into three parts based on their objectives.

The first part includes strategies, infrastructures, and products. This part mainly solves the planning or strategy-related issues.

The second part comprises service operations related to daily activities. These operations can be divided into two categories: function-facing and people-facing. Function-facing operations include: service readiness, service fulfillment, service assurance, and service billing. People-facing operations can be further divided into four types: customer-facing (e.g., customer relationship management), internal worker-facing (e.g., service management and operation), physical and people resource-facing (e.g., resource management and operation), and partner and supplier-facing (e.g., supplier/partner relationship management).

The third part comprises enterprise management components that span the first part and the second part. This part covers most of the business administration works, such as strategic and enterprise planning, enterprise risk management, enterprise effectiveness management, knowledge and research management, financial and asset management, stakeholder and external relations management, and human resource management.

1.7 Relationship Between IT and Non-IT Services in a Services Ecosystem

The trend of the evolution of business ecosystems is that, businesses increasingly depend on IT technologies as a source of innovation and differentiation, while IT is moved to a higher level to align with business needs. In the past, IT people mainly focused on technology itself; at present, people have recognized that IT should be aligned with business in the whole service lifecycle. As a matter of fact, both the delivery of IT services and the enablement of IT to business changes require sound understanding of the principles of the uniqueness of IT services. This section will compare the lifecycle of an IT service with that of a known healthcare service. The goal is to identify their commonalities and illustrate why Services Computing is needed to build modern services industries.

1.7.1 Overview of a Services Ecosystem

A variety of service industries (a.k.a., vertical service) exist, such as aerospace and defense, automotive, banking, chemicals and petroleum, consumer products, education, electronics, energy and utilities, financial markets, government, healthcare, insurance, life sciences, media and entertainment, retail, wholesale distribution, telecommunications, and travel and transportation. All services can be divided into two basic categories: pure IT services (e.g., software as services) and IT-enabled services (e.g., Customer Relationship Management (CRM) services and some vertical services such as banking services, telecommunication services, automotive services, and chemicals services). However, no matter which category one service falls in, it shares some commonalities that are summarized in Fig. 1.7.

Figure 1.7 shows a high-level view of a simplified services ecosystem. A service consumer may enjoy services from different service industries simultaneously. Each of these services is typically constructed on top of some reusable cross-industry common services (a.k.a. horizontal services), which are in turn divided into two categories: common business services and common IT services.

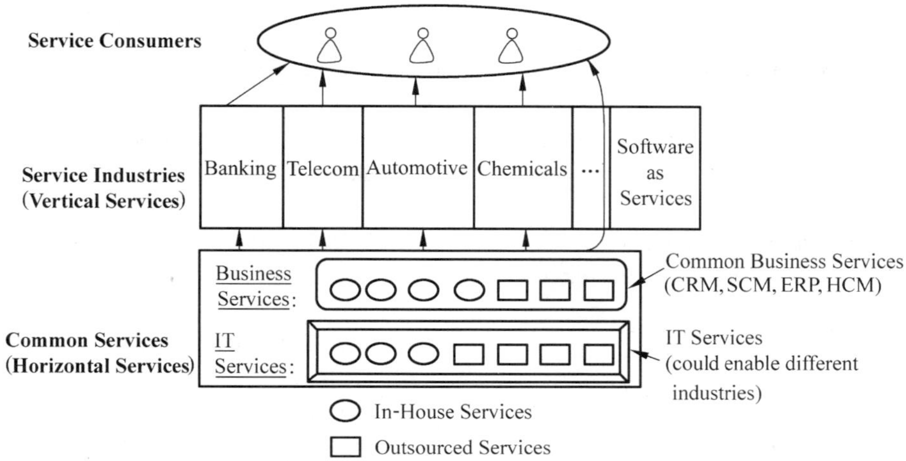

Figure 1.7 Overview of a services ecosystem

Common IT services refer to highly reusable IT-oriented supporting services, such as monitoring services, remote control services, and Web hosting services. Common business services refer to business logic-included supporting services, such as Customer Relationship Management (CRM), Supply Chain Management (SCM), Enterprise Resource Planning (ERP), and Human Capital Management (HCM). As shown in Fig. 1.7, the common services can be developed either in-house or through outsourcing. What a service consumer sees as one service may actually be provided by multiple service providers and service partners in an agreed-upon approach through a service value chain.

There exist significant differences between the two fundamental service categories. Healthcare industry is taken as an example from (vertical) IT-enabled service industry to be compared with a pure (horizontal) IT service.

1.7.2 Comparisons Between IT and Non-IT Services

Table 1.1 shows the comparisons of the features of a healthcare service lifecycle and an IT service lifecycle.

As shown in Table 1.1, both healthcare service and IT service share two major common features. The first commonality is that both services follow the same principle of a services lifecycle, which follows the order of services consulting, services engagement and services delivery, services operation and monitoring, and contracting and billing processes. The second commonality is that both services possess the same set of elements of a services system: people, resources, activities/processes, partners, and so on. Within a services lifecycle, it is required that all these elements collaborate to provide the services required by service consumers, and gather feedback information to continuously improve the services systems.

Table 1.1 Comparisons between a healthcare service lifecycle and an IT service lifecycle

A Healthcare Service Lifecycle	An IT Service Lifecycle
■ **Healthcare Service** **Objectives**: Health, Quick Treatment & Recovery	■ **IT Service** **Objectives**: Grow Business & Core Competency
■ **Service Environment:** Front (e.g., patient, doctor, pharmacist) Back (e.g., nurse, assay)	■ **Service Environment:** Front (e.g., customer, project manager, architect) Back (e.g., IT specialist)
Phases in the service lifecycle: ■ Healthcare Consulting – Shaping – ... ■ Diagnosis – Check – Watch – Ask... ■ Treatment – Surgery – Dose – Psychotherapy – Transplant ■ Clinical Support – Laboratory Information System – Radiology Information Systems – Pharmacy Information Systems – Blood Bank Information System ■ Visit back & Monitoring – Frequent visit back ■ Billing	**Phases in the service lifecycle:** ■ IT/Business Consulting Services – CRM, ERP, SCM, HCM – Insight: data collection ■ Services (Solutions) Delivery – Project management – Business component analysis – IT (cost) analysis, – Architecture design – Hardware (HW) configuration – Software (SW) development ■ Capability of Services Provisioning – People skill – HW/SW maturity – Number of experts – Assertion – Methodology and SSM / management ■ Services Operation (e.g. Data Center) – Design new architecture – IT change management – Education – IT enabled BTO/BPO ■ Service Quality Monitoring – Event-driven method... ■ Billing

Three major differences exist between these two types of services. First, they use different Key Performance Indicators (KPIs) as measurements. These KPIs are often owned by specific roles at a service provider side. For example, for a healthcare service, customer satisfaction is decided by whether its patients receive prompt services (e.g., query measured in hours), whether its doctors provide correct diagnosis (e.g., patients being cured in 2 – 3 days), and the time required for its clinical laboratories to provide correct data (e.g., 20 minutes for a simple check or 2 days for a complex check). While in an IT service, customer satisfaction is often decided by the success of a project (meaning whether it is completed on schedule, within budget, and meet the requirements).

Second, requirements managements in the two types of services are different. The requirements from the healthcare industry are typically mature and stable. The requirements from IT service consumers, on the other hand, often come from different stakeholders. Even worse, they often undergo significant changes, especially for those dynamic industries (e.g., telecommunication industry, banking industry, and electronic industry) or in those dynamic locations (e.g., developing countries).

Third, the paces of changes in the two types of services are different. The healthcare industry typically only needs to adapt to customers' infrequent changes of request. IT industries have to adapt to quick changes, not only coming from customers' changes of request but also coming from the advancement of IT technologies and IT services.

Because of these differences, a healthcare service may tolerate manual processes. However, an IT service can hardly bear processes that are not well integrated with other solution architectures, because they imply more efforts and cost for future changes thus lead to lower competitiveness.

1.8 Emergence of Services Computing Technology

The rise of Services Computing technology family intends to create, operate, manage and optimize these processes in a well-defined architecture for higher flexibility facing future business dynamics[5]. Therefore, it is time that we look inside the services to establish the foundation of Services science, technologies. Furthermore, the introduction of Services Computing into a traditional industry (e.g., the healthcare industry) may add new values and innovative functions and improve the internal and external integration of industry-specific applications. For example, the introduction of SOA may help integrating the diagnosis and prescription processes within a hospital and the medicine pick-up process within pharmacies, which can greatly simplify the medical treatment process for patients.

With the emergence of Service-Oriented Architecture and Web services technology, more companies have been exposing their business applications through well-defined interfaces in a platform-independent manner to increase the interoperability with partners' applications to streamline the whole business collaboration chain. As a result, IT infrastructure paradigm is shifting to service-oriented architecture. At the same time, the business models are also evolving to be component-based to achieve agile and on-demand business. In order to align with this trend in the IT industry, many initiatives have been formed. The formal creation of Services Computing discipline in 2003 is the very first step of this adjustment.

Services Computing covers various aspects of business and IT services. For business services, Services Computing covers: service-oriented business consulting methodology and utilities, business process modeling, transformation, integration, business performance management, and industry solution patterns. For IT services, Services Computing covers: application integration services, infrastructure services (e.g., utility business services, service-level automation and orchestration, and resource virtualization services), and IT-level autonomous system management services.

In summary, Services Computing, as an emerging cross-discipline, covers the science and technology of effectively creating and leveraging computing and information technology to model, create, operate, and manage business services. The core technology suite includes SOA and Web services, business process integration and business performance management, and services innovation methodologies.

IEEE Technical Committee on Services Computing[6] under Computer Society is a key community of promoting Services Computing paradigm. Rich resources can be found at the sites of Technical Committee on Services Computing in IEEE Computer Society and SOA/Web Services-related conferences, such as IEEE International Conference on Web Services (ICWS)[7] and IEEE International Conference on Services Computing (SCC)[8].

1.9 Summary

A services system significantly differentiates from a manufacturing system in their respective operation models, which require deep understanding of the characteristics of a services system and using Service-Oriented thinking. The goal of a services system is to provide efficient business services and align IT services with business services. A service lifecycle has many phases with different roles and requires different skills.

Because of the natural differences between a manufacturing system and a services system, there is more space to improve the quality of services system through technology innovation. IT services (components) and IT architectures are critical to enable IT resources to be best leveraged in services fulfillment process.

In the remaining parts of this book, different methods and technologies will be introduced, which can be leveraged to bridge the gap between business services and IT services.

References

[1] Fitzsimmons JA (2005) Service management: operations, strategy, information. 5th edn. McGraw-Hill/Irwin

[2] Gronroos C (2000) Service management and marketing: a customer relationship management approach. John Wiley & Sons

[3] Sasser WE (1978) Management of service operations: text, cases, and readings. Allyn and Bacon

[4] The Enhanced Telecom Operations Map (eTOM). http://www.tmforum.org/browse.aspx?catID = 1648

[5] Zhang LJ (2005) Services Computing: a new discipline. Editorial Preface. International Journal on Web Services Research (JWSR) 2(1)

[6] IEEE Services Computing Technical Committee. http://tab.computer.org/tcsc

[7] IEEE International Conference on Web Services (ICWS). http://conferences.computer.org/icws

[8] IEEE International Conference on Services Computing (SCC). http://conferences.computer.org/scc

2 e-Business Evolution

2.1 Phases of e-Business Adoption

Chapter 1 introduces and defines some basic concepts of Services Computing; this chapter will discuss the emergence and necessity of Services Computing in the context of Electronic Business (e-Business) evolution. Referring to enterprise-level business solutions and infrastructures over the Internet, e-Business has become a popular term with high exposure in the modern society. In retrospect, however, its original inception in the mid-nineties did not cause a sensation. Rather, as shown in Fig. 2.1, e-Business started as a common technical innovation aiming at supporting simple Internet browsing and interaction utilizing Hyper Text Transfer Protocol (HTTP). In order to enable global access, companies publish static information (e.g., business name, address, contact information, company history) on their Hypertext Markup Language (HTML) homepages on the Internet.

Enterprises did not stop at static information sharing; instead, they tried to explore the Internet as a new business medium to conduct business activities. Soon afterwards, online transactions emerged, such as online shopping, online auction, and online payment. These transaction-based catalog management and shopping carts applications are commonly referred to as Electronic Commerce (e-Commerce). At present, these e-Commerce activities have entered people's daily lives.

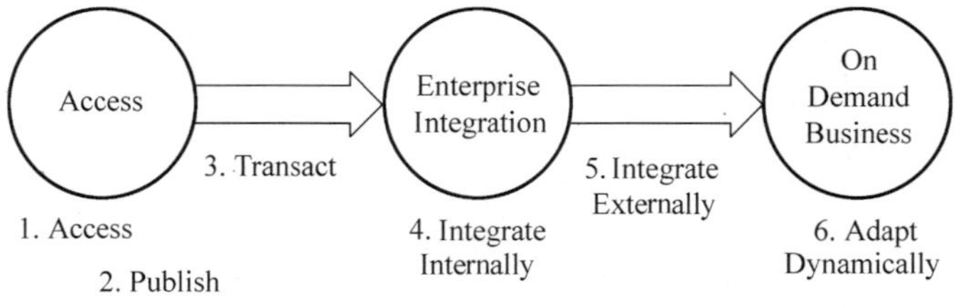

Figure 2.1 Evolution phases of e-Business adoption

Since the beginning of the 21st century, the advancement of e-Business has been catching significant attention from various occupations and society in general. The business world is now facing an electronic information revolution; thus, the term "e-Business" was coined to represent enterprise-level business transformation. In this information revolution, enterprise-internal information transformation has great importance in facilitating resource utilization and management effectively and efficiently. Meanwhile, inter-enterprise communications and interactions become inevitable. A modern enterprise can no longer stand alone; instead, it has to constantly interact with and rely on its interrelated enterprises, its suppliers, and its clients, thus establishing a functioning enterprise-level service chain. This level of e-Business is called enterprise conformity. After these enterprises are synergistically integrated with each other, their mutual interdependencies become tremendous. To ensure that this sophisticated enterprise service chain adapts itself with stochastic adjustments, when the market fluctuates, remains a big challenge. As a matter of fact, this "self-adaptable e-Business" or "on-demand business" represents the highest level of e-Business.

Figure 2.2 gives a snapshot of an on-demand business model. Assume that a user discovers an interesting merchandise from an online search engine, then clicks the associated link to connect to the corresponding supplier. After filling a purchase order with payment information (e.g., credit card number, name shown on the card, and expiration date), the user sends the request to the supplier. The supplier then dynamically connects to the corresponding payment service provider (e.g., the credit card company) to perform a real-time transaction and acknowledges the customer. After the payment is conducted, the supplier interacts with available shipping service providers to arrange a timely shipment to the user. This simple example shows that the modern business models require seamless runtime interaction and collaboration among suppliers, partners, and customers on an on-demand basis.

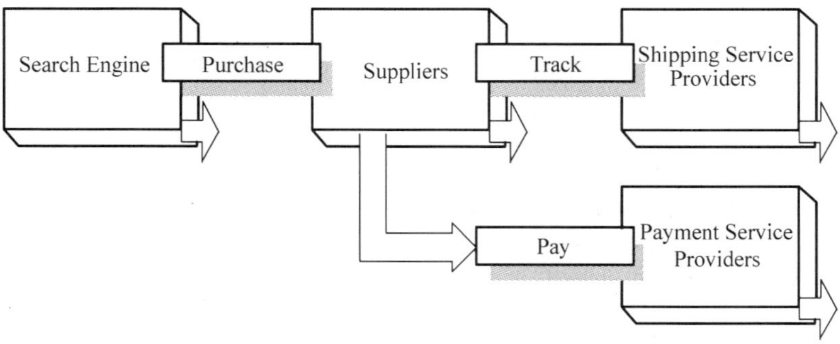

Figure 2.2 An e-Business snapshot

To date there has been no uniformly accepted explanation for the highest boundary of e-Business. However, although this term may have various notations with different enterprises, there exist some commonly accepted criteria and views denoting the ultimate phase of e-Business. First, throughout the whole lifecycle of an enterprise, its enterprise service chain must adapt with random changes according to market changes. Second, the power of adjustment comes from both internal and external sources to meet market demand. Third, the adaptation should be achieved based on advanced information technologies, software architectures, and business management experiences. IBM defines an *On-Demand*

Business as follows[1]:

> *"**An On-Demand Business** is an unprecedented enterprise whose business processes—integrated end-to-end across the company and with key partners, suppliers and customers—can respond with flexibility and speed to customer demand, market opportunity or external threat."*

Many major industry companies have realized the paramount importance of On-Demand Business. Samuel J. Palmisano, the CEO of IBM, delivered a message to the *Business Week*, "*On-Demand Business is our way of describing a fundamental shift in computing architecture and how it is applied to business—a shift toward integrated solutions and quantifiable business value, not just technology features and functions.*"

2.2 Top Trends of e-Business

It has been more than ten years since the inception of e-Business, which has caused tremendous changes in the world. As a matter of fact, along with the emergence and rapid development of Internet technology, nowadays most business companies have close relationships with e-Business, though they may not always acknowledge the fact or they may not even realize it. In general, e-Business covers any service, transaction, and management conducted on the network. Different designs and implementations of these electronic activities engender various business models, leading to the existence of various enterprises.

What direction is e-Business heading to? What demands more attention and momentum? The rest of the chapter will discuss the top trends of e-Business in the following four categories:

- IT innovations to flatten the world;
- "Open" trends for technologies and services ecosystem;
- Debuts of new services-oriented business models;
- The discipline: Services Computing.

2.3 IT Innovations to Flatten the World

The current IT innovations[2] intend to flatten the world through the following three major directions: interactive multimedia services, office online services, and globalization of businesses.

2.3.1 Interactive Multimedia Services

Ubiquitous interactive multimedia provisioning of communication is worth anticipating. Underlying are three key technologies: Voice over IP (VoIP), interactive digital TV, and wireless broadband.

Also known as Internet Voice Telephony, VoIP allows telephone calls using a broadband Internet connection instead of traditional analog phone lines. VoIP first converts voice signals from a voice device into digital signals, propagates them over the Internet, then converts the digital signals back to voice signals at the recipient end. As shown in Fig. 2.3, after connecting a computer to the Internet, one can make phone calls to local computers, local land phones, local mobile phones, and other computers or phones in long distance or even across the world. Meanwhile, one can also receive calls from regular land phones or cell phones by sitting in front of a computer connected to the Internet. Telecommunication technology intends to enable universal, cost-effective, and superior-quality voice calls via its next-generation peer-to-peer protocols. With VoIP phones, one can enjoy reliable and high-quality voice calls via the Internet. In short, VoIP technolgy has been attracting so much public attention. In 2005, eBay acquired Skype[3], a world leading VoIP-based telephony company, for $4 billion.

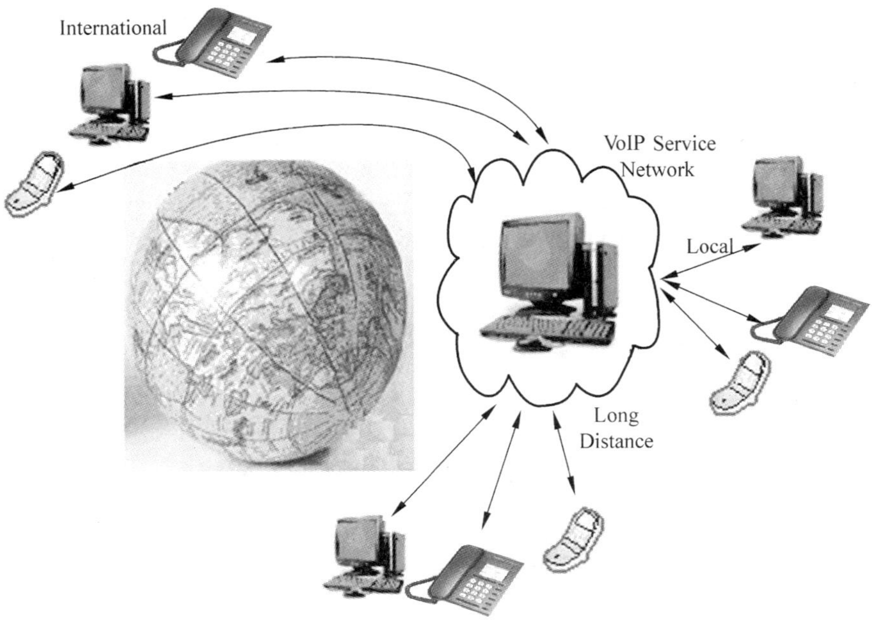

Figure 2.3 VoIP services

Interactive digital TV, or Internet Protocol TV (IPTV), intends to deliver high-quality video streams, either live or recorded, synchronized with Web contents. Figure 2.4 shows an example of such a video-on-demand IPTV screen layout. The basic idea is to extend the well-known hyperlink concept from ordinary texts and images to objects in motion[4]. As shown in Fig. 2.4 hyperlinks are embedded into moving objects in digital video streams. When watching television, one can track any interested moving object and check its related information on the Internet simultaneously. For example, in Fig. 2.4, if one clicks on *Object* 1 shown on the right screen, the system underneath the IPTV will go to the Internet and search for the sales information of *Object* 1. Assume that a corresponding seller is found from an online virtual mall. Then the related information of *Object* 1 at the seller will be shown on the left screen, such as product description and the contact information of the company. In other words, IPTV brings forth significant business opportunities. Such an e-Business application can either support real-time transmission or provide a downloadable version.

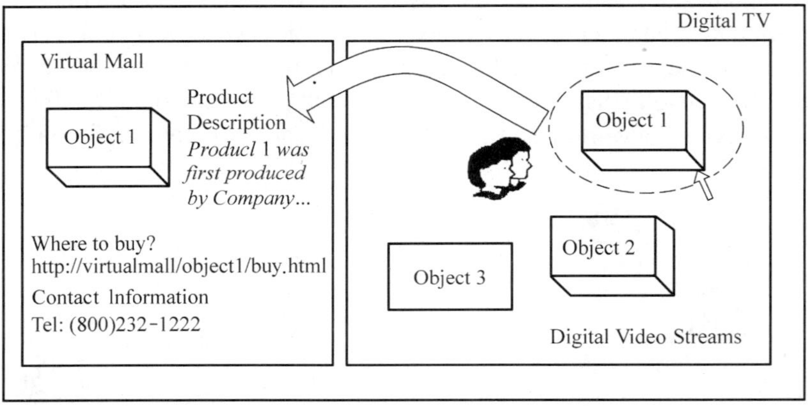

Figure 2.4 Interactive digital TV Service

Wireless broadband technology aims to enable mobile customers to access high-speed Internet from anywhere at any time. Currently, two major types of phones are selected as examples in this book. One is the Third Generation (3G) phone and the other is the Wi-Fi phone. The 3G technology intends to leverage the most advanced mobile communication technology to transmit multimedia information, such as image, video, audio, and instant message. As a matter of fact, many 3G wireless phones have already been produced. 3G phone is able to receive many television programs through digital signals. Wi-Fi technology, also known as IEEE 802.11, is a term coined by the Wireless Ethernet Compatibility Alliance (WECA)[5]. Wireless phones certified as Wi-Fi by WECA have unprecedented power, so that they can be used anywhere in a wireless network environment. Meanwhile, Wi-Fi certified products are interoperable with each other even if they are from different manufacturers. A user with a Wi-Fi product can use any brand of Access Point with any other brand of client hardware as long as it is built conforming to the Wi-Fi standard. The reason why Wi-Fi phones are not yet popular is that the present wireless network is not stable enough.

SOA has led to the emergence of converged network, a term representing a common network[6] that seamlessly connects mobile and fixed networks based on the key telecommunication technologies. The Parlay Group[7] has been formed as a consortium to develop open technology-independent Application Programming Interfaces (APIs) that enable the development of applications operating across converged networks. The organization has developed Parlay X standards which simulate a set of Web services interfaces for general telecom capabilities. The standards exploit lower-level network services provided by both telecommunication service providers and higher-level service network services provided by Web-based applications. Conforming to the Parlay X standards, portable network-independent applications can be developed to connect the IT and telecommunication worlds.

2.3.2 Office Online Services

The second trend of e-Business is to move office online. As modern business demands flexible mobility, it is almost impossible to require that one person keep everything needed on personal computer during a trip. Moreover, this kind of information may include various categories of data, ranging from personal emails to a variety of business data. Regarding emails, one may expect to be able to check multiple email accounts from anywhere with Internet access. Regarding to business data, a business manager may need to dynamically monitor the operation of a company, including resource distribution as well as sales achievements. This universal office model is in fact a novel business model, as many corporations are moving towards this direction.

Figure 2.5 shows an online office screen for consulting manager John Smith. He can conduct his everyday business work on this portal from anywhere he has Internet access. For example, he can continue his work while he is waiting at an airport. As shown in Fig. 2.5, this online office allows him to check email, review and sign his consultants' weekly reports, manage business accounts, monitor consultant availability, overview client requests, and examine up-to-date consultant performance.

As Fig. 2.5 illustrates, this online office portal is personalized according to the user's (i.e., John Smith) profiles. His incoming emails are automatically organized into various folders: consultants, sales, clients, company, and personal. His managed consultants submit work reports on a weekly basis; the reports are automatically accumulated into corresponding folders by the week. Information about his managed clients is also organized into different folders. The online office portal also keeps John up to date with consultant availability. As shown by the left-hand screen on the lower row of Fig. 2.5, John can check the real-time information about every consultant's name, skill sets, status (i.e., on site of client or on bench), and the date of availability for new projects. For example,

Consultant #1 has expertise on Java; he is currently on site at Client #1; he will finish the current project and become available again on 5/1/2006. As shown by the middle screen on the lower row of Fig. 2.5, John can check the real-time information about client requests, their names, required skill sets, number of consultants, priorities, and required dates. For example, Client #1 requires one consultant with skill sets Java and C# to start from 5/1/2006. Finally, as shown by the right-hand screen on the lower row of Fig. 2.5, John can check the real-time information about consultant performances. For example, up to 4/6/2006, Consultant #1, with rank as Senior Consultant, has utilization of 80% and has written one paper to show thought leadership.

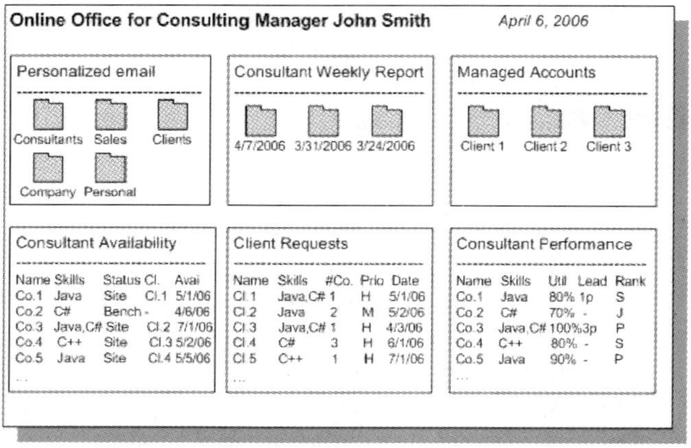

Figure 2.5 Online office

Office online also implies real-time collaboration. For example, multiple users (e.g., managers and partners) cooperate on editing a shared design document synchronously. Any proposed changes from a participant are distributed to all collaborators and shown on their screens. A mechanism is provided to allow the participants to vote for accepting or rejecting the changes.

2.3.3 Globalization of Businesses

The third trend is that businesses have unprecedented opportunities to grow globally, as shown in Fig. 2.6. These businesses have two directions. First is to utilize the outsourcing model[8]. A lot of new business patterns emerge through the outsourcing model in order to lower costs and boost profits quickly. Many small businesses often started in developing countries, such as China and India. For example, as illustrated in Fig. 2.6, a typical form is to found a small company in the US that cooperates with outsourcing companies in China and India with large number of employees.

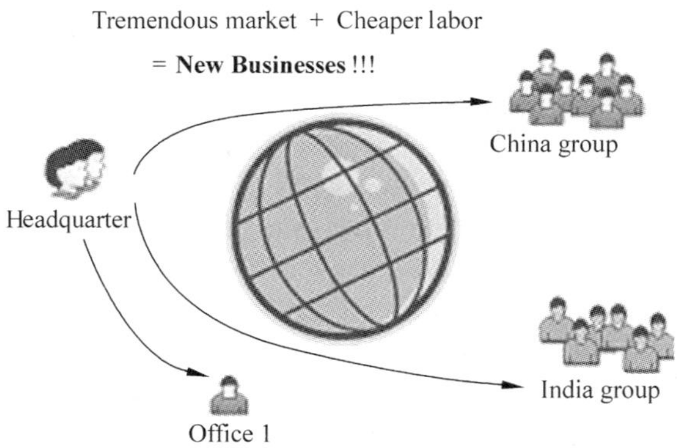

Figure 2.6 New global business model

Critical decisions and integrations are made at the headquarter, while most of the day-to-day business operations, such as software development and product manufacturing, are conducted by collaborative partners located in developing countries. These global businesses are further strengthened by localized "Silicon Valley" models with free competitions. The second direction is to target bigger overseas opportunities. A typical example is the tremendous cell phone overseas market in China—think about a market of over 1.3 billion people! A number of small telecommunication companies are founded to design, produce, and sell new types of cell phones oriented to the Chinese market.

In his best-selling book, *The World Is Flat: A Brief History of the Twenty-first Century*[9], Thomas L. Friedman analyzes the progress of globalization in the early twenty-first century. According to him, the world becomes "flattening". Individuals and businesses are empowered throughout the process of globalization, where accelerated changes are made possible by intersecting technological advances and social protocols, such as cell phones, the Internet, and open-source software.

To sum up, these businesses intend to utilize both the unexplored market potentials and the cheaper labor in developing countries. By positioning with optimized resource combinations, they are more likely to attract investors for further expansion. As a matter of fact, according to their rapid development trends, these global businesses can go public (i.e., IPO) or be bought by bigger companies after a few years.

2.4 "Open" Trends for Technologies and Services Ecosystems

From the technology perspective, an emerging "open" trend has been fundamentally changing the way of software design and development: open standards, open sources, and open architecture: Service-Oriented Architecture (SOA).

2.4.1 Open Standards

The fourth trend is to establish uniform open standards. The success of this direction has paramount importance to other trends. Open standards set up innovation agendas and higher starting points. For example, one may notice that modern railway systems all share the same gauge. This was not the case historically until the nineteenth century, when the United Kingdom and European countries formulated the standards for railway construction. With the same railway gauge standard, a train is able to travel between different railway systems developed by different railway construction companies. Afterwards, railroad rapidly became one of the major transportation methods. Furthermore, connected railroads further fueled their own growth and created new business opportunities. When these railroad networks and related services formed a tremendous transportation industry, their new distribution models fundamentally changed the marketplace and the way it operated. It is safe to say that the standardization of the railway network made industrialization possible in the America and Europe.

History has witnessed other technologies that bear the same effects, such as the electricity grid and national highway systems. Standards simplify the interaction rules and policies between enterprises and drive innovations; thus they can be transformed into business values. In the recent Internet era, Web services and a whole stack of industry-specific standards are significant examples of global standardization for Internet enterprises interoperation and intercommunication. At present, many countries and organizations are dedicated to the global standardization efforts, since it is easy to understand that if an organization or a country has authority on standardization of a technology or a field, its economy will be greatly influenced.

In short, open standards help in streamlining an industry and introduce a new platform for further innovation.

2.4.2 Open Sources

The open source initiative is another well-known trend. “Open source software” is software whose source code is made public for everyone to copy, modify or redistribute without paying fees under some predefined license terms. Typical open source initiatives are Linux, Eclipse[10], Apache[11], Mozilla[12], various projects hosted on SourceForge.net, and other open source Web sites.

The open source trend greatly encourages collaboration and competition. The open source revolution forms an open-source community including an ever-growing mass of software developers. If a software product is expensive, members from the open-source community may soon create similar software products with the same or similar functions but at a much cheaper price. Big companies have to face the challenge. For example, IBM has set up a strategy that intends to support open sources by donating some patents.

The open source initiatives lead us to stand on "shoulders of giants". A typical scenario is like the following: when a company needs to develop a software, instead of starting from scratch, the company searches and downloads open source software pieces first. Software developers then integrate new ideas and update the open source code to create a customized version. Numerous successful cases have proven the effectiveness and efficiency of this new software engineering pattern.

The open source model also allows individuals to show their value quickly. In the past, a person working in a big company may only be known if his/her code is integrated and announced in a product. With the open source approach, an individual may publish his/her innovative work on the Internet and obtain credits easily and quickly.

However, since the open source trend leads to a more complicated solution pool including open sources, third-party Independent Service Vendor (ISV) applications, and solutions from big vendors, how to integrate these solutions becomes a critical challenge.

2.4.3 Open Architecture: Service-Oriented Architecture (SOA)

The sixth trend is the Service-Oriented Architecture (SOA), which is currently a keyword in the software industry and Internet[13]:

> *"Service-Oriented Architecture (SOA) is a business-centric IT architectural approach that supports integrating your business as linked, repeatable business tasks, or services. SOA helps users build composite applications, which are applications that draw upon functionality from multiple sources within and beyond the enterprise to support horizontal business processes."*

SOA will be a central topic of the software industry during the decade of 2005 – 2015. Although SOA is a novel concept, from the technical perspective it is not really new. Instead, it is derived from *component engineering* and *distributed computing* and brings them to an extreme end. The building blocks of an SOA solution are not arbitrary components or distributed objects. Instead, an SOA solution is built on reusable services accessible from the Internet or services registries. Nevertheless, SOA turns into reality what we wanted to do but could not do in the last several decades. It enables the interoperability and integration of complex software systems in a standard way. In the past, an often-encountered problem was the inexistency of standards. At present, standards are being established. Using the open standards and open platforms, various software components (i.e., services) written in different languages can be seamlessly integrated, in order to realize resource sharing and achieve the maximum efficiency that is one of the ultimate goals of the software industry. In the next ten years, SOA, as an open architectural model, will act in more important roles and impact the design and development of every software product as well as business solutions of every organization.

As shown in Fig. 2.7, SOA is not merely a technical concept. Instead, it intends to bridge IT and business requirements. Modern flexible business demands flexible IT support. Consider a business in terms of various business components (e.g., departments), each requiring the synergistic operation of a set of optimized business processes, each in turn being implemented by IT resources. As business requirements are ever changing, supporting IT foundations need to bear corresponding flexibility. This is why SOA has been catching unprecedented attention and momentum from both academia and industry.

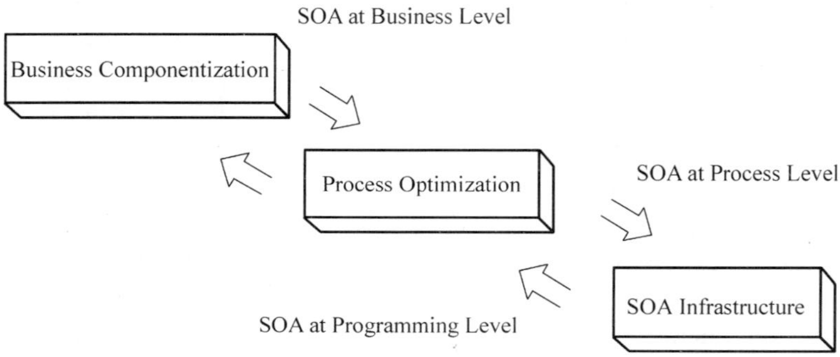

Figure 2.7 SOA at various business and IT levels

SOA can be used to guide activities at various levels. At the programming level, SOA can be used to guide low-level IT technologies, such as Simple Object Access Protocol (SOAP)[14], binary SOAP messaging for data transportation, and Service Component Architecture (SCA)[15]. From the middleware perspective, SOA can be used to guide design and development of common product and open-source software. For example, SOA can be utilized to help architects select from different models (e.g., single Enterprise Service Bus (ESB) or multiple ESBs, message-oriented or event-based infrastructures) according to different enterprise maturities. At the process level, SOA can be used to guide event-driven business process integration and management. At the enterprise level, SOA can be used to componentize an enterprise into reusable and configurable business components and support high-level enterprise transformation consultation. For example, SOA can help executives decide whether to implement a business process using an SOA service package or divide the workflow using the SOA concept.

Figure 2.7 also illustrates a bilateral view of how SOA realizes business and IT linkages. One is a top-down approach that further decomposes business components into business processes, each being realized by IT processes. The other one is a bottom-up approach that provides SOA-based IT resources, which can be seamlessly integrated to rapidly create new business processes that lead to new business opportunities.

In either top-down or bottom-up approaches, SOA offers essential guidance at various granularities: business level, process level, or middleware level / programming level. At each level, SOA guides to decompose a big unit into smaller service-centered units in the top-down method, and guides to aggregate available smaller units into larger units providing new services in the bottom-up method.

2.5 Debuts of New Service-Oriented Business Models

With the emergence of the open trends, business models are going through a transformation. New service-oriented business models are emerging, they are: services modernization, software as services, and services as software.

2.5.1 Services Modernization

The SOA model was originally proposed from software programming and development processes. In its recent years' growth, the SOA concept is no longer limited as a software architectural model for software development; instead, it has been extended as a guidance to help better manage business processes and enterprises. In more detail, SOA guides to prioritize and (re)organize enterprise's internal structures. SOA can be used to guide organic division and conformity of an enterprise, identifying key components, thus leading to development plans more suitable for the enterprise.

Meanwhile, SOA can be further extended to lead to a revolution in the service industry. The modern service industry considers every profession as a type of service to society. Figure 2.8 shows the classification of the US service industry[16]. Data reveals that various service industries occupy fifty to seventy percent of a country's industrial output.

As shown in Fig. 2.8, the service industry covers all traditional and modern professions including: traditional transportation and warehousing, information, finance, stock market, rental and leasing, scientific and technical services, administration, and entertainment. How to further enhance the effectiveness and efficiency of the service industry has become a critical topic. One core question of the modern service industry is how to exploit modern IT solutions and business models to further enhance these service professions for maximum efficiency, and how to share and reuse the resources that include contractors and reusable software assets among various professions. SOA is widely acknowledged as such a candidate to engender service modernization through new business models and IT solutions. In other words, SOA, as an architecture aspect of Services Computing technology, helps to transform the traditional service industries into modern service industries.

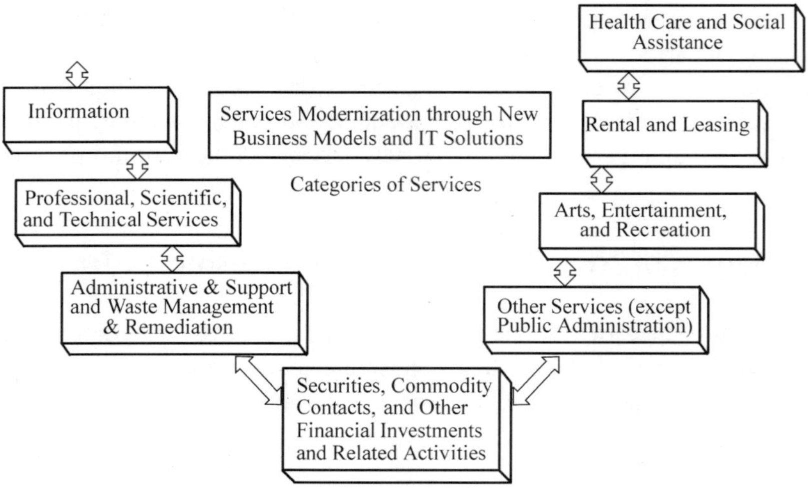

Figure 2.8 Services modernization

2.5.2 Software as Services

Software is being leveraged to deliver domain-specific services. Consider an example. In the US there appeared a management service software product that is capable of managing customer relationships. The software product is then installed onto the Internet for public access. If an enterprise wishes to use the product to manage its customer relationships, it can register as a user with a monthly fee of $100, thus utilizing the service remotely. Such a single registration allows one employee of the enterprise to use the service. If the enterprise needs to allow multiple employees to access the same service, it needs to register as multiple users and pay more usage fees. Such a service can typically support multiple enterprises as customer groups with separate dedicated domains.

This simple example illustrates how software can be used as services. More generally, enterprises will use the Internet and Web services standards to make software systems universally accessible to customers, partners, and other application service providers.

Using the idea of "Software as Services", an unprecedented business operation model becomes feasible. Figure 2.9 shows how a new business can be established with this new model. Assume that you want to open Company A from scratch. You begin from a great idea. You grasp a comprehensive business process that integrates various service suppliers, such as shipping services, Purchase Order (PO) creation services, and credit checking services. There exist enterprises that provide these services. As shown in Fig. 2.9, Enterprise B provides PO creation service and credit checking service, while another enterprise provides shipping services. In the past, without owning these services or building direct relationships with all of these service providers (e.g., Enterprise B), there was no way to start this business. With the emergence of Web services and SOA, all of the above service providers publish their services on a public services registry, via SOAP and eXtensible Markup Language (XML)[17]. These services thus become accessible to the public based on subscription or open-access business models. As a result, you can discover the interested service providers and remotely invoke the services through the Internet. As shown in Fig. 2.9, you can easily establish your own company by managing the business process and utilizing published services.

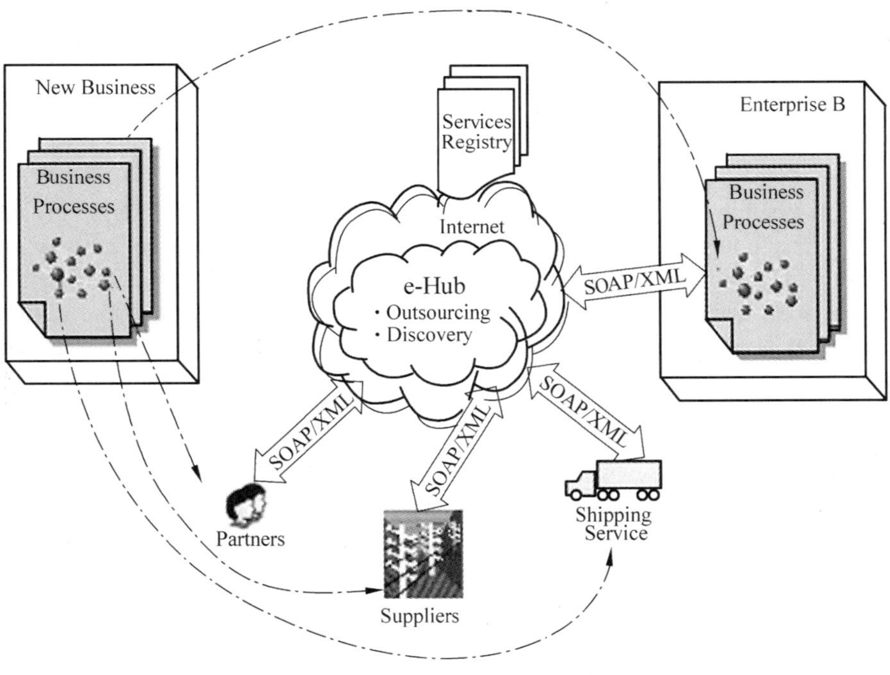

Figure 2.9 Software as services

Figure 2.9 also illustrates a running business service integration prototype with a simple, scalable service that allows for control, visibility, and security. An e-Hub is established as an integration platform on top of Internet and open Web services standards. It offers easy access to customers, partners, and other application service providers. A business process outsourcing manager is constructed to aggregate services based on business requirements, in order to enhance business service outsourcing capability: service-oriented business process on-demand.

2.5.3 Services as Software

The ninth trend is to transform services into software. It refers to transform the current consulting experience into software products, which can be shared by others. Let us look at one example of consulting services. Assume a consultant, who has three critical cases at hand, has to take a week of sick days off. His/her absence may directly cause delay of services to the three critical clients. If a new employee is hired to temporarily take over the position, the problem is that the new person may need months of training before being able to face clients independently. This example illustrates the big issue of how to modernize consulting services from knowledge sharing and transfer perspective. One solution is to exploit the emerging technique of services as software. Using this example, the experiences of the first consultant may be transformed into software to guide his/her substitute to take over the task quickly.

2.6 New Discipline: Services Computing

As introduced in Chapter 1, a cross-discipline space is rapidly emerging: Services Computing. It has been extensively accepted that the modern service industry has paramount importance in modern information society. However, when the service industry poses more and more demands, how to leverage the current manpower to provide an on-demand service remains challenging. Although it is easy to find job market professionals in various fields (e.g., computer science, electronic engineering, physics, and so on), it is difficult to find enough well qualified service-oriented business consultants and service-oriented solution developers. A new discipline oriented to services is in demand. We call it Services Computing, defined as follows:

> *"With the mission of bridging the gap between business services and IT services, and further enhancing business services, Services Computing covers the science and technology of leveraging computing and information technology to model, create, operate, and manage business services."*

Services Computing requires seamless collaboration from various professions and disciplines, centering around computing and information technology. Many countries and organizations in the world have been promoting this new discipline. IEEE (Institute of Electrical and Electronics Engineers)[18] Computer Society[19], the world's leading organization of computer professionals, establishes a dedicated technical committee on Services Computing[20].

Meanwhile, the growth of services has an impact on the academia. The society has realized the importance of educating services-oriented professionals. In the US, more and more universities have been opening new courses related to services and Services Computing. Other countries are conducting similar efforts.

Some traditional areas are under revision towards the service-oriented field. For example, a discipline such as Operation Research born in the manufacturing era, is being revised to reflect services and extended to Service Operations.

Similarly, Marketing is being revised to Service Marketing; Management Science to Service Management; Industrial and System Engineering to Service Engineering with enterprise transformation; Finance to Activity Based Costing; Contracts and Negotiations to eSourcing; and Computer Science to Services Computing. New areas also arise, such as Management of Technology and Innovation, Service professions, Personal Security Management (PSM), and Entrepreneur. Within these service-related areas, Services Operations, Services Management, and Services Computing form the Modern Science landscape. It should be noted that Services Operation and Services Management have been explored and investigated by the traditional industries (e.g., telecommunications industry and banking industry) and business management practitioners and researchers for decades. However, Services Computing, the core technical foundation for the modern services science, describes a new discipline innovated by the newly emerging SOA concept, consulting methods, delivery platforms, and tools. This new paradigm provides innovative sources to further enhance and facilitate more effective services operation and services management. At the early stage of the revolution in academia, these fields are aggregated together as a multidisciplinary subject. New subjects will emerge and join in. This trend has started at a variety of universities. Down the road, these various disciplines will be synergistically integrated.

It should be noted that Services Computing implies a much broader field than SOA and Web services. Its ultimate goal is to investigate how to use IT and computing technology to create, operate, and manage business services in an effective and efficient manner. All supporting science and technologies forms the discipline of Services Computing. This evolution path is sort of re-illustrating the creation history of Computer Science created from Electrical Engineering, Mathematical Science, and other related disciplines. Computer Science was driven by powerful computing technology. Services Computing is being driven by the growing services industry's modernization requirements. SOA is merely one recent model (i.e., a triangular model) that enables the concept of Services Computing from architecture perspective, and Web services is one recent technology that implements SOA.

2.7 Summary

In this chapter we discussed e-Business evolution, its inception, its development in the last ten years, its current state-of-art, and its future in the next ten years. E-Business has been developed over the last ten years through a six-stage process. On-demand business poses significant challenges to e-Business. The top trends in e-Business are examined in four categories: IT innovations to flatten the world, "open" trends for technologies and service ecosystem, debuts of new services-oriented business models, and the discipline: Services Computing.

References

[1] IBM On Demand Business. http://www.ibm.com/ondemand
[2] Seyfer J, Johnson S, Chmielewski D, Marshall M, Bazeley M (2005) Top 10 tech trends for 2006. http://www.transmediacorp.com/news/releases/2005/mercury1224.htm
[3] Skype. http://www.skype.com
[4] Zhang LJ, Liu LK, Lipscomb JS, Zhou Q, Xie D, Chung JY (2004) A per-object-granularity tracking mechanism and system for interactive TV viewership estimation and program rating in real time. Multimedia System 9: 466 – 476
[5] WiFi Alliance. http://www.wi-fi.org
[6] Cai H, Lu W, Yang B, Tang LH (2002) Session initiation protocol and Web services for next generation multimedia applications. In: Proceedings of 2002 Fourth International Symposium on Multimedia Software Engineering, pp 70 – 80
[7] Paylay. http://www.parlay.org/en/index.asp
[8] Ripin KM, Sayles LR (1999) Insider strategies for outsourcing information systems: building productive partnerships, avoiding seductive traps. Oxford University Press
[9] Friedman TL (2006) The world is flat: a brief history of the twenty-first century. Farrar Straus Giroux
[10] Eclipse—an open development platform. http://www.eclipse.org/
[11] The Apache Software Foundation. http://www.apache.org
[12] Mozilla Foundation. http://www.mozilla.org
[13] IBM SOA Software. http://www-306.ibm.com/software/solutions/soa/
[14] SOAP Specifications. http://www.w3.org/TR/soap/
[15] Service Component Architecture. http://www-128.ibm.com/developerworks/library/specification/ws-sca/
[16] U.S. Census Bureau: Service Annual Survey, Industry Summary Pages. http://www.census.gov/svsd/www/services/sas/sas_summary/summaryhome.htm
[17] XML. http://xml.coverpages.org/xml.html
[18] Institute of Electrical and Electronics Engineers (IEEE). http://www.ieee.org
[19] IEEE Computer Society. http://www.computer.org
[20] IEEE Technical Committee on Services Computing. http://tab.computer.org/tcsc

3 Web Services Modeling

3.1 Basic Concept of Web Services

A Web service[1] is a programmable module with standard interface descriptions that provide universal accessibility through standard communication protocols. The functions offered by Web services can be implemented in different programming languages on different platforms. Meanwhile, Web services can be composed to build domain-specific applications and solutions.

Figure 3.1 illustrates the concept of Web services. To a certain degree, the concept of Web services is a significant extension to that of an object in Object-Oriented design. Similar to an object that encapsulates its implementation details and can only be accessed through its interface, a Web service encapsulates its functionality implementation details and can only be accessed through its published interfaces. In contrast to a common object, a Web service typically carries comprehensive business logic, can be searched through the Web, and has to be accessed through the Internet or Intranet environment. Above all, a Web service is published in a standard language and accessed through a standard protocol.

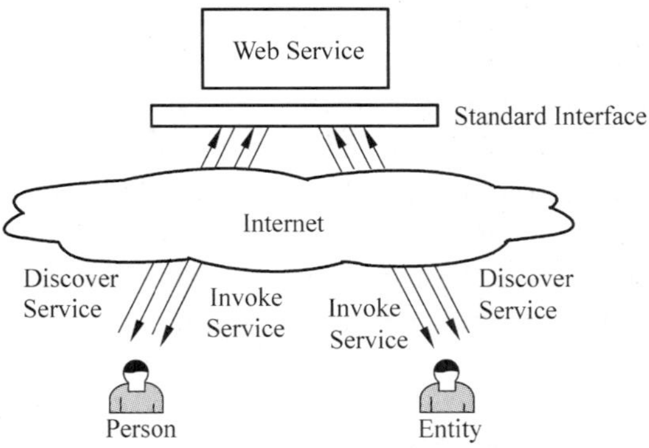

Figure 3.1 Concept of Web services

The paradigm of Web services is changing the Internet from a repository of Web content into a repository of services in three significant ways. First, by means of each organization exposing its business applications as services on the Internet and making them accessible via standard programmatic interfaces, this model of Web services offers a promising way to facilitate Business-to-Business

(B2B) collaboration within and across enterprise boundaries[2,3]. Second, the Web services technology provides a uniform and loosely coupled integration framework to increase cross-language and cross-platform interoperability for distributed computing and resource sharing over the Internet, inside or outside of firewall[4,5]. Third, the paradigm of Web services opens a new cost-effective way of engineering software to quickly develop and deploy Web applications, by dynamically integrating other independently published Web service components into new business processes[6].

3.2 Modeling of a Web Service

In order to publish a business application on the Internet as a Web service, one necessary step is to define its interfaces in a standard way[7], so that interested users can discover and access the service in a standard manner. The Web Services Description Language (WSDL)[8] and Simple Object Access Protocol (SOAP)[9] have become *de facto* industry standards for describing and accessing a Web service, respectively. Their specifications are published by the international standard body World Wide Web Consortium (W3C). As a matter of fact, W3C has formed working groups for WSDL and SOAP: "Web Services Description Working Group" and "W3C XML Protocol Working Group," respectively. As the versions of the specifications are still evolving, this chapter introduces the basic concepts and structures of WSDL and SOAP, both based on their basic versions 1.1.

A Web service does not have to be developed from scratch. In theory, any existing application can become a Web service, as long as it is wrapped by a Web service interface (i.e., in WSDL) and then published in a registry. Service requestors can locate the service and access its functions through Remote Process Calls (RPCs) embedded in SOAP messages. Meanwhile, for a Web service to be developed from scratch, the best practice is to start by modeling its potential interfaces before moving to implementation details.

3.2.1 Basic Concepts of WSDL Modeling

WSDL is "an XML[10,11] format for describing network services as a set of endpoints operating on messages containing either document-oriented or procedure-oriented information"[8]. It is created to define the public interface of a Web service, including its functionalities and how to invoke them. A WSDL document also defines the message formats and protocol bindings that are required to interact with the Web services. Message formats define how to interpret the data types passed in messages; protocol bindings define how to map the messages onto concrete network transports. In addition, WSDL is designed for both synchronous (procedure-oriented) and asynchronous (document-oriented) interaction patterns.

In short, WSDL provides a notation to answer the following "what, where, and how" questions: What is the service about? Where does it reside? How can it be invoked? The data types used are embedded in the WSDL file in the form of XML Schema[12], so WSDL is often used in combination with SOAP and XML schema to define a Web service over the Internet. A client program reads a WSDL document to understand what a Web service can do; then it uses SOAP to actually invoke the functions listed in the WSDL document. This process can be automated.

WSDL Constructs

Figure 3.2 shows the basic elements of WSDL. A Web service is defined as a set of ports (service access points), each publishing a collection of port types that bind to network addresses using a common binding mechanism. Every port type is a published operation that is accessible through messages, which are in turn categorized into input messages containing incoming data arguments and output messages containing results. Each message consists of data elements; every data element must belong to a data type, either an XML Schema Definition (XSD) simple type or an XSD complex type. XSD is the canonical type system of WSDL; however, WSDL also allows other data type systems, such as CORBA[13] Interface Definition Language (IDL) data types.

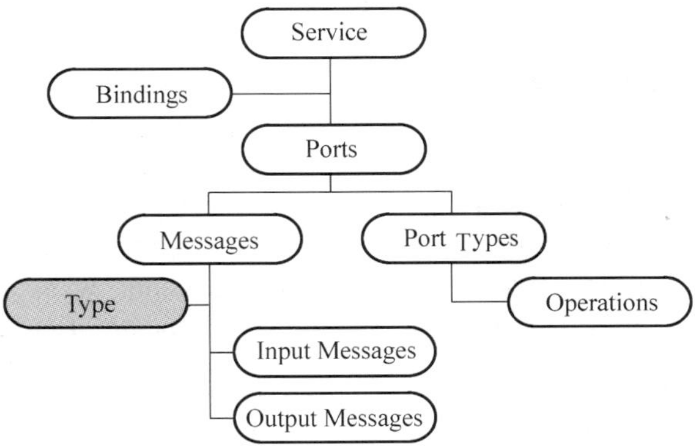

Figure 3.2 WSDL constructs

WSDL Example

Figure 3.3 shows a simplified segment of a WSDL document *Product.wsdl*. A WSDL document is stored as an ASCII file with a *.wsdl* extension, typically on the same server where the Web service is deployed. The tag *portType* defines "productPrice" as the name of a *port*, and "getPrice" as the name of an *operation*.

The "getPrice" operation defines an *input message* named "getPriceRequest" and an *output message* "getPriceResponse." The tag *message* defines the parameters and associated data types of the *input message* and the *output message*. Compared to traditional programming languages, "productPrice" can be mapped to a function library, "getPrice" to a function; "getPriceRequest" to an input parameter; and "getPriceResponse" to a return parameter. As shown in Fig. 3.3, in a WSDL document, it is typical to first define input and output messages, then describe operations with defined input and output messages included in corresponding portTypes.

```
<message name="getPriceRequest">
   <part name="productid" type="xs:string"/>
</message>

<message name="getPriceResponse">
   <part name="value" type="xs:string"/>
</message>

<portType name="productPrice">
   <operation name="getPrice">
      <input message="getPriceRequest"/>
      <output message="getPriceResponse"/>
   </operation>
</portType>
```

Figure 3.3 An example WSDL segment of Product.wsdl

WSDL defines four types of operations: *one-way*, *request-response*, *solicit response*, and *notification*. Note that these four types of operations are defined from a service provider perspective. The one-way operation receives a message but does not return a response message. Note that these four types of operations are defined from a service provider perspective. The request-response operation is the most frequently used operation type; it receives a request and returns a response. The solicit-response operation sends a request for a response. The notification operation sends a message but does not wait for a response. Figure 3.3 defines a request-response operation named "getPrice".

WSDL Data Types

WSDL allows comprehensive data types to be specified for service invocation. Its data type definitions are based on XML Schema, and can be defined either in separate files or in the same file. Figure 3.4 rewrites Fig. 3.3 by defining a complex data type for input parameter *productInfo* in the same WSDL file. As shown in Fig. 3.4, the definition of the data type *ProductInfo* includes three elements: *id*, *name*, and *vendor*. Each element is defined as an XSD simple type *string*. Then the message *getPriceRequest* takes a parameter with the defined *ProductInfo* as data type.

```
<types>
  <schema targetnamespace="http://servicescomputing.org/ProductInfo"
           xmlns="http://www.w3.org/2001/XMLSchema"
           xmlns:wsdl=http://servicescomputing.org/wsdl/>
      <xs:element name="id" type="xsd:string"/>
      <xs:element name="name" type="xsd:string"/>
      <xs:element name="vendor" type="xsd:string"/>
      <xs:complexType name="ProductInfo">
          <xs:sequence>
              <xs:element ref="tns:id"/>
              <xs:element ref="tns:name"/>
              <xs:element ref="tns:vendor"/>
          </xs:sequence>
      </xs:complexType>
  </xs:schema>
</types>

<message name="getPriceRequest">
   <part name="productInfo" type="xs:ProductInfo"/>
</message>

<message name="getPriceResponse">
   <part name="value" type="xs:string"/>
</message>

<portType name="productPrice">
   <operation name="getPrice">
      <input message="getPriceRequest"/>
      <output message="getPriceResponse"/>
   </operation>
</portType>
```

Figure 3.4 An example WSDL segment with data type definitions

3.2.2 Web Services Communication Protocol: SOAP

After the interface of a Web service is modeled in WSDL, its access of and communication with other Web services or programs should go through a standard communication protocol. Simple Object Access Protocol (SOAP) is such a standard protocol designed for Web services communications.

SOAP Basics

SOAP is a simple and lightweight protocol for exchanging structured and typed information among Web services. In other words, it defines the format of messages used to communicate with a Web service. SOAP is XML-based and independent of any operation system, programming language, or distributed computing platform. Note that SOAP needs to bind to existing Internet protocols, such as Hypertext Transfer Protocol (HTTP) or Simple Mail Transfer Protocol (SMTP), as underlying communication protocols. In general, SOAP provides a way to communicate between Web services running on different operating systems and implemented by different technologies and programming languages. SOAP has been endorsed by W3C and many major industry vendors such as IBM, Microsoft, and Sun Microsystems. Detailed information about SOAP can be found at the W3C Web site[9].

SOAP mainly supports two types of interaction patterns: Remote Procedure Call (RPC) pattern and document-oriented pattern. The RPC pattern refers to a synchronous request/response interaction approach. A service requestor sends a SOAP request message with input arguments and output parameters, formatted specifically to be mapped to a single service operation, and waits for response. Upon receiving the service request, the service invokes corresponding service operation and responds with a SOAP response message. On the other hand, the document-oriented pattern refers to an asynchronous interaction approach. A service requestor sends a SOAP message taking the form of a complete XML document intended to be processed as a whole. Upon receiving the service request, the service responds right away with an acknowledgement of the receipt of the message. The message then will be handled asynchronously. After the whole process is finished, the result is sent back to the service requestor.

SOAP Constructs

SOAP-based communications are performed through SOAP messages. As shown in Fig. 3.5, a SOAP message is an ordinary XML-formatted text string document containing four elements: a required *Envelope* element that represents the root element and specifies the XML document as a SOAP message, an optional *Header* element that contains application-specific control information (e.g., authentication and payment) about the specified SOAP message, a required *Body* element that contains the actual SOAP message (either as a request message or a response message) intended for the ultimate endpoint, and an optional *Fault* element that is part of SOAP *Body* and indicates error messages.

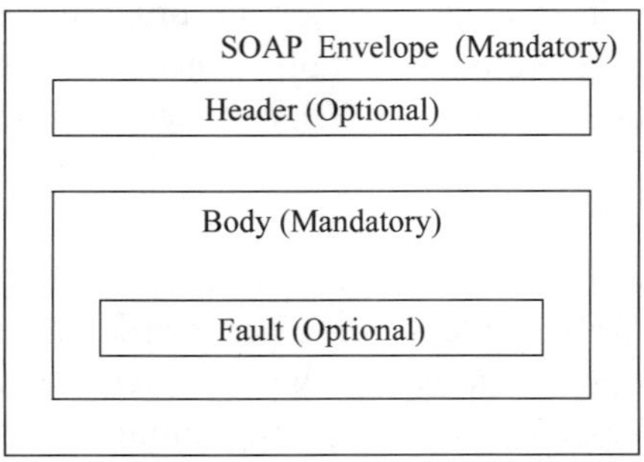

Figure 3.5 SOAP constructs

SOAP Example

SOAP defines three attributes in the default namespace (http://www.w3.org/2001/12/soap-envelope): *actor*, *mustUnderstand*, and *encodingStyle*. The attributes defined in the SOAP Header define how a recipient should process the SOAP message. The *actor* attribute is used to address the Header element to a particular endpoint along the message path; the *mustUnderstand* attribute is used to indicate whether a header entry is mandatory (i.e., with value "1") for the recipient to process; the *encodingStyle* attribute is used to define the data types used in the document. Figure 3.6 gives an example of SOAP request message and response message associated with the WSDL definition in Fig. 3.3. The example defines a SOAP message header including a "Payment" element with a value of "123", associated with an "actor" attribute with a recipient of "http://www.servicescomputing.org/appml/" and a "mustUnderstand" attribute with a value of "1".

```
POST /InServicesComputing HTTP/1.1
Host: www.servicescomputing.org
Content-Type: application/soap+xml; charset=utf-8
Content-Length: 100

<?xml version="1.0"?>
<soap:Envelope xmlns:soap="http://www.w3.org/2001/12/soap-envelope"
   soap:encodingStyle="http://www.w3.org/2001/12/soap-encoding">

   <soap:Header>
      <m:Payment xmlns:m="http://www.servicescomputing.org/payment/"
        soap:actor="http://www.servicescomputing.org/appml/"
        soap:mustUnderstand="1">
          123
      </m:Payment>
   </soap:Header>

   <soap:Body>
      <!-- Request message -->
      <m:GetPrice xmlns:m="http://www.servicescomputing.org/prices">
         <m:Item>Product</m:Item>
      </m:GetPrice>

      <!-- Response message -->
      <m:GetPriceResponse xmlns:m="http://www.servicescomputing.org/prices">
         <m:Price>70</m:Price>
      </m:GetPriceResponse>
  ...
      <soap:Fault>
   ...
      </soap:Fault>
   </soap:Body>
</soap:Envelope>
```

Figure 3.6 A SOAP message (including both request and response body)

In the *Body* element, the example shown in Fig. 3.6 requests the price of *Products* by calling the method *GetPrice* with a parameter *Item*. Note that the *m*:*GetPrice* and the *Item* elements above are application-specific elements. They are not a part of the SOAP standard. To save space, in Fig. 3.6 we also show a SOAP response message: the price of *Product* is $70. Again the *m*:*GetPriceResponse* and the *Price* elements are application-specific elements. In reality, SOAP request messages and response messages are always separate messages.

The top section of the SOAP message example in Fig. 3.6 also shows its binding to HTTP. A SOAP client connects to an HTTP server and sends the SOAP request message. If successful, the server returns a standard HTTP success status code of "200". The *Content-Type* header defines the MIME type (here application/soap+xml) for the message and the character encoding (here utf-8) used for the XML body. The *Content-Length* header specifies the number of bytes in the message body (here 100 bytes).

3.2.3 Binding of WSDL to SOAP

In addition to defining service operations, a WSDL document needs to define how to access the service operations using the element *binding*: the message format and protocol details for each port. Figure. 3.7 shows how to add the binding information on the basis of Fig. 3.3. The *binding* tag has two attributes: *name* and *type*. The name attribute defines the name of the binding, and the type attribute points to the port for the binding, in this case the "productPrice" port. The body of the binding contains two elements: binding specification (in tag *soap:binding)* and binding details of the operation (in tag *operation)*. The tag *soap:binding* has two attributes: *style* and *transport*. The style attribute defines how the operation can be accessed. SOAP currently supports two approaches: either through RPC calls or through document processing. These two approaches are denoted as "rpc" or "document", respectively; in this example, it is "rpc". The transport attribute defines the underlying protocol that SOAP binds to, in this example "HTTP". The tag *operation* is needed for each operation that the port exposes. For each operation, the corresponding SOAP action needs to be defined. One needs to specify how the input and output messages are encoded. In this simple example, the way of "literal" encoding is used for both input and output messages.

In addition to this SOAP RPC mapping for HTTP, WSDL can also map abstract messages and operations onto other transports. The WSDL specification includes several other examples: a SOAP one-way mapping for Simple Mail Transfer Protocol (SMTP), a SOAP mapping to HTTP GET and POST, and a mapping example for the Multipurpose Internet Messaging Extensions (MIME) multipart binding for SOAP.

```
<message name="getPriceRequest">
   <part name="productid" type="xs:string"/>
</message>

<message name="getPriceResponse">
   <part name="value" type="xs:string"/>
</message>

<portType name="productPrice">
   <operation name="getPrice">
      <input message="getPriceRequest"/>
      <output message="getPriceResponse"/>
   </operation>
</portType>

<binding type="productPrice" name="b1">
  <soap:binding style="rpc"
             transport="http://schemas.xmlsoap.org/soap/http/"/>
   <operation>
      <soap:operation soapAction="http://servicescomputing.org/getPrice"/>
      <input>
         <soap:body use="literal"/>
      </input>
      <output>
         <soap:body use="literal"/>
      </output>
   </operation>
</binding>
```

Figure 3.7 An example WSDL binding segment

3.2.4 Publishing a Web Service in Registry

After a Web service is modeled in WSDL, it needs to be made available to other users. Typically, the implementation of the Web service is first deployed onto an application server accessible to the Internet, and then published to a service registry on the Internet so that it can be discovered by any user. Note that such a service registry does not contain the actual implementation of the Web services; instead, it provides the information that service requestors need to discover service providers and their Web services, e.g., service name, service provider's name, and URL of the WSDL file describing a service. The actual Web service implementation program and associated WSDL files are located at corresponding service providers' servers and maintained by service providers.

Universal Description, Discovery, and Integration (UDDI)[14] is a specification that provides a "meta service" for publishing and locating Web services by enabling robust queries against rich metadata. The UDDI Specification Technical Committee at OASIS includes representatives from leading technology vendors, such as IBM, Microsoft, and SAP. Detailed information about UDDI can be found at its official Web site[14].

In concept, UDDI is similar to a Yellow Page directory. UDDI defines a mechanism to store descriptions of registered Web services in term of XML messages. The UDDI specifications record several types of information about a Web service that help service requestors determine the answers to the questions as "who, what, where and how":

- *Who*: basic information about a business, such as its name, business identifiers, and contact information;
- *What*: classification information that includes industry codes and product classifications, as well as descriptive information about the registered Web services;
- *Where*: registration information (e.g., the Uniform Resource Locator (URL) or email address) through which each type of service can be accessed;
- *How*: registration references about interfaces and other properties of a given service.

A UDDI data model contains four main elements: *businessEntity* represents a physical business by describing its information (e.g., name, description, and contacts) and its offered services; *businessService* represents a service offered by a business, *bindingTemplate* indicates how to invoke a service, and *Technical Models* (*tModel)* represents unique concepts or constructs.

UDDI uses the XML Schema to formally describe its data structures. As an example, the following sample segment specifies the *discoveryURL* of a business entity representing a URL pointing to Web addressable discovery documents. It is generated by a UDDI node that is accessible at "www.servicescomputing.org" and rendered by the publisher of the *businessEntity* that is identified by the *businessKey* "uddi:servicescomputing.org:registry:sales:100". The specification contains a *useType* attribute designating the name of the convention that the referenced document follows. The value of the *useType* is a reserved convention value "businessEntity," meaning that the *discoveryURL* points to an XML document of the type *businessEntity*.

```
<discoveryURL useType="businessEntity">
   http://www.servicescomputing.org?
   businessKey=uddi:servicescomputing.org:registry:sales:100
</discoveryURL>
```

3.2.5 Stateful Web Services Modeling

Stateless vs. Stateful Web Services

What WSDL can model is a *stateless* Web service, meaning that its state is not captured and maintained. This is probably enough for a read-only Web service, such as a catalog retrieval service. However, due to various business requirements, a Web service typically needs to serve various types of consumers and provide personalized services. In addition, instead of providing simple and isolated transactions, such a Web service needs to maintain persistent information (for example, user historical data) to serve consumers better. Furthermore, many such services are comprehensive enough to require a stateful session for a specific consumer in the whole period of a process. Thus, conversational information needs to be kept and tracked during a transaction. For example, a purchasing service of an online store should have the ability to record and retrieve what a customer has put into his/her shopping cart before he/she checks out. In short, under these circumstances stateful Web services may be required.

In general, stateless services scale better and are more fault-tolerant; stateful services, on the other hand, can support more comprehensive business transactions and provide more personalized services by remembering historical information. It is up to an SOA architect to make decisions about which alternative to choose. If the system intends to provide simple read-only services (e.g., catalog service) with no user information (e.g., preferences and historical activities) needed to be remembered, or provide one-time interactions (e.g., the system does not remember a user, and the user always logs in as a visitor or new user), a stateless alternative is sufficient. If the system provides comprehensive enterprise services requiring multi-step interactions or provides personalized services for multiple entries, a stateful alternative is needed. Enterprise services typically possess a level of sophistication to provide their consumers with personalized and individualized services. This in many cases means that the system has to remember user input preferences and historical activities.

A stateful service requires more coding and additional processing resources. Therefore, it typically has a definite impact on the performance of the service (e.g., cost, configurability and re-configurability of the service). Furthermore, it takes longer time to develop the mechanism and the application. Moreover, it may affect the scalability of the service. Therefore, it should be used only when necessary.

Modeling Stateful Web Services in WSRF

Initiated by IBM, Computer Associates (CA), Oracle, and other collaborators, Web Services Resource Framework (WSRF)[15] defines a system of specifications for managing and accessing stateful resources using Web services.

In short, WSRF is an XML-based presentation method to capture resources. WSRF contains four sets of specifications: *WS-ResourceProperties*, *WS-Resource-Lifetime*, *WS-BaseFaults*, and *WS-ServiceGroup*, which enable access to internal states of a resource via Web service interfaces, i.e., data values that persist across and evolve as a result of Web services interactions. In addition, WSRF supports dynamic creation of resource properties and associated values. In other words, WSRF describes how the state of a WS-Resource is made accessible through a Web service interface, and defines related mechanisms concerned with WS-Resource grouping and addressing.

Figure 3.8 shows a simple example resource properties document "Sample-StatefulResource," assuming that the product described in Fig. 3.3 is a stateful resource.

```
<xs:schema
   targetNamespace="http://servicescomputing.org/SampleStatefulResource"
   xmlns:tns="http://servicescomputing.org/SampleStatefulResource"
   xmlns:xs="http://www.w3.org/2001/XMLSchema">

   <xs: elements>
   <xs:element name="name" type="xsd:string"/>
   <xs:element name="leftNumberInStorage" type="xsd:string"/>
   <xs:element name="SampleStatefulResource">
      <xs:complexType>
         <xs:sequence>
            <xs:element ref="tns:name"/>
            <xs:element ref="tns:leftNumberInStorage"/>
         </xs:sequence>
      </xs:complexType>
   </xs:element>
…
</xs:schema>

<!-- Association of resource properties document to a portType -->
<wsdl:definitions
   targetNamespace="http://servicescomputing.org/SampleStatefulResource"
   xmlns:wsdl="http://schemas.xmlsoap.org/wsdl/"
   xmlns:xs="http://www.w3.org/2001/XMLSchema"
   xmlns:wsrp="http://www.ibm.com/xmlns/stdwip/web-services/ws-
resourceProperties"
   xmlns:tns="http://servicescomputing.org/SampleStatefulResource">
…
   <wsdl:types>
      <xs:schema>
         <xs:import
            namespace="http://servicescomputing.org/SampleStatefulResource"
            schemaLocation="…"/>
      </xs:schema>
   </wsdl:types>
…
   <wsdl:portType name="ProductPrice"
      wsrp:resourceProperties="tns:SampleStatefulResource">
      <operation name="getPrice"/>
…
   </wsdl:portType>
…
</wsdl:definitions>
```

Figure 3.8 A segment of an example stateful resource definition using WSRF

As shown in Fig. 3.8, the WS-Resource properties specification document is defined using XML Schema. The state of the modeling resource contains two components: *name* and *leftNumberInStorage*, both with XSD type *String* (xsd:string). In order for a service requestor to know that the "SampleStatefulResource" defines the WS-Resource properties document associated with the Web service, the WS-Resource properties document declaration is associated with the WSDL portType definition in the WSDL definition of the Web service interface, with the use of a standard attribute *resourceProperties*. As a result, as shown in Fig. 3.8, the *portType*, with the associated resource properties document, defines the type of the WS-Resource.

Granularity Enablement of State Management

Regarding a stateful Web service, another decision made by a solution or application architect is the granularity enablement of state management. Several questions have to be answered: To which granularity will the state information be captured and tracked? Will all interactions and activities be logged? What kind of consumer preferences will be captured and stored?

Three approaches exist: predefined state management, reconfigurable state management, and hybrid state management. A predefined state management approach means that a state management method, either coarse-grained or fine-grained, is predefined and remains unchangeable for a service. A reconfigurable state management approach means that administrators can dynamically adjust the granularity levels of state management, based upon enterprise requirements such as cost and performance. A hybrid state management approach means that a hybrid granularity level of state management and its configurability are adopted, based upon enterprise requirements including cost, development time and efforts, resources, and performance.

In general, different granularities of state management imply different performance impacts and governance levels. Coarse-grained state management is cheaper to implement and requires less resources. It also has less effect on service performance. Fine-grained state management, on the other hand, provides comprehensive state information and allows various levels of control and management over the service. However, the tradeoff is not only the expense to implement and maintain the state management ability, but also that it requires a significant amount of resources at run time, and thus it may affect performance significantly. Reconfigurable state management offers re-configurability, flexibility, and extensibility to both the service and customers. However, it requires significant development efforts. Hybrid state management takes into consideration various system requirements (e.g., flexibility, extensibility, configurability, re-configurability, maintainability, and performance) and enterprise requirements (e.g., cost, development time and efforts, and resources) and leads to a domain-specific solution.

For a specific service, the solution architect should take into consideration all related enterprise requirements as well as system requirements, and choose an application-specific state management mechanism.

3.2.6 Web Services Interoperability

The combination of WSDL+SOAP+UDDI depicts a process as follows: modeling a Web service using WSDL, binding it to SOAP, and then publishing the service onto a service registry such as UDDI. Although this combination provides an example way to model and publish a Web service, different vendors may implement these specifications in different ways. Thus, Web services published onto the Internet with different vendors' implementations may still have issues interacting with each other. The Web Services Interoperability (WS-I) Organization[16] was thus formed to tackle the challenges of interoperability among Web services.

In general, Web services interoperability addresses the integration issues for Web services that are deployed on multiple platforms, shared by multiple applications, or implemented in multiple programming languages. The goal of the WS-I is to encourage Web services adoption by introducing conventions and the best practices. Its Basic Profile 1.0 specification has been released as a key milestone for Web services interoperability. Based on the Basic Profile, each Web service defines its own specific profile. Therefore, various Web services can understand each other through their Basic Profiles. Meanwhile, WS-I also defines some individual profiles for specific purposes, e.g., WS-I Security Profile. These complementary profiles allow Web services to expose more comprehensive information. Furthermore, the flow of the WS-I working group covers scenarios and sample applications, Web services basic profiles, and testing tools and materials. The detailed guidelines simplify developers' jobs of selecting from various development tools or from different vendors.

3.3 Modeling a Composite Web Service

A business process typically involves multiple parties. Thus, multiple Web services may be required to collaborate with each other to form a composite Web service. For example, a travel booking Web service may include three sub-processes: flight reservation, hotel reservation, and car reservation. These three sub-processes may be performed by three individual Web services provided by corresponding service providers. The travel booking Web service thus becomes a composite Web service involving three collaborative Web services. The Business Process Execution Language for Web Services (BPEL4WS)[17,18] is such a flow representation developed to facilitate coordination of Web services into a comprehensive business process. BPEL4WS and its variations such as WS4BPEL are also known as BPEL.

3.3.1 Basic Concepts of BPEL

By extending the Web services interaction model and enabling it to support business transactions, BPEL defines an interoperable integration model to facilitate the expansion of automated process integration in both intra-corporate and inter-corporate environments.

BPEL focuses on describing the behaviors of a business process based on the interactions between the process and its partners. The interactions occur through Web service interfaces, and the structure of the relationship at the interface level is encapsulated in a *partner link*. A BPEL process defines how multiple business interactions are coordinated to achieve a common business goal, as well as the state and the logic necessary for this coordination. A rich process description notation is defined in BPEL to precisely define essential service behaviors for cross-enterprise business protocols, such as the data-dependent behaviors (e.g., the delivery deadline), exceptional conditions and their consequences (e.g., recovery sequences), and the long-running interactions at various levels of granularity.

BPEL separates the public behaviors of a business process from its internal implementations. A business process can be modeled in two ways, either an executable model or an abstract model. An executable process models actual behaviors of the participants in a business interaction; an abstract model specifies the mutually visible message exchange behaviors of involved parties without revealing their internal behaviors.

3.3.2 BPEL Basic Structure: via an Example

To better illustrate the basic structure of a BPEL document and how to use BPEL to define a business process, recall the on-demand business order example shown in Fig. 2.2, where three service providers collaborate to fulfill the business process. A user sends a purchase order (PO) request to an online supplier, who identifies a payment service provider to handle the payment transaction and a shipping service provider to schedule the shipping, before returning to the user with a result including a payment receipt and a shipping schedule.

This business process can be modeled as a composite Web service *OrderService*, as shown in Fig. 3.9. From a customer's perspective, he/she faces one single Web service *OrderService*. This composite Web service invokes two self-contained Web services from corresponding service providers: a payment Web service from a payment service provider and a shipping Web service from a shipping service provider. In order to construct this composite Web service, a business workflow needs to be identified.

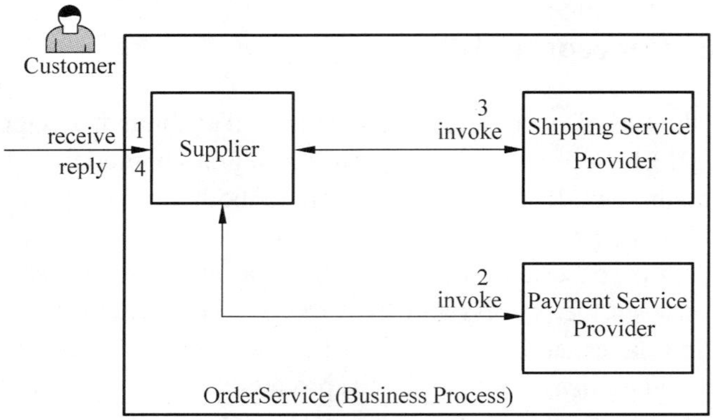

Figure 3.9 A simple composite Web service OrderServicde

Without losing generality, the workflow can be simplified in four steps. First, the user submits a PO request to the supplier; second, the supplier submits a payment request to a payment service provider and the latter responds to the supplier with a payment receipt; third, the supplier submits a shipping request based on customers' requirements to a shipping service provider and the latter responds to the supplier with a shipping schedule; fourth, the supplier returns to the user the result including a payment receipt and a shipping schedule. As shown in Fig. 3.9, steps 2 and 3 are synchronous calls, meaning that the caller (i.e., supplier) waits for a response after sending a request. This simple workflow forms a sequential procedure.

In order to create this business process in BPEL, a two-phase procedure should be followed: the first is to create service descriptions; the second is to create business processes.

Create Service Descriptions

First, involved business parties as well as the messages to be exchanged and manipulated should be formally defined. A business process in BPEL relies on WSDL descriptions to refer to the message types, the operations, and the portTypes to which these operations belong. Using the example shown in Fig. 3.9, descriptions are needed for the payment service, the shipping service, and the exchanged message formats. Since the payment service and the shipping service belong to different service providers, they are defined by corresponding service providers' WSDL definition documents. To simplify the presentation, the related *portType* definitions for both payment service and shipping service are shown in one place in Fig. 3.10.

```
<!-- portType supported by the payment service provider -->
<portType name="paymentPT">
   <operation name="submitPayment">
      <input message="pos:paymentRequestMessage"/>
      <output message="pos:paymentResponseMessage"/>
   </operation>
</portType>

<!-- portType supported by the shipping service provider-->
<portType name="shippingPT">
   <operation name="requestShipping">
      <input message="pos:shippingRequestMessage"/>
      <output message="pos:shippingResponseMessage"/>
   </operation>
</portType>
```

Figure 3.10 WSDL definition segments for required services

Figure 3.10 shows the related WSDL definitions for the supplier. The WSDL document first defines the *namespace* of the document for later references: "http://servicescomputing.org/xsd/po". Six types of messages to be used by the process are defined: *PurchaseOrderMessage*, *ResultMessage*, *paymentRequest-Message*, *paymentResponseMessage*, *shippingRequestMessage*, and *shipping-ResponseMessage*. Three portTypes (*purchseOrderPT, shippingPT,* and *paymentPT*) *each* contains a request-response operation: *submitPurchaseOrder*, *shipping*, and *payment*, respectively. (*shippingPT* and *paymentPT* are defined in Fig. 3.10.) In this example, the composite order service includes three synchronous communications: one between the customer and the supplier; one between the supplier and the payment service provider; one between the supplier and the shipping service provider.

Notice that no binding information is defined in the WSDL document. This BPEL process is defined "in the abstract", meaning that it only references the *portTypes* of the involved services without their deployments. In this way, the related business process definitions can be reused for multiple deployments of compatible services.

Observe that in the last section of the WSDL document in Fig. 3.11, three *partnerLinkTypes* are defined: *supplyLT*, *shippingLT*, and *paymentLT*. These partner link types represent the interactions or dependencies between the supplier service and the parties with whom it interacts. According to BPEL specifications, each partner link type defines up to two "roles", each associated with the portType that the role supports. As shown in Fig. 3.11, the *paymentLT* partner link represents the dependency between the supplier and the payment service provider, where a service function *paymentPT* is supported; the *shippingLT* partner link represents the dependency between the supplier and the shipping service provider, where a service function *shippingPT* is supported. They all support one role. As shown in Fig. 3.11, the business process acts as a requestor to both the payment service and the shipping service.

```
<definitions targetNamespace="http://servicescomputing.org/wsdl/po"
   xmlns:sns="http:// servicescomputing.org/xsd/po"
   xmlns:pos="http:// servicescomputing.org/wsdl/po"
   xmlns:xsd="http://www.w3.org/2001/XMLSchema"
   xmlns="http://schemas.xmlsoap.org/wsdl/"
   xmlns:plnk="http://schemas.xmlsoap.org/ws/2003/05/partner-link/">

<import namespace="http:// servicescomputing.org/xsd/po"
   location="http:// servicescomputing.org/xsd/po.xsd"/>

<!-- definitions of messages -->

<message name="PurchaseOrderMessage">
   <part name="purchaseOrder" type="sns:purchaseOrder"/>
</message>
<message name="ResultMessage">
   <part name="result" type="sns:Result"/>
</message>
<message name="shippingRequestMessage">
   <part name="purchaseOrder" type="sns:purchaseOrder"/>
</message>
<message name="shippingResponseMessage">
   <part name="shippingSchedule" type="sns:shippingSchedule"/>
</message>
<message name="paymentRequestMessage">
   <part name="purchaseOrder" type="sns:purchaseOrder"/>
</message>
<message name="paymentResponseMessage">
   <part name="paymentReceipt" type="sns:paymentReceipt"/>
</message>

<!-- portTypes supported by the supplier -->
<portType name="purchaseOrderPT">
   <operation name="submitPurchaseOrder">
      <input message="pos:PurchaseOrderMessage"/>
      <output message="pos:resultMessage"/>
   </operation>
</portType>

<!-- partner link types definitions -->
<plnk:partnerLinkType name="supplyLT">
   <plnk:role name="purchaseOrderService">
      <plnk:portType name="pos:purchaseOrderPT"/>
   </plnk:role>
</plnk:partnerLinkType>

<plnk:partnerLinkType name="shippingLT">
   <plnk:role name="shippingServiceRequestor">
      <plnk:portType name="pos:shippingPT"/>
   </plnk:role>
</plnk:partnerLinkType>

<plnk:partnerLinkType name="paymentLT">
   <plnk:role name="paymentServiceRequestor">
      <plnk:portType name="pos:paymentPT"/>
   </plnk:role>
</plnk:partnerLinkType>

</definitions>
```

Figure 3.11 An example WSDL definition for a business order process

Create Business Processes

After service definitions are created, it is ready for business processes to be designed in BPEL. Using the definitions of the portTypes, operations, and message types, the process can be elaborated as shown in Fig. 3.12. In the first step, the customer calls the *submitPO* operation with a message *PurchaseOrderMessage*; in the second step, the supplier calls the *submitPayment* operation with a message *paymentRequestMessage* and receives a message *paymentResponseMessage*; in the third step, the supplier calls the *submitShipping* operation with a message *shippingRequestMessage* and receives a message *shippingResponseMessage*; in the fourth step, the supplier returns to the customer a message *ResultMessage*.

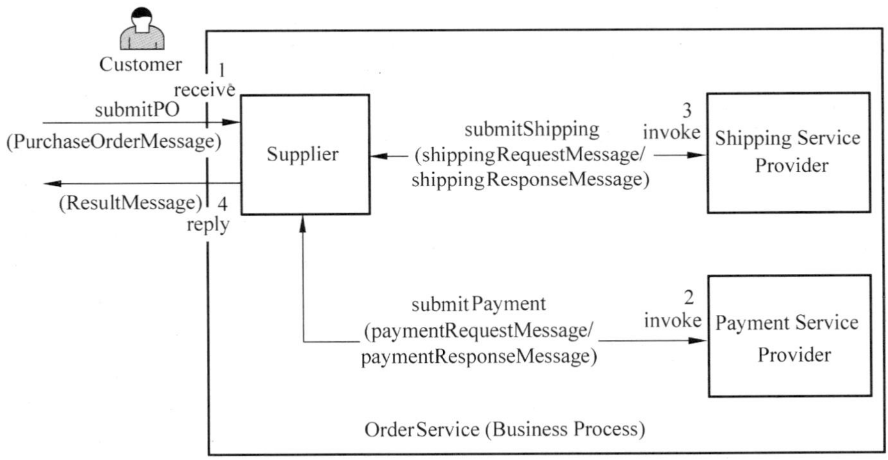

Figure 3.12 Elaborated OrderService business process

This process can be defined in BPEL as shown in Fig. 3.13. A BPEL process starts with a tag *process,* and includes the namespace that allows it to refer to the required WSDL information ("http://servicescomputing.org/wsdl/po"). As shown in Fig. 3.13, a typical BPEL process definition contains three sections: partner link definitions, variable definitions, and process definitions.

In the partner link definition section, involved business parties are grouped by a tag *partnerLinks*, as shown in Fig. 3.13. Each partner link is characterized by a tag *partnerLink*. In this example, three partner links are defined: *purchasing*, *payment*, and *shipping*. The myRole/partnerRole attribute of a partner specifies how the partner and the process interact given the *partnerLinkType*. The *myRole* attribute refers to the role in the serviceLinkType that the process will play, while the *partnerRole* specifies the role that the partner will play. For example, for the partner *payment,* the supplier acts as a *paymentRequestor* and the payment service provider offers the service; for the partner *shipping,* the supplier acts as a *shippingRequestor* and the shipping service provider offers the service.

```
<process name="orderService"
  targetNamespace="http://servicescomputing.org/bpel4ws/purchase"
  xmlns="http://schemas.xmlsoap.org/ws/2003/03/business-process/"
  xmlns:lns="http://servicescomputing.org/wsdl/po">

<!-- Define partner links -->
  <partnerLinks>
    <partnerLink name="purchasing"
                 partnerLinkType="lns:supplyLT"
                 myRole="purchaseService"/>
    <partnerLink name="payment"
                 partnerLinkType="lns:paymentLT"
                 myRole="paymentRequestor"
                 partnerRole="paymentServiceRequestor"/>
    <partnerLink name="shipping"
                 partnerLinkType="lns:shippingLT"
                 myRole="shippingRequestor"
                 partnerRole="shippingServiceRequestor"/>
 </partnerLinks>

<!-- Define variables -->
 <variables>
   <variable name="PurchaseOrder" messageType="lns:PurchaseOrderMessage"/>
   <variable name="Result" messageType="lns:ResultMessage"/>
   <variable name="ShippingRequest" messageType="lns:shippingRequestMessage"/>
   <variable name="ShippingResponse" messageType="lns:shippingResponseMessage"/>
   <variable name="PaymentRequest" messageType="lns:paymentRequestMessage"/>
   <variable name="PaymentResponse" messageType="lns:paymentResponseMessage"/>
 </variables>

<!-- Define process -->
 <sequence>
   <receive partnerLink="purchasing"
            portType="lns:purchaseOrderPT"
            operation="submitPurchaseOrder"
            variable="PurchaseOrder">
   </receive>

   <invoke partnerLink="payment"
           portType="lns:paymentPT"
           operation="submitPayment"
           inputVariable="PaymentRequest"
           outputVariable="PaymentResponse">
    </invoke>

    <invoke partnerLink="shipping"
            portType="lns:shippingPT"
            operation="submitShipping"
            inputVariable="ShippingRequest"
            outputVariable="ShippingResponse">
    </invoke>

    <reply partnerLink="purchasing"
           portType="lns:purchaseOrderPT"
           operation="submitPurchaseOrder"
           variable="Result"/>
 </sequence>
</process>
```

Figure 3.13 An example BPEL definition for a business order process

The section of *variables* in Fig. 3.13 defines the data variables used by the business process, based upon their definitions in terms of WSDL message types, XML Schema simple types, or XML Schema elements. For example, the variable *PurchaseOrder* refers to the *PurchaseOrderMessage* defined in the WSDL document in Fig. 3.11; *Result* refers to *ResultMessage*; and *ShippingRequest* refers to *ShippingRequestMessage*. Variables allow processes to maintain state data and process history based on messages exchanged.

In the process definition section, as shown in Fig. 3.13, the structure of the main processing section is defined by a pair of *sequence* tags, indicating that four activities are performed sequentially: *receive, payment, shipping,* and *reply*. The first activity is a *receive* activity, which accepts incoming customer messages. The definition of a *receive* activity includes the partner who sends the message, the port type, and the operation of the process to which the partner is targeting this message. Based on this information, once the process receives a message, it searches for an active *receive* activity that has a matching quadruple <partnerLink, portType, operation, variable> and hands it the message. In Fig. 3.13, the *receive* activity invokes the *submitPurchaseOrder* operation from the *purchaseOrderPT* portType with the variable *PurchaseOrder* (i.e., *PurchaseOrderMessage*).

As shown in Fig. 3.13, after the *receive* activity, the process invokes two Web services sequentially, each being delimited using an *invoke* tag. First, the process invokes the operation *submitPayment* from the portType *paymentPT*, with an input message *PaymentRequest* (i.e., *PaymentRequestMessage*) and an output message *PaymentResponse* (i.e., *PaymentResponseMessage*). Then the process invokes the operation *submitShipping* from the portType *shippingPT*, with an input message *ShippingRequest* (i.e., *ShippingRequestMessage*) and an output message *ShippingResponse* (i.e., *ShippingResponse*Message).

The fourth and the last activity is a *reply* activity, which allows the business process to send a message in reply to the customer. Once a reply activity is reached, the quadruple <partnerLink, portType, operation, variable> is used to send the result back to the customer. In Fig. 3.13, the *reply* activity invokes the *getResult* operation from the *purchaseOrderPT* portType with the variable *Result* (i.e., *ResultMessage*). Note that the combination of a pair of *receive* and *reply* forms a request-response operation on the WSDL portType for the process, in this example *submitPurchaseOrder* operation in the portType *purchaseOrderPT*.

3.3.3 BPEL Key Elements

The simple example above illustrates the basic structure of a BPEL document. BPEL defines 9 key elements: *partners*, *partner link types*, *partner links*, *business partners*, *endpoint references*, *activities*, *data handling*, *correlation*, and *scope*. The example above shows the utilization of part of the elements. This section briefly discusses the meaning of each of the 9 elements. Their detailed usages and examples can be found in BPEL specifications[17,18].

Partners

The concept of *partner* defines the relationships between a business process under construction and its partner processes. A process can be considered as a partner process if it fits into one of the following three roles: a consumer of a service provided by a business process, a provider of a service that is used by a business process, or a service that activates a business process.

Partner Link Types

A partner link type defines the conversational relationship between two Web services in terms of the role that each service acts in the conversation and the portType (function) it provides. Each role in a partner link type specifies exactly one WSDL portType.

Partner Links

A partner link models the partner services that a business process interacts with. Each partner link is characterized by a partner link type. Multiple partner links can be characterized by the same partner link type. This concept defines the static shape of the relationships within a business process. Two roles can be specified: *myRole* represents the role of the business process, and *partnerRole* represents the role of the partner service.

Business Partners

In order to model the relationships with a business partner who requires more than one conversational relationship, BPEL uses the *partner* element to represent the capabilities required by a business partner. It allows the grouping of partner links based on expected business enterprise relationships. This concept is defined as a subset of the partner links of the process. Partner definitions must not overlap, meaning that a partner link must not appear in more than one partner definition.

Endpoint References

The concept of endpoint references is to provide a mechanism for dynamic binding with port-specific data for services. An endpoint reference makes it possible in BPEL to dynamically select a provider for a particular type of service and to invoke its operations. In other words, the binding of an actual service to a partner link is described by its endpoint reference. Every partner role in a partner link within a BPEL process instance is assigned a unique endpoint reference during the deployment of the process, or dynamically by an activity within the process.

Activities

BPEL supports two types of activities: basic activities and structured activities. A basic activity is a primitive activity that does not contain other activities, such as receive, reply, and invoke. A structured activity defines a collection of activities with some predefined order to form a business process. BPEL defines three types of structured activities: *sequence, switch, and while* define a sequential order; *flow* defines a concurrent order; and *pick* defines a non-deterministic choice. An activity may have some optional attributes, such as *name* (name of the activity), *joinCondition* (a Boolean expression to specify the requirements of concurrent paths reaching at an activity), *source*, and *target*.

Data Handling

A business process typically requires modeling stateful interactions, including messages received and sent, as well as other relevant data, such as time-out values. BPEL provides three ways to handle stateful interactions: state variables, expressions, and assignments. *Variables* are used to maintain the state of a business process in state variables. *Expressions* are used to extract data from the state and combine them in a way to control the behavior of the process. *Assignments* can be used to update state. BPEL provides these three features for both XML data types and WSDL message types.

Correlation

The concept of *correlation* in BPEL is coined to handle long-lasting (e.g., days or months) stateful conversations between business processes. Message correlation is used to match returning customers to long-running business processes. When a request is issued by a partner, it is necessary to identify if a new business process should be instantiated or whether the request should be directed to an existing process instance.

Scope

The *scope* element provides a context for the behavior of each activity. A scope can provide five kinds of contexts: fault handlers, event handlers, compensation handlers, data variables, and correlation sets. Each scope specifies a primary activity that defines the normal behavior of the scope. The primary activity can be either a basic activity or a structured activity containing nested activities. A scope is shared by all nested activities.

3.4 Three-Dimensional Web Services Modeling

WSDL and BPEL can be used to model a single Web service using WSDL and a composite Web service. However, both WSDL and BPEL only focus on describing static information about a Web service. WSDL describes a Web service's abstract interface, its bindings to particular message formats and protocols, as well as the location of the service. BPEL describes the invocation relationships among Web service components within a business process. In short, they both provide static modeling of Web services.

However, Web services inherently contain other information that should be covered, such as their dynamic information and the relationships with each other, as shown in Fig. 3.14.

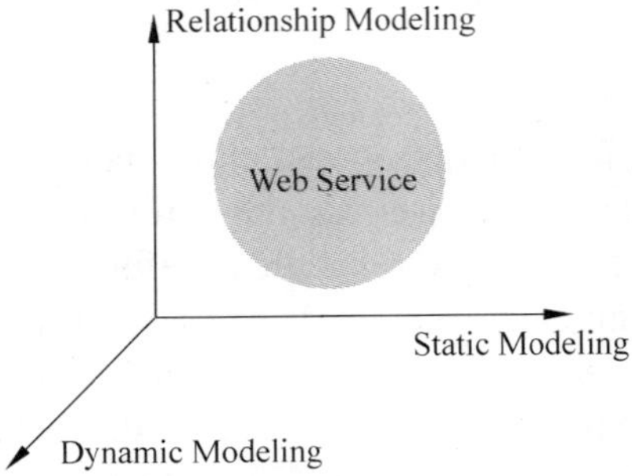

Figure 3.14 Three-dimensional modeling of Web services

A three-dimensional model[19] is needed to cover three types of information about a Web service. Static information describes a Web service. Dynamic information describes dynamic behaviors of a Web service, including invocation history of a Web service and some Quality of Services (QoS) measurements (e.g., its reliability in a specific time frame or its successful access rate). Relationship information describes the relationships among Web services and their corresponding service providers.

The major goal of this three-dimensional description model is two-fold: first is to help extract or exchange information from or within Web services registries; second is to automatically analyze, cluster, and index Web services. The three-dimensional model acts as a fundamental concept that represents not only the semantic information of individual Web services, but also the relationships among Web services. Furthermore, a business services database should be built as a reliable source to carry category information as well as Web services reputation and recommendation ratings to help service requestors access/use Web services quickly. Relationships between Web services will be discussed in detail in Chapter 6; QoS of Web services and SOA will be discussed in Chapter 8.

3.5 Discussions on Web Services Modeling

When talking about Web services modeling, people typically discuss how to abstract a WSDL interface from a traditional application, how to design a WSDL interface, how to bind to SOAP, or how to design a BPEL workflow for a services-based business process. Based on these basic concepts and techniques of Web services modeling, this book presents the concept of a three-dimensional Web services modeling. In addition to covering static modeling, it emphasizes the importance of dynamic modeling and relationships modeling. WSRF is introduced to be used to model schemas-based extensible Web services, as well as stateful Web services.

WSDL provides the ability of defining basic functionality of a Web service. However, as Web services become popular, more and more Web services are published on the Internet on the daily basis. How to distinguish among Web services bearing similar functionalities remains a big challenge for Web services adoption. Many researchers have proposed various ways to extend WSDL for a Web service provider to describe richer information about a Web service, including semantics of Web services, quality of Web services, context of a Web service, and so on. How to establish a comprehensive, flexible, and extensible Web services modeling standard system remains a challenging research topic open to researchers and practitioners.

In theory, Web services can be carried by any underlying transportation protocol. For example, as a connectionless transportation protocol, it is difficult for HTTP to handle mission-critical service invocations. Thus, Internet Engineering Task Force (IETF) working groups are proposing a peer-to-peer protocol standard, Blocks Extensible Exchange Protocol (BEEP), for connection-oriented services that intend to deliver dedicated connection-based services.

In order to support real B2B-based Web interactions, several additional technologies beyond basic Web services technology may be needed. For example, the Electronic Business XML (ebXML)[20] consortium has defined a comprehensive set of specifications for XML document exchange between business trading partners. Also based on SOAP as a messaging framework, ebXML has started to leverage Web services. Specially, ebXML favors several qualities of service, such as security, guaranteed messaging, and compliance with business process interaction patterns. Meanwhile, ebXML centers on document-oriented interactions.

This chapter discusses the contents and basic elements of WSDL, SOAP, and BPEL documents. In real Web services modeling, however, one rarely has to handle the actual contents and syntaxes of those documents. Instead, those information is normally generated and handled by vendor-provided tools. Various vendors provide this type of facility usally through particular wizards. For example, when creating a new Web service, a wizard will typically create the corresponding WSDL file; when using a Web service by pointing to its associated WSDL file, a wizard typically will create a client proxy to locate and invoke the service.

Finally, it should be noted that all of the aforementioned specifications and technologies (WSDL, SOAP, UDDI, BPEL, WSRF, and WS-I) keep on evolving. They should be viewed as present examples of infrastructure enablement technologies for services-oriented environment. With the development of Services

Computing, industry leaders and standard bodies may agree on new common specifications, and these aforementioned technologies will continuously evolve to their next generations.

3.6 Summary

This chapter discussed Web services modeling techniques. WSDL is an XML-based description language for modeling the public interface (including the protocol bindings and message formats) of a single Web service. BPEL is a description language for modeling a composite Web service. SOAP is an XML-based protocol supporting service messaging. In addition, a multi-dimensional model is introduced to depict various aspects of a Web service: static information about the descriptions of individual Web services, dynamic information about the behaviors of individual Web services, and the relationships among Web services and their corresponding service providers.

References

[1] Ferris C, Farrell J (2003) What are Web services? Communications of the ACM 46: 31

[2] Fremantle P, Weerawarana S, Khalaf R (2002) Enterprise services. Communication of the ACM 45: 77 – 82

[3] High JR, Kinder S, Graham S (2005) IBM SOA foundation – architecture overview. http://download.boulder.ibm.com/ibmdl/pub/software/dw/webservices/ws-soa-whitepaper.pdf

[4] Papazoglou MP (2003) Service-oriented computing: concepts, characteristics and directions. In: 2003 Proceedings of the Fourth International Conference on Web Information Systems Engineering (WISE 2003), pp 3 – 10

[5] Stal M (2006) Using architectural patterns and blueprints for service-oriented architecture. IEEE Software 23: 54 – 61

[6] Zhang J, Chang CK, Zhang LJ, Hung PCK (2007) Phased transformation toward services-oriented architecture. IEEE Transactions on Systems, Man, and Cybernetics, Part A

[7] (2004) Web services architecture. http://www.w3.org/TR/ws-arch/

[8] (2001) Web Services Description Language (WSDL). http://www.w3.org/TR/wsdl

[9] SOAP specifications. http://www.w3.org/TR/soap/

[10] Ron S, Vandersypen T, Bloomberg J, Siddalingaiah M (2002) XML and Web services unleashed. SAMS Publishing

[11] XML. http://xml.coverpages.org/xml.html

[12] XML Schema. http://www.w3.org/XML/Schema

[13] OMG CORBA. http://www.corba.org/

[14] UDDI. http://www.uddi.org/specification.html

[15] (2004) Web Services Notification and Web Services Resource Framework (WSRF). http://www-106.ibm.com/developerworks/webservices/library/ws-resource/
[16] Web Services Interoperability (WS-I). http://wsi.org/
[17] Business Process Execution Language for Web Services Version 1.1. http://www.ibm.com/developerworks/library/ws-bpel
[18] OASIS (2003) Business Process Execution Language (BPEL4WS, version 1.1). http://xml.coverpages.org/BPELv11-May052003Final.pdf
[19] Zhang LJ (2004) Challenges and opportunities for Web services research. International Journal of Web Services Research 1(1)
[20] ebXML. http://www.ebxml.org/

4 Web Services Publishing and Discovery

4.1 Web Services Publishing

In Chapter 3, Universal Description, Discovery and Integration (UDDI)[1] is introduced as typical specification for Web services registries. In general, as illustrated in Fig. 4.1, a Web service can be published in one of two major ways[2]: to a centralized services registry or to a distributed services registry. The UDDI registry is one typical example of a centralized services registry, whereas the Web services Inspection Language (WS-Inspection or WSIL)[3] is an example of publishing a Web service as a distributed document.

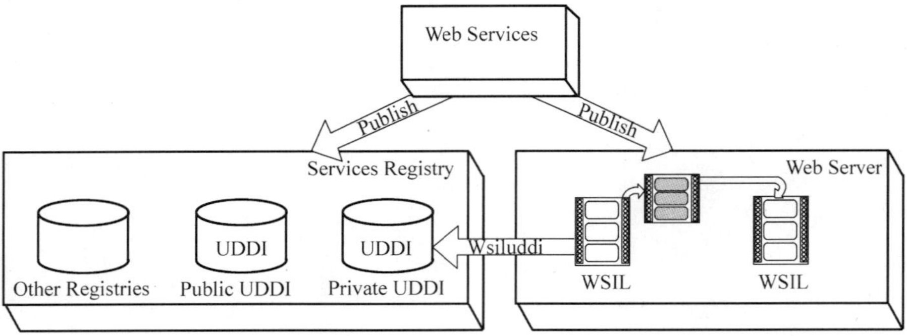

Figure 4.1 Web services publishing approaches

4.1.1 Public/Private UDDI Publishing

A UDDI registry is a centralized repository that maintains a set of links for published Web services. UDDI also provides information about corresponding service providers[4] such as company profiles and project development team profiles. All information for registered Web services is stored in the UDDI registry. Meanwhile, a UDDI registry provides a SOAP[5] interface to enable SOAP message-based services publishing.

UDDI registries can be further divided into two categories in terms of their access control policies, namely public UDDI registries and private UDDI registries. The public UDDI registry allows public access, while the private UDDI registry only permits access from users with access control enablement. A service provider can always publish a Web service to an existing public UDDI registry. However, if a Web service needs to be kept confidential or for internal use only, the best way is to publish it to a private UDDI registry.

4.1.2 WSIL Publishing

The second approach of Web services publishing is for testing purpose or for small-scale integration. In this approach, a Web service is published to a regular Web server as a plain XML[6] document, as shown in Fig. 4.1. A WSIL document also provides a means for aggregating references from existing service description documents, which may be authored in either a standard format (e.g., UDDI entries) or in a specific format (e.g., MetaWSDL that will be introduced in Chapter 5). In addition, one can use both approaches in one application. UDDI registries and WSIL documents can be tightly associated by a WSIL data tag *wsiluddi*. In a WSIL document, a reference pointer can be used to connect to a service published in a UDDI registry, as illustrated in Fig. 4.1.

As shown in Fig. 4.1, the WSIL document can also link to another WSIL document, which in turn may link to the third WSIL document, and so on. These WSIL documents may link through multiple levels. Thus, they are referred to as WSIL chains or Web services representation chains.

An Example of WSIL Chain

Recall the simple scenario from the on-demand e-Business example shown in Fig. 2.2. An online supplier requests services from both a payment service provider and a shipping service provider. The payment service provider in turn requests services from a bank service provider. Focusing on the core aspects without losing generality, this service description document chain contains four service description documents, as shown in Fig. 4.2. The chain has a root WSIL document *supply.wsil*, which links to two sub-documents: *shipping.wsil* and *payment.wsil*. The WSIL document *payment.wsil* in turn links to another WSIL document *bank.wsil*.

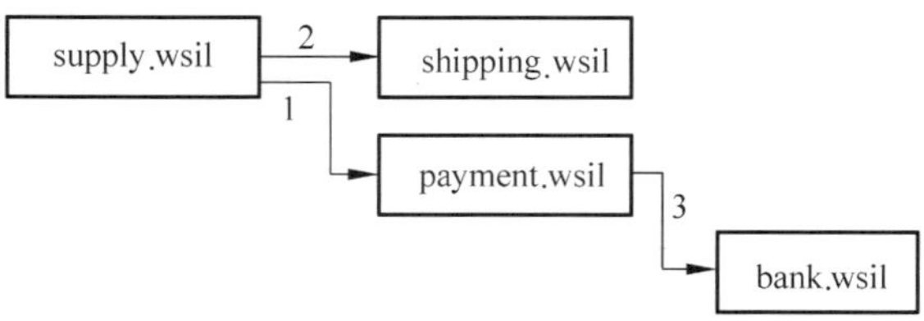

Figure 4.2 Example service description document chain

The content of the root WSIL document *supply.wsil* is shown in Fig. 4.3. This WSIL document specifies some basic information of the Web service: the name of the service *SupplyService,* its corresponding WSDL[7] document *supply.wsdl,* abstract of the service, and description location. The document also specifies two linked WSIL documents: *shipping.wsil* and *payment.wsil*, with their locations and their abstract information. Note that a WSIL document is an XML document.

```
<?xml version="1.0" encoding="UTF-8" ?>
<inspection xmlns="http://servicescomputing.org/wsdl/"
  xmlns:wsilwsdl="http://servicescomputing.org/wsdl/">

  <service>
      <abstract>This supply service provides an online purchase order
handling service.</abstract>
      <name xml:lang="en-US">SupplyService</name>
      <description location="supply.wsdl"
               referencedNamespace="http://servicescomputing.org/wsdl/"/>
         <unknown:service-description type="unknown" />
      </description>
  </service>

  <link location="payment.wsil"
         referencedNamespace="http://servicescomputing.org/wsdl/">
      <abstract>Link to the WSIL document for payment service</abstract>
  </link>
  <link location="shipping.wsil"
        referencedNamespace="http://servicescomputing.org/wsdl/">
      <abstract>Link to the WSIL document for shipping service</abstract>
  </link>
</inspection>
```

Figure 4.3 Content of the root Service Description Document (supply.wsil)

Figure 4.4 shows the content of the WSIL document *shipping.wsil.* It specifies the name of the service *ShippingService*, the corresponding WSDL file *shipping.wsdl*, and the abstract of the service. Note that *shipping.wsil* is already a leaf node in the service description document chain; thus, it does not have linked WSIL documents defined.

```
<?xml version="1.0" ?>
<inspection xmlns="http://schemas.xmlsoap.org/ws/2001/10/inspection/"
xmlns:wsilwsdl="http://schemas.xmlsoap.org/ws/2001/10/inspection/wsdl/">
  <service>
    <abstract xml:lang="en-US">The WSDL service description for the shipping
service</abstract>
    <name xml:lang="en-US">ShippingService</name>
    <description referencedNamespace="http://schemas.xmlsoap.org/wsdl/"
                 location= "shipping.wsdl"/>
  </service>
</inspection>
```

Figure 4.4 Content of shipping.wsil

Figure 4.5 shows the content of the WSIL document *payment.wsil*. It specifies the name of the service *OnlinePaymentService*, the corresponding WSDL file *payment.wsdl*, and the abstract of the service. Note that the service name *OnlinePaymentService* is different from the name of the WSIL document *payment.wsil*. The WSIL document also specifies that there is another WSIL document *bank.wsil* linked to this document and the abstract of the linked WSIL service.

```
<?xml version="1.0" ?>
<inspection xmlns="http://schemas.xmlsoap.org/ws/2001/10/inspection/"
xmlns:wsilwsdl="http://schemas.xmlsoap.org/ws/2001/10/inspection/wsdl/">
  <service>
     <abstract xml:lang="en-US">The WSDL service description for online
payment service.</abstract>
     <name xml:lang="en-US">OnlinePaymentService</name>
     <description referencedNamespace="http://schemas.xmlsoap.org/wsdl/"
                  location="payment.wsdl" />
  </service>

  <link referencedNamspace
="http://schemas.xmlsoap.org/ws/2001/10/inspection/" location="bank.wsil">
    <abstract>Link to a specific bank service provider.</abstract>
  </link>
</inspection>
```

Figure 4.5 Content of payment.wsil

4.1.3 UDDI Publishing *vs.* WSIL Publishing

The major differences between UDDI and WSIL lie in the cost and complexity. UDDI can be viewed as a traditional Yellow Pages directory that categorizes and organizes published Web services from various organizations. Organizations can share and use UDDI registries to maintain a number of Web services under different categories. UDDI is thus considered as a core building block that enables organizations to quickly, easily, and dynamically locate and transact with each other *via* their preferred applications. WSIL, on the other hand, is a cheaper solution for organizations to share Web services. Carried by XML files, WSIL enables Web services discovery, deployment, and invocation through regular Web servers without a comprehensive and complex services registry infrastructure. In short, the choice between using UDDI or WSIL is analogous to the one between using Yellow Pages or asking around for information.

4.2 Simple Web Services Discovery

According to the two Web services publishing channels, there exist some simple solutions for Web services discovery in each way. As shown in Fig. 4.6, a WSIL document can contain a link pointing to another WSIL document or a UDDI registry, which can be either a private UDDI registry or a public UDDI registry. Therefore, Web services searching can span across UDDI registries and WSIL documents.

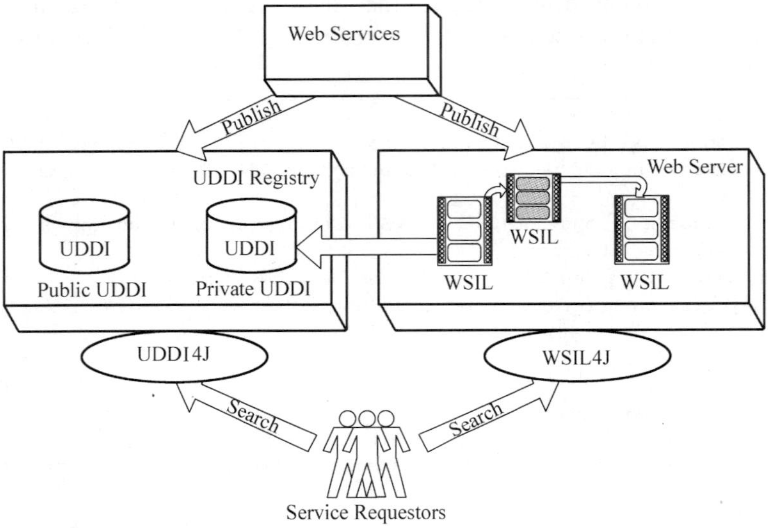

Figure 4.6 Simple Web services discovery

4.2.1 Simple UDDI Search

A simple UDDI search usually adopts a UDDI client to look up a Web service in a UDDI registry. One example of a UDDI client is UDDI for Java (UDDI4J, http://sourceforge.net/projects/uddi4j), an open-source project initialized by IBM. UDDI4J is a Java class library that provides an Application Programming Interface (API) to interact with a UDDI registry. UDDI4J supports the UDDI specifications, SOAP transports, debug logging, and configuration capabilities.

Generally, a UDDI search intends to follow one of three directions: *search for business*, *search for service*, and *search for service type*.

Search for Business

Search for business allows one to find business entities (organizations) according to some criteria, which can be any combination of *keywords*, *identifiers*, *locators*, *service types*, and *discovery URLs*. Only business organizations that match *all* of the specified criteria are returned. Such a search query has to contain at least one search criterion.

Search by business name By using the *BusinessName* tag, this search criterion specifies the name of the targeting business. The business organizations with their names starting with the specified characters will be returned.

Search by identifier A UDDI registry allows each of its stored entities to be annotated with information that can uniquely identify itself. This information is called an *identifier*. By using the *Identifier* tag, this search criterion specifies a (name, value) pair representing the type of a targeting identifier and its value.

Search by category In order to facilitate service searching, a UDDI registry typically classifies its entities with various categorization taxonomies, such as *North American Industry Classification System* (*NAICS*), *Universal Standard Products and Services Classification* (*UNSPSC*), and *Geographic* (*GEO*). These classification taxonomies are called *locators*. By using the *Category* tag, this search criterion specifies a (name, value) pair representing the type of a targeting locator and its value.

Search by discovery URL UDDI allows each of its stored entities to be associated with the address that points to a URL-addressable discovery document containing the information about the business registered. This address is called a *discovery URL*. By using the *DiscoveryURL* tag, this search criterion specifies the value of a discovery URL to look for. The business organizations whose discovery URLs starting with the specified characters will be returned.

Search for Service

Search for service allows one to find published business services according to some criteria, which can be any combination of service name and service category. Only business services that match *all* of the specified criteria are returned. Such a search query has to contain at least one search criterion. Meanwhile, since business services depend on business entities (organizations), searching for business services normally requires that business names be specified. Otherwise, all business entities registered within a public UDDI or private UDDI have to be examined, which is obviously time-consuming.

Search by service name By using the *ServiceName* tag, this search criterion specifies the name of the service to look for. The business services with their names starting with the specified characters will be returned.

Search by category By using the *Category* tag, this search criterion specifies a (name, value) pair representing the type of a service category to look for and its value.

Search for Service Type

Search for service type allows one to find published business service types according to some criteria, which can be any combination of service type name and service type category. Only business service types that match *all* of the specified criteria will be returned. Such a search query has to contain at least one search criterion.

Search by service type name By using the *ServiceTypeName* tag, this search criterion specifies the name of the service type to look for. The business service types with their names *starting with* the specified characters will be returned.

Search by category By using the *Category* tag, this search criterion specifies a (name, value) pair representing the type of a service type category to look for and its value.

4.2.2 Simple WSIL Search

As just discussed, WSIL documents provide an easy and convenient way to allow business partners and suppliers to publish their services on the Web with flexible linkages to other published services. Currently, a WSIL discovery mechanism is mainly based upon an iterative search process through a WSIL document chain, which typically includes the following five steps:

Step 1: Identify the location of a starting WSIL document (e.g., http://www.servicescomputing.org/start.wsil).

Step 2: Perform the search for the specified WSIL document.

Step 3: Display a list of links contained in the WSIL document.

Step 4: Select a link to launch the content of the selected WSIL document. If the launched document contains other links, chase down the links to retrieve further documents.

Step 5: Repeat Steps 3 and 4 to iterate through all interested links until intended information is found.

Apparently, to discover all the services a WSIL references by hand in such a service document chain is not an easy task. Therefore, WSIL crawling usually adopts a search tool built on top of a WSIL parser. For example, the Web Services Inspection Language for Java API (WSIL4J)[8] provides a Java interface that can be used to parse existing WSIL documents or programmatically create new WSIL documents. Most of the WSIL4J classes represent the elements that can appear in a WSIL document. In addition, a *WSILProxy* class is usually used to access certain types of information within a WSIL document. One can use the proxy interface to browse a WSIL document, then directly access interested UDDI business services.

As shown in Fig. 4.6, a Web services search requestor can use WSIL4J to look into WSIL documents. If one wants to look up a UDDI registry, he/she needs to utilize a UDDI client such as UDDI4J. UDDI operators can provide their own Web browser interfaces to allow users to specify search criteria from their own UDDI registries.

4.2.3 Issues of the Simple UDDI/WSIL Search

In general, with the UDDI approach, one can locate business services whose identities are well-known: one can find out what services a business is offering and how to access the services. However, simple search mechanisms have inherent issues with efficiency, accuracy, complexity, and interoperability[9]. First, a public UDDI registry typically contains thousands of distinct entities. Thus, it is unlikely that a simple search will yield a manageable size of result sets. Second, simple UDDI searching mechanisms require that service requestors know which directories to search ahead of time (e.g., search by business or search by service). Third, developers must manually write comprehensive search code, because simple UDDI search APIs are insufficient. This situation becomes more severe when a UDDI search request aims to include multiple search criteria or span over multiple UDDI registries. Fourth, typical UDDI search engines for simple UDDI searching only support specific types of UDDI registries. For example, a company's UDDI search technology may only allow its users to search its own UDDI registries. Fifth, a basic UDDI query only allows searching for one category (i.e., search for business, search for service, or search for service type) at a time, which is obviously inefficient.

Meanwhile, simple WSIL search approaches also exhibit two apparent drawbacks. First, they lack a capability to aggregate found services when traversing linked WSIL documents. Second, there is no uniform discovery mechanism for aggregating search results from multiple data sources, such as UDDI registries and WSIL documents.

To overcome these drawbacks, advanced UDDI and WSIL discovery techniques are introduced in the following section.

4.3 UDDI Search Markup Language

UDDI Search Markup Language (USML)[10] is a comprehensive XML-based description language, aiming to formalize UDDI search queries and enable complex UDDI search queries across UDDI registries[2,11]. A USML-based search request typically incorporates multiple search queries, UDDI sources, and aggregation operators. Such a query navigates through single or multiple UDDI registries according to multiple search criteria, including keywords, identifiers, and categories. The search results are aggregated before responding to search requestors.

Using a simple example, Fig. 4.7 shows the basic structure of a USML search request. The search script defines a composite query containing two UDDI search queries: the first query is to look up a private UDDI registry installed on server *servicescomputing.org* in the category of *business* with the business name starting with *COMPUTER*; the second query is to look up a public UDDI registry installed on server *pubuddi* in the category of *business* with the business name starting with *ELEC*. Then an aggregation operator *OR* is used to indicate that the search results gathered from the two different UDDI registries need to be aggregated into the final result.

According to the UDDI specification, there are three core data types that can be queried: *business*, *service*, and *service type* (*tModel*). Therefore, USML search criteria typically include businesses, services, and service types. The search type is delimited by *FindBy* tag. In Fig. 4.7, both queries choose to search by *Business*.

Finally, the search script also specifies the format of returned data. In Fig. 4.7, the returned data should be organized by their "Business".

```
<?xml version="1.0"?>
<UDDISearch xmlns="http://www.servicescomputing.org"
   xmlns:xsi="http://www.w3.org/2001/XMLSchema-instance"
   xsi:schemaLocation="http://www.servicescomputing.org/UDDISearch.xsd">

<Search>
   <Query>
      <Source>Private UDDI</Source>
      <SourceURL>http://servicescomputing.org/services/uddi
/inquiryAPI</SourceURL>
      <BusinessName>COMPUTER</BusinesName>
      <FindBy>Business</FindBy>
   </Query>

   <Query>
      <Source>Public UDDI</Source>
      <SourceURL>http://pubuddi/services/uddi/servlet/uddi</SourceURL>
      <BusinessName>ELEC</BusinesName>
      <FindBy>Business</FindBy>
   </Query>

   <AggOperator>OR</AggOperator>
   <RequestTypeName>Business</RequestTypeName>
</Search>
```

Figure 4.7 A simple USML script

4.3.1 USML Schema

USML Search Schema

At the top of Fig. 4.7, the USML file has a link to an XML Schema[12] file "UDDISearch.xsd". A USML script is an XML document that contains a set of search queries, each being associated with predefined criteria. In order for these USML scripts to be parsed and handled automatically by services registries, it is imperative for them to be associated with schema files describing the structure of each search query and criterion. In other words, an associated XML Schema file describes how the USML script should be interpreted. It defines the elements that a USML search request can contain, such as their attributes, values, and so on. A valid USML document must conform to its associated XML Schema document. It should be noted that any kind of metadata description language can be used for this purpose, for example, Document Type Definition (DTD). XML Schema is just an example of an XML-based metadata description language capable of defining comprehensive metadata information.

Figure 4.8 shows the content of the *UDDISearch.xsd* associated with the USML file shown in Fig. 4.7. As illustrated in Fig. 4.8, a USML search query (delimited by the *Search* tag) contains three parts: a one to many occurrences of

```
<?xml version="1.0" encoding="ISO-8859-1"?>
<xs:schema xmlns:xs="http://www.w3.org/2001/XMLSchema"
   targetNamespace="http://www.servicescomputing.org"
   xmlns="http://www.servicescomputing.org"
   elementFormDefault="qualified">

   <xs:element name="FindBy">
      <xs:complexType>
         <xs:choice>
            <xs:element name="Business" type="xs:string"/>
            <xs:element name="Service" type="xs:string"/>
            <xs:element name="ServiceType" type="xs:string"/>
         </xs:choice>
      </xs:complexType>
   </xs:element>

   <xs:element name="Query">
      <xs:complexType>
         <xs:element name="Source" type="xs:string"/>
         <xs:element name="SourceURL" type="xs:string"/>
         <xs:element name="BusinessName" type="xs:string"/>
         <xs:element ref="FindBy"/>
      </xs:complexType>
   </xs:element name="Query">

   <xs:element name="AggOperator">
      <xs:complexType>
         <xs:choice>
            <xs:element name="AND" type="xs:string"/>
            <xs:element name="OR" type="xs:string"/>
         </xs:choice>
      </xs:complexType>
   </xs:element>

   <xs:element name="RequestTypeName" type="xs:string"/>

   <xs:element name="Search">
      <xs:complexType>
         <xs:sequence>
            <xs:element ref="Query" minOccurs="1" maxOccurs="unbounded"/>
            <xs:element ref="AggOperator"/>
            <xs:element ref="RequestTypeName"/>
         </xs:sequence>
      </xs:complexType>
   </xs:element>
</xs:schema>
```

Figure 4.8 An example of USML-associated XML Schema specifications

queries (delimited by *Query* tag), an aggregation operator (delimited by *AggOperator* tag), and a request type name (delimited by *RequestTypeName* tag) that specifies how the returned data are to be organized (e.g., in business or in business service).

The element *Query* specifies a single query condition, which combines *Source*, *SourceURL*, *BusinessName,* and *FindBy*. The element *Source* specifies the name of the UDDI source for the query. It can be a *public UDDI,* a *private UDDI*, or other sources. The element of *SourceURL* specifies the URLs of the UDDI sources for a search engine to access. The element *BusinessName* specifies the name of the business entity. The element *FindBy* specifies the searching keywords: *Business*, *Service*, and *ServiceType* (*tModel*).

The XML element *AggOperator* specifies the logical relationships among search queries. As shown in Fig. 4.8, *AggOperator* have two values: *OR* or *AND*. If *OR* is specified, all results obtained from *FindBy* for each individual query will be aggregated and returned. If *AND* is specified, on the other hand, only results obtained from all individual queries will be returned.

USML Response Schema

Both a USML search script and its response are represented as an XML documents. Therefore, in order for a USML response to be automatically and correctly interpreted, it should also be associated with an XML Schema document. In other words, a USML response schema describes the structure of a UDDI search response in the format of an XML file. Figure 4.9 shows such an example.

The USML response contains a list of items, each containing information about a found business. Note that the response can contain zero to many items. A Business description is a quintuple of strings <*BusinessName*, *BusinessKey*, *Description*, one or more associated *URLs*, *Operator*>.

4.3.2 Composite Search Options

As discussed earlier, a simple UDDI search intends to find one of the three categories of information: search for business, search for service, and search for service type. As shown in USML search schema in Fig. 4.8, the USML provides an integrated search mechanism, which allows a search script to query a combination of any of the three search categories for more precise results. For example, as shown in Fig. 4.10, the USML query is comprised of three UDDI search queries: one for business, one for service type, and one for service. The query intends to discover *software_project consulting* services from *company* 1.

```
<?xml version="1.0" encoding="ISO-8859-1"?>
<xs:schema xmlns:xs="http://www.w3.org/2001/XMLSchema"
   targetNamespace="http://www.servicescomputing.org"
   xmlns="http://www.servicescomputing.org"
   elementFormDefault="qualified">

   <xs:element name="Business">
      <xs:complexType>
         <xs:element name="BusinessName" type="xs:string"/>
         <xs:element name="BusinessKey" type="xs:string"/>
         <xs:element name="Description" type="xs:string"/>
         <xs:element name="URL" type="xs:string" minOccurs="0"
maxOccurs="unbounded"/>
         <xs:element name="Operator" type="xs:string"/>
      </xs:complexType>
   </xs:element name="Business">

   <xs:element name="SearchResults">
      <xs:complexType>
         <xs:sequence>
            <xs:element ref="Business" minOccurs="0" maxOccurs="unbounded">
         </xs:sequence>
      </xs:complexType>
   </xs:element>
</xs:schema>
```

Figure 4.9 An example of USML Response Schema

4.3.3 Aggregation Operators

The *AggOperator* defined in USML can take different values, which can be either a simple *AND* (or *OR*) as discussed in the previous section, or a comprehensive function that requires a script to perform an aggregation task (e.g., an XOR function). If a response contains redundant information, it can be filtered by the use of such operators. This feature is especially useful for business searching. For example, since every business organization is associated with a business key and every service has a service key, an aggregation operator can help in combining the results of different keys and eliminate the repetitive information with the same key.

OR Search Criteria

The *OR* operator aggregates search results regardless of their relationships. For example, if one intends to search in a UDDI registry for any businesses starting with *Company* A or any services starting with *Web*, he/she should make two requests accordingly, and the results will be aggregated.

```
<?xml version="1.0"?>
<UDDISearch xmlns="http://www.servicescomputing.org"
   xmlns:xsi="http://www.w3.org/2001/XMLSchema-instance"
   xsi:schemaLocation="http://www.servicescomputing.org/UDDISearch.xsd">

<Search>
   <Query>
      <Source>Public UDDI</Source>
      <SourceURL>http://servicescomputing.org/uddi/inquiryapi</SourceURL>
      <BusinessName>company1</BusinessName>
      <FindBy>Business</FindBy>
   </Query>
   <Query>
      <Source>Public UDDI</Source>
      <SourceURL>http://servicescomputing.org/inquire</SourceURL>
      <ServiceTypeName>consulting</ServiceTypeName>
      <FindBy>ServiceType</FindBy>
   </Query>
   <Query>
      <Source>Public UDDI</Source>
      <SourceURL>http://servicescomputing.org/inquire</SourceURL>
      <BusinessName>company1</BusinessName>
      <ServiceName>software_project</ServiceName>
      <FindBy>Service</FindBy>
   </Query>
   <AggOperator>AND</AggOperator>
   <RequestTypeName>Business</RequestTypeName>
</Search>
```

Figure 4.10 Search options

AND Search Criteria

The *AND* operator defines the search query that all search criteria need to be satisfied. For example, as shown in Fig. 4.10, one intends to search for service *software_project,* with service type *consulting,* from business *company* 1. Three queries are specified: one for service, one for service type, and one for business. Then *AND* is used as the *AggOperator* tag. In other words, the *AND* operator is an indicator to aggregate and filter the results obtained from the user's multiple criteria requests.

4.4 USML-Based Advanced UDDI Search Engine (AUSE)

Using USML, a service requestor can write one compound USML request to search across multiple UDDI registries with specified search criteria. On the side of UDDI registries, in order to facilitate USML interpretation and handling, the Advanced UDDI Search Engine (AUSE)[10] is established. The goal of an AUSE is to automatically interpret incoming USML requests, dispatch and conduct search queries to corresponding UDDI registries, aggregate search results from different UDDI registries, and send back results to search requestors in the format of a USML response. The architecture of an AUSE is shown in Fig. 4.11.

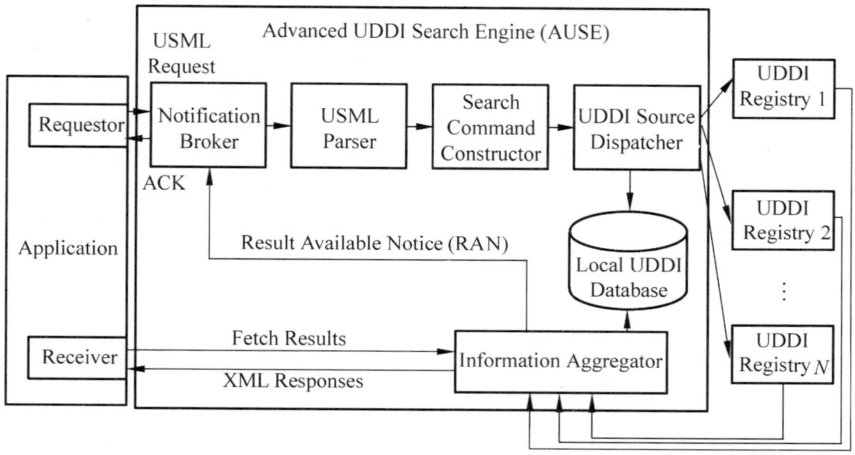

Figure 4.11 Advanced UDDI Search Engine (AUSE) architecture

4.4.1 AUSE Structure

As shown in Fig. 4.11, the AUSE typically contains one database component (*Local UDDI Database*) and five executing components: a *Notification Broker*, a *USML Parser*, a *Search Command Constructor*, a *UDDI Source Dispatcher*, and an *Information Aggregator*.

The *Local UDDI Database* acts as a local cache for quicker service. In general, the *Local UDDI Database* stores and re-organizes published UDDI category information (i.e., UDDI semantics information and the access information of available UDDI registries, each being either a public UDDI registry or a private UDDI registry) based on carried knowledge and self-updating mechanisms.

The *Notification Broker* enables an asynchronous search mode for a search requestor. As shown in Fig. 4.11, when a research requestor submits a USML request, the request is first registered at the *Notification Broker*. An acknowledgement is instantly sent back to the service requestor, which thus does not need to stay online waiting for search results. Instead, after the *Information Aggregator* finishes the aggregation of search results from different UDDI registries, it sends out a Results Available Notice (RAN) to the *Notification Broker*, which in turn notifies the search requestor. Afterwards, the receiver in the application can arrange to retrieve the results from the AUSE at its convenient time.

After receiving a USML search request, the *Notification Broker* forwards it to the *USML Parser*, which interprets the search script in accordance with its associated USML schema document. If the search script is a valid XML document, it is forwarded to the *Search Command Constructor*.

The *Search Command Constructor* generates individual UDDI search commands based upon the results from the *USML Parser* and forwards them to the *UDDI Source Dispatcher*.

Upon receiving a search request, the *UDDI Source Dispatcher* first searches the *Local UDDI Database*. If information is found, results can be quickly sent back without launching remote UDDI registries. Meanwhile, the *Local UDDI Database* is updated in real time when a search command is executed. Successful search results are always stored in the *Local UDDI Database* for later use. If information is not found, the *UDDI Source Dispatcher* dispatches the search queries to corresponding UDDI registries based upon the UDDI category information retrieved from the *Local UDDI Database*. The *Local UDDI Database* can also be updated during a programmed time period through its own updating mechanism, which automatically sends search commands to available UDDI registries and organizes the returned results in a well-formatted way. Note that the *UDDI Source Dispatcher* shown in Fig. 4.11 is an intelligent component, in the sense that it can dynamically dispatch the constructed UDDI search commands to the pre-selected UDDI registries based on the USML requests. If there is no source information defined in the USML request, the *UDDI Source Dispatcher* automatically dispatches the UDDI search commands to a known UDDI registry based on its knowledge base and intelligence carried.

The search results from various UDDI registries are gathered by the *Information Aggregator*, which parses and re-organizes the returned results based on aggregation operators and predefined rules. The final result is represented as an XML-based USML response. A cascading search mechanism is used for refining the search results at different levels of granularity. Filtering and aggregation mechanisms are applied to the search results returned from different UDDI registries.

4.4.2 AUSE-Based Search Process

Figure 4.11 illustrates a step-by-step search procedure using an AUSE engine.

Step 1: A service requestor generates a USML request and sends it to an AUSE engine. The request is registered at the *Notification Broker*.

Step 2: The *Notification Broker* sends an acknowledgement of receipt to the service requestor.

Step 3: The *Notification Broker* forwards the search request to the *USML Parser* to interpret the request.

Step 4: The *USML Parser* validates the search script in accordance with corresponding USML Schema, and forwards the search script to the *Search Command Constructor*.

Step 5: The *Search Command Constructor* generates one or more individual UDDI search queries and forwards them to the *UDDI Search Dispatcher*.

Step 6: The *UDDI Search Dispatcher* first checks the *Local UDDI Database*. If information is not found, it checks the availability of requested UDDI registries and their access information. Search queries are also stored to the database for later use by the *Information Aggregator*.

Step 7: The *UDDI Search Dispatcher* dispatches the search queries to corresponding UDDI registries.

Step 8: The *Information Aggregator* retrieves information from the *Local UDDI Database*, then listens and gathers search results from the corresponding UDDI registries, and aggregates search results into an XML-based USML response based upon the aggregation operators defined in the USML request.

Step 9: The *Information Aggregator* sends a Result Available Notice (RAN) message to the *Notification Broker*, informing availability of the corresponding search results.

Step 10: The *Notification Broker* in turn sends a notification message to the service requestor.

Step 11: The service requestor tries to fetch the search results from the *Information Aggregator*.

Step 12: The *Information Aggregator* sends the search results back to the service requestor in the format of an XML-based USML response.

In summary, an AUSE engine can largely improve the efficiency of business-level search facilities in four ways. First, the AUSE mechanism dramatically reduces the network traffic from service requestor's perspective by using only one USML-based search request and one XML-based response for a service requestor. Second, it simplifies a developer's effort by avoiding mastering the UDDI search programming skills for different UDDI registries. Third, a cascading search mechanism is used for refining the search results at different levels of granularity. Service requestors can use USML to define criteria of filtering and aggregating search results. Fourth, a local UDDI database is used as a cache for providing quicker service.

IBM implements the AUSE engine in Java, called Business Explorer for Web Services (BE4WS)[13,14]. BE4WS provides a comprehensive set of APIs to enable UDDI clients like UDDI4J to conduct complex UDDI searches based upon USML documents. BE4WS engines can be either directly embedded into Java programs or wrapped into a BE4WS Web service, and can be shared by different Web components.

4.5 WSIL-Oriented Dynamic Services Discovery Framework (DSDF)

As UDDI-oriented advanced search techniques have been introduced, this section will introduce WSIL-oriented advanced search techniques[11].

WSIL documents typically link together and nest multi-level deep into a WSIL chain, as shown in Fig. 4.12. Manually searching through a WSIL chain is obviously both time-consuming and error prone. Therefore, a WSIL-oriented Dynamic Service Discovery Framework (DSDF) is introduced to provide a mechanism to automatically search Web services in WSIL chains, aggregate Web services found in each WSIL document, and return results to the requestor for real-time feedback. As shown in Fig. 4.12, a service requestor, either from a program or from a Web browser, makes a request to the DSDF. The DSDF then searches the Internet for appropriate WSIL chains starting from a specified Web link to find proper Web services that are available. DSDF also provides an aggregation mechanism to group all Web services found in each WSIL document and return organized results to the service requestor at once. Thus, service requestors are released from manually tracking down WSIL documents for candidate Web services.

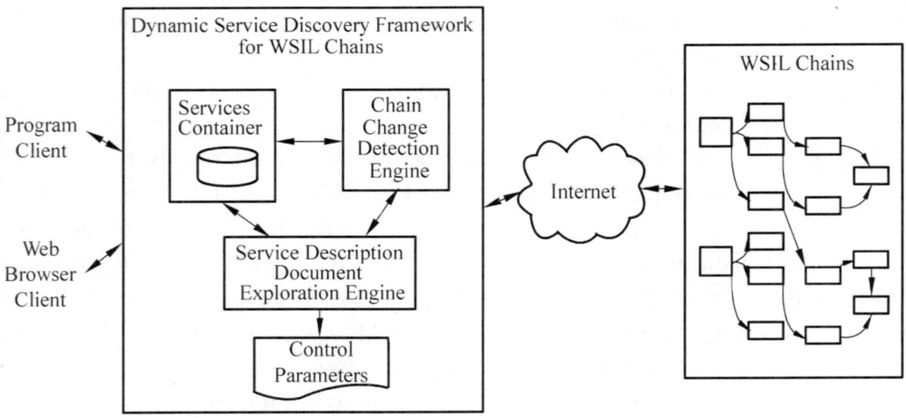

Figure 4.12 Dynamic Service Discovery Framework (DSDF) for WSIL chains

4.5.1 Architecture of DSDF

Figure 4.12 shows an architecture diagram of the DSDF, which contains four major components: a *Service Description Document Exploration Engine*, a *Services Container*, a *Chain Change Detection Engine*, and a list of *Control Parameters*.

Service Description Document Exploration Engine

The *Service Description Document Exploration Engine* is a key component that provides the mechanism for automatic and deep exploration of service description documents linked together. The engine adopts a depth-first algorithm to navigate through WSIL documents searching for qualified services. For example, Fig. 4.12 shows the exploration of a book and its related references using the *Service Description Document Exploration Engine*. Assume that the book is divided into 17 chapters, each being contained in an individual WSIL document. One separate WSIL document contains the table of content of the book. A separate WSIL document contains a reference list of all the papers. Assume that each WSIL document is published on a Web site. These WSIL documents are linked together to form a WSIL chain, as shown in Fig. 4.13. Starting from *TableOfContent.wsil*, the engine navigates to *Chapter* 1.*wsil* for the first chapter, then to *Reference* 1.*wsil* to the reference list of the first chapter, and then to *Paper* 1.*wsil* to the first reference paper and *Paper* 2.*wsil* to the second reference paper of the first chapter. After navigating through all reference papers of the first chapter, the engine navigates to *Chapter* 2.*wsil* and its references, and so on. In this way, the engine navigates through all chapters and every reference paper.

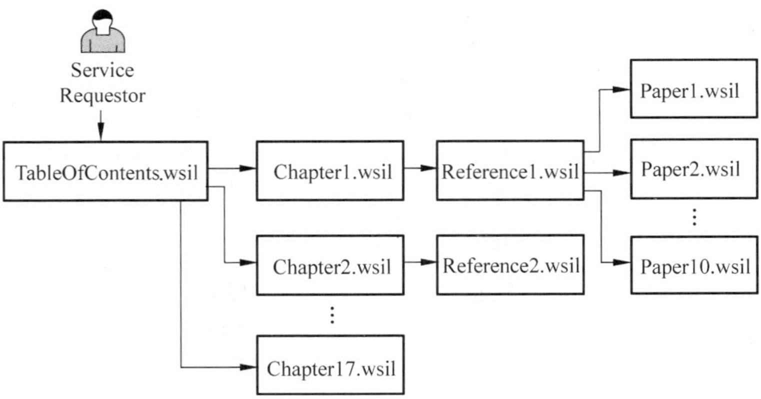

Figure 4.13 Sample service description document chain for book service navigation

Services Container

The *Services Container* stores cached information of each service description document chain and Web services contained in the chain. This information is retrieved and used by the *Chain Change Detection Engine*. At minimum, service names and sources (e.g., the WSIL signature) are captured for each Web service in the appropriate *Service Container*. The container also stores cached most-recently-accessed data and metadata of the service description document chain and Web services specified in the chain, thus eliminating frequent chain access (meaning that cached data can be quickly accessed without following the chain for intended data), except for the exceptional cases.

The *Services Container* component consists of the following two parts: cached information about services in each service description document chain and utilities to accept requests from external components, such as *Chain Change Detection Engine* and *Service Description Document Exploration Engine*, to maintain the cached content. The architecture of an example *Service Container* is shown in Fig. 4.14.

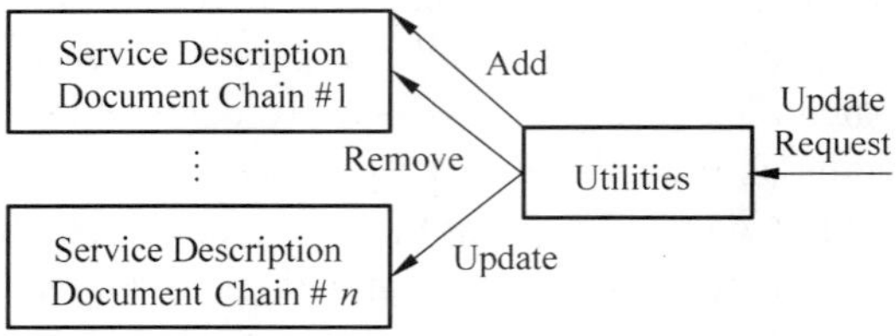

Figure 4.14 Service Container architecture

For each service description document chain, the *Service Container* maintains the following two types of information: category name and description for the category. *Category name* describes a category of services within a service description document chain. The category name should adopt human friendly terms, such as *travel*, *finance*, *car*, *food*, and *clothing*. For each service description document linked in the chain and each Web service found, relevant metadata should also be stored, such as *creation time*, *document size*, *name*, and *location*. *Description for the category* is built based on service abstracts and service names to create additional metadata and keywords to facilitate search processes.

Chain Change Detection Engine

DSDF provides automatic change detection and caching of WSIL chains. This feature is important because the Web services contained in WSIL documents can change frequently, as new Web services are published and old ones are removed. The ability to dynamically re-explore the linked and nested WSIL documents is extremely valuable to businesses that require access to up-to-date lists of Web services. DSDF achieves such a goal through pre-fetched link calculation and caching methods through the *Chain Change Detection Engine*.

The *Chain Change Detection Engine* provides a caching capability that automatically detects changes in the service description documents using various attributes, such as creation time, size, and other signatures of a service description document. The *Chain Change Detection Engine* also checks service description document chains on a time-initiated basis against the contents cached in the *Service Container*.

Additionally, the *Chain Change Detection Engine* supports the configuration of different granularities for different conditions. The first condition is to stop checking for changes and immediately return when it detects the first change. The second condition is to activate the *Chain Change Detection Engine* by either time-initiated checking or on-demand checking. *Time-initiated checking* is based on configurable intervals of time to kick off the chain change detection process. This mode can be configured as the default behavior as well. *On-demand basis* allows the *Chain Change Detection Engine* to accept requests from the *Service Description Document Exploration Engine* to detect changes of a specific service.

Control Parameters

The *Control Parameters* are the initial set of configuration data established for the *Service Description Document Exploration Engine*. Some examples are maximum depth or level to traverse and the indicator of a caching mechanism. The maximum depth or level is the configurable granularity, i.e., how deep the *Service Description Document Exploration Engine* will explore in a depth-first fashion for a given link before the peer links are explored. As for the indicator of the caching mechanism, it can be turned on or off.

4.5.2 DSDF Implementation

One example implementation of DSDF is IBM's WSIL discovery tool, *WSIL Explorer*. Being part of the IBM Emerging Technologies Toolkit (ETTK) 2.3[15], the *WSIL Explorer* can automatically start from the root WSIL document of a WSIL document chain and navigate through the whole WSIL document chain, digging deeply into all of the linked WSIL files regardless of their locations, either local or remote. The WSIL Explorer then aggregates all the results in one XML document as a return.

4.6 Federated Web Services Discovery Framework

As discussed in the previous sections, UDDI and WSIL coexist as two major Web services publishing mechanisms. This coexistence adds significant complexity in services discovery because UDDI and WSIL adopt different search mechanisms. In this section, a federated Web services discovery framework will be introduced for generic Web services discovery.

4.6.1 Basic Ideas

The federated framework provides a uniform interface for both UDDI-based and WSIL-based services discoveries; thus, it hides the complexity and differences between UDDI and WSIL programming models. As a result, a search over UDDI registries and WSIL chains becomes transparent to application developers. An application developer can use the same interface for any service searching and write all search queries in one document. The federated framework searches proper repositories and aggregates the results before returning to the user.

For example, these objectives can be realized by an advanced search portal embedded on a Web application server. The script-based search agent plays an important role in simplifying the application developers' jobs when developing browser-based clients or e-Business applications for Web services discovery. The federated Web services discovery framework with the search agent is shown in Fig. 4.15. The advanced Web services search agent is accessible from either a regular application client or a Web browser.

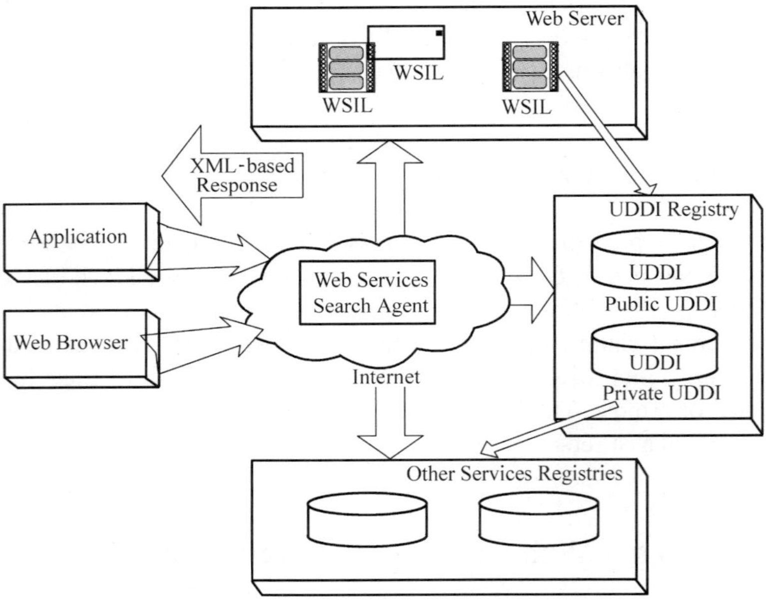

Figure 4.15 Agent-based advanced Web services discovery

The federated Web services search agent implements comprehensive result aggregation mechanisms, and communicates with multiple UDDI registries and WSIL documents. When a service requestor looks for a Web service, the search agent responds with one or all of the basic data types, *businessEntity*, *business-Service*, and *ServiceType* (a.k.a. Technical Model, or *tModel*) retrieved from UDDI registries or WSIL document chains. Example aggregation includes, but is not limited to, operations of intersection, union, and script-based logic to operate on the responses from multiple sources.

It should be noted that the advanced Web services search agent is not limited to search two popular services repositories (i.e., UDDI registries and WSIL chains). Instead, it can search other services registries, as shown in Fig. 4.15.

The final response to a search requestor may be a new XML format or an existing XML format such as WSIL. Standardized response messages allow to cache searching data to further enhance search efficiency. In the meantime, the Web services search agent may automatically invoke selected Web services to obtain the actual results or just to explore the Web services capabilities. This feature may be extended and realized to largely advances the ability of such a Web services discovery agent. The search agent could be deployed on a separate machine, or on the same machine with the services registries or service description documents.

4.6.2 Search Language

In addition to UDDI discovery, USML is extended to serve federated Web services discovery. Figure 4.16 presents an example of extended USML search script that intends to search a UDDI registry and a service description document chain. The search query identifies two search destinations: the first is the UDDI registry "Public UDDIV2" from the URL http://uddi.company1.com/inquire and the second is the WSIL root document "organizations.wsil". For the UDDI search, the query requests to search by business with the business name starting with "Computer" and service name starting with "UDDI". For the WSIL search, the query requests to search for "Computer" from the corresponding WSIL chains. The query also predefines an "OR" aggregate operator.

```
<?xml version="1.0"?>
<Search>
   <Query>
      <Source> Public UDDIV2</Source>
      <SourceURL>http://uddi.company1.com/inquire</SourceURL>
      <ServiceName>UDDI</ServiceName>
      <BusinessName>Computer</BusinessName>
      <FindBy>Business</FindBy>
   </Query>

   <Query>
      <wsilUrl>organizations.wsil</wsilUrl>
      <wsilCriteria>Computer</wsilCriteria>
   </Query>

   <AggOperator>OR</AggOperator>
</Search>
```

Figure 4.16 Example of an extended compound USML search script

As shown in Fig. 4.16, the federated search framework facilitates services discovery in the following four ways. First, it provides a unified search query interface. Second, it provides a framework for integrating aggregation algorithms to manipulate data. Third, it allows aggregating result data according to predefined targets. Fourth, by organizing response messages in a formalized XML format, it facilitates caching for search efficiency.

4.6.3 Comparison with Generic Web Search Engine

Finally, Table 4.1 compares the federated search framework with generic Web search engine from five perspectives: usages, search targets, support interfaces, output, and search criteria. The federated framework intends to discover qualified Web services from available services registries, while a generic search engine intends to discover related Web contents from available Web sites. Both of them support Web service interfaces and HTTP interfaces. The output data of the federated framework supports XML-based format only, whereas the output of a generic search engine can be either HTML or XML data. Finally, the federated framework supports combinations of three categories of search options (search by business, search by service, and search by service type), while a generic search engine typically supports free keyword-based search options. The former is a unified search engine for Web services discovery, while the latter is a search engine for generic Web content discovery. Considering search targets, the federated search framework searches multiple services registries, as opposed to a generic Web search engine searching multiple Web sites. Considering supporting interfaces, the federated services search framework supports Web service interfaces and HTTP interfaces, same as a generic Web search engine. Considering output data, the federated services search framework supports XML-based format, while a generic Web search engine supports either HTML or XML format.

Table 4.1 Comparison between federated search framework with generic Web search engine

	Federated search framework	Web search engine
Usages	Unified search engine for Web services discovery	Unified search engine for Web content discovery
Search targets	Multiple services registries	Multiple Web sites
Support interfaces	Web services/HTTP	HTTP/Web services
Output	XML	HTML/XML
Search criteria	Combinations of three types of search options	Keywords (not sensitive to Web services)

4.7 Discussions on Web Services Publishing and Discovery

Services publishing and discovery usually refers to UDDI-based techniques. In order to support lightweight, flexible services publishing and discovery, this chapter introduces WSIL as a complementary technique for UDDI. Moreover, this chapter introduces in detail an advanced services discovery framework and technique, aiming at standardizing and optimizing a generic services discovery approach over various types of services registries such as UDDI registry or other services repositories.

As more and more Web services are published onto the Internet, it is common for a set of popular services registries to maintain information about thousands to millions of registered services. How to effectively store and organize these registration information to enable and facilitate efficient queries remains a big challenge. Considering the fact that a popular services registry may have to support thousands of service queries intensively at any time, this issue becomes much more severe. Many traditional database techniques, such as indexing and sorting, partitioning, transactional control, and various query approaches, will definitely be useful for solving this issue. However, services-oriented registry management may raise new issues. For example, since stored information relates to published Web services maintained by corresponding service providers, how to control the integrity of a service item with proper version number remains a challenge.

In other words, services publishing and discovery remains an open area with many challenges for researchers and practitioners. Here we just name a few challenges for a services registry management.

In order to promote discovery of services, a service registry should provide powerful service classification facility, based on both business and IT, with configurable taxonomy support and validation. An individual organization should be able to easily define its own classifications to align with specific requirements.

A service registry must secure access to business services and assets. Fine-grained access control facility needs to be provided and should be able to be configured and re-configured based on policies.

A service registry should support efficient version control and change management facility equipped with automatic notifications based on the publisher / subscriber pattern. Whenever changes happen at service providers, alerts need to be triggered in a timely manner to be sent to corresponding service consumers to eliminate disruptions to consuming applications.

A service registry should control the consistency and integrity of registered services, meaning that a structured and streamlined approval process is needed to assure business services are properly reviewed before they can be published on the services registry.

Finally, it is critical to provide user-friendly interfaces for services registration, browsing, and discovery. Users should be allowed to easily configure personalized query interfaces, such as how information will be edited, searched, and displayed.

4.8 Summary

In this chapter, Web services publishing and discovery technologies were discussed. Web services can be published to either centralized service registries (e.g., UDDI) or distributed services registries (e.g., WSIL). Advanced search techniques are on demand to facilitate efficient Web services discovery. USML associated with an AUSE engine could facilitate UDDI discovery; DSDF could help WSIL discovery. A federated search framework can be established, which hides complexity and provides a uniform way of performing discovery over various types of services registries.

References

[1] UDDI. http://www.uddi.org/specification.html
[2] Zhang LJ (2002) Next-generation Web services discovery. Web Services Journal, September
[3] IBM Web Services Inspection Language. http://www-128.ibm.com/developerworks/library/specification/ws-wsilspec/
[4] Rocco D, Caverlee J, Liu L, Critchlow T (2005) Domain-specific Web service discovery with service class descriptions. In: 2005 IEEE International Conference on Web Services (ICWS'05), pp 481 – 488
[5] SOAP specifications. http://www.w3.org/TR/soap/
[6] XML. http://xml.coverpages.org/xml.html
[7] Erik Christensen, et al. (2001) Web Services Description Language (WSDL). http: // www.w3.org/TR/wsdl
[8] IBM Web Services Inspection Language for Java (WSIL4J). http://www-128.ibm.com/developerworks/webservices/library/ws-wsilover/
[9] Web Services Interoperability (WS-I). http://wsi.org/
[10] Zhang LJ, Chao T, Chang H, Chung JY (2003) XML-based advanced UDDI search mechanism for B2B integration. Electronic Commerce Research 3(1-2): 25 – 42
[11] Zhang LJ, Zhou Q, Chao T (2004) A dynamic services discovery framework for traversing Web services representation chain. In: 2004 IEEE International Conference on Web Services, pp 632 – 639
[12] XML Schema. http://www.w3.org/XML/Schema
[13] Zhang LJ, Zhou Q (2002) Aggregate UDDI searches with business explorer for Web services. http://www-128.ibm.com/developerworks/webservices/library/ws-be4ws
[14] Zhang LJ, et al. (2001) IBM Business Explorer for Web Services (BE4WS). http: // www.alphaworks.ibm.com/ tech/be4ws
[15] IBM Emerging Technologies Toolkit (ETTK). http://www.alphaworks.ibm.com/ettk

5 Service-Oriented Architecture

5.1 Concept of Service-Oriented Architecture (SOA)

SOA stands for Service-Oriented Architecture. It is the fundamental architectural model that supports the overall paradigm of Services Computing from architecture perspective. As proved by the history of software and system development in the last fifty years, software architecture plays an essential role in software systems, by providing plausible insights, triggering the right questions, and offering general tools for thoughts. An architectural model is a representation of blueprint that contains certain building blocks common to all similar applications, along with certain variable aspects unique to each specific application. Building "conceptual constructs" is critical not only for a single software design but also for all large-scale applications and systems.

Basically, SOA is a business-IT-aligned approach in which applications rely on available services to facilitate business processes. A service is a self-contained reusable software component provided by a service provider and consumed by service requestors. SOA creates a vision of IT flexibility enabling business agility. Implementing an SOA mainly involves componentizing enterprise and/or developing applications that use services, making applications available as services for other applications to use, and so on.

5.1.1 Triangular SOA Operational Model

As shown in Fig. 5.1, traditionally, service providers notify service requestors of available services; service requestors then invoke services[1,2]. This end-to-end services delivery model is now replaced by a triangular SOA operational model[3 - 13] that provides an underlying backbone for the creation, registration, discovery, and composition of distributed services. In this model, three roles are identified based on their behaviors and responsibilities over a service: *service provider*, *service registry*, and *service requestor*. A service provider offers services; a service requestor invokes services; a service *registry* helps service providers publish services and help service requestors find service providers for proper services.

SOA thus defines a formalized triangular SOA operational model between the three roles, as shown in Fig.5.1. A service provider publishes services at a service *registry*. A service *registry* registers and organizes published services and provides search services. Such a service *registry* generally contains a service repository associated with two access interfaces: a publishing interface serving service providers, and a query interface serving service requestors. As illustrated in Fig. 5.1, published services are hosted by the corresponding service providers. A service requestor queries the service *registry* for an interested service and obtains the location information of the corresponding service provider. Then the service requestor binds to the service provider, and remotely invokes the service from the service provider. Definitely, if a service requestor is aware of a proper service provider, it may decide to directly contact the service provider without consulting a service registry. However, the SOA triangular model provides a generic way for a service requestor to search and discover an appropriate service from a repository of published services.

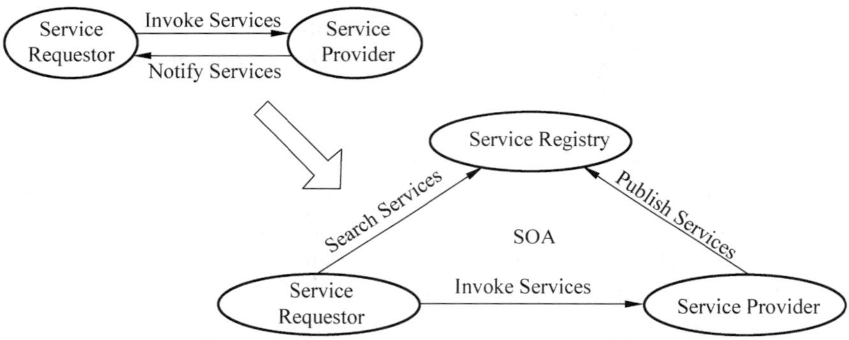

Figure 5.1 Service Oriented Architecture (SOA)

5.1.2 Web Services-Based SOA

SOA is a conceptual-level architectural model, meaning that it needs to be implemented and embodied by an IT technology. The Web services technology is such a popular technique to date that realizes the SOA model. In the rest of the book, Web services will be adopted as the default underlying technology to realize SOA. However, it should be noted that SOA could be implemented by other technologies, including component engineering and distributed objects.

SOA is built on top of industry standards[14]. As shown in Chapter 3, the Web services community has created a set of standards to enable standardized communication among the entities in the SOA model. As shown in Fig. 5.2, a service provider publishes services at a service registry using Universal Description, Discovery, and Integration (UDDI)[15]. The public interfaces and binding information of the registered services are clearly defined in a standard Web Services Description Language (WSDL)[16]. A service requestor communicates with a service provider through a lightweight messaging protocol, Simple Object Access Protocol (SOAP)[17]. UDDI, WSDL, and SOAP are being adopted for Web services. More detailed information about SOA and Web services standards will be discussed in Chapter 7.

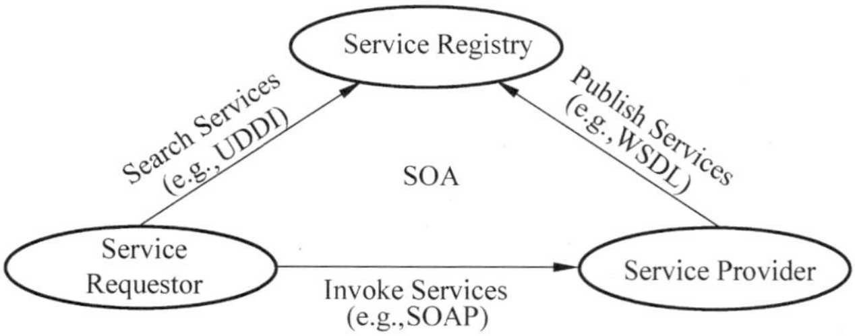

Figure 5.2 A simplified Web services-based SOA

5.2 Services Invocation

As shown in Fig. 5.1 and Fig. 5.2, the SOA model identifies three major processes between Web services interactions: services publishing, services discovery, and services invocation. The first two processes were discussed in Chapter 4. As a natural extension, this section will focus on services invocation techniques.

5.2.1 Simple Services Invocation

After a desired Web service is discovered and located, the service requestor will directly invoke the Web service from the corresponding service provider. Using the network address retrieved from the service registry, the service requestor binds to the located service provider. After negotiating with the service provider as appropriate, the service requestor invokes the required Web service and executes the service remotely provided by the service provider.

How to enhance services invocation and how to automate services invocation remain challenging. As discussed earlier, services can only be remotely accessed through their service interfaces defined in WSDL. Since the current form of WSDL specifications only exposes limited information for Web services interfaces, parameter interpretations and adaptations are typically required prior to and after actual services invocations. In a WSDL service method signature, only the method name and the data types of the parameters are defined. This information is usually too generic and is inadequate for a program to properly invoke the target Web service. There is no semantic information available to help correctly construct input parameters[18]. The WSDL description in Fig. 5.3 shows such an example. The Web service defines an operation named *getShippingPrice*, which takes one input parameter as the weight of merchandise and responds with one output parameter as the calculated shipping price of the merchandise.

```
<message name="getShippingPriceRequest">
   <part name="weight" type="xs:float"/>
</message>

<message name="getShippingPriceResponse">
   <part name="price" type="xs:float"/>
</message>

<portType name="shippingPrice">
   <operation name="getShippingPrice">
      <input message="getShippingPriceRequest"/>
      <output message="getShippingPriceResponse"/>
   </operation>
</portType>
```

Figure 5.3 An example WSDL segment of calculating shipping price

As shown in Fig. 5.3, the WSDL document defines a float number type for the input parameter *weight*. From the name of the parameter, one may guess its semantic meaning, as it represents a measure of the heaviness of a good instead of something else (e.g., temperature). However, what does the number actually represent? What is the unit of the measurement? Is it in the unit of kilogram, or pound, or ounce, or some other units? If it is known that the service provider is an American company, then probably one can guess that the unit of the measurement is *pound*. But this is not precisely defined in the WSDL document in Fig. 5.3. Taking the output parameter as another example, as shown in Fig. 5.3, the WSDL document defines a float number type for the output parameter *price*. From the name of the parameter, one may guess its semantic meaning, as it represents the amount of money required to be paid for the shipping instead of something else (e.g., length). However, what does the number actually represent? What is the monetary unit? Is it in the unit of US dollar, or British pound, or Chinese yuan, or some other units? If it is known that the service provider offers the service oriented to US users, then probably one could guess that the unit of the price is *dollar*. But again, this is not precisely defined in the WSDL document.

These two examples show that unless the semantic definitions are clearly specified, it may be difficult for programmers to correctly prepare input parameters and interpret output parameters, thus may cause subsequent services invocation failure. In other words, adaptation of input parameters will ensure that a Web service can be invoked correctly, and interpretation and adaptation of output parameters will ensure that the results from the Web service are meaningful.

5.2.2 Introduction to MetaWSDL

In order to formally define the semantic information of Web service interfaces and enable automatic parameter adaptation, MetaWSDL[19] is introduced as a superset of WSDL and is complementary to the current WSDL by enriching the semantic definitions of Web services. Two mechanisms are set up to specify two main types of adaptations: specifications for input parameter adaptation and specifications for output result adaptation.

Introduction of MetaObject

In order to encapsulate data transformation and adaptation information, MetaWSDL introduces the concept of *MetaObject* as a wrapper for normal data objects in a WSDL document.

A MetaObject is a self-describing object encapsulating data conversion functions. Each MetaObject contains a required part *unit*, several optional parts *nativeunits*, and the conversion functions between the *unit* and the *nativeunits*. A *unit* represents a parameter carried by a Web service with specific semantic meanings. A *nativeunit* represents a parameter that may be used by a service requestor also with specific semantic meanings.

Each MetaObject is denoted by the *unit*. Figure 5.4 shows two MetaObjects, one for input parameters on the left and the other for output parameters on the right. For the input parameters, the semantic meaning carried by the Web service is *kg*; therefore, the corresponding MetaObject is denoted by *kg*. For the output parameters, the semantic meaning carried by the Web service is *meter*; therefore, the corresponding MetaObject is denoted by *meter*. The MetaObject *kg* is capable of converting between the unit *kg* with three *nativeunits*: *pound, g,* and *oz*. The MetaObject *meter* is capable of converting between the unit *meter* with three *nativeunits*: *mile, km,* and *foot*.

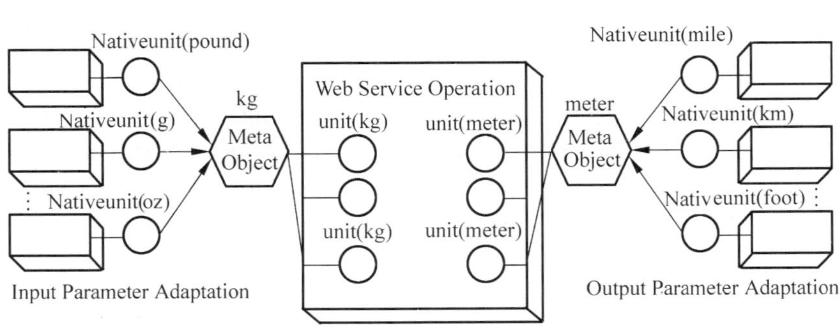

Figure 5.4 Concept of MetaObject

The mapping between "nativeunit" and "unit" in an input adaptation is a many-to-one relationship, meaning that there may exist many "nativeunits" mapping to one "unit", as shown in Fig. 5.4. When the "nativeunit" of an argument of an invoking application is not the same as the "unit" of the corresponding input parameter of the target Web service, the argument needs to be converted into the specified "unit", before invoking the Web service.

As shown in Fig. 5.4, the mapping between "unit" and "nativeunit" in an output adaptation is a one-to-many relationship, meaning that one "unit" can be translated into many "nativeunits". When an output "unit" of a Web service operation is not the same as a "nativeunit" for a locale, it needs to be converted into the specified "nativeunit" before it can be used by the corresponding application.

Each MetaObject carries the conversion functions between its *unit* and all the *nativeunits*, so that it can automatically handle data conversions between *unit* and the *nativeunits*. For example, for the MetaObject shown on the left in Fig. 5.4, it carries the conversion functions between "kg" and "pound", "kg" and "g", and "kg" and "oz".

Every type of input parameter is assigned a dedicated MetaObject, as shown in Fig. 5.4. For example, a MetaObject denoted by "kg" is constructed to serve all the input parameters with MetaWSDL unit "kg". The MetaObject encapsulates the parameter type and handles the corresponding type conversions for the parameter on behalf of the Web service. For example, the MetaObject denoted by "kg" embodies the actual kilogram unit and handles conversions from itself to other known units such as *pound.*

Note that MetaObjects are inheritable Object-Oriented objects, which can be extended to create new sub-MetaObjects, each handling one type of parameter conversion. Sub-MetaObjects automatically inherit all conversion functions defined in the super-MetaObjects. New conversion functions can be added. Existing conversion functions can also be overwritten. Related MetaObjects thus form a hierarchical tree of inheritance. Therefore, the introduction of MetaObject provides a flexible and extensible approach to facilitate services invocation type conversions.

Specifications for Input Parameter Adaptation

In MetaWSDL, two keywords *unit and nativeunit* are thus introduced to represent the concepts of *unit* and *nativeunit.* Every input parameter in each exposed operation (i.e., method) is denoted by its keyword "unit". Different parameters measured by the same unit type are denoted as the same unit. The keyword "nativeunit" denotes the unit format, native to the locale, as obtained by business applications. Figure 5.5 shows a sample MetaWSDL specification for the input parameter of the example shown in Fig. 5.3.

As shown in Fig. 5.5, a pair of "metaWsdl" tags delimits a MetaWSDL specification. A pair of "messageMeta" delimits the specification of the *unit* of a parameter and the possible *nativeunits* it can be converted from. A verbose name "getShippingPriceRequestMeta" is provided for an input adaptation. The *unit* of

```
<?xml version="1.0" encoding="UTF-8" ?>
<metaWsdl xmlns:m="http://schemas.servicescomputing.org/ws/metaWsdl/">
   <messageMeta name="getShippingPriceRequestMeta"/>
      <part name="weight" unit="m:kg"/>
      <nativeunit name="m:pound"/>
      <nativeunit name="m:ounce"/>
      <nativeunit name="m:ton"/>
   </messageMeta>
   <extension>
      <description>
         The input parameter can be in kg, pound, ounce, and ton.
      </description>
   </extension>
</metaWsdl>
```

Figure 5.5 A sample MetaWSDL for weight unit input adaptation

the parameter of the method is "kg", meaning that the input argument should be in the unit of "kg". The MetaWSDL also defines three *nativeunits*: "pound", "ounce", and "ton". The definitions of the *nativeunits* mean two-fold. First, it means that three types of input data are allowed, in addition to the exact type "kg". Second, if input data belong to one of the three *nativeunit* types, conversions are required. As shown in Fig. 5.5, a MetaWSDL can also include an optional tag "extension". This pair of extension tags can be used to carry more verbose information to further specify an invocation process, such as showing a sample native data within this tag. As shown in Fig. 5.5, a verbose description describing the acceptable input data type is defined within the pair of "extension" tags.

Specifications for Output Result Adaptation

In MetaWSDL, the type of each output parameter of a Web service is also denoted by a keyword "unit". Different parameters measured by the same unit type are denoted as the same unit. Same as for input parameters, the keyword "nativeunit" denotes the unit format, native to the locale, as obtained by business applications. Figure 5.6 shows a sample MetaWSDL specification for the output parameter of the example shown in Fig. 5.3.

```
<?xml version="1.0" encoding="UTF-8" ?>
<metaWsdl xmlns:m="http://servicescomputing.org/ws/metaWsdl/">
   <messageMeta name="GetShippingPriceResponseMeta">
      <part name="price" unit="m:dollar">
         <nativeunit name="m:pound"/>
         <nativeunit name="m:yuan"/>
      </part>
   </messageMeta>
</metaWsdl>
```

Figure 5.6 MetaWSDL for Output parameters of getShippingPrice Web service

As shown in Fig. 5.6, the keyword “unit” specifies that the output parameter from the Web service method “getShippingService” is in US dollar. The keyword “nativeunit” specifies that an application may expect to receive results in either British pound or Chinese yuan. If an application expects “pound” as the “nativeunit”, a conversion is required to convert the result from the “unit” of “dollar” to the “nativeunit” of “pound”. Similarly, if an application expects “yuan” as the “nativeunit”, a conversion is needed to convert the result from the “unit” of “dollar” to the “nativeunit” of “yuan”.

Specifications for Custom Type Adaptation

In addition to defining simple data adaptation for simple XML[20] types, MetaWSDL can be used to enable dynamic method signature transformation for custom complex data types. The example in Fig. 5.7 shows a Web service that accepts an input parameter as of type USML script. As discussed in Chapter 4, USML is an XML-based script language for advanced Web services discovery. As shown in Fig. 5.7, a MetaObject is thus constructed, meaning that when the Web service receives user input, a conversion is required to parse the user input and transform it into a valid USML search script. This implies that since the MetaObject is of a custom complex type, a conversion mapping must be specified for the data transformation. As shown in Fig. 5.7, user *nativeunit* input is considered as plain text (xsd:string); a *conversion_mapping* keyword specifies a data transformation mechanism “String2USML_MetaObject” to be adopted. Figure 5.7 also shows that in the section of *extension,* a sample input can be listed to guide users how to prepare a valid input argument, in the example a valid USML script.

```
<?xml version="1.0" encoding="UTF-8" ?>
<metaWsdl xmlns:m="http://servicescomputing.org/ws/metaWsdl/">
   <messageMeta name="getUSMLScriptMeta">
      <part name="usmlRequest" unit="m:USML"/>
      <nativeunit name="xsd:string"
       conversion_mapping="String2USML_MetaObject"/>
   </messageMeta>
   <extension>
     <sampleinput>
       Business
       COMPUTER
       Private UDDI
       http://servicescomputing.org/uddi/computer
       Business
       PRINTING
       Private UDDI
       http://privateUDDI/uddi/computer
       AND
      </sampleinput>
   </extension>
</metaWsdl>
```

Figure 5.7 MetaWSDL for custom data type conversion

It should be noted that the example shown in Fig. 5.7 illustrates another important usage of MetaObject, as it can be used to perform data validation. As shown in Fig. 5.7, a user input search script is checked by the data transformation mechanism "String2USML_MetaObject" to verify whether it is a valid USML search script or not.

5.2.3 MetaWSDL Publishing

As a complement of WSDL, MetaWSDL documents should be published to the Internet and be associated with the original WSDL documents by using the same file name but different file extensions: ".wsdl" for the original WSDL documents and ".mws" for the corresponding complementary MetaWSDL documents. MetaWSDL and WSDL documents can be either stored in the same place or at distributed places.

Different approaches can be used to link them together, for example, by storing the mapping information between them. WSIL[21] is one such method through its description elements building block. The description elements can point to various forms of service description documents; they are extensible and customizable as well. Therefore, this building block enables adding pointers to MetaWSDL documents for original WSDL documents.

Figure 5.8 gives a simple example of a WSIL document that associates a MetaWSDL document with its original WSDL document. As shown in Fig. 5.8, a service *getShippingPrice* is defined, enclosed between the <service> and </service> tags. Each service contains two description elements, one for WSDL document and the other for MetaWSDL document.

```
<inspection xmlns="http://schemas.xmlsoap.org/ws/2001/10/inspection/">
   <service>
       <description referencedNamespace="http://schemas.xmlsoap.org/wsdl/"
location="http://servicescomputing.org/services/getShippingPrice.wsdl"/>
       <description referencedNamespace="http://schemas.xmlsoap.org/metawsdl/"
location="http://servicescomputing.org/MetaWSDLs/getShippingPrice.mws"/>
   </service>
</inspection>
```

Figure 5.8 Sample WSIL document associating MetaWSDL with WSDL documents

Each description element contains attributes "referencedNamespace" and "location". The "referencedNamespace" attribute specifies the namespace to which the referenced document belongs. It helps users determine if the referenced description document is of interest. In this example, semantic information is used as the value to the attribute "referencedNamespace" that specifies whether the document is a WSDL document or its complementary MetaWSDL document, by using either "http://schemas.xmlsoap.org/wsdl/" or "http://schemas.xmlsoap.org/metawsdl/". The "location" attribute specifies the location from which the document can be retrieved. For the original WSDL document, it can be retrieved from "http://servicescomputing.org/services/getShippingPrice.wsdl"; for its complementary MetaWSDL document, it can be retrieved from "http://servicescomputing.org/MetaWSDLs/getShippingPrice.mws".

5.2.4 MetaWSDL-based Advanced Services Invocation Framework

The combination of WSDL, MetaWSDL, and WSIL enables a dynamic invocation pattern for a Web service request. WSDL specifies the basic method signatures for a Web service; MetaWSDL carries semantic information for method signatures not included in WSDL; WSIL links together WSDL and MetaWSDL documents. Therefore, a MetaWSDL-based advanced services invocation framework can be established, as shown in Fig. 5.9. WSDL documents and associated MetaWSDL documents are all published to services registries.

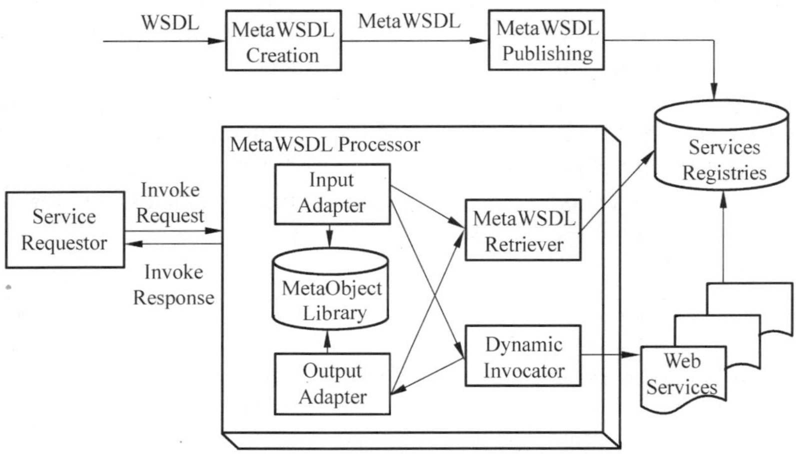

Figure 5.9 MetaWSDL-based advanced Web services invocation framework

As shown in Fig. 5.9, the center of the framework is a MetaWSDL processor. Instead of invoking a Web service directly, a service requestor now sends the invocation request to and receives invocation responses from the MetaWSDL processor. The essential idea of the MetaWSDL process is three-fold. First, before invoking a Web service, the MetaWSDL processor retrieves the corresponding MetaWSDL document associated with the target Web service to find out data transformation mechanisms. Second, the MetaWSDL processor transforms the input data and invokes the Web service. Third, the MetaWSDL processor transforms the responses from the Web service and sends back to the service requestor adapted output data.

As shown in Fig. 5.9, the MetaWSDL process contains one repository (*MetaObject library*) and four major components: an *input adapter*, an *output adapter*, a *MetaWSDL retriever*, and a *dynamic invocator*. The *MetaObject library* is a configurable and extensible repository containing MetaObjects; the *input adapter* realizes input data transformation; the *output adapter* realizes output data adaptation; the *MetaWSDL retriever* queries the services registries to retrieve proper MetaWSDL documents; the *dynamic invocator* invokes the corresponding Web service using adapted input arguments.

The *MetaObject library* contains simple-type, complex-type, or custom-type MetaObjects. It typically holds a configuration file that defines all the MetaObjects that the MetaWSDL processor knows and provides extensibility to the library. Newly created user-defined MetaObjects, whether simple or custom-type, are specified in the configuration file, so that the MetaWSDL processor can invoke it at runtime. Thus, custom MetaObjects can be added into the MetaObject library without any code change.

When a service requestor sends an invocation request to the WSDL processor, the *input adapter* triggers the *MetaWSDL retriever* to obtain corresponding MetaWSDL documents, and then automatically transforms the input data into service-compatible input arguments using the MetaObjects in the *MetaObject library* based upon the transformation mechanisms defined in the MetaWSDL documents, and then passes the adapted request to the *dynamic invocator*. Then the *dynamic invocator* uses the adapted input arguments to invoke the method from the target Web service, receives responses, and passes the responses to the *output adapter*. Before returning the service responses to the service requestor, the *output adapter* interacts with the *MetaWSDL retriever* and transforms the output results to the correct formats as defined in the corresponding MetaWSDL documents.

5.3 SOA: Bridging Business and IT Architecture

As shown in Fig. 5.10, SOA is not merely a technical concept. Instead, it is capable of bridging IT and business requirements. Modern flexible business demands flexible IT support. Consider a business in terms of various business components (e.g., departments), each requiring interacting operations of a set of optimized business processes, each in turn being implemented by IT resources. As business requirements are ever changing, supporting business processes and IT foundations have to change accordingly. SOA is such a model that guides the establishment of a loosely coupled system with flexibility and extensibility. This is why SOA has been catching unprecedented attention and momentum from both academia and industry.

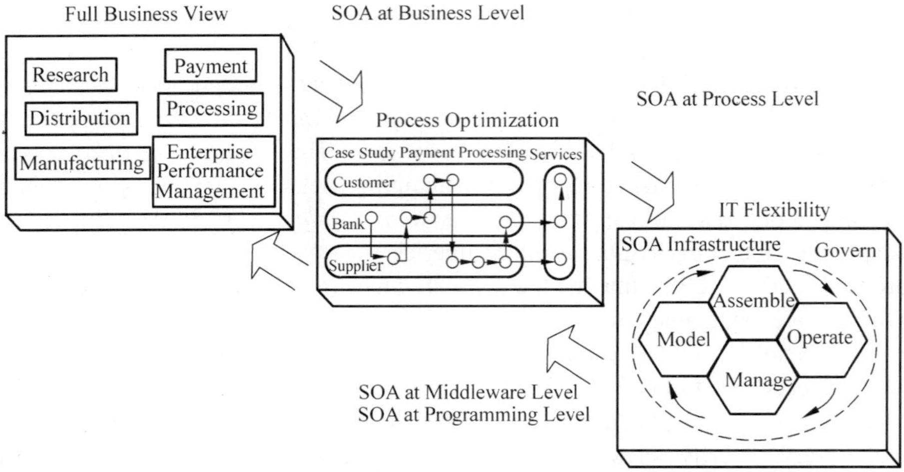

Figure 5.10 SOA at various business and IT levels

SOA at Three Levels

SOA can be used to guide activities at various levels. At the programming level, SOA can be used to guide low-level IT technologies, such as Simple Object Access Protocol (SOAP) and binary SOAP messaging for data transportation. One recent SOA programming model is Service Component Architecture (SCA)[22].

At the middleware level, SOA can be used to guide design and development of common product and open-source software. For example, SOA can be utilized to help select from different models (e.g., single Enterprise Service Bus (ESB)[23] or multiple ESBs, message-oriented or event-based infrastructures) according to different enterprise maturities. SOA infrastructure supports simplified version of an SOA lifecycle from modeling, assembling, operating/deploying and management to achieve IT flexibility. Finally, as shown in Fig. 5.10, governance is used to provide normative guidance and exception handling mechanism to the iterative phases in an SOA lifecycle.

At the process level, SOA can be used to guide business process integration and management, as well as the design of event-driven architecture. For example, a payment processing business process may require customers, banks, and suppliers to be involved through service-oriented integration model, as shown in Fig. 5.10.

At the enterprise level, SOA can be used to componentize an enterprise and support high-level transformation consulting. For example, SOA can help executives decide whether to implement a business process using an SOA service package or to divide the business process into sub-processes using the SOA concept. As shown in Fig. 5.10, an enterprise could be componentized into key business areas (e.g., research, payment, distribution, development, manufacturing, and enterprise performance management (EPM)) for higher flexibility and extensibility.

SOA on a Bilateral View

Figure 5.10 also illustrates a bilateral view of how SOA realizes business and IT linkages. One is a top-down approach that decomposes business components into business processes, each being realized by IT processes. The other is a bottom-up approach that provides SOA-based IT resources, which can be seamlessly integrated to rapidly create new business processes that lead to new business opportunities.

In either top-down or bottom-up approach, SOA offers essential guidance at various granularities: business level, process level, middleware level, and programming level. At each level, SOA guides to decompose a big unit into smaller service-centered units in the top-down method, and guides to organize available small units into larger unites providing new services in the bottom-up method.

5.4 SOA Solution Lifecycle

With the basic concept of the paradigm and the three basic operations of SOA, it is time to discuss how to apply the SOA model to design and develop business solutions. A concept of lifecycle of an SOA solution is introduced[24], which consists of services modeling, development, deployment, publishing, discovery, composition, collaboration, monitoring, and management with analytical control. Note that the Web services technology is used as the underlying technology, but the SOA solution lifecycle is independent from Web services.

In an SOA-centered software system, services are considered as the most fundamental construction units. Each software component is constructed as a service; each service possesses a standard interface so that it can interact with other service components in a standard way. SOA sheds a light on building a business solution by leveraging existing systems and applications. In a simple case, one can wrap up a legacy application with a Web service interface and then publish it to service registries (e.g., a UDDI registry or WSIL documents). Thus, the application can be universally accessed as a normal Web service. For example, in J2EE, JAX-RPC[25] is widely used to wrap existing applications and expose them as Web services. In a more sophisticated case, one can use a Web services composition language (e.g., BPEL)[26,27] to capture an invocation sequence of a set of available Web services into a comprehensive business process[28 – 30].

With the SOA paradigm, the lifecycle of a service exhibits significant differences from that of a traditional software component. A service's *lifecycle* refers to the period of time that begins when a service is conceived and ends when the service is no longer used. Explicit recognition of the lifecycle of a service encourages service practitioners to address particular issues at the appropriate time; for example, to model a service before actual development work begins.

The service lifecycle provides a diachronic view of the solution engineering process. Figure 5.11 illustrates the lifecycle of a Web services-based solution, which covers how a Web service is created, published, used, composed, and managed in a solution context. A typical lifecycle of an SOA solution consists of nine phases: modeling, development, deployment, publishing, discovery, invocation, composition, collaboration, as well as monitoring and management. These phases may overlap or be performed iteratively.

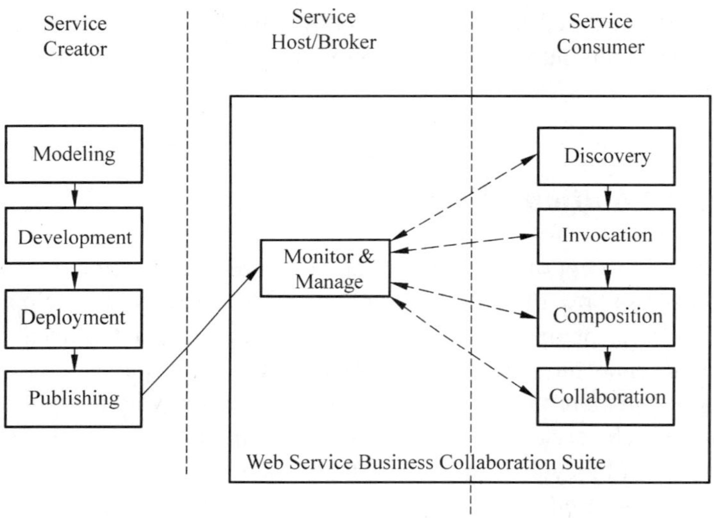

Figure 5.11 SOA service lifecycle for development and management

In the lifecycle of an SOA solution, multiple parties may be involved dynamically in one or more stages. As shown in Fig. 5.11, all involving parties can be categorized into three roles: creator, host/registry, and consumer. Creators are responsible for modeling, developing, deploying, and publishing Web services. Hosts/registries and users leverage Web services via discovery, invocation, composition, and collaboration processes, while monitoring and managing Web services in the process of usages. Consumers consume Web services. An entity can act in multiple roles. For example, a creator can also consume created Web services; a creator can also host its own Web services.

5.4.1 Modeling

The first stage of a service lifecycle is to design the service using conceptual modeling techniques. To date the dominant Web services modeling approach is a

WSDL-based top-down decomposition method. Before code development, the interface of the Web service is first defined in platform-independent WSDL. Fundamentally, this method is no different from the traditional interface-first design approach. One of the challenges on Web services modeling is to find a way to carry more semantic information about method signature adaptations for dynamic Web services invocations. For example, in previous section, MetaWSDL is introduced to represent the semantic information of WSDL for adaptive Web services invocations, including the information for describing and quantifying the input and output parameters. OMG's UML-based Model Driven Architecture (MDA) is another modeling approach that can be used to model the complexities of a business solution using Web services and SOA.

5.4.2 Development

After the interface of a Web service is defined using a standard service definition language, the detailed implementations of the service can be realized using any programming languages (e.g., Java, C#, and C++). The development phase of a service refers to several stages of a typical software lifecycle, including design, development, and testing[31]. Software development methodologies can be used to guide through the development process of a Web service, such as Rational Unified Process (RUP)[32], Agile methodology[33], or even the waterfall model[34]. The outcome is a well-tested service that implements the predefined WSDL interfaces and is ready to be published to the service registry for global access or controlled access[31]. SOAP is used as the message protocol for expressing requests and responses to and from a Web service. In J2EE platform, JAX-RPC is widely used as a mechanism to pack and marshall/unmarshall parameters and return values to and from Web services.

5.4.3 Deployment

In theory, a service can be deployed on any platforms. The deployment binds the abstract service definition to the XML-based protocols, such as SOAP over HTTP. Typically, a service is deployed to a server machine according to the type of the implementation of the service. For example, an EJB-based Web service is deployed to an EJB container in a J2EE-based Web application server.

5.4.4 Publishing

After a service is modeled, developed, and deployed, it needs to be published onto the Internet for users to access at any time from anywhere. This is where the binding information is described, as about how to connect and interact with the service. The details of Web services registries and publishing mechanisms can be found in Chapter 4.

5.4.5 Discovery

Web services discovery refers to the process of dynamically finding appropriate Web services from heterogeneous Web services registries. Typically, services publication/discovery processes are realized using the well-known publisher/ subscriber model. Services discovery through UDDI is normally complemented by subscription services. Using predefined subscription profiles carrying preferences on desired services, service requestors browse various catalogs of available services. Detailed information on Web services discovery is given in Chapter 4.

5.4.6 Invocation

After an expected Web service is discovered, a service requestor directly invokes the Web service from the corresponding service provider using the binding information obtained from the service registries. Typically, the service requestor and the service provider negotiate on Service Level Agreements (SLAs). After achieving mutual agreements, the service requestor invokes the required Web service and executes the service remotely at the site of the service provider. SOAP is typically used in conjunction with other transport protocols or mechanisms (e.g., HTTP, SMTP[35], or MQ[36]) to carry out the invocation requests and responses. On both sides of the service provider and service requestor, marshall / unmarshall of information needs to be performed. For example, on the service provider side, a SOAP listener receives incoming requests, validates the message against XML schemas[37] as described in WSDL, unmarshall the SOAP message, and dispatch the message to appropriate service code. In J2EE, JAX-RPC is typically used to send SOAP method calls to remote parties and to receive results.

5.4.7 Composition

A comprehensive business process typically requires supports from multiple services. Web service composition refers to a process of adaptively composing a set of available Web services into a business process flow, according to predefined business requirements. To standardize and formalize the specification of business processes, several business process languages are created, such as Business Process Execution Language for Web Services (BPEL4WS, a.k.a. BPEL)[27] and Web Service Choreography Interface (WSCI)[29]. Chapter 9 will discuss requirements-driven services composition, aiming at modeling flexible business requirement representation, automating search process based on business requirements, and composing an optimal business process.

5.4.8 Collaboration

In a comprehensive business process, multiple services may need to collaborate toward a common goal. Since these services are typically provided and invoked by different service providers, they need to be well coordinated. Information exchange between collaborating services requires special attention. Semantic meanings should be considered to realize proper interactions between services. In addition, assurance of the coexistence of service components in a business process is also the most important.

5.4.9 Monitoring and Management

Since Web services are designed to be used by service requestors through the Internet or Intranet, it is critical to monitor and control its execution. Typical service monitoring and controlling include access control, performance monitoring, Service Level Agreement (SLA) enforcement, and exception handling. Access control ensures availability of a Web service through appropriate authorization. Performance monitoring examines closely the status of a Web service under parallel execution and assures its Quality of Service (QoS). SLA defines mutual agreements between service providers and service requestors. SLA enforcement guarantees the satisfaction levels for service requestors. Whenever there is a business exception, some control mechanisms are needed for exception handling. Furthermore, there is a need to monitor and track the status of the exchanged information in a distributed environment, which is a typical visibility control issue in a service-to-service collaboration chain. Moreover, a comprehensive business solution typically involves multiple parties across business boundaries. When a Web service is used in such a business solution, its monitoring and tracking involves multiple parties.

One of the challenges for monitoring the status of a SOA solution across multiple organizations is to define a federated access control policy, which is used to coordinate the access control scope and access rights by leveraging existing trust and access control components provided in individual software components. After monitoring the real-time activities, data analysis and information analysis are needed for adjusting the current major steps for better modeling, deployment, discovery, composition, collaboration, and monitoring, if necessary.

5.5 Enterprise Service Bus (ESB)

The concept of Enterprise Service Bus (ESB)[38] paves a new way of systematically constructing and deploying enterprise services. An ESB is a conceptual software infrastructure that facilitates dynamic integration, message routing, mediation, and control of service components and their interactions. The concept of ESB, as a matter of fact, is not completely new. It is similar to Common Object Request Broker Architecture (CORBA)[39] *object bus* and Java 2 Platform, Enterprise Edition (J2EE)[40] *application server*. The differences are: CORBA *object bus* integrates Object-Oriented software components; J2EE *application server* integrates JavaBeans[41] and J2EE applications; while ESB integrates services and service components conceptually.

As shown in Fig. 5.12, an ESB provides a common SOA-based platform that allows various service components to plug in and communicate with each other. As shown in Fig. 5.12, ESB favors a key feature of platform-neutral. An application component developed in any technologies (e.g., Java, .Net, and mainframe) can be easily integrated to the ESB and form a new business process. In its most basic form, an ESB provides a management framework to support integration, message routing, and simple transformation. The framework may also provide real-time monitoring and management capabilities for system health and availability. It also includes capabilities to ensure configurable security control and management. The integration part provides service orchestration engines to construct both stateful (long-running) and stateless (short-running) processes from available service components. The message routing part provides a way for service components to send data via messages through standard protocols. Routing and filtering of messages to/from service components are plugged-in (registered) in the ESB. In short, ESB framework can offer a synchronous/asynchronous store-and-forward message delivery mechanism. The simple transformation facilities enable various plugged-in service components to exchange XML data based on XML Schema.

As shown in Fig. 5.12, an ESB product usually provides a dashboard that allows a user to create a user-friendly services-oriented application rapidly. This dashboard also allows a user to configure message formats, specify routing policies, and define necessary message transformation rules. Meanwhile, the dashboard should also allow a user to create a personalized portal that aggregates services from multiple sources.

Figure 5.12 shows a basic form of ESB. More advanced ESBs typically offer a number of additional value-added features. For example, a comprehensive ESB may contain tools for services discovery and provisioning, dynamically adjusting Service Level Agreement (SLA) based on performance and error events, and so on. As another example, an ESB may provide advanced Web services discovery as presented in Chapter 4. Moreover, particular adapters may be applied to enable connectivity into packages, custom enterprise applications, and other emerging technologies.

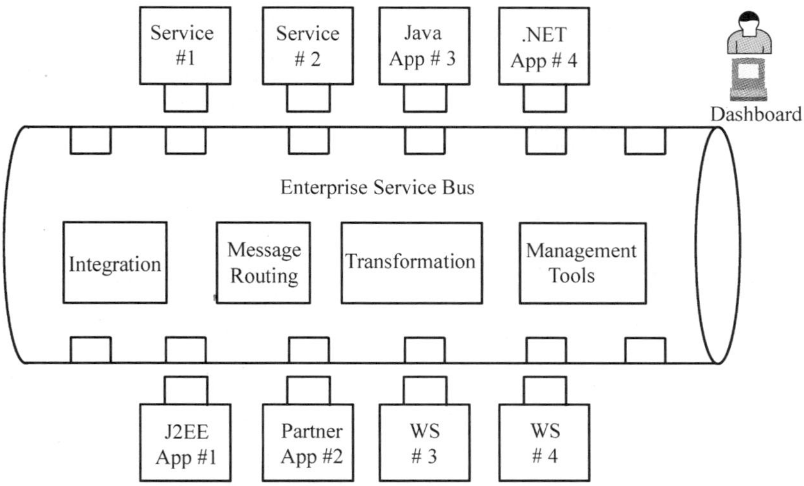

Figure 5.12 Enterprise Service Bus (ESB)

In short, an ESB provides an infrastructure that enables interoperability and reusability of service components from integration and messaging perspectives.

5.6 SOA Reference Architecture (SOA-RA)

This section will introduce an SOA Reference Architecture (SOA-RA)[46], as shown in Fig. 5.13, which can be used as a guidance for IT architects to design the overall architecture of an SOA solution[42].

SOA-RA

As shown in Fig. 5.13, SOA-RA partitions an SOA-based system into a two-dimensional architecture with five horizontal layers and four vertical layers. The horizontal dimension implements functional requirements, while the vertical dimension provides system-support facilities and enablement. The four vertical layers of the system include: Integration layer, Data Architecture layer, Quality of Service (QoS) layer, and Governance layer. The five horizontal layers are further divided into two tiers: services provider tier and services consumer tier. The services provider tier acts as the back-end of the application, while the services consumer tier acts as the front-end serving application users. As shown in Fig. 5.13, Service layer is shared by the services provider tier and the services consumer tier.

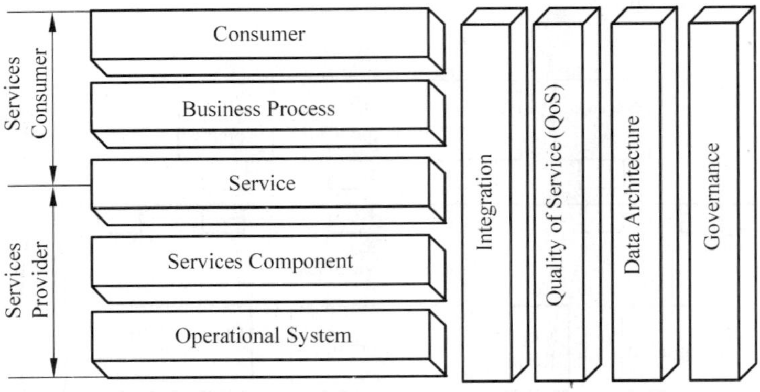

Figure 5.13 SOA Reference Architecture (SOA-RA)

For the five horizontal layers, the Operational System layer contains existing packaged applications (applications provided by individual service vendors (ISVs)), customer applications (applications developed in-house or to-be- developed), and legacy systems (existing applications developed in traditional ways). Traditionally, these applications could only be used for one purpose and serve one specific user. With the aid of SOA, an application can be exposed as a service with standard interfaces; so that it can be reused by other upper-level services.

The Services Component layer provides code containers that implement services (i.e., service interfaces) defined in the Service Layer. A services component may rely on some packaged components from the Operational System layer, some services from the Service layer, and some business processes from the Business Process layer. For example, a services component can be implemented in a Java Class, EJB, or .Net Component. In addition, a services component may include the implementations of multiple methods, while some methods exposed as services in the Service layer. Moreover, the Services Component layer is responsible for automate input transformation and output adaptation from invocation perspective.

The Service layer extends the known triangular SOA model into a comprehensive logical layer enabling and facilitating service registration, decomposition, discovery, binding, interface aggregation, as well as service lifecycle management. The Service layer introduces a concept *service cluster*, which refers to a collection (category) of Web services conceptually serving a common business function. These Web services may be published by different service providers, and differentiated with each other by specific features. For example, a shipping service cluster may include various services from various service providers such as UPS, USPS, and FedEx. For each service cluster decomposed from a business process in the Business Process layer, the Service layer is responsible for locating appropriate service provider and binding to the target Web service interface. In addition, the Service layer is also capable of aggregating multiple service interfaces into a new service.

The Business Process layer handles all business logics regarding services composition and decomposition. For services composition, this layer leverages the Service layer to quickly compose and choreograph services and to coordinate business processes to fulfill customer requirements. For services decomposition, this layer provides facilities to decompose business requirements into tasks comprising conceptual service clusters, each being realized by existing business processes, services, and services components. It should be noted that the Business Process layer does not focus on individual business process representation, which can be fulfilled by workflow description languages such as Business Process Execution Language (BPEL). Rather, this layer focuses on building SOA solutions using business processes from the perspective of coordination and management of a set of processes.

The Consumer layer is responsible for presentation that leverages the Business Process layer, the Service layer, or other layers, to quickly construct the user interfaces of business services to fulfill customer requirements. In other words, this layer is responsible for building a front-end interface to interact with users for an SOA solution. The Service consumer layer typically should provide caching facility to enhance presentation performance. In addition, this layer should simultaneously support various types of users or channels, such as B2B, desktop, wireless, and Personal Digital Assistant (PDA).

The Integration layer is a key enabler for an SOA solution as it provides the capability to mediate, route, and transform service requests between service requestors and service providers. Enterprise Service Bus (ESB) is one example that fulfills the responsibility of this layer.

The Quality of Services (QoS) layer provides solution-level QoS management in various aspects, such as availability, reliability, security, and safety. Note that this layer does not focus on service-level QoS control; instead, this layer concentrates on providing a mechanism to support, track, monitor, and manage solution-level QoS control. The details of solution-level QoS control will be introduced in Chapter 8.

The Data Architecture layer provides a unified representation and enablement framework that integrates with domain-specific data architecture to facilitate value chain integration (i.e., integration of services developed by different parties). Typical domain-specific data architecture examples are: the Shared Information and Data model (SID) in eTOM[43] of telecommunication industry, and the RosettaNet Technical Dictionary and RosettaNet Business Dictionary defined by RosettaNet[44] for electronics industry.

The Governance layer provides design guidance to ensure the proper design of the SOA solution architecture. Typically, the layer helps to establish best practices or their references (e.g., Center of Excellence of SOA/Web services), to establish principles of how to define SOA solution in each layer, and to establish principles of how to monitor in running system and how to handle exceptions at runtime.

Practices and Services Engineering Methodology for SOA

In short, SOA-RA shows an abstraction of how to construct an SOA solution as a set of logical layers. It should be noted that an SOA-RA is a loosely-coupled architecture in that each layer is not strictly hidden from the layers above. For example, the Consumer lay may choose to access a service through the Business Process layer or the Service layer directly; the Service lay may choose to leverage two styles of service implementation: either services components like EJBs or .NET components from the Services Component layer, or packaged applications such as SAP or Siebel or other SOA-enabled legacy applications from the Operational System layer. For another example, a service provider may provide an implementation of a service in a services component or through the wrapping of an existing system or packaged application. Furthermore, the service provider will ensure quality of service through the security, monitoring, and management supplied by the QoS layer. The communication between a service and its services component implementation or operational system will occur via the Integration layer. If there is a point-to-point connection (although it is discouraged), it will come through this layer. Moreover, if there is an Enterprise Service Bus (ESB), it will also reside in the Integration layer.

The SOA reference architecture is an enterprise architectural template that guides the creation of SOA solutions at the enterprise level by defining reference architecture. Organizations may start from this reference model, customize it, and apply it to develop solutions for one or more lines of business. In fact, organizations may have different lines of business use this architectural template, customizing it for their own needs and integrating and interacting among themselves.

In order to define an SOA-oriented system architecture applying the SOA-RA model, a best practice called Service-Oriented Modeling and Architecture (SOMA)[45] from IBM guides a generic engineering process. SOMA depicts detailed steps to configure components in SOA-RA layers. Three steps are defined: identification of services, specification of services, and realization of services.

The *service identification* step comprises a combination of top-down, bottom-up, and middle-out techniques of domain decomposition (i.e., decompose domain knowledge into controllable components), existing asset analysis, and goal-service modeling.

The *service specification* step comprises service classification or categorization, subsystem analysis, and component specification.

The *service realization* step comprises service allocation (i.e., assigning services to the subsystems that have been identified) and making decisions for service realization (e.g., select from vendor, custom built, integration, transformation, subscription, and outsourcing part of services).

5.7 Discussions on SOA

When talking about SOA, people will typically discuss the known triangular SOA operational model. This chapter goes beyond that and introduces advanced SOA techniques and SOA Reference Architecture oriented to an SOA solution. First, advanced services invocation techniques are introduced along with advanced services publishing and services discovery capability discussed in Chapter 4. Then, this chapter introduces how SOA can bridge the gap between business models and IT models at the conceptual level, the lifecycle of an SOA solution, and the advanced ESB technique. Finally, SOA Reference Architecture and services engineering methodology are introduced.

Although SOA has been widely considered as a promising enabling technology to bridge the gap between business and IT, a systematic SOA-based engineering methodology associated with integrated development environment (IDE) and tool sets is still missing. Such a methodology should provide end-to-end guidance and assistance to refine and transform business models created by business experts into IT models understandable by IT architects and engineers, and then from IT models to IT implementation code. Such an IDE environment and tool sets should provide SOA best practice-based templates and patterns to capture the knowledge from service consumers and service providers and help SOA practitioners quickly establish a prototype for an SOA solution based on reusable assets. In addition, such an environment should provide corresponding algorithms and solutions, as well as verification facilities, to assist SOA practitioners to design valid and optimal architectural models. How to ensure an SOA system built from these techniques conforms to business requirements is another critical issue. In short, all of these topics and issues are open to researchers and practitioners.

5.8 Summary

In this chapter, we have introduced the basic concept of SOA as the fundamental architectural model of Services Computing, the triangular SOA operational model and three critical processes. The lifecycle of an SOA solution is introduced, followed by SOA Reference Architecture aiming at guiding IT architects to design the architecture of an SOA solution.

References

[1] Maximilien EM, Singh MP (2005) Toward Web services interaction styles. In: 2005 IEEE International Conference on Services Computing (SCC'05), pp 147 – 154

[2] Baresi L, Heckel R, Thone S, D V (2003) Modeling and validation of service-oriented architectures: application vs. style. In: ACM SIGSOFT Software Engineering Notes, Proceedings of the 9th European software engineering conference held jointly with 11th ACM SIGSOFT international symposium on Foundations of software engineering ESEC/FSE-11, pp 68 – 77

[3] Erl T (2005) Service-Oriented Architecture: a field guide to integrating XML and Web services. Prentice Hall

[4] Erl T (2004) Service-Oriented Architecture (SOA): concepts, technology, and design. Prentice Hall

[5] Marks EA, Bell M (2006) Service-Oriented Architecture (SOA): a planning and implementation guide for business and technology. John Wiley & Sons

[6] Cerami E (2002) Web services essentials. 1st edn. O'Reilly Media

[7] Tsai W, Fan C, Chen Y, Paul R, Chung JY (2006) Architecture classification for SOA-based applications. In: 2006 Ninth IEEE International Symposium on Object and Component-Oriented Real-Time Distributed Computing (ISORC 2006), pp 24 – 26

[8] Falkl J (2005) Service Oriented Architecture compliance: initial steps in a longer journey. http://download.boulder.ibm.com/ibmdl/pub/software/dw/webservices/soa-compliance.pdf

[9] Alonso G, Casati F, Kuno H, Machiraju V (2003) Web services. 1st edn. Springer

[10] Krafzig D, Banke K, Slama D (2004) Enterprise SOA: service-oriented architecture best practices. Prentice Hall

[11] Newcomer E, Lomow G (2005) Understanding SOA with Web services. Addison-Wesley

[12] Singh MP, Huhns MN (2005) Service-Oriented Computing. John Wiley & Sons

[13] Zhang J, Chang CK, Chung JY, Kim SW (2004) S-Net: a petri-net based specification model for Web services. In: IEEE International Conference on Web Services (ICWS 2004), San Diego, CA, USA, pp 420 – 427

[14] Clark M, Fletcher P, Hanson JJ, Irani R, Waterhouse M, Thelin J (2003) Web services business strategies and architectures. A-Press

[15] UDDI. http://www.uddi.org/specification.html

[16] (2001) Web Services Description Language (WSDL). http://www.w3.org/TR/wsdl

[17] SOAP specifications. http://www.w3.org/TR/soap/

[18] McIlraith SA, Son TC, Zeng H (2001) Semantic Web services. IEEE Intelligent Systems 16: 46 – 53

[19] Zhang LJ, Chao T, Chang H, Chung JY (2002) Automatic method signature adaptation framework for dynamic Web service invocation. In: 6th World Multi Conference on Systemics, Cybernetics and Informatics (SCI 2002), pp 541 – 546

[20] XML. http://xml.coverpages.org/xml.html

[21] IBM Web Services Inspection Language. http://www-128.ibm.com/developerworks/library/specification/ws-wsilspec/

[22] Service Component Architecture assembly model specification, version 0.9. http://download.boulder.ibm.com/ibmdl/pub/software/dw/specs/ws-sca/SCA_Assembly-Model_V09.pdf
[23] Keen M, Bishop S, Hopkins A, Milinski S, Nott C, Robinson R, Adams J, and Verschueren P (2004) Patterns: implementing an SOA with the enterprise service bus. IBM Press
[24] Zhang LJ, Jeckle M (2003) The next big thing: Web services collaboration. Lecture Notes on Computer Science 2853, Springer, pp 1 – 10
[25] JAX-RPC. http://java.sun.com/webservices/jaxrpc/
[26] OASIS (2003) Business Process Execution Language (BPEL4WS, version 1.1). http://xml.coverpages.org/BPELv11-May052003Final.pdf
[27] Business Process Execution Language for Web Services Version 1.1. http://www.ibm.com/developerworks/library/ws-bpel
[28] Peltz C (2003) Web services orchestration and choreography. IEEE Computer 36: 46 – 52
[29] Web Service Choreography Interface. http://www.w3.org/TR/wsci/
[30] Simmons S (2005) Introducing the WebSphere integration reference architecture: a service-based foundation for enterprise-Level business integration. http://www-128.ibm.com/developerworks/websphere/techjournal/0508_simmons/0508_simmons.html
[31] Zhang J, Chang CK, Zhang LJ, Hung PCK (2007) Phased transformation toward services-oriented architecture. IEEE Transactions on Systems, Man, and Cybernetics, Part A
[32] Kruchten P (2000) The Rational Unified Process: An Introduction (2nd Edition). Addison-Wesley Professional
[33] Martin RC (2002) Agile software development, principles, patterns, and practices. Prentice Hall
[34] Sommerville I (2000) Software engineering (6th Edition). Addison Wesley
[35] Simple Mail Transfer Protocol (SMTP). http://www.ietf.org/rfc/rfc0821.txt
[36] IBM MQSeries. http://www-306.ibm.com/software/integration/wmq/
[37] XML Schema. http://www.w3.org/XML/Schema
[38] Enterprise Service Bus (ESB). http://en.wikipedia.org/wiki/Enterprise_Service_Bus
[39] OMG CORBA. http://www.corba.org/
[40] Sun Java 2 Platform, Enterprise Edition (J2EE). http://java.sun.com/j2ee/1.4/download.html?cid=101309
[41] Sun JavaBeans. http://java.sun.com/products/javabeans/
[42] IBM Service-Oriented Architecture. http://www.ibm.com/soa
[43] The Enhanced Telecom Operations Map (eTOM). http://www.tmforum.org/browse.aspx?catID = 1648
[44] RosettaNet. http://www.rosettanet.org/
[45] Arsanjani A (2004) Service-oriented modeling and architecture. http://www-128.ibm.com/developerworks/webservices/library/ws-soa-design1/
[46] Ali Arsanjani, Liang-Jie Zhang, Michael Ellis, Abdul Allam, Kishore Channabasavaiah (2007) S3: A Service-Oriented Reference Architecture. IEEE IT Professional, May/June

6 Services Relationship Modeling

6.1 Introduction to Services Relationship Modeling

Interface-based services discovery discussed in Chapter 4 is actually a function-oriented services discovery. In the real world, business services discovery typically has to consider other features in addition to business functions. Business relationship is an important one. For example, consider that a business organization *A* intends to decide from two business services serving the same functionality: service *b* produced by business *B* and service *c* produced by business *C*. Assuming that business *A* has formed an alliance relationship with business *B*, business *A* thus will be more likely to choose service *b* due to this existing business relationship. For another example, suppose an enterprise E_1 needs to compose a business process including service *s*. Enterprises E_2 and E_3 both provide similar service *s*. However, there is a partnership between E_1 and E_2 leading to a service discount, and there is no specific relationship between E_1 and E_3. If price is a requirement of consideration for E_1, the partnership between E_1 and E_2 shall be counted in order to form the most appropriate business process.

These two simple examples illustrate that business relationships usually play an important role in business services discovery. Well-captured relationships can facilitate services discovery by providing sufficient information for precise judgment. In addition, by modeling relationships between services, services registry can be enhanced to capture more comprehensive information and better categorize registered services according to their features and interrelationships.

Based on these considerations, in recent years, business relationship modeling has gained significant attention in business services discovery and integration. By describing business relationships in addition to service functionalities, services registry owners can further strengthen service requestors' confidences about the trustworthiness and legitimacy of business services found from the services registries. Furthermore, SOA-based e-Business solutions are typically comprised of multiple services. Its unprecedented openness demands comprehensive understanding and management of the business relationships between the contained services, in order to maintain the relationships between them in case of any changes of the e-Business systems. For example, if a service is changed, its related services with dependency relationship shall be examined.

SOA-oriented business integration can be divided into two levels, each involving specific types of business relationships. The first level of business integration refers to creating simple connections between existing business applications. Business entities and activities are represented and implemented by services; services interact with each other to realize business integrations and collaborations. This level of integration specifies structural and temporal relationships between services.

The second level of business integration requires effective interactions between services, which need more than simple dependency relationships. These kinds of relationships, such as partnership, alliance, and exclusion, are critical to the success of realistic business process integration. For example, assuming several business entities (e.g., service providers) form an alliance, business scenarios conducted in the domain of the alliance will receive a higher priority or a larger discount. A business entity thus prefers to consider the services provided by the partners in the alliance than those with the same functions but provided by other entities out of the alliance. Another example is that a business entity may be a competitor of some service providers. Thus, it may not select services provided by its competitors.

As a result, creating a relationships binding mechanism for business services is becoming an emerging requirement for dynamic business services integration.

6.1.1 UDDI Specifications on Simple Relationships

UDDI[1] specification defines assertions of business relationships between two parties. Due to their comprehensive nature, large-scale enterprises or marketplaces can hardly be represented by one single unit *businessEntity*. Therefore, a structure comprising several *businessEntity* units is often used to represent individual subsidiaries of a large enterprise or individual participants of a marketplace. In order to explicitly declare the relationships between integral parts in their UDDI registrations, related businesses use the *xx_publisherAssertion* messages to indicate business relationships. In a case that a publisher is responsible for related businesses, the corresponding relationships automatically become visible after the publisher publishes one assertion. The *publisherAssertion* structure consists of the following three elements: *fromKey* (the first *businessKey*), *toKey* (the second *businessKey*), and *keyedReference*. The *keyedReference* designates the type of the asserted relationship in terms of a (keyName, keyValue) pair within a *tModel* (technical model or service type), which is uniquely referenced by a *tModelKey*.

6.1.2 Other Relationship Specification Languages

The underpinning of the UDDI assertion infrastructure is the Resource Description

Framework (RDF)[2], whose central idea is a concept of assertion, associated with a concept of quotation that makes assertions about assertions. The rationale of a quotation is two-fold: first, comprehensive relationships require hierarchical assertions; second, most initial RDF-based applications center around data about data (or so-called "metadata"), in which assertions about assertions are natural to represent the relationships between data even without logic. RDF has been widely considered as a disciplined methodology for XML[3] development by annotating documents with metadata.

However, RDF is not, and it was not meant to be, a general-purpose knowledge representation language. Therefore, DARPA Agent Markup Language (DAML)[4] was originally coined for this purpose. Later releases of DAML incorporate the European Community's Ontology Interface Layer (OIL)[5]. The resulting DAML+ OIL[5] is known as a semantic markup language for Web resources. It builds on earlier W3C standards RDF and RDF Schema[2], and extends these languages with richer modeling primitives[5].

Meanwhile, Web Ontology Language for Web Services (OWL-S)[6] (formerly DAML-S)[4] provides a markup language support to Web service providers for describing the properties and capabilities of their Web services in an unambiguous computer-interpretable manner. OWL-S markup of Web services intends to facilitate the automation of Web service tasks, including automated Web services discovery, execution, interoperation, composition, and execution monitoring.

Furthermore, eXtensible Customer Relationships Language (xCRL)[7] from Organization for the Advancement of Structured Information Standards (OASIS)[8] focuses on an effective single customer view to achieve interoperability between different systems, processes, and platforms. xCRL identifies three types of customer relationships: organization-to-organization relationship, organization-to-person relationship, and person-to-person relationship. OASIS also illustrates some simple examples of organization-to-organization relationships: Company *A* "TRADING AS" Company *B*; Company *A* is the subsidiary of Company *B*; Company *A* is the parent of Company *B*; Company *A*, Company *B* and Company *C* are the subsidiary companies of Company *D*, and so forth.

In general, DAML-S focuses on describing the advertisements of the service properties and capabilities. It does not provide facilities to describe the relationships among services, businesses, and operations. xCRL describes the relationships among general service providers, similar to the *publisherAssertion* defined in UDDI specification. However, all of these works are not designed for describing the relationships among Web services in standard services registries, such as UDDI and WSIL documents. In short, the current Web services world suffers from a lack of formalization in terms of metadata formats for relationship bindings.

6.2 Web Services Relationship Language (WSRL)

Since Web services is currently the best enabling technology to implement SOA, a business relationship description language is developed based on the Web services technology, which is called Web Services Relationship Language (WSRL)[9]. WSRL intends to seek a dynamic and extensible solution by defining a richer and broader range of relationships at various levels oriented to dynamic business service integration.

WSRL is an XML-based description language for formal description of the semantic relationships between Web services. In detail, WSRL identifies three levels of relationships for Web services: business entity level, Web service level, and operation level. At the business entity level, WSRL defines four types of relationships: partnership, parent-child relationship, exclusion, and alliance. At the Web service level, WSRL also defines four types of relationships: parent-child, exclusion, binding, and community. At the operation level, WSRL defines another four types of relationships: constraint, exclusion, community, and parent-child. All of these relationships are straightforward based on common sense and can be easily understood from their names.

6.2.1 Structure of a WSRL Document

Figure 6.1 shows the basic structure of a WSRL document. The tag <wsrl> represents a WSRL definition file, which includes four elements: *bbr*, *ssr*, *oor*, and *wsrl-link*. The tag <bbr> declares that the relationship is a business-level relationship. The tag <partnership> in turn specifies a partnership relationship with a unique id *p*1; the tag <alliance> specifies an alliance relationship with a unique id *a*1. The tag <ssr> declares that the relationship is a Web service-level relationship. The tag <parent-child> in turn specifies a parent-child relationship with a unique id *pc*1. The tag <oor> declares that the relationship is an operation-level relationship. The tag <constraint> in turn specifies a constraint relationship with a unique id *oc*1. The element "wsrl-link" is used to point to another WSRL file.

6.2.2 WSRL Discussions

WSRL provides a declarative mechanism to create and describe the relationships between Web services at three levels[9]. It defines an XML-based representation to encapsulate comprehensive relationships among business entities, services, and service types.

```
<?xml version="1.0"?>
<wsrl>
  <bbr>
     <partnership id=p1>
 ...
     </partnership >
     <alliance id=a1>
      ...
     </alliance >
  </bbr>
  <ssr>
     <parent-child id=pc1>
  ...
     </parent-child>
  </ssr>
  <oor>
     <constraint id=oc1>
  ...
     </constraint>
  </oor>
  <wsrl-link>
  ...
  </wsrl-link>
</wsrl>
```

Figure 6.1 Structure of a WSRL document

A WSRL specification document can be embedded into other documents via a link tag. A WSRL document can be created for a specific business purpose and represents a value-added Web service. For example, a mortgage agent can use WSRL to build a relationship tree for its potential service providers, trading partners, and provided services. In order to describe a complex relationship tree, nested WSRL documents can be created with links to other WSRL documents. In other words, a WSRL document can be referenced in three ways: in a WSIL document, on a Web server, or be published and referenced in an UDDI registry as a *tModel*.

However, WSRL only defines business-to-business, service-to-service, and operation-to-operation relationships. In real life, there exist other types of relationships, such as business-to-service relationship. For example, a business organization may only be interested in searching for shipping services. In addition, the Web services technology is merely one current IT approach to realize business services, although it is currently the recommended enabling technology to implement SOA. Therefore, a more comprehensive and generic services-oriented business relationship description language is needed.

6.3 Layered Services Relationship Modeling

In order to represent comprehensive SOA-oriented business relationships, a layered model is introduced as shown in Fig. 6.2. Four types of entities are identified: BusinessEntity, BusinessService, WebService, and Operation. A business entity refers to a business organization that either provides services, or consumes services from other business entities, or both. A business entity can be either an entire enterprise or a business unit inside of an enterprise. A business service realizes some business functions in an enterprise. Note that from IT's perspective, a business service is a conceptual service independent of IT technologies. A Web service implements a business service using the Web services technology. It publishes a business service (e.g., using WSDL)[10] on the Internet for consumption. From IT's perspective, a Web service may be independent of implementation platforms. An operation refers to a specific function provided by a service. It involves internal implementation of a service and corresponding infrastructure support.

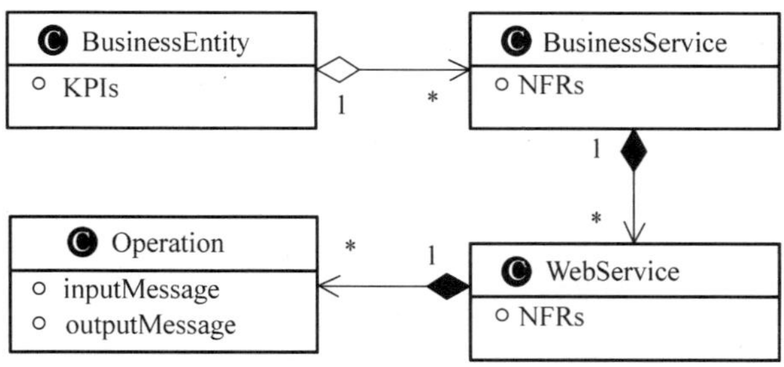

Figure 6.2 SOA-based services relationship diagram

Figure 6.2 uses a Unified Modeling Language (UML)[11] class diagram to illustrate the relationships between the four entities. These four entities exhibit a layered relationship: a business entity may provide multiple business services; a business service can be implemented by multiple Web services in different ways; a Web service may contain multiple operations. The association between *business entity* and *business service* is an aggregation relationship; the two associations (one is between *business service* and *Web service*, and the other one is between *Web service* and *operation*) belong to the composition relationship.

The layered model describes business relationships at four levels: business entity level, business service level, Web service level, and operation level. As shown in Fig. 6.3, the layered model captures services-oriented relationships at 9 different granularities: (1) business-to-business relationship (B-B-R); (2) business_service-to-business_service relationship (BS-BS-R); (3) Web_service-to-Web_service relationship (WS-WS-R); (4) operation-to-operation relationship (O-O-R); (5) business-to-business_service relationship (B-BS-R); (6) business-to-Web_ service relationship (B-WS-R); (7) business-to-operation relationship (B-O-R); (8) business_service-to-Web_service relationship (BS-WS-R), and (9) Web_service-to-operation relationship (WS-O-R). These relationships facilitate selecting and composing a set of services that meet predefined business requirements. In other words, in order to discover and locate appropriate services, all of these 9 types of relationships should be considered and examined. It can be seen that WSRL is an example that partially realizes the layered model of business relationships in SOA.

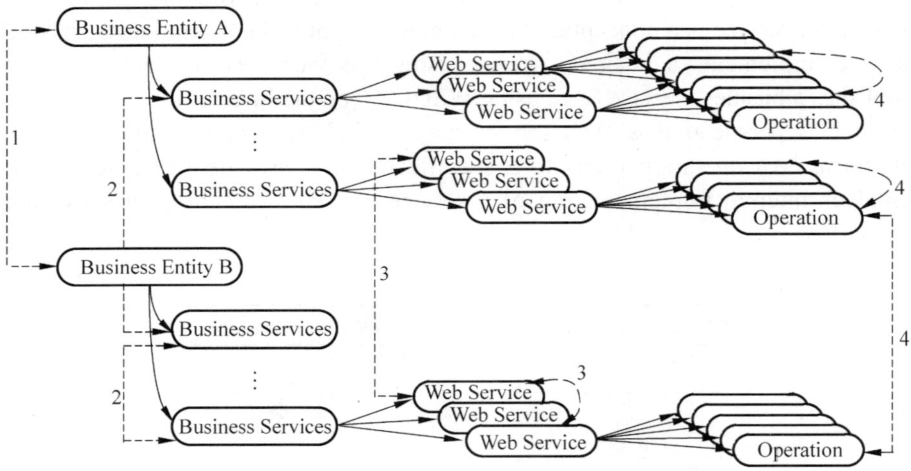

Figure 6.3 Relationships overview in SOA

6.4 SOA-Based Relationship Modeling Language (SOA-RML)

The above layered business relationship model can be embodied by an SOA-based Relationship Modeling Language (SOA-RML), which supports generic services-related relationship descriptions for generic services. As an extension of WSRL, SOA-RML is an XML-based description language to formalize the semantic relationships between business services and other entities in SOA. An SOA-RML specification document can be embedded into other documents via a link tag.

6.4.1 Business Services Relationships at Business Entity Level

At the business entity level, SOA-RML defines the relationships among business entities as a Business-to-Business Relationship (B-B-R). Four types of B-B-Rs are identified: partnership, parent-child relationship, exclusion, and alliance.

Partnership

A partnership relationship describes two business entities that provide complementary services and tend to collaborate for a specific business process. For example, a typical shipping transaction process includes a shipping service and a payment service, each having multiple service providers available. Assume that Company *X* provides shipping service and Company *Y* provides payment service. If they have formed a partnership, they tend to collaborate in a shipping process. In more detail, if Company *X* has already been selected to provide shipping service in a shipping process, it tends to recommend Company *Y* to provide payment service, instead of other payment service providers, and vice versa. Meanwhile, a business can have partnerships with multiple other businesses. For example, Company *X* can also build up a partnership with Company *Z*, in addition to Company *Y*. The example SOA-RML file shown in Fig. 6.4 describes the partnership relationship between Company *X* and Company *Y*, and that between Company *X* and Company *Z*.

```
<?xml version="1.0"?>
<SOA-RML xmlns="http://www.servicescomputing.org"
  xmlns:xsi="http://www.w3.org/2001/XMLSchema-instance"
  xsi:schemaLocation="http://www.servicescomputing.org/SOA-RML.xsd">

<SOA-RML>
  <bbr>
    <partnership id=p1>
        <source>
           <name> Company X </name>
           <link type="uddi-location" >
              <location>http://www.servicescomputing.org/uddi?4C9AACD0-
5C39-11D5-9FCF-BB3200333F79</location>
           </link>
        </source>
        <target>
           <name> Company Y </name>
           <link type="uddi-location">
             <location>http://www.servicescomputing/uddi?4C9DADD0-
5C39-11D5-3FCF-BB4500333F88</location>
          </link>
       </target>
       <target>
           <name> Company Z </name>
           <link type="wsil-location">
               <location>http://www.servicescomputing.org/uddi?4C9DADD0-
5C39-11D5-3FCF-AA4500333F99</location>
          </link>
       </target>
    </partnership>
  </bbr>
</SOA-RML>
```

Figure 6.4 Business entity-level partnership relationship in SOA-RML

As shown in Fig. 6.4, the tag <SOA-RML> represents an SOA-RML definition file. The tag <bbr> declares that the relationship is a business-to-business relationship. The tag <partnership> in turn specifies a partnership relationship with a unique id "p1". The partnership relationship always needs to define two involved business entities: one in a tag <source> and the other in a <target> tag. Figure 6.4 defines two partnerships in the same tag <bbr>, one between Company *X* and Company *Y*, and the other between Company *X* and Company *Z*. In other words, Fig. 6.4 specifies a one-to-many relationship between Company *X* and its two partners, Company *Y* and Company *Z*. A many-to-many relationship among business entities can also be defined in a similar way by SOA-RML.

As shown in Fig. 6.4, for each involved business entity, only the link of its definition document is included in an SOA-RML document delimited by <link> tags. One can specify the type and the location of a link. Taking Company *X* as an example, its definition document is stored at a UDDI registry at location "http://www.servicescomputing.org/uddi?4C9AACD0-5C39-11D5-9FCF-BB3200333F79". Meanwhile, these links can point to existing services registries, such as UDDI registries or WSIL documents. For example, the definition document of Company *Z* is stored in a WSIL document.

Parent-Child

A parent-child relationship describes businesses that have a belonging relationship. For example, a parent-child relationship between Company *X* and *A* may define that the latter is a subsidiary of the former. An example SOA-RML specification between Company *X* and *A* is shown in Fig. 6.5.

As shown in Fig. 6.5, the tag <bbr> declares that the relationship is a business-to-business relationship. The tag <parent-child> in turn specifies a parent-child relationship with a unique id "pc1". The relationship defines the parent-side entity Company *X* in a tag <source> and the child-side entity Company *A* in a <target> tag. The location of the both sides' definition documents is also specified in the document.

There is one special parent-child relationship that refers to the relationships between individual participants of a marketplace and the marketplace itself. This kind of relationship is equivalent to the *PublisherAssertion* defined in UDDI specification.

Exclusion

An exclusion relationship describes businesses that do not coexist under certain circumstances. For example, if business entities *A* and *B* are competitors in shipping service area, it is likely that their services may not work together in a business process. Such a competitive relationship can be modeled as an exclusion relationship. An example of exclusion relationship between Company *A* and Company *B* is illustrated in Fig. 6.6.

```
<?xml version="1.0"?>
<SOA-RML xmlns="http://www.servicescomputing.org"
   xmlns:xsi="http://www.w3.org/2001/XMLSchema-instance"
   xsi:schemaLocation="http://www.servicescomputing.org/SOA-RML.xsd">

<SOA-RML>
   <bbr>
      <parent-child id=pc1>
          <source>
             <name> Company X </name>
             <link type="uddi-location">
                 <location>http://www.servicescomputin.org/uddi?4C9DADD0-
5C39-11D5-9FCF-BB3200335F03</location>
             </link>
          </source>
          <target>
             <name> Company A </name>
             <link type="uddi-location">
                 <location>http://www.servicescomputing.org/uddi?4C9DADD0-
5C39-11D5-3FCF-BB4500334F05</location>
             </link>
          </target>
      </parent-child>
  </bbr>
<SOA-RML>
```

Figure 6.5 Business entity-level parent-child relationship in SOA-RML

```
<?xml version="1.0"?>
<SOA-RML xmlns="http://www.servicescomputing.org"
    xmlns:xsi="http://www.w3.org/2001/XMLSchema-instance"
    xsi:schemaLocation="http://www.servicescomputing.org/SOA-RML.xsd">

<SOA-RML>
   <bbr>
      <exclusion id=ex1>
          <source>
             <name> Company A </name>
             <link type="uddi-location">
                 <location>http://servicescomputing.org/uddi?4C9DADD0-
5C38-11D5-6FCF-BB3200335F07</location>
            </link>
         </source>
         <target>
            <name> Company B </name>
            <link type="uddi-location">
               <location>http://servicescomputing.org/uddi?4C9DADD0-
5C69-11D5-2FCF-BB4500334F02</location>
             </link>
          </target>
      </exclusion>
  </bbr>
<SOA-RML>
```

Figure 6.6 Business entity-level exclusion relationship in SOA-RML

The exclusion relationship is represented in a tag <exclusion> with attribute (i.e., id with value "ex1"). The tag <source> specifies one business entity, and the tag <target> specifies the other business entity that has exclusion relationship with the former. It should be noted that similar to the specification of partnership relationship, one tag <exclusion> could specify multiple exclusive relationships between one source business entity and multiple target business entities.

Alliance

An alliance relationship describes businesses that are loosely coupled in nature. For example, an e-Business solution community is formed by several enterprises, each providing related services or capabilities. Businesses belonging to the same alliance may receive preferential price, delivery, or selection over non-alliance members. For example, *Airline A* and *Airline B* are two airline companies with an alliance relationship. An *Airline A* mileage plus member can also earn mileage if he/she books ticket from *Airline B*. An example of alliance relationship between *Airline A* and *Airline B* is illustrated in Fig. 6.7.

```
<?xml version="1.0"?>
<SOA-RML xmlns="http://www.servicescomputing.org"
  xmlns:xsi="http://www.w3.org/2001/XMLSchema-instance"
  xsi:schemaLocation="http://www.servicescomputing.org/SOA-RML.xsd">

<SOA-RML>
  <bbr>
     <alliance id=a1>
         <source>
            <name> Airline A </name>
            <link type="uddi-location">
               <location>http://servicescomputing.org/uddi?4C9DADD0-
5C38-11D5-6FCF-BB3200335F07</location>
            </link>
         </source>
         <target>
            <name> Airline B </name>
            <link type="uddi-location">
               <location>http://servicescomputing.org/uddi?4C9DADD0-
5C69-11D5-2FCF-BB4500334F02</location>
            </link>
         </target>
      </alliance>
  </bbr>
<SOA-RML>
```

Figure 6.7 Business entity-level alliance relationship in SOA-RML

The alliance relationship is represented in a tag <alliance> with attribute (i.e., id with value "a1"). The tag <source> specifies one business entity, and the tag

<target> specifies the other business entity that has alliance relationship with the former. It should be noted that similar to the specification of partnership relationship, one tag <alliance> could specify multiple alliance relationships between one source business entity and several target business entities.

Comparison with xCRL

As discussed earlier, xCRL from OASIS defines some customer relationships. It defines some types of the organization-to-organization relationships, such as parent-child relationship, partner relationship, and supplier relationship. However, the xCRL schema focuses on customer relationships only, and the data specified are static in nature. For example, an xCRL file may describe the contact information and business address of a business entity, as well as its relative relationships. However, all of the data are hard-coded in the xCRL document. In contrast with xCRL, SOA-RML only specifies the links of the description documents of business entities in services registries. Therefore, the detailed information about the business entities can be dynamically changed without changing corresponding SOA-RML documents. Therefore, SOA-RML provides a dynamic and distributed means to describe SOA-based business relationships.

6.4.2 Business Services Relationships at Business Service Level

At the service level, SOA-RML defines the relationships among services as a business_service-to-business_service relationship (BS-BS-R). SOA-RML divides all BS-BS-Rs into two types: inter-BS-BS-R and intra-BS-BS-R. An inter-BS-BS-R refers to the relationship between two business services across multiple business entities; an intra-BS-BS-R refers to the relationship between two business services within the same business entity. Both inter-BS-BS-R and intra-BS-BS-R contain four types of relationships: parent-child, exclusion, binding, and community.

Parent-Child

A parent-child relationship describes two business services with an "is a" relationship, meaning that one service is a generalization of the other service, or say one service is a specialization of the other. The example SOA-RML specification shown in Fig. 6.8 describes such a kind of parent-child relationship between two services *S*1 and *S*2. *S*1 is a generic e-Business solution service and *S*2 is a messaging service. Since a messaging service is a specific type of e-Business solution service, the two services thus form a parent-child relationship.

As shown in Fig. 6.8, the tag <bsbsr> declares that the relationship is a business_service-to-business_service relationship. The parent-child relationship is represented in a tag <parent-child> with attribute (i.e., id with value "spc1"). The tag <source> specifies one business service *S*1, and the tag <target> specifies the other business entity *S*2 that has a parent-child relationship with the former.

```
<?xml version="1.0"?>
<SOA-RML xmlns="http://www.servicescomputing.org"
   xmlns:xsi="http://www.w3.org/2001/XMLSchema-instance"
   xsi:schemaLocation="http://www.servicescomputing.org/SOA-RML.xsd">

<SOA-RML>
   <bsbsr>
      <parent-child id=spc1>
           <source>
               <name> S1 </name>
               <description>e-Solution service</description>
                <link type="wsil">
                    <location>http://servicescomputing.org/
e-business/s1.wsdl</location>
               </link>
            </source>
            <target>
               <name> S2 </name>
               <description>messaging service</description>
               <link type="uddi">
                   <location>http://servicescomputing.org/uddi/
inquiryapi</location>
                   <servicekey>D85D8F70-E8E6-11D5-B61C-
970107B90C83</servicekey>
               </link>
           </target>
       </parent-child>
  </bsbsr>
<SOA-RML>
```

Figure 6.8 Service- level parent-child relationship in SOA-RML

As shown in Fig. 6.8, for each involved business service, only the link of its definition document is included in an SOA-RML document delimited by <link> tags. One can specify the type and the location of a link. Taking service *S*1 as an example, its definition document is stored as a WSIL document at location "http://servicescomputing.org/e-business/s1.wsdl". These links can point to existing services registries, such as UDDI registries. For example, the definition document of service *S*2 is stored in a UDDI registry at location "http://servicescomputing.org/uddi/inquiryapi" with service key "D85D8F70-E8E6-11D5-B61C-970107B90C83".

Exclusion

An exclusion relationship describes services that cannot coexist in a business process. For example, the relationship between a shipping service using credit card and a payment service using bank transfer have an exclusion relationship because they accept different payment methods.

Binding

A service binding relationship means that two business services are tightly coupled, or so-called dependent. Assume that two services *S*1 and *S*2 have a binding relationship. If service *S*1 is selected in a business process, then service *S*2 has to be selected in the same composition, and vice versa.

Community

A community relationship describes two services that provide similar or equivalent functionalities. For example, the *Shipping* 1 service, *Shipping* 2 service, *Shipping* 3 service are some examples of the shipping service community. A business process may decide to choose one service from the community based upon various criteria, such as cost, time, and personal preference.

6.4.3 Layered Relationships Summary

Table 6.1 summarizes SOA-based business relationships defined in SOA-RML.

Table 6.1 Summary of layered relationships

Relationship categories	Relationship sub-categories		Comments
	Business	IT	
B-B-R	partnership, parent-child, alliance	exclusion	
BS-BS-R		exclusion, parent-child, binding, community	intra /inter
WS-WS-R		parent-child, exclusion, binding, community	
O-O-R		constraint, exclusion, cluster, parent-child	
B-BS-R		containment, consumption, none	
B-WS-R	Ownership	none	
B-O-R	Ownership	none	
BS-WS-R		implementation, none	
WS-O-R		inclusion, none	

As shown in Table 6.1, 9 categories of business relationships are caught: (1) B-B-R; (2) BS-BS-R; (3) WS-WS-R; (4) O-O-R; (5) B-BS-R; (6) B-WS-R; (7) B-O-R; (8) BS-WS-R; and (9) WS-O-R. If a pair of elements are not shown in the table, it means that no direct relationship is recommended between them.

As shown in Table 6.1, for each considered pair of elements, their relationships can be further divided into two sub-categories: business and IT. By business, we mean that the relationships are business-related and can be re-organized if necessary, for example, partnership between business entities. By IT, we mean that the relationships substantially exist and cannot be re-organized, for example, inclusion relationship. It should be noted that a "none" relationship declared in the table emphasizes that there is no relationship between the corresponding entities. Such a denotation is meant for eliminating confusion or guessing of whether there could be some relationships between two entities. This denotation also helps in deciding relationship annotations in the implementation phase.

B-B-R & BS-BS-R

As discussed in the previous sections, B-B-R contains four types of relationships (partnership, parent-child, exclusion, and alliance); BS-BS-R contains four types of relationships: parent-child, exclusion, binding, and community.

WS-WS-R

Similar to BS-BS-R, WS-WS-R also contains four types of relationships: parent-child, exclusion, binding, and community. Contrasted with BS-BS-R that focuses on business-level services, WS-WS-R focuses on relationships between Web service interfaces.

O-O-R

O-O-R defines the relationships among service operations as an operation-to-operation relationship. A business service typically exposes one or more methods as access points. Each method corresponds to a specific operation. For example, an *airline booking* service may publish the following three major methods (i.e., operations): *fareFinder* that allows a user to check possible air ticket availability and price, *ticketBooking* that performs online air ticket purchase, and *easyCheck-in* that allows passengers to check in online.

At the operation level, SOA-RML identifies four types of relationships: constraint, exclusion, community, and parent-child. A constraint relationship describes two service methods that have invocation restrictions between their usages. For example, in an *airline booking* service, a user needs to invoke *fareFinder* operation first, then *ticketBooking*, and finally *easyCheck-in*. In other words, there is a temporal constraint relationship between the three operations. An exclusion relationship describes two service methods that cannot be invoked simultaneously. For example, there is an exclusion relationship between the method *fareFinder* and the method *easyCheck-in* at the same time. A community relationship describes a set of service methods with common functionality. For example, an airline service may include two methods, namely *bookBusinessClass* and *bookEconomic-Class*. Each of these methods can be used to book a ticket in the same airplane. The differences are their prices. A parent-child relationship describes two service methods where one method derives from the other. For example, a method can declare that it extends another method, making a derived operation. Of course the “derived” method and its parent method cannot have a conflict between their method specifications. For example, the method *bookBusinesClass* may derive from a generic method *bookTicket*.

B-BS-R

B-BS-R defines the relationships between a business entity and a business service. Three types of relationships exist: inclusion, consumption, and none. An inclusion relationship defines whether a business service belongs to a business entity. In other words, if a business entity contains a business service, it means that the business entity is the service provider of the business service. A consumption relationship defines whether a business entity consumes and utilizes a business service. In other words, it defines whether a business entity is a service consumer of the business service. A none relationship implies that there is no relationship between a business entity and a business service.

B-WS-R

B-WS-R defines the relationships between a business entity and a Web service. The hierarchical business relationship tree suggests that there is no direct provider/consumer relationship between a business entity and a Web service. The relationship exists: ownership or none. An ownership relationship defines whether a business entity directly owns a Web service. A none relationship implies that there is no relationship between a business entity and a Web service.

B-O-R

B-O-R defines the relationships between a business entity and an operation. A business entity may directly own a Web service to which the operation belongs. Based on this association, two types of relationship are defined: ownership and none. If a business entity owns the Web service to which an operation belongs, there is an ownership relationship between them. Otherwise, there is no relationship between them.

BS-WS-R

BS-WS-R defines the relationships between a business service and a Web service. Two types of relationship are identified: implementation and none. A business service can be implemented by various Web services. Therefore, if a Web service implements one or more business services, there is an implementation relationship between them. Otherwise, there is no relationship between them specifically.

WS-O-R

WS-O-R defines the relationships between a Web service and an operation. A Web service may contain multiple operations. Therefore, two types of relationships are identified: inclusion and none. If an operation is contained and exposed by a

Web service, there is an inclusion relationship between them. Otherwise, there is no relationship between them.

6.5 SOA-RML-Enriched Services Registry

One major purpose of SOA-RML is to enhance services discovery and composability by enriching a services registry. A relationships-binding engine is added to a services registry to create the relationships among businesses, among services, and among service types. SOA-RML is used to create an XML-based representation encapsulating these comprehensive relationships.

Figure 6.9 illustrates the framework of services registry enhancement enriched by SOA-RML and the corresponding exploring engine. As shown in Fig. 6.9, an SOA-RML-based exploring engine consists of three major components: a Relationship Binding Broker (RBB), an SOA-RML Processor (including an Internal SOA-RML Processor and an External SOA-RML Processor), and an Advanced Services Discovery Engine (ASDE).

The RBB provides a standard service API for gathering business relationships and discovery requirements from service consumers. Using the internal information about business entities, business services, Web services, and operations, the Internal SOA-RML Processor builds the relationship representations in SOA-RML within a services registry. The External Processor builds the relationship representations in SOA-RML from external services registries. The ASDE (e.g., Advanced UDDI Search Engine (AUSE) as discussed in Chapter 4) supplies application developers with standard interfaces to search businesses and services information from one or multiple services registries.

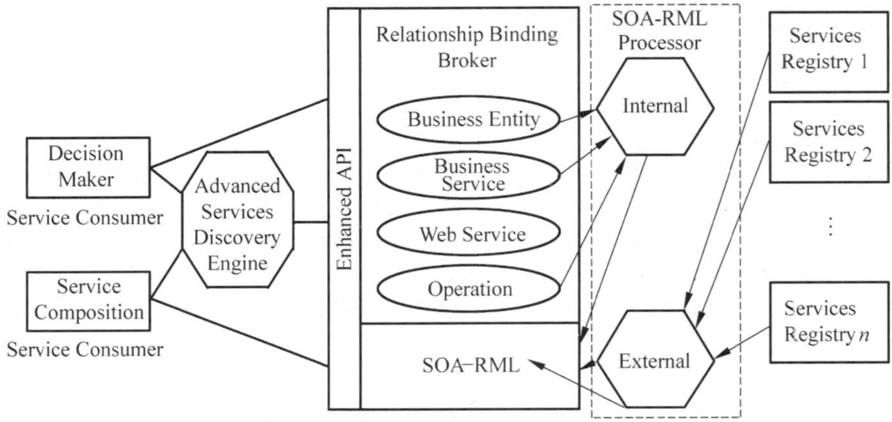

Figure 6.9 SOA-RML-enriched services registry

6.5.1 SOA-RML Schema

Note that at the top of Fig. 6.4 – Fig. 6.8, the SOA-RML files all have a link to an XML Schema[12] file "SOA-RML.xsd." An SOA-RML file is an XML document that contains a set of definitions of business relationships between elements (i.e., business entities, business services, Web service, and operations). In order for these SOA-RML scripts to be parsed and handled automatically by the SOA-RML processor shown in Fig. 6.9, it is imperative for them to be associated with the same schema files describing the structure of each relationship definition. In other words, an associated XML Schema file describes how the SOA-RML script should be interpreted. It defines the elements that an SOA-RML file can contain,

```
<?xml version="1.0" encoding="ISO-8859-1"?>
<xs:schema xmlns:xs="http://www.w3.org/2001/XMLSchema"
   targetNamespace="http://www.servicescomputing.org"
   xmlns="http://www.servicescomputing.org"
   elementFormDefault="qualified">

   <xs:element name="source">
      <xs:complexType>
         <xs:sequence>
            <xs:element name="name" type="xs:string"/>
            <xs:element name="link type" type="xs:string"/>
         </xs:sequence>
      </xs:complexType>
   </xs:element>

   <xs:element name="target">
      <xs:complexType>
         <xs:sequence>
            <xs:element name="name" type="xs:string"/>
            <xs:element name="link type" type="xs:string"/>
         </xs:sequence>
      </xs:complexType>
   </xs:element>
<xs:element name="partnership">
      <xs:complexType>
         <xs:attribute name="id" type="xs:string"/>
         <xs:sequence>
            <xs:element ref="source">
            <xs:element ref="target" minOccurs="1" maxOccurs="unbounded">
         </xs:sequence>
      </xs:complexType>
   </xs:element>
</xs:schema>
```

Figure 6.10 An example of SOA-RML Schema specifications for partnership

their attributes, values, and so on. A valid SOA-RML document must conform to the associated XML Schema document: SOA-RML.xsd. XML Schema is used for this purpose as a popular XML-based metadata description language capable of defining comprehensive metadata information.

Figure 6.10 shows a segment of the content of the *SOA-RML.xsd* that defines the schema for the *partnership* relationship between business entities defined in Fig. 6.4. As shown in Fig. 6.10, the definition of a *partnership* (delimited by *partnership* tag) contains three parts: an attribute named *id*, an element of source entity (delimited by *source* tag), and a one-to-many occurrence of element target entity (delimited by *target* tag).

As shown in Fig. 6.10, the attribute type of *id* of a *partnership* should be a string. For defining a source entity, two elements are required: its *name* and its *line type,* both being strings. For defining each target entity, two elements are required: its *name* and its *line type*, both being strings.

6.6 Discussions on SOA-Based Relationship Modeling

When talking about services discovery, it is common to analyze static functionalities and dynamic quality measurements to differentiate various services. This chapter adds another dimension of consideration as services relationship modeling. Based on a hierarchical SOA-based business relationship framework, this chapter presents a relationship modeling language to describe the relationship information about businesses, business services, Web services, and operations. This information could potentially facilitate services searching, matching, selection, composition, and automation with an attempt to bridge the gap between primitive and composite services.

The services relationship model discussed in this chapter focuses on static relationships regarding published services. Dynamic relationships between services, (e.g., prerequisite and temporal relationships between services in a specific services composition) can be gradually introduced in SOA-RML in the future. Since services discovery and services composition are typically driven by business processes, how to model dynamic relationships between candidate services to satisfy the specific business processes remains open to researchers and practitioners.

6.7 Summary

In this chapter, we introduced the concept of SOA-based relationship modeling and how to define and model semantic business relationships. A layered business relationship model identifies 9 types of relationships between business entities, business services, Web services, and operations. SOA-RML is one implementation of the layered business relationship model and can be used to enrich services registries for effective services discovery.

References

[1] UDDI. http://www.uddi.org/specification.html

[2] Resource Description Framework (RDF). http://www.w3.org/RDF/

[3] XML. http://xml.coverpages.org/xml.html

[4] The DAML Services Coalition. (2002) DAML-S: Semantic Markup For Web Services. http://www.daml.org/services/daml-s/ 2001/ 10/daml-s.html

[5] Connolly DEA (2001) Annotated DAML+OIL Ontology Markup. http://web4.w3.org/TR/daml+oil-walkthru/

[6] OWL-S: Semantic Markup for Web Services. http://www.daml-s.org/owl-s/1.0/owl-s.html

[7] OASIS eXtensible Customer Relationships Language (xCRL). http://www.oasis-open.org/committees/ciq/ciq.shtml#8

[8] Organization for the Advancement of Structured Information Standards (OASIS). http://www.oasis-open.org/home/index.php

[9] Zhang LJ, Chang H, Chao T (2002) Web Services Relationships Binding for Dynamic e-Business Integration. In: International Conference on Internet Computing (IC'02), Las Vegas, NE, USA, pp 561 – 570

[10] Erik Christensen, et al. (2001) Web Services Description Language (WSDL). http://www.w3.org/TR/wsdl

[11] OMG Unified Modeling Language (UML). http://www.uml.org/

[12] XML Schema. http://www.w3.org/XML/Schema

7 SOA and Web Services Standards

7.1 Introduction

As discussed in the previous chapters, the foundation of the Web services paradigm is a set of emerging standards that enable seamless integration between heterogeneous information technology processes and systems. A variety of standardization organizations and leading industrial organizations have been collaborating on Web services standards. Among them, the World Wide Web Consortium (W3C)[1], the Organization for the Advancement of Structured Information Standards (OASIS)[2], the Internet Engineering Task Force (IETF)[3], United Nations Centre for Trade facilitation and Electronic Business (UN/CEFACT)[4], WS-Integration (WS-I)[5] are selected standardization bodies. W3C develops interoperable technologies (i.e., specifications, guidelines, software, and tools) to lead the Web to its full potential. OASIS is a non-profit, global consortium that drives the development, convergence, and adoption of e-Business standards. IETF is a large open international community concerned with the architectural evolution and the smooth operation of the Internet. UN/CEFACT covers worldwide policy and technical development in the area of trade facilitation and e-Business. WS-I is an open industry group formed in 2002 to promote Web services interoperability across platforms, operating systems, and programming languages. Among industry vendors, IBM, BEA, and Microsoft are leading industry organizations and key contributors. With their joint efforts, currently the Web services field has developed a stack of standard protocols, categorized into a five-layer structure: transport, messaging, description/publication/discovery, Quality of Service (QoS), and service composition.

This stack of protocols is specific to the Web services technology. Some industries set up industry-specific services-oriented standards, such as the electronics industry, insurance industry, telecommunication industry, and banking industry. Up till now, there still lacks a set of generic SOA solution-oriented standards. This chapter will first introduce the Web services-oriented standard protocol stack, then discuss several industry-specific service standards, and finally depict a picture of a generic view of SOA solution-oriented standard.

7.2 Web Services Standard Stack

In order for the Web services protocols to become interoperable across diverse systems and suitable for business applications, standards bodies such as W3C,

OASIS, and WS-I collaborate with key industry leaders to formally standardize the protocols into a known Web services standard stack[6,7] fitting within the context of a Web services framework.

As shown in Fig. 7.1, the current Web services standard stack can be categorized into a five-layer structure[8]: transport, messaging, description/publishing/discovery, Quality of Service (QoS), and service composition.

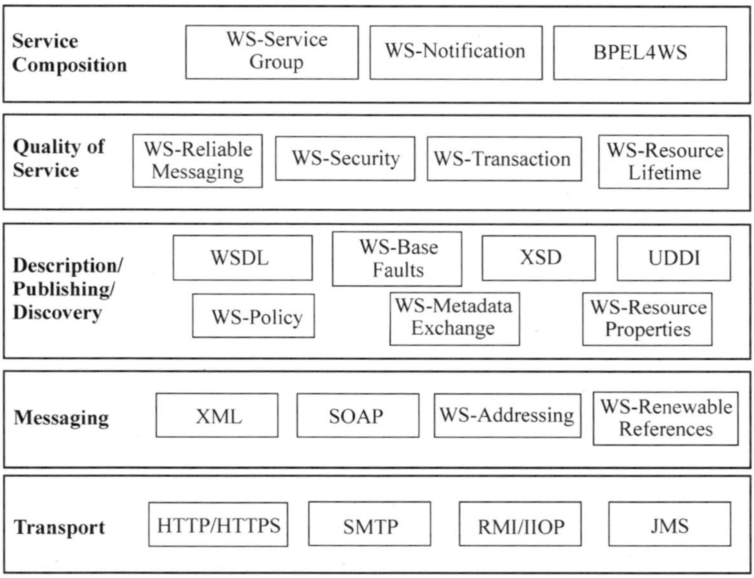

Figure 7.1 Web services standard stack

Each layer together with related *specifications* will be discussed in the following. Some industry-adopted specifications, such as SOAP[9], WSDL[10], UDDI[11], and BPEL4WS[12,13], were discussed in the previous chapters. However, for the completeness of the standards stack, they will be briefly summarized again.

7.2.1 Transport

This layer provides a set of protocols defining core communication mechanisms for Web services communications and interactions. The transport layer provides the fundamental support for any Web services-related activities. Its typical protocols include HTTP/HTTPS (Hyper Text Transport Protocol[14]/HTTP over SSL (Secure Sockets Layer)[15], SMTP (Simple Mail Transfer Protocol)[16], RMI/IIOP (Remote Method Invocation/Internet Inter-Operability Protocol)[17], and JMS (Java Messaging Service)[18].

HTTP/HTTPS

Typical Internet transport protocols are: Hyper Text Transfer Protocol (HTTP), HTTP over Secure Socket Layer (SSL) (HTTPS), and Simple Mail Transport Protocol (SMTP). Web service implementations may support additional transports, but it is critical to provide support for standard interoperable protocols.

HTTP is widely used as a method to transfer or convey information over the Internet. It is an open Internet protocol whose original purpose was to provide a way to publish and receive HyperText Markup Language (HTML) pages. In detail, HTTP is a request/response protocol between clients and servers. An HTTP client initiates an HTTP request by establishing a Transport Control Protocol (TCP) connection to a particular port on a remote host (port 80 by default); an HTTP server listens to the specific port. Upon receipt of a request, the server sends back an HTTP response, including a status line such as "HTTP/1.1 200 OK", together with a message body, containing answers to the client.

Strictly speaking, HTTPS is not an individual protocol, but refers to the combination of an HTTP over a secure SSL mechanism that protects messages in transportation. HTTPS uses a different default TCP port (443) compared to HTTP (80).

SMTP

SMTP is the *de facto* standard for sending emails over the Internet; it is a relatively simple text-based protocol where message texts can be transferred to one or more recipients. SMTP uses TCP port 25. Note that SMTP is a "push" protocol instead of a "pull" protocol, meaning that email receivers have to use different protocols, such as Post Office Protocol version 3 (POP3) to download emails from remote mail servers. SMTP requires extensions such as *8BITMIME*[19] to transfer binary files in addition to ASCII text-based messages.

RMI/IIOP/JMS

Java Remote Method Invocation (RMI) enables developers to create distributed Java technology-based applications. Using RMI, the methods of a remote Java object can be invoked from another Java client, possibly residing on different host. RMI uses object serialization method to marshal and unmarshal parameters and does not truncate types.

Internet Inter-ORB Protocol (IIOP) is a transport protocol used for communication between Common Object Request Broker Architecture (CORBA)[20] object request brokers. As part of the CORBA standard, IIOP is an Object-Oriented protocol that enables distributed programs written in different programming languages to communicate over the Internet.

The Java Message Service (JMS) defines a standard for reliable enterprise messaging (a.k.a. Messaging Oriented Middleware (MOM)[21]), which allows application components based on the Java 2 Platform, Enterprise Edition (J2EE) to create, send, receive, and read messages. It enables distributed communication that is loosely coupled, reliable, and asynchronous[22].

7.2.2 Messaging

The layer of messaging intends to provide a framework for exchanging information between Web services in a distributed environment. This layer of protocols defines an interoperable mechanism for encoding Web service messages for transportation. In other words, these protocols define how to appropriately format messages.

Extensible Markup Language (XML)

Based on the common Web transports, Web services require a common language—XML—for universal data exchange. Endorsed by W3C in February 1998, XML is a meta-language of markup languages that makes the data portable by defining a standard format for structured documents and data definitions on the Web[23].

Recall that the essential goal of Web services is to enable interoperability of distributed business services within any platform and language. Just as in the real world a common language is necessary for effective and efficient communications among a group of people coming from different countries and cultures, XML has become a "common language" for various business services to exchange information and interact with each other without human interventions. Based on pure text, XML provides a system-independent way of describing data. Like static HTML, XML encloses data in tags. Unlike HTML that only accepts its predefined set of tags, XML allows users to define application-specific tags that describe the contents of any specific type of document. In addition, unlike HTML tags that describe how to display the enclosed content, XML tags represent semantic meanings of enclosed content. Moreover, XML adopts schema languages (e.g., Document Type Definition (DTD) and XML Schema[24]) to represent the rules that compilers can use to interpret the structure of a specific type of XML document. Therefore, XML provides a way of representing portable data. In other words, together with the associated schemas, XML data can be exchanged by different applications. In the field of Web services, XML provides a message structure between Web services.

Simple Object Access Protocol (SOAP)

Simple Object Access Protocol (SOAP) is a simple and lightweight protocol for exchanging structured and typed information among Web services. In the core of the Web services model, SOAP acts as the messaging protocol for transport with binding to existing Internet protocols, such as Hypertext Transfer Protocol (HTTP) and Simple Mail Transfer Protocol (SMTP), as the underlying communication protocol. By defining a uniform way of passing XML-encoded data, SOAP also enables a way of conducting Remote Procedure Calls (RPCs) binding with HTTP.

A SOAP message is specified as an XML information set. SOAP consists of three major parts: an *envelope*, a set of *encoding rules*, and a *RPCs convention*. An *envelope* defines a framework for describing the content of the message and how to process it. An *encoding rule* defines a serialization mechanism for exchanging application-defined data types. An *RPC convention* enables basic request/response interactions.

SOAP is endorsed by the W3C and key industry vendors. Detailed information about SOAP can be found at the W3C Web site at http://www.w3c.org/TR/SOAP.

WS-Addressing

WS-Addressing[25] was previously known as WS-Routing, WS-Referral, and SOAP Routing Protocol (SOAP-RP). Originally proposed by BEA Systems, IBM, and Microsoft, OASIS publishes Web Services Addressing (WS-Addressing), which enables messaging systems to support message transmission in a transport-neutral manner. WS-Addressing defines XML elements to identify Web service endpoints and to secure end-to-end identifications in messages.

WS-Addressing defines two constructs, namely *endpoint references* and *message information headers*, to normalize underlying transportation protocols and messaging systems into a uniform format that can be processed independent of transportations and applications. A Web service endpoint is defined as a referable entity, processor, or resource where Web service messages can be targeted. A *message information header* allows uniform addressing of messages, including the source address, the destination address, and the message identity.

WS-Renewable

WS-Renewable is built on WS-Addressing. It is a reference that refers to a stateless Web service or a stateful WS-Resource. WS-Renewable provides a mechanism for renewing a new reference to the same WS-Resource if the old reference becomes stale.

7.2.3 Description/Publishing/Discovery

The transport and message specifications enable Web services to communicate using messages. The description layer defines a standard way to describe a Web service, its interfaces and capabilities, as well as the messages it sends and receives. XML Schema and Web Services Description Language (WSDL) are the accepted specifications at present.

XSD

An XML Schema Definition (XSD) is an instance of an XML Schema written in the XML Schema language. XML Schema describes the structure and contents of XML-based messages. XSD provides a way to describe and validate data in an XML document. An XSD defines a type of XML document in terms of some predefined constraints, such as what elements and attributes may appear, their mutual relationships, what types of data they carry, and so on. It can be used with validation software to ensure whether a particular XML document is of the right type.

Web Services Description Language (WSDL)

Web Services Description Language (WSDL)[10] is an XML format for describing Web services and their access information. The W3C specifies WSDL as:

> *"...an XML format for describing network services as a set of endpoints operating on messages containing either document-oriented or procedure-oriented information. The operations and messages are described abstractly, and then bound to a concrete network protocol and message format to define an endpoint. Related concrete endpoints are combined into abstract endpoints (services)."*

WSDL is used to describe the metadata information of a Web service as what functionalities it has, where it is located, and how to invoke it. A service provider uses WSDL specifications to publish Web services; a service broker uses WSDL specifications to find published services; and a service requestor uses WSDL specifications to invoke deployed services dynamically.

Using WSDL, a Web service is defined as a set of ports, each publishing a collection of port types that bind to network addresses using common binding mechanisms. Every port type is a published operation that is accessible through messages. Messages are in turn categorized into input messages containing incoming data arguments and output messages containing results. Each message consists of data elements; every data element must belong to a data type, either a simple type (e.g., XML Schema Definition (XSD)) or a complex type. Detailed information about WSDL can be found at the W3C Web site[10].

WS-Resource Properties

The WS-Resource Properties specification is a part of the WS-Resource Framework (WSRF)[26]. It describes how service requestors can view and modify the types and values of a WS-Resource's state through a Web services interface. WS-Resource states are defined in an XML resource property document using XML Schema. The WS-Resource Properties specification associates the definition of a resource's properties to a Web service by annotating a WSDL *portType* with the type definition of the resource property document. It also defines a standard set of message exchanges that allow a service requestor to query or update the property values of the implied resource instance.

WS-Base Faults

WS-Base Faults[27] defines an XML schema type for base faults, along with rules for how these base fault types can be used and extended by Web services.

WS-Policy

WS-Policy[28] describes the capabilities, requirements, and general characteristics of Web services using an extensible grammar. Web service policies are defined as collections of one or more policy assertions.

WS-Metadata Exchange

Web services use metadata to describe what other endpoints need to know in order to interact with them. WS-Metadata Exchange[29] specification intends to facilitate communications between Web services and retrieval of metadata from Web services. It defines two types of request-response interactions. First, if a service requestor knows the type of metadata to search for (e.g., WS-Policy), then it can be indicated that only that type of data should be returned. Second, if a service requestor needs additional types of metadata, or all of the metadata relevant to subsequent interactions with an endpoint needs to be retrieved, it can be indicated that all available metadata, regardless of their types, should be returned. It should be noted that the interactions defined are intended for the retrieval of metadata (i.e., service description information) only. The specifications do not aim to provide a general-purpose query or retrieval mechanism for other types of data associated with a service, such as state data, properties, and attribute values.

Universal Description, Discovery, and Integration (UDDI)

Universal Description, Discovery and Integration (UDDI) provides a "meta service" for locating Web services by enabling robust queries against rich metadata. UDDI defines a standard mechanism for service brokers to store descriptions of registered Web services in term of XML messages. In addition, by querying the UDDI registries, service requestors locate Web services so they can invoke the services from the corresponding service providers.

UDDI registries can be either private registries or public registries. The former type publishes services within an enterprise or a community, while the latter type publishes services to the global business community on the Internet. UDDI specifications record several types of information about a Web service that help service requestors determine the answers to the questions "who, what, where and how":

- *Who*: UDDI records simple information about a business, such as its name, business identifiers, and contact information;
- *What*: UDDI records classification information that includes industry codes and product classifications, as well as descriptive information about the registered Web services;

- *Where*: UDDI records registration information (e.g., the Uniform Resource Locator (URL) or email address) through which each type of service can be accessed;
- *How*: registration references (i.e., tModels in the UDDI documentation) about interfaces and other properties of a given service.

7.2.4 Quality of Service (QoS)

In order to serve business purposes, a Web service needs to satisfy non-functional requirements (Quality of Service or QoS in short) in addition to functional requirements. The Web services community has been starting to put significant efforts on addressing these non-functional perspectives of Web services. To date, four categories of QoS standards have arisen: security, transaction, reliable messaging, and resource lifetime management.

WS-Security

Web Services Security (WS-Security)[30] provides a set of mechanisms to help Web service developers secure SOAP message exchanges. It is a family of protocols that enhances the messaging technique to solve three basic problems about the quality of protection of Web services: authentication and authorization of users, message integrity, and message encryption. Focusing on secure communications, these mechanisms can be used to accommodate a wide range of security models and encryption technologies.

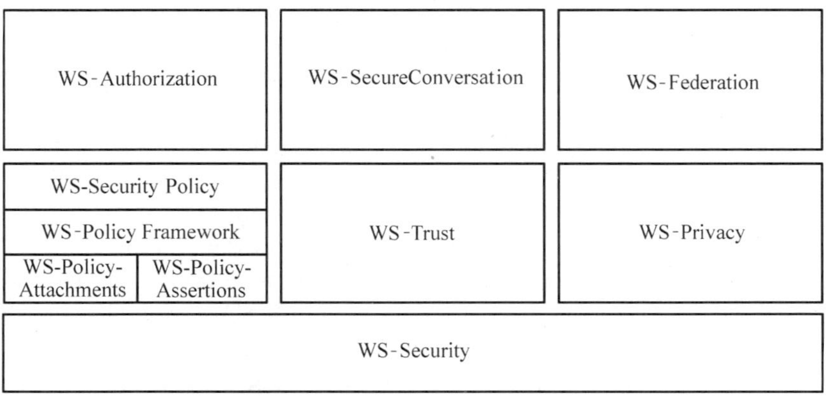

Figure 7.2 WS-Security roadmap

Based on the WS-Security, six enhanced models, as shown in Fig. 7.2, are proposed to help establish secure interoperable Web services: *WS-Policy*, *WS-Trust*[31], *WS-Privacy*[32], *WS-Authorization*[33], *WS-SecureConversation*[34], and *WS-Federation*[35]. *WS-Policy* provides a syntax-wired model to specify Web services endpoint policies; *WS-Trust* defines methods to request and issue security tokens for establishing trust relationships; *WS-Privacy* specification describes a model for expressing privacy claims inside of WS-Policy descriptions and associating privacy claims with messages; *WS-Authorization*[33] defines how Web services manage authorization data and policies; *WS-SecureConversation*[34] defines a security context based on security tokens for secure communication; and *WS-Federation*[35] defines mechanisms to enable federation of identity, account, attribute, authentication, and authorization across different trust realms.

As shown in Fig. 7.2, the WS-Policy is further refined by including the four elements: *WS-Security Policy*, *WS-Policy Framework*, *WS-Policy-Attachment*, and *WS-Policy-Assertions*. The WS-Security Policy defines a grammar for expressing Web service policies. In other words, it is a language to support the WS-Security specifications. The WS-Policy Framework is designed to allow extensibility to express generic policies not limited to security policies. The WS-Policy Framework intends to accommodate expressions of domain-specific policy languages within a consistent Web services framework. WS-Policy-Attachment offers ways to advertise policy assertions with Web services. It builds on the existing WSDL and UDDI specifications and also supports extensibility. The WS-Policy Assertions language offers common policy expressions, which define a generic set of policy assertions for Web services.

WS-Transaction Management (WS-TM)

Business activities typically require the transaction feature, or so-called all-or-nothing attribute. The actions taken prior to a commitment are tentative, meaning that they are not persistent thus not visible to other activities. WS-TM[36] defines three transaction protocols (i.e., WS-Coordination[37], WS-AtomicTransaction[38], and Asynchronous Service Access Protocol) that can be plugged into a service coordination framework for interoperability across existing transaction managers, long running compensations, and asynchronous business process flows. It also includes a solution to bridge diffèrent transaction models (e.g., MQSeries[10] and JMS[18]).

WS-Coordination WS-Coordination[37] is a general mechanism for starting and coordinating the outcome of multiparty multi-message Web services. WS-Coordination defines a coordinator service and a coordination context. A coordinator service provides a service, described in WSDL, which has the ability of starting a coordinated task, terminating a coordinated task, allowing a participant to register in a task, and producing a coordination context within a group. A coordination service also includes an interface in WSDL, which the other participating services could use to be notified of the outcome of a coordinated task. A coordination context supports all messages that Web services exchange during a conversation. It contains a WS-Addressing endpoint reference to the coordination service, which in turn contains information to identify the specific task being coordinated.

In short, WS-Coordination is a framework for coordinating Web services interactions. The other two protocols, WS-AtomicTransaction and WS- Business-Activity, extend this framework to permit distributed participants to make decisions on the collaboration work.

WS-Atomic Transaction (WSAT) WSAT[38] replaces Part I of the WS-Transaction. This specification provides the definition of the atomic transaction coordination type to be used with the extensible coordination framework described in the WS-Coordination specification. The specification defines three specific agreement coordination protocols for the atomic transaction coordination type: *completion*, *volatile two-phase commit*, and *durable two-phase commit*. Service developers can use any or all of these protocols when building applications that require all-or-nothing transaction requirements. WSAT defines protocols that enable existing transaction processing systems to wrap their proprietary protocols and interoperate across different hardware and software vendors.

Asynchronous Service Access Protocol (ASAP)[22] ASAP is currently a working draft at OASIS, which intends to define a way to integrate asynchronous Web services across the Internet and manage their interactions. The integration and interactions consist of controlling and monitoring the services. *Controlling* includes creating a service, setting up a service, starting a service, stopping a service, being informed of exceptions, being informed of the completion of a service, and getting the results of a service. *Monitoring* includes keeping track of the current status and execution history of a Web service. ASAP aims to create a very simple extension of SOAP to enable generic asynchronous Web services or long running Web services. In ASAP, a new set of SOAP methods is defined to accomplish the controlling and monitoring of generic asynchronous services.

WS-Reliable Messaging

It is critical to ensure messages to be delivered reliably between distributed Web services, even in the presence of network failures. Proposed by OASIS, Web Services Reliability (WS-Reliability)[39] is a SOAP-based protocol designed to ensure reliable message exchanges, i.e., with guaranteed delivery, without duplications, and assured message ordering. Its current version binds to HTTP; however, it should be independent of underlying transport protocols. WS-Reliability is defined as SOAP header extensions.

In order to ensure reliable messaging, WS-Reliability proposes a reliable messaging model, in which a sender sends a SOAP message to a receiver directly, and the receiver sends back an acknowledging SOAP message to the sender. In other words, in order to support reliable messaging, upon receipt of a SOAP message, the receiver *must* send a reply, either an *acknowledging* message or a *fault* message. An acknowledgment message is correlated with a normal SOAP message by referencing its message Identifier, which is a globally unique message identifier, to confirm that the receiver has received the message. In case the sender does not receive an acknowledge message, it would resend the same message with the same message Identifier, unless a predefined threshold of the total number of resend attempts has been reached.

In order to ensure duplication-free and message ordering, WS-Reliability suggests mechanisms on the receiver side. Upon receipt of messages, the receiver examines associated message identifier. Duplicated messages with the same message identifier are eliminated right away. In addition, a sequence number is used to track and enforce the correct order of a sequence of messages with a common grouping identification number. Furthermore, WS-Reliability extends the *SOAP Fault Specifications* with fault codes to specify reliable messaging-specific fault values.

WS-Resource Lifetime

WS-Resource Lifetime[40] specification defines message exchanges to standardize the means as to how a WS-Resource can be destroyed, and how resource properties (WS-ResourceProperties) can be used to inspect and monitor the lifetime of a WS-Resource. This specification defines two means of destroying a WS-Resource: immediate destruction and time-based scheduled destruction.

7.2.5 Service Composition

SOAP+WSDL+UDDI guides service requestors to locate one Web service. However, business interaction models typically require synchronous/asynchronous sequences of peer-to-peer message exchanges within stateful interactions involving multiple parties. Thus, multiple Web services may be required to collaborate with each other for the common business interactions. For example, a travel planning process may include collaborative Web services such as flight scheduling, hotel reservations, and car rentals. Service composition allows developers to "compose" services that exchange SOAP messages and define their interfaces into an aggregate solution. The aggregate is a composed Web service or a so-called composite Web service.

BPEL

The Business Process Execution Language for Web Services (BPEL) is proposed for formal specification of synergistically coordinating and organizing Web services into business processes. By extending the Web services interaction model and enabling it to support business transactions, BPEL defines an interoperable integration model that facilitates the expansion of automated process integration in both intra- and inter-corporate environments.

Services composition has three aspects: *structure, information* and *behavior*. BPEL introduces three constructs to support each composition aspect: *partnerLink*, *variable*, and *activity*, respectively. BPEL focuses on describing the behaviors of a business process based on the interactions between the process and its partners.

The interactions occur through Web service interfaces, and the structure of the relationship at the interface level is encapsulated in a *partnerLink*. A BPEL process defines how multiple business interactions are coordinated to achieve a common business goal, as well as the state and the logic necessary for this coordination. A rich process description notation is defined in BPEL to precisely describe essential service behaviors for cross-enterprise business protocols, such as data-dependent behaviors (e.g., the delivery deadline), exceptional conditions and their consequences, including recovery sequences, and long-running interactions at various levels of granularity.

WS-Service Group[41]

A ServiceGroup is a by-reference collection of heterogeneous Web services. ServiceGroups can be used to form a wide variety of collections of services or WS-Resources, including services registries and associated WS-Resources. Members of a ServiceGroup are represented using components called *entries*. As a matter of fact, a ServiceGroup entry is a WS-Resource.

WS-Notification

WS-Notification is a set of specifications that provide support for events using Web services technologies. It makes use of the specifications that compose the WS-Resource Framework (WSRF)[26].

7.3 Industry-Specific Service-Oriented Standards

Industry-specific standards are moving to Web services and SOA. For example, electronics industry, insurance industry, and telecommunication industry have started to leverage Web services standards.

7.3.1 Electronics Industry

In the electronics industry, a set of standards, known as RosettaNet's[42] standards, has been established. Instead of focusing on specific business units, elements and/or proprietary solutions, RosettaNet's standards provide generic business frameworks that allow individual companies to enhance their interoperability of business processes across the global supply chain. In addition, RosettaNet leverages existing protocols, guidelines, and specifications to quickly create standards for efficient business communications across multiple platforms, applications, and networks. Furthermore, RosettaNet's standards are global and open. They describe how to implement collaborative business processes between supply-chain trading partners, using networked applications. In short, RosettaNet provides a common platform of communication, or a common language, which allows different trading partners involved in a business process to automate the process and to conduct it over the Internet.

As shown in Fig. 7.3, RosettaNet's specifications include the business process definitions and technical elements for interoperability and communication: *Partner Interface Processes* (*PIPs*), *PIP Directory*, *Dictionaries*, *RosettaNet Implementation Framework* (*RNIF*), and *Trading Partner Implementation Requirements*. PIPs define business processes between trading partners. PIP Directory facilitates a faster access to the PIP information in a search. Dictionaries provide a common set of properties for PIPs. Specially, RosettaNet Business Dictionary designates the properties used in basic business activities; RosettaNet Technical Dictionaries provide properties for defining products. RNIF provides an infrastructure supporting the packaging, routing, and transporting of PIP messages and business signals. Trading Partner Implementation Requirements enable trading partners to create, view, and respond to RosettaNet PIPs without requiring backend integration.

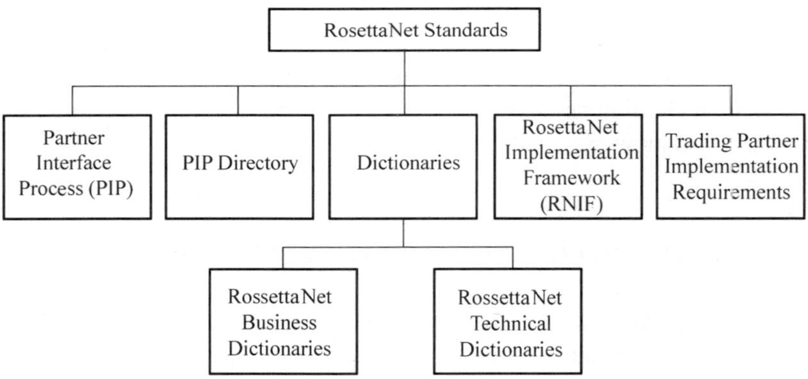

Figure 7.3 RosettaNet Standards

A working group in RosettaNet is working on WSDL-enabled interface definitions for describing the data structures used in PIPs[43].

7.3.2 Insurance Industry

At present, real-time responsiveness to customers and adaptability to changing business requirements have become two critical factors for insurance carriers. The insurance industry is increasingly recognizing the power of standards to help insurance carriers improve their business efficiency and profitably increase their customer base. Insurance standards have evolved over time, starting with the usage of standardized data formats, to standardized forms, and to standardized messages, and now towards the adoption of standardized process services definitions. For example, standardized forms and electronic interchange protocols are expediting business communication between carriers, producers, and third-parties. Standards-based collaboration is helping insurance companies achieve their business goals by making it easier for people, systems, and processes to work together and for businesses to communicate and interoperate within an ecosystem. In short, the insurance industry is evolving away from monolithic silo-based organizations toward networked models, where enterprises collaborate to offer more value to their customers and partners.

The insurance industry has a set of key standards bodies, each focusing on specific areas of the common insurance processes such as e-commerce and infrastructure. Several major standards bodies are: The Association for Cooperative Operations Research and Development (ACORD)[44], Collision Industry eCommerce Association (CIECA)[45], Centre for the Study of Insurance Operations (CSIO)[46], and Western Europe EDIFACT Insurance Group (eEG7)[47]. Among them, CIECA is a standards body based in the United States.

ACORD standards have become widely adopted, and almost all business solutions in the insurance industry leverage these standards in the integration and collaboration of producers and insurance companies. As the leader in global insurance standards, ACORD has developed messaging standards (including standardized forms, data models, and XML standards) for Life and Annuity (L&A), Property and Casualty (P&C), and reinsurance products for the insurance industry. The ACORD approach intends to map insurance-specific applications onto Web services capabilities[47,48].

7.3.3 Telecommunication Industry

The telecommunication (telecom) industry has been putting significant efforts on standardization to increase interoperability. In recent years, a new force "converge" has emerged: the companies whose individual identities were the foundation of the industry are merging, and the companies whose identities were shaped by their services are shedding familiar lines of business. Its essential goal is to converge various existing networks (including wireless networks, wired networks, and IP networks) and various existing services to provide consumers value-added services in the present competitive market. This new force is driving the telecommunication industry into the next generation of "anytime, anywhere" communication networks, which implies the intense competitive demands for standardization in the field. SOA has been considered as a decision factor in this trend.

The Parlay Group[49] is a consortium formed to develop open, technology-independent Application Programming Interfaces (APIs) that enable the development of applications operating across converged networks. Proposed by the Parlay group, Parlay X is an open architecture that abstracts and simplifies the Parlay specifications oriented to the Web services technologies. In detail, Parlay X[49] abstracts telecom network capabilities and masks the telecom-specific features, so that they become independent of network equipments. By mapping Parlay UML specifications into WSDL specifications, Parlay X automatically translates telecom-specific applications into Web services, which are called Parlay X Web services or Parlay Web services. Messages transferred between Parlay Web services and Parlay Web services servers are based on XML. As a result, with Parlay X, IT developers are able to quickly understand and develop Parlay X Web services without deep telecom knowledge.

In Parlay X Web Services specification version 1.0, eight basic services are predefined to allow IT developers to access telecom network capabilities: third-party call control, network-initiated third-party call control, short messaging system, multimedia messaging system, billing, account management, user status, and location of end user device.

Parlay X also decouples service development from service deployment. At the service development phase, developers do not need to consider realization methods in the Parlay X gateways and Parlay gateways. While at the service deployment phase, UDDI service discovery mechanism of Parlay X Web services can be leveraged to bind to Parlay X gateways possessing required capabilities.

7.4 Generic SOA Solution Standards are Evolving

As illustrated in the previous section, individual industries have been standardizing various aspects of their domain-specific business processes, such as interface definitions, best practice benchmarking, and even whole business processes. Industry-specific standards are a key aspect of any strategy for getting closer to customers and becoming more efficient, while facilitating business processes. The increasing adoption of standardized business processes by carriers leads to the necessity and feasibility of automation of standardized business processes. Service-Oriented Architecture (SOA), one of the most open, adaptable, and scalable solution platforms available today, sheds a light on building such an architectural framework to greatly facilitate standardized business processes.

Meanwhile, these industry-specific standards have not fully leveraged the power of the emerging Web services technology and SOA. Web services provide a standardized approach for publishing and accessing services, enabling organizations to easily collaborate within and across business boundaries. In addition, Web services provide a quick approach for building flexible innovative solutions by reusing available published services.

In short, Web services could potentially bridge the gap between IT and business via SOA; however, the current Web services standard protocol stack is basically IT-oriented. This limitation can be diminished from two directions: the first is to leverage the Web services technology to enhance the current industry-specific standards; the second is to establish an SOA-oriented business solution standard stack. Individual industry standards organizations have started to work in the first direction. Each industry may eventually come up with its own industry-specific Web services-based standards. However, there is still no generic SOA solution framework that can be reused and shared to guide both the existing standards and future industry standards.

The industries currently with specific business standards can link the values of their standards with the benefits of SOA to achieve strategic business values and business flexibility. SOA can be leveraged as a foundation to establish an information technology infrastructure, where business processes can be constructed from component modules or "services". These services are independent of specific applications and the computing platforms on which they run, meaning that each service can be reused across a wide range of applications on many different platforms; changes in response to business needs thus become less costly and easier to implement.

7.5 Discussions on SOA and Web Services Standards

Beyond systematically introducing the SOA and Web services standards stack, this chapter discusses several cutting-edge industry-specific standards, and presents a bilateral direction for the emergence of the SOA standards and industry-specific standards.

For the Web services standards stack, each layer will soon have more standards joining in. For example, the QoS layer currently only has four standards. In order to support better QoS control, more standards are needed in SOA, such as solution-level QoS enablement and management standards. IEEE Standards Association formed *SOA Working Group* to dedicate to the creation of SOA standards in 2006. IEEE SOA Working Group has been working on a set of new foundational SOA standards, solution-level SOA reference architectures, and composite application level standards, which are being gradually released to the community (www.soa-standards.org).

7.6 Summary

In this chapter, we discussed Web services standards. The *ad hoc* Web services industry standards stack was introduced as a five-layer structure: transport, messaging, description/publication/discovery, QoS, and service composition. Then three industry-specific standards were discussed: the electronics industry, the insurance industry, and the telecommunication industry. Finally, a picture of unified SOA solution standards was envisioned to be reusable and shared by various industries to establish industry-independent standards for realizing cross-industry interoperability.

References

[1] World Wide Web Consortium (W3C). http://www.w3.org/

[2] Organization for the Advancement of Structured Information Standards (OASIS). http: //www.oasis-open.org/home/index.php

[3] Internet Engineering Task Force (IETF). http://www.ietf.org/

[4] United Nations Centre for Trade facilitation and Electronic Business (UN/CEFACT). http: //www.unece.org/cefact/

[5] Web Services Interoperability (WS-I). http://www.ws-i.org/

[6] Standards and Web services. http://www-128.ibm.com/developerworks/webservices/standards/

[7] Staab S, van AW, Benjamins VR, Sheth A, Miller JA, Bussler C, Maedche A, Fensel D, Gannon D (2003) Web services: been there, done that? IEEE Intelligent Systems 18: 72 – 85

[8] Simmons S (2005) Introducing the WebSphere Integration Reference Architecture: A Service-based Foundation for Enterprise-Level Business Integration. http://www-128.ibm.com/developerworks/websphere/techjournal/0508_simmons/0508_simmons.html

[9] SOAP Specifications. http://www.w3.org/TR/soap/

[10] (2001) Web Services Description Language (WSDL). http://www.w3.org/TR/wsdl

[11] UDDI. http://www.uddi.org/specification.html

[12] OASIS Business Process Execution Language for Web Services Version 1.1. http: //www.ibm.com/developerworks/library/ws-bpel

[13] (2003) Business Process Execution Language (BPEL4WS, version 1.1). http: //xml.cover-pages.org/BPELv11-May052003Final.pdf

[14] Hyper Text Transport Protocol (HTTP). http://www.w3.org/Protocols/

[15] Secure Sockets Layer (SSL). http://en.wikipedia.org/wiki/SSL

[16] Simple Mail Transfer Protocol (SMTP). http://www.ietf.org/rfc/rfc0821.txt

[17] RMI / IIOP (Remote Method Invocation / Internet Inter-Operability Protocol). http: //java.sun.com/products/rmi-iiop/

[18] Java Messaging Service (JMS). http://java.sun.com/products/jms/

[19] 8BITMIME. http://en.wikipedia.org/wiki/8BITMIME

[20] OMG CORBA. http://www.corba.org/

[21] Messaging Oriented Middleware (MOM). http://www.sei.cmu.edu/str/descriptions/momt_body.html

[22] Asynchronous Service Access Protocol. http://www.oasis-open.org/committees/tc_home.php?wg_abbrev=asap

[23] XML. http://xml.coverpages.org/xml.html

[24] XML Schema. http://www.w3.org/XML/Schema
[25] (2002) WS-Addressing. http://www.w3.org/2002/ws/addr/
[26] (2004) Web Services Notification and Web Services Resource Framework (WSRF). http://www-106.ibm.com/developerworks/webservices/library/ws-resource
[27] (2004) WS-Base Faults. http://docs.oasis-open.org/wsrf/2004/06/wsrf-WS-BaseFaults-1.2-draft-02.pdf
[28] Web Services Policy Framework. http://xml.coverpages.org/ws-policyV11.pdf
[29] (2004) WS-Metadata Exchange. http://specs.xmlsoap.org/ws/2004/09/mex/WS-Metadata-Exchange.pdf
[30] WS-Security. http://www.oasis-open.org/committees/wss/
[31] (2005) WS-Trust. http://specs.xmlsoap.org/ws/2005/02/trust/WS-Trust.pdf
[32] (2003) WS-Privacy. http://xml.coverpages.org/ni2003-07-09-a.html
[33] WS-Authorization. http://download.boulder.ibm.com/ibmdl/pub/software/dw/specs/ws-fed/ws-authorization.xsd
[34] WS-SecureConversation. http://www-28.ibm.com/developerworks/library/specification/ws-secon/
[35] WS-Federation. (2006). Web Services Federation Language (WS-Federation). http://www-128.ibm.com/developerworks/webservices/library/specification/ws-fed/
[36] (2002) WS-Transaction. http://xml.coverpages.org/WS-Transaction2002.pdf
[37] (2004) WS-Coordination. http://specs.xmlsoap.org/ws/2004/10/wscoor/wscoor.pdf
[38] (2004) WS-AtomicTransaction. http://specs.xmlsoap.org/ws/2004/10/wsat/wsat.pdf
[39] (2005) WS-Reliable Messaging. http://specs.xmlsoap.org/ws/2005/02/rm/ws-reliablemessaging.pdf
[40] WS-Resource Lifetime. http://docs.oasis-open.org/wsrf/2004/06/wsrf-WS-ResourceLifetime-1.2-draft-03.pdf
[41] WS-ServiceGroup. http://xml.coverpages.org/WS-ServiceGroup20040331.pdf
[42] RosettaNet. http://www.rosettanet.org/
[43] Papazoglou MP (2003) Web services and business transactions. World Wide Web 6: 49 – 91
[44] The Association for Cooperative Operations Research and Development (ACORD). http://www.acord.org/
[45] Collision Industry eCommerce Association (CIECA). http://www.cieca.com/
[46] Centre for Studies of Insurance Operations (CSIO). http://www.csio.com/
[47] Western Europe EDIFACT Insurance Group (eEG7). http://www.eeg7.org/
[48] Hinkelman S, Buddenbaum D, Zhang LJ (2006) Emerging patterns in the use of XML for information modeling in vertical industries. IBM Systems Journal 45: 373 – 388
[49] Paylay. http://www.parlay.org/en/index.asp

8 Solution-Level Quality of Service in SOA

8.1 State-of-the-art of QoS on Web Services

The flexibility of Web services-centered computing is not without penalty since the value added by this new paradigm can be largely defeated if its quality cannot be guaranteed. In order to address the issues of QoS related to Web services[1], the Web services community has been putting significant efforts. Recall the current *Web services standard stack* discussed in Chapter 7. A dedicated layer of QoS shown in Fig. 8.1 is identified to accumulate standards and protocols that aim at enhancing the trustworthiness of Web services in various aspects.

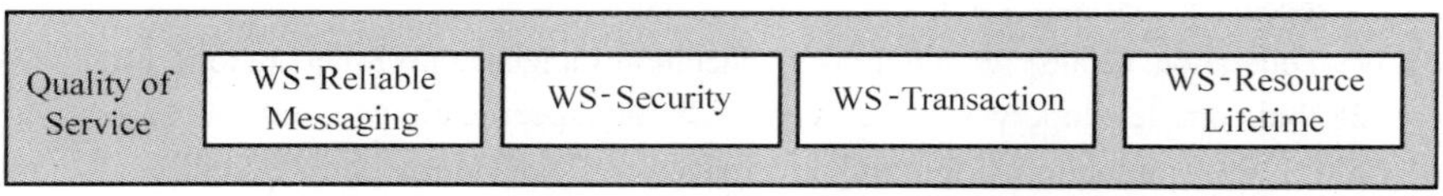

Figure 8.1 QoS layer in Web services standard stack

In the current QoS layer, four standards have been specified regarding four perspectives: security, transaction, reliable messaging, and resource lifetime management. The four standards was discussed in Chapter 7.

The QoS layer of the current Web services standard stack defines a set of standards to help developers and service providers enhance the quality of Web services at the message level and the transaction level. In order to convince enterprises to adopt external Web services into their business processes, however, Web services quality needs to be assured at the solution level that provides integrated QoS control at various granularity levels. An SOA solution may comprise multiple services, each exhibiting component-level QoS attributes. Managing QoS of the entire solution requires not only QoS information of the individual services but also QoS information at the solution level.

It should be noted that the current Web services QoS standards focuses on a couple of QoS attributes, such as security and reliability. Major requirements supporting QoS in Web services should include a holistic set of attributes, such as availability, accessibility, integrity, performance, reliability, regulatory, and security. Meanwhile, the discipline of Software Engineering has contributed a wealth of theories and technologies to assess and ensure these attributes for generic software systems; many researchers are currently investigating how to exploit and apply these technologies and methodologies in the field of Web services[2–4]. Still, these researches focus on individual QoS attributes at the Web services level.

Therefore, there is clearly a necessity and demand for a method that guides software engineers to create a fine-grained solution-level QoS control and management framework for SOA. In more detail, solution-level QoS management needs to address representation, measurement, monitoring, and management of QoS of the federated and aggregated services.

8.2 SOA-QoS

To tackle the QoS issue at the solution level[5], the rest of the chapter introduces a method for creating a data-driven QoS management framework. This technique addresses QoS data enablement from five perspectives: how to represent context-aware QoS data in a unified form; how to communicate QoS data through high-level message exchange under constraints; how to propagate QoS data in system architecture at various granularities; how to detect QoS events at run time; and how to handle QoS events.

The framework addresses QoS management through a logical QoS layer associated with a logical Data Architecture layer, each comprising a closure of configurable and re-configurable constructs based on the best practices in SOA solution development. These fine-grained constructs are associated with relationships and interaction patterns between them as extensible rules to enable adaptability to evolutionary changes.

8.2.1 Context-Aware QoS Model

A solution-level QoS model is needed to qualitatively and quantitatively define the quality of an SOA solution. This concept is defined as a combination of a set of attributes: reliability (Re), security (Se), safety (Sa), availability (Av), and so on. Meanwhile, the measurement of the quality of an SOA solution is not isolated; instead, it should be based on its surrounding contexts. Therefore, a set of SOA-oriented contextual parameters should be identified, including business-level requirements such as key performance indicators (KPIs, e.g., delivery time and execution cost), delivery environment, and SOA relationships. In other words, the quality of an SOA solution s can be represented as a function of the specified attributes:

$$QoS(s) = f(a\text{Re}, b\text{Se}, c\text{Sa}, d\text{Av}, \cdots) \mid (\text{KPIs, environment, relationships})$$

where a, b, c, and d are quantitative or qualitative measures of particular attributes, which fact implies that each attribute may contribute differently to the quality of an SOA solution in a specific context[6], including KPIs, environment, and relationships.

8.2.2 Representation of QoS Model

In order to enable the QoS model over the entire SOA solution, it is necessary to identify a uniform, flexible, and extensible way to model QoS data (i.e., requirement). Instead of creating a new description method, the Web Services Resource Framework (WSRF) is applied as an example to define QoS data as universal resources. As an XML-based presentation method to capture resources, WSRF defines a system of specifications for managing and accessing stateful resources using Web services. Since QoS information may need to be carried by system or system components and should be able to persist across and evolve as a result of Web service interactions, it is suitable and feasible to be modeled as a stateful resource using WSRF.

A QoS requirement can be modeled using WS-Resource properties specifications. Figure 8.2 illustrates relative segments of a sample resource properties document definitions for *QoSRequirement*. As shown in Fig. 8.2, the WS-Resource properties specification document is defined using XML Schema.

```
    <xs:schema
targetNamespace="http://servicescomputing.org/scbook/qos/QoSRequirement"
   xmlns:tns="http://servicescomputing.org/scbook/qos/QoSRequirement"
   xmlns:xs="http://www.w3.org/2001/XMLSchema">

   <xs:element name="QosRequirementId" type="xs:string"/>
   <xs:element name="Description" type="xs:string"/>

   <xs:element name="attribute" type="xs:string"/>

   <xs:simpleType name="QosTypeEnumeration">
     <xs:restriction base="xs:string">
       <xs:enumeration value="Reliability"/>
       <xs:enumeration value="Security"/>
       <xs:enumeration value="Safety"/>
       <xs:enumeration value="Availability"/>
     </xs:restriction>
   </xs:simpleType>

   <xs:simpleType name="OperatorEnumeration">
      <xs:restriction base="xs:string">
        <xs:enumeration value="GREATERTHAN"/>
```

Figure 8.2 A segment of a QoSRequirement shema for resource properties definition

```
        <xs:enumeration value="GREATERTHANOREQUALTO"/>
        <xs:enumeration value="EQUALTO"/>
        <xs:enumeration value="LESSTHAN"/>
        <xs:enumeration value="LESSTHANOREQUALTO"/>
      </xs:restriction>
  </xs:simpleType>

  <xs:element name="constraint">
    <xs:complexType>
        <xs:sequence>
        <xs:element ref="attribute"/>
        <xs:element ref="operator" type="operatorEnumeration"/>
        <xs:element ref="attribute"/>
        </xs:sequence>
    </xs:complexType>
  </xs:element>

  <xs:element name="PreCondition">
    <xs:complexType>
      <xs:sequence>
        <xs:element ref="constraint" minOccurs="1"
maxOccurs="unbounded"/>
      </xs:sequence>
    </xs:complexType>
  </xs:element>

  <xs:element name="PostCondition">
    <xs:complexType>
      <xs:sequence>
        <xs:element ref="constraint" minOccurs="1"
maxOccurs="unbounded"/>
      </xs:sequence>
    </xs:complexType>
  </xs:element>

  <xs:element name="QoSRequirement">
     <xs:complexType>
       <xs:sequence>
          <xs:element ref="QosRequirementId"/>
          <xs:element ref="Description"/>
          <xs:element name="QosType" type="QosTypeEnumeration"/>
          <xs:element ref="PreCondition"/>
          <xs:element ref="PostCondition"/>
       </xs:sequence>
     </xs:complexType>
  </xs:element>
…
  </xs:schema>
```

Figure 8.2 (Continued)

As shown in Fig. 8.2, the state of a *QoSRequirement* contains five elements: *QosRequirementId*, *Description*, *QosType*, *PreCondition*, and *PostCondition*. Each element is of a XML Schema Definition (XSD) type, either a simple XSD data type or a user-defined data type. *QosRequirementId* denotes the unique identifier of the QoS requirement, with an XSD type *String* (xsd:string). *Description* denotes the verbose descriptions of the QoS requirement, with an XSD type *String* (xsd:string). *QosType* denotes to which one of the four software attributes the requirement is related, with defined type *QosTypeEnumeration* containing four predefined values (Reliability, Security, Safety, and Availability). *PreCondition* denotes the precondition of the requirement. *PostCondition* denotes the post-condition of the requirement. Both *PreCondition* and *PostCondition* contain one or multiple *constraints*, each being a triple <attribute, operator, attribute>. An *attribute* is of an XSD type *String* (xsd:string). *Operator* denotes one of the five operators, with defined type *operatorEnumeration* containing five predefined values (>, >=, ==, <, <=).

```
  <wsdl:definitions
 targetNamespace="http://servicescomputing.org/scbook/qos/QoSRequirement"
    xmlns:wsdl="http://schemas.xmlsoap.org/wsdl/"
    xmlns:xs="http://www.w3.org/2001/XMLSchema"
    xmlns:wsrp="http://www.servicescomputing.org/scbook/qos/web-
 services/ws-resourceProperties"

 xmlns:tns="http://www.servicescomputing.org/sccbook/qos/QoSRequirement">
   ...
    <wsdl:types>
       <xs:schema>
          <xs:import
 namespace="http://servicescomputing.org/scbook/qos/QoSRequirement"
 schemaLocation="..."/>
       </xs:schema>
   </wsdl:types>
   ...
   <wsdl:portType name=" QoSRequirement PortType"
                 wsrp:resourceProperties="tns: QoSRequirement">
      <operation name="getQoSRequirementId"/>
      <operation name="getDescription"/>
      <operation name="getQoSType"/>
      <operation name="getPreCondition"/>
      <operation name="getPostCondition"/>
   ...
    </wsdl:portType>
   ...
  </wsdl:definitions>
```

Figure 8.3 Association of the QoSRequirement resource properties document to a portType

In order for a *QoSRequirement* user to know that the "QoSRequirement" defines the WS-Resource properties document associated with a Web service, the WS-Resource properties document declaration is associated with the WSDL *portType* definition in the WSDL definition of the Web service interface, through the use of a standard attribute *resourceProperties*. As shown in Fig. 8.3, the *portType*, with the associated resource properties document, defines the type of the WS-Resource. The *portType* "QoSRequirementPortType" in Fig. 8.3 defines a set of five operations to allow users to access the state information of the defined *QoSRequirement* (*getQoSRequirementId*, *getDescription*, *getQoSType*, *getPreCondition*, and *getPostCondition*).

8.2.3 QoS Data Management

After a QoS requirement is represented as a universal Web service resource, it can be communicated between various architectural components through high-level message exchange as a common service resource. In more detail, each component is equipped with corresponding QoS requirements as validators. For such a component, its related components and propagated QoS requirements can be analyzed. For example, if another component has a child-parent relationship with it, its QoS requirement will be inherited by the child component. The QoS data is communicated through message delivery of QoS metrics and carried by business protocols. In order to decide whether a QoS requirement needs to be propagated to another component, the relationships between the two components need to be analyzed first. Business relationship model discussed in Chapter 6 can be used to address this need.

At run time, if a QoS requirement cannot be satisfied at one architectural component, a QoS validation failure event will be generated and be propagated to all related components. Each receiving component will then validate its corresponding QoS requirements. If they cannot be satisfied, the component will in turn propagate the QoS events to its related components. Such a chained QoS event propagation will help to perform runtime variation impact analysis.

8.2.4 Business Relationship Model

In order to represent comprehensive SOA-oriented business relationships, a layered model is introduced in Chapter 6. Four types of entities are identified: business entity, business service, Web service, and operation. A business entity refers to a business organization; a business service realizes some business functions in an enterprise; a Web service implements a business service; and an operation refers to a specific function provided by a service.

The layered model captures services-oriented relationships at 9 different granularities, which define the hierarchical relationships between SOA-related elements: (1) business-to-business relationship (B-B-R); (2) business_service-to-business_service relationship (BS-BS-R); (3) web_service-to-web_service relationship (WS-WS-R); (4) operation-to-operation relationship (O-O-R); (5) business-to-business_service relationship (B-BS-R); (6) business-to-web_service relationship (B-WS-R); (7) business-to-operation relationship (B-O-R); (8) business_service-to-web_service relationship (BS-WS-R); and (9) web_service-to-operation relationship (WS-O-R).

8.3 QoS Framework in an SOA Solution

A logical QoS framework intends to control and manage the quality of an SOA solution, as shown in Fig. 8.4. The internal structure of the QoS framework comprises 16 fundamental constructs: solution-level QoS manager (s-QoS manager), representation manager, capability manager, solution-level QoS context (s-QoS context) manager, solution-level QoS enabler (s-QoS enabler), solution-level instance manager (s-level instance manager), lifecycle manager, delivery time manager, execution cost manager, delivery environment manager, relationship manager, solution-level QoS content (s-QoS content) manager, reliability manager, availability manager, security manager, and safety manager.

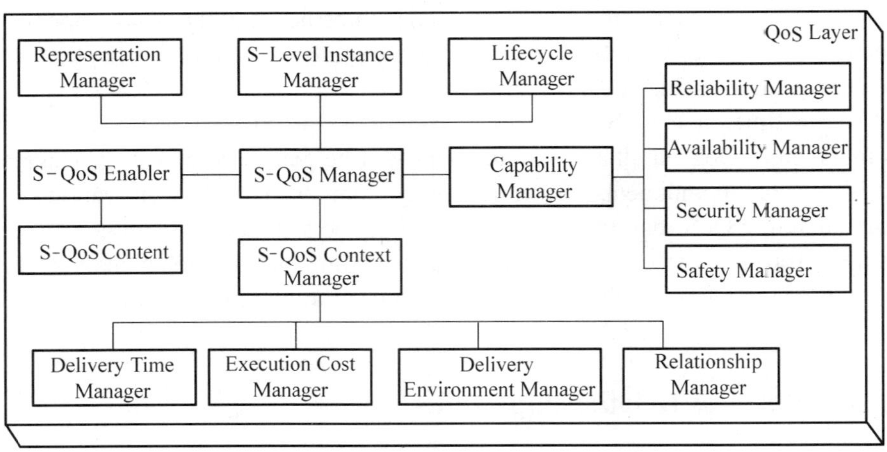

Figure 8.4 QoS framework

8.3.1 QoS Framework Descriptions

As shown in Fig. 8.4, the s-QoS manager is the centralized controller of the QoS framework coordinating other constructs. It has 6 first-level child constructs: representation manager, s-level instance manager, lifecycle manager, s-QoS enabler, capability manager, and QoS context manager. The s-QoS enabler construct is associated with the s-QoS content construct as a support. The capability manager contains a cluster of four sub-constructs: reliability manager, availability manager, security manager, and safety manager. The s-QoS context manager in turn contains four sub-constructs: delivery time manager, execution cost manager, delivery environment manager, and relationship manager. As shown in Fig. 8.4, sub-constructs are part of their corresponding parent constructs.

S-QoS Manager

An s-QoS manager construct is the center of the SOA-QoS framework. It coordinates all other constructs. It is called an s-QoS manager instead of a QoS manager to emphasize that it refers to solution-level QoS management. As shown in Fig. 8.4, the s-QoS manager construct is a six--tuple <representation manager, s-level instance manager, lifecycle manager, s-QoS enabler, capability manager, s-QoS context manager>.

Representation Manager

A representation manager construct is responsible for providing a unified description interface for QoS requirements. The purpose is to hide proprietary presentation details on specific QoS requirements. Web Services Resource Framework (WSRF) and WS-Policy are two possible candidates because they help to define requirements in a uniform manner.

Capability Manager

A capability manager construct is responsible for handling how to represent, measure, monitor, and manage the detailed solution-level QoS requirements in terms of traditional software-related attributes. As shown in Fig. 8.4, four QoS capabilities are captured as default sub-constructs: reliability manager, availability manager, security manager, and safety manager. It should be noted that more software-related attributes can be plugged into the QoS framework as sub-constructs for the capability manager construct.

S-QoS Context Manager

An s-QoS context manager maintains contextual information for solution-level QoS management. It contains four categories of information: delivery time, execution cost, delivery environment, and relationship. This construct implies that the solution-level QoS measurement and assessment are based on surrounding contexts.

S-QoS Enabler

An s-QoS enabler construct is responsible for adapting solution-level QoS requirements into solution-specific QoS requirements. For example, a solution-level QoS requirement may imply different QoS requirements to other components in a specific solution.

S-Level Instance Manager

An s-level instance manager construct is responsible for managing running instances of various services or components under control of solution-level QoS requirements.

Lifecycle Manager

A lifecycle manager construct is responsible for managing solution-level QoS requirements during the period of a solution's lifecycle, from the time when the solution is delivered to a specific deployment environment to the time when the solution is terminated.

Delivery Time Manager

A delivery time manager construct is responsible for recording, tracking, and monitoring the time needed to deliver a specific solution.

Execution Cost Manager

An execution cost manager construct is responsible for recording, tracking, and monitoring the cost needed to execute a specific solution.

Delivery Environment Manager

A delivery environment manager construct is responsible for defining the required running environment needed to deliver a specific solution.

Relationship Manager

A relationship manager construct is responsible for defining SOA-oriented business relationships between services in a specific system (or solution). These business relationships are important supplement of functionalities for solution-level quality control.

S-QoS Content

An s-QoS content construct is responsible for storing solution-specific <name, value> pairs of QoS attributes and required values.

Reliability Manager

A reliability manager construct is responsible for handling the reliability feature of a solution. It refers to how much percentage that a solution can be successfully executed without failure during a certain period of time. This construct handles how to represent, measure, monitor, and manage application-specific solution-level reliability on top of multiple comprised services with component-level reliability.

Availability Manager

An availability manager construct is responsible for handling the availability feature of a solution. This construct handles how to represent, measure, monitor, and manage application-specific solution-level availability on top of multiple comprised services with component-level availability.

Security Manager

A security manager construct is responsible for handling the security feature of a solution. This construct handles how to represent, measure, monitor, and manage application-specific solution-level security on top of multiple comprised services with component-level security.

Safety Manager

A safety manager construct is responsible for handling the safety feature of a solution. This construct handles how to represent, measure, monitor, and manage application-specific solution-level safety on top of multiple comprised services with component-level safety.

8.3.2 Relationships Between Constructs in QoS Framework

Figure 8.5 uses a Unified Modeling Language (UML) component diagram to illustrate a static view of the relationships between the constructs in the QoS framework. All identified constructs are represented as components in the diagram, with "construct" as stereotype. The SOA-QoS is represented as a package containing all identified constructs.

Certain relationships exist between the identified constructs:

There is a one-to-one relationship between s-QoS manager construct and a list of other constructs: representation manager, s-level instance manager, lifecycle manager, s-QoS enabler, capability manager, and s-QoS context manager.

There is a one-to-one relationship between s-QoS enabler construct and s-QoS content construct.

There is a one-to-one relationship between capability manager construct and a list of sub-constructs: reliability manager, availability manager, security manager, and safety manager.

There is a one-to-one relationship between s-QoS context construct and a list of sub-constructs: delivery time manager, execution cost manager, delivery environment manager, and relationship manager.

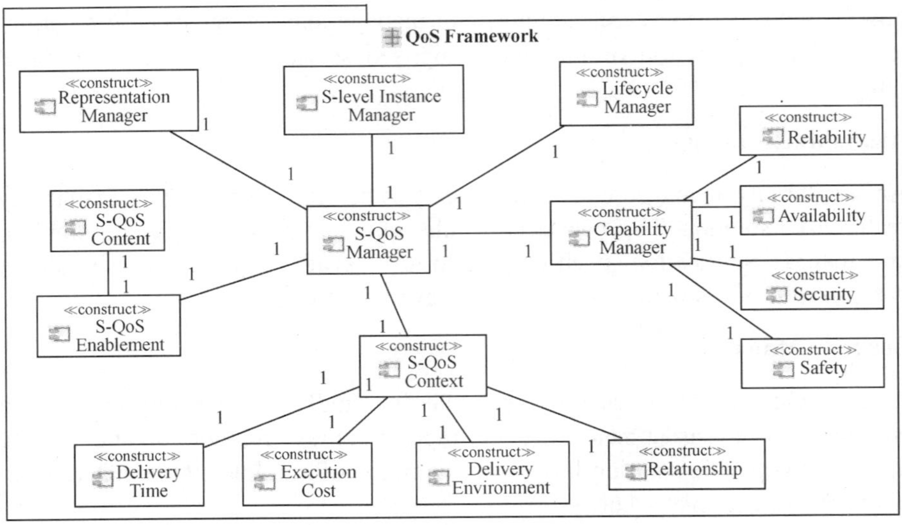

Figure 8.5 Component relationships in the QoS framework

8.4 Data Architecture Framework

In order to separate data manifestation and manipulation from QoS control, a dedicated logical data architecture framework is introduced to be associated with the QoS framework. The data architecture framework provides a unified representation and enablement framework that integrates with domain-specific data architecture to facilitate services integration. Typical domain-specific data architecture examples are: the Shared Information/Data model (SID) in Enhanced Telecom Operations Map (eTOM)[7] of telecom industry, as well as the RosettaNet Technical Dictionary and RosettaNet Business Dictionary defined by RosettaNet for electronics industry[8].

8.4.1 Data Architecture Framework Descriptions

Figure 8.6 shows the internal structure of the data architecture framework. Seven basic constructs are identified: data services gateway, data aggregator, data mining manager, access control manager, traceability enabler, data representation manager, and data sources manager. As shown in Fig. 8.6, the data aggregator is the centralized controller of the data architecture framework coordinating other constructs. The data services gateway construct acts as the gateway of the data architecture framework. Other components in the same solution typically go through the data services gateway to obtain data-related services from the data architecture framework.

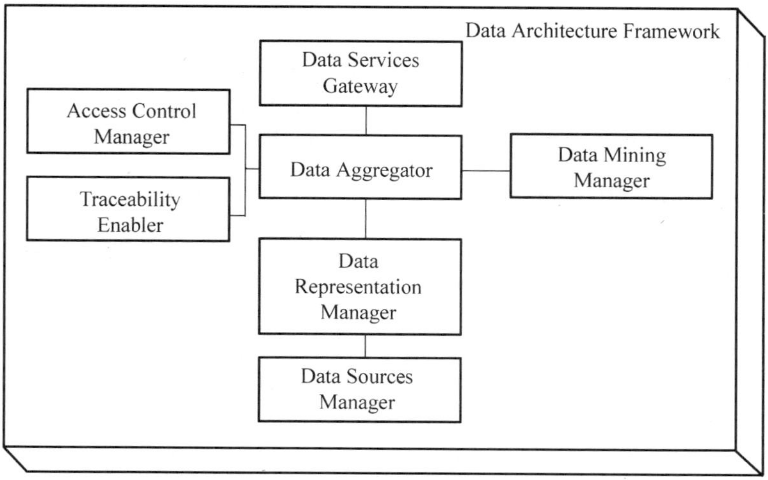

Figure 8.6 Data architecture framework

Data Services Gateway

A data services gateway construct acts as the gateway (front desk) of the data architecture framework. It mainly has three responsibilities. First is to expose data as services. Second is to add, remove, and manipulate data entries in different services or service components. Third is to disable some data from outside access.

Data Aggregator

A data aggregator construct is the federated data manager of the data architecture framework. Its major responsibilities are three-fold: first is to dispatch requests to other constructs; second is to handle data transformation (including transformation of data types and contents); third is to aggregate data from multiple data sources.

Data Mining Manager

A data mining manager construct is responsible for analyzing data access history and providing optimization algorithms and business intelligence for data optimization.

Access Control Manager

An access control manager construct is responsible for handling access privileges of various participants. It typically involves authorization and authentication functionalities for registered participants. The access control manager normally defines access control attributes. For example, the access control manager construct handles who can see or access which portion of a data source (documents), as well as who can change it.

Traceability Enabler

A traceability enabler construct is responsible for monitoring and managing data usages through a log-like facility. Typical traceability log includes: who has accessed the data, when, and what part of the data has been accessed.

Data Representation Manager

A data representation manager construct is responsible for handling representation of data from various data sources in a unified data format. In other words, the data representation manager intends to hide various data sources and present data in uniform formats to other constructs for data handling. It should be noted that the data representation manager construct may link to various data sources and handle relationships between the data sources.

Data Sources Manager

A data sources manager construct deals with the actual data repositories in various types, such as a database or an ASCII file. It should be noted that the data sources manager construct in the data architecture framework intends to build and manage high-level links associated with metadata to real data sources in the real implementation platforms. For example, instead of containing (e.g., attaching) a huge document, the data sources manager construct here typically handles an on-demand link to the original document, together with some metadata describing the document (e.g., goals, purposes, and short descriptions) that help users decide whether there is a need to access the original document (e.g., a CEO may decide not to download a detailed design document while a project architect may decide to download and review). In addition, it should be noted that data sources manager here typically handles industry-specific data structure; therefore, transformation may be needed for further processing.

8.4.2 Relationships Between Constructs in Data Architecture

Figure 8.7 uses a UML component diagram to illustrate a static view of the relationships between the constructs within the data architecture framework. All identified constructs are represented as components in the diagram, with "construct" as stereotype. The data architecture framework is represented as a package containing all identified constructs.

Certain relationships exist between the identified constructs:

First, there is a one-to-one relationship between data aggregator construct with a list of other constructs: data services gateway, access control manager, traceability enabler, data mining manager, and data representation manager.

Second, there is a many-to-many relationship between data representation manager construct and data sources manager construct.

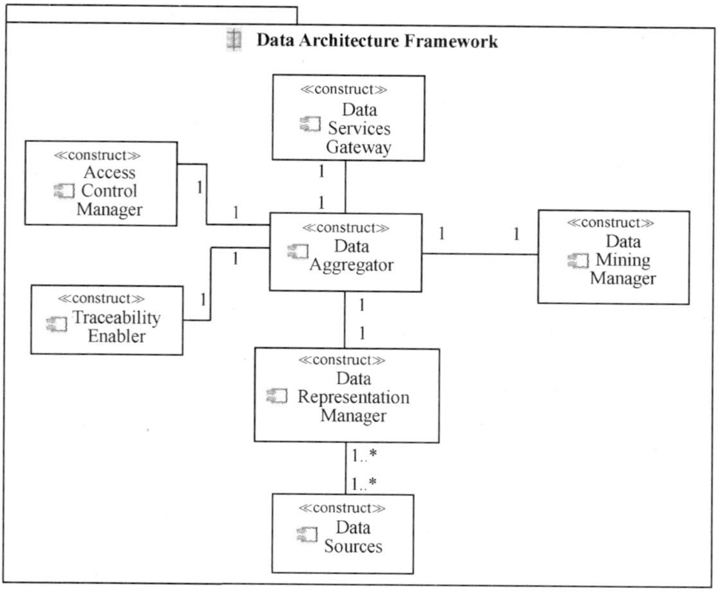

Figure 8.7 Component relationships within the data architecture framework

8.5 Modeling the Key Elements in QoS Management

In order to ensure solution-level QoS control, the modeling of two elements needs to be given special attention, namely resources and validation processes[9]. The lifecycle of an SOA solution involves different types of participating entities, including physical entities, human resource, and abstract entities. Example entities are organizations, users, and people who engage in the software lifecycle by acting in different roles (e.g., developers, testers, and analysts). Every entity can be treated as a reusable resource. Each resource needs to take responsibility to assure the QoS-related policies over its involved activities. In addition that each resource assures QoS-related policies, a validation process should be explicitly defined and associate with the policy. A validation process is a procedure that documents how the policies are to be achieved and verified. As an example, involved resources can be modeled using WSRF; QoS assurance processes can be modeled using BPEL4WS.

8.5.1 Modeling of Resources

A services-oriented system typically involves various types of participating entities, each taking different responsibilities to ensure the quality of the system. Earlier studies in the field of software engineering have revealed that accountability structure (i.e., proper definition of roles and responsibilities) is important in ensuring the success of a software project. Therefore, four types of resources are identified: organization, user, role player, and abstract entity.

An *organization* resource refers to a service provider of Web services. A *user* resource refers to a service requestor of an application system. A *role player* resource refers to a person who engages in the service lifecycle by acting in different roles, such as developer, tester, analyst, and project manager. An *abstract entity* resource refers to other entities involved, including hardware devices and software components.

Moreover, the role of QoS testers can be identified. Minimally, three sub-roles are in turn predefined: a program manager (PM) accountable for delivering a system that meets the QoS expectation; a technical project lead accountable for delivering a system to the PM that meets the PM's stated QoS requirements; and a quality assurance (QA) manager responsible for developing the QA Plan and for measuring, assessing, and reporting QoS performances against objectives.

These roles can be considered as WS-Resources due to the three characteristics that the roles possess:

- Uniqueness: each role has a distinguishable identity and lifetime;
- Statefulness: each role maintains a specific state that can be materialized using XML;
- Accessibility: the information of each role should be accessed through one or more Web services to provide another level of quality assurance.

```
<xs: schema targetNamspace=
"http://servicescomputing.org/QualityControllerPropertiesExample"
  xmlns:tns="http://servicescomputing.org/QualityControllerPropertiesExample"
  xmlns:xs="http://www.w3.org/2001/XMLSchema"
... >

  <xs:element name="RoleID" type="xs:string"/>
  <xs:element name="Responsibility" type="xs:string"/>
  <xs:element name="Mandatory" type="xs:string"/>
  <xs:element name="RoleRequirements" type="xs:string"/>

  <xs:element name="QualityControllerProperties">
    <xs:complexType>
       <xs:sequence>
          <xs:element ref="tns:RoleID"/>
          <xs:element ref="tns: Responsibility"/>
          <xs:element ref="tns: Mandatory"/>
          <xs:element ref="tns: RoleRequirements"/>
        </xs:sequence>
    </xs:complexType>
    </xs:element name="QualityControllerProperties">
```

Figure 8.8 Fragment of resource properties document QualityControllerProperties

Figure 8.8 defines a QA manager role *QualityController* using WS-Resource specifications. The state of a *QualityController* is composed of four resource property components: its unique identification number, its responsibility related to QoS, whether the role is mandatory, and the skill set that the role requires. Its resource properties document, named *QualityControllerProperties*, is defined as shown in Fig. 8.8.

```
<wsdl:definitions
   targetNamespace="http://servicescomputing.org/QualityControllerProperties"
   xmlns:wsdl="http://schemas.xmlsoap.org/wsdl/"
   xmlns:xs="http://www.w3.org/2001/XMLSchema"
   xmlns:wsrp=
"http://www.ibm.com/xmlns/stdwip/web-services/ws-resourceproperties"
   xmlns:tns="http:// servicescomputing.org /QualityControllerProperties">
...
   <wsdl:types>
     <xs:schema>
<xs:import namespace=http://servicescomputing.org/QualityControllerProperties
schemaLocation="..."/>
    </xs:schema>
  </wsdl:types>
...
  <wsdl:portType name="QualityControllerInfo"
wsrp:ResourceProperties="tns:QualityControllerResourceProperties">
   <operation name="...
...
   </wsdl:portType>
...
</wsdl:definitions>
```

Figure 8.9 Fragment of QualityController role

Figure 8.9 shows how the defined *QualityController* role can be published as part of the Web service by embedding the code into the WSDL description of the Web service. Then the WS-Resource properties document declaration of *QualityController* is associated with the WSDL *portType* definition via the use of the Resource Properties attribute, as highlighted in Fig. 8.9. Afterwards, service requestors may obtain and examine this XML schema definition of the WS-Resource properties document, which represents the type of stateful resource *QualityController*. A sample SOAP request to the *QualityController* resource is shown in Fig. 8.10. The SOAP message requests two properties of the specific *QualityController* of a system: the identification number and the skill sets.

8.5.2 Modeling the QoS Assurance Process

QoS assurance processes are meant to provide reasonable assurance that the system

```
<QualityControllerProperties>
  <QCID></QCID>
  <RoleID>QualityController</RoleID>
  <Responsibility>Certify Quality</Responsibility>
  <Mandatory>yes</Mandatory>
  <RoleRequirements></RoleRequirements>
</QualityControllerProperties>
```

Figure 8.10 A sample SOAP request to the QualityController resource.

of QoS control is relevant, adequate, and complied with in practice. Validation processes normally include the development of a general strategy and the preparation of a detailed approach to the corresponding policies, while outlining the supervision and review responsibilities and other QoS control procedures specific to QoS requirement.

As a language that can be used to specify business processes and business interaction protocols, BPEL can be used to model the process. Consider a process of validating a flight reservation service. If a remote flight reservation Web service generates an invalid number as return, it should be considered as an exception. The system then needs to handle the *InvalidNo* fault. As shown in Fig. 8.11, the system uses the <invoke> section to invoke the Web service *FlightRESerivce*. A <faultHandlers> section is embedded to handle the exception. The fault handlers define the activities that must be performed in response to *InvalidNo* faults resulting from the invocation of the assessment and approval services. The WSDL fault *InvalidNo* is identified by a qualified name formed by the target namespace of the WSDL document in which the relevant *portType* and fault are defined.

```
<scope containerAccessSerializable="no">
  <faultHandlers>
    <catch faultContainer="frError" faultName="frs:InvalidNo">
      <!-- send assertion to the service requestor -->
...
    </catch>
</faultHandlers>
<sequence>
   <invoke inputContainer="frInput"
           name="flightRE"
           operation="process"
           outputContainer="frOutput"
           partner="flightREService"
           portType="frs:FlightREService"/>
 </sequence>
</scope>
```

Figure 8.11 A sample QoS assurance process represented in BPEL

8.6 Discussions on QoS in SOA

In addition to discussing the QoS layer of the current Web services standard stack, this chapter introduces a data-driven QoS management framework at the SOA solution level. This model addresses the two major limitations of the known SOA solution: lack of solution-level QoS support and lack of holistic QoS considerations. Organizations may start with this data-driven QoS model, customize it and apply it for developing reusable, flexible, and extensible solution-level QoS services for SOA solutions. This method is especially suitable to be used by software architects who are responsible for designing software architecture for enterprise-level QoS control for SOA solutions. The presented model can be quickly configured and customized into an architectural proposal to customers, based upon specific business requirements. Moreover, the customized data-driven QoS model and data architecture model can be directly delivered to the corresponding development team as architecture template for the final solution development.

Due to the specific properties of Web services-based SOA solution, these existing software testing models and methodologies deserve reinspection in the domain of Web services and SOA. In more detail, three critical questions need to be tackled: How to precisely define the quality of SOA, and what are the criteria? How to measure and test the quality of SOA? How to enhance and guarantee qualified Web services in the whole lifecycle of an SOA solution? All of these questions are open to researchers and practitioners.

8.7 Summary

In this chapter, we introduced a framework for creating a data-driven, solution-level, and SOA-based QoS modeling and management, as well as data architecture. A QoS framework, associated with a data architecture framework, is introduced. The two frameworks both comprise configurable and re-configurable constructs. Furthermore, relationships and interaction patterns are predefined, within and across the frameworks as extensible rules, to enable adaptability to evolutionary changes.

References

[1] Zhang LJ (2004) Challenges and opportunities for Web services research. International Journal of Web Services Research 1

[2] Zhang J (2006) A mobile agents-based approach to test reliability of Web services. International Journal of Web and Grid Services 2: 92 – 117

[3] Zhang J, Zhang LJ (2005) Criteria analysis and validation of the reliability of Web services-oriented systems. In: IEEE International Conference on Web Services (ICWS 2005), Orlando, FL, USA, pp 621 – 628
[4] Zhang J (2004) An approach to facilitate reliability testing of Web services components. In: IEEE 15th International Symposium on Software Reliability Engineering (ISSRE 2004), Saint-Malo, Bretagne, France, pp 210 – 218
[5] Zhang LJ, Li B (2004) Requirements driven dynamic business process composition for Web services solutions. Journal of Grid Computing 2: 121 – 140
[6] Chen IYL, Yang SJH, Zhang J (2006) Ubiquitous provision of context aware Web services. In: IEEE International Conference on Services Computing (SCC 2006), Chicago, IL, USA
[7] The Enhanced Telecom Operations Map (eTOM). http://www.tmforum.org/browse.aspx?catID = 1648
[8] RosettaNet. http://www.rosettanet.org/
[9] Zhang J, Zhang LJ, Chung JY (2004) WS-trustworthy: a framework for Web services centered trustworthy computing. In: Proceedings of 2004 IEEE International Conference on Services Computing (SCC 2004), pp 186 – 193

Part 2 Realization of Services Computing

9 Requirements Driven Services Composition

9.1 Introduction

Business requirements from customers normally exhibit in various kinds of forms and keep on changing all the time. Some current tools exist to help catch the requirements and store them in a consistent way, such as IBM's *Rational Requisite Pro*[1]. However, how to rapidly establish a business process meeting dynamic and evolving business requirements remains a big challenge.

The concept of Services Computing paves a new way of rapid business process integration and management, by leveraging existing business services[2,3]. Instead of developing a new business process from scratch, available business services are discovered, organized, re-configured, and grouped into a new business process to satisfy customer requirements. To standardize and formalize the specification of business processes, several business process languages were created, such as Business Process Execution Language for Web Services (BPEL4WS, a.k.a. BPEL)[4] and Web Service Choreography Interface (WSCI)[5].

As business requirements are ever changing, dynamic and automatic business process composition poses significant challenges. First, business processes are driven by business requirements, which typically tend to be informal, subjective, and difficult to quantify. Therefore, it is critical to properly formulate the descriptive and subjective requirements into quantifiable, objective, and machine-readable formats to enable automatic business process composition. Second, existing Web services-based business process description languages do not adequately accommodate detailed requirement specifications, which makes it difficult to create optimal business process composition. Third, the present Web services specifications generally lack facilities to define comprehensive services-related relationships, which are important to optimize business process composition. Readers can refer to Chapter 6 for detailed discussions about services-oriented relationships. Fourth, as more and more services are published to the Internet on the daily basis, how to clearly specify search requirements to discover proper service candidates remains a challenge. Fifth, a typical business process generally requires multiple services to collaborate on comprehensive business requirements. Therefore, each service not only needs to satisfy individual requirements, but also needs to coexist with other services in order to best fit the overall composed business process. In other words, the entire business process should be optimized prior to execution.

An information architectural model is needed to precisely capture comprehensive business requirements, preferences, Web service features, event-action mapping, as well as the relationships among Web services. An automated mechanism is needed to generate search scripts, which can dynamically discover appropriate Web services for a specific task from various services registries, including public UDDI registries, private UDDI registries, WSIL documents, and other services registries. A seamless integration mechanism is needed to perform model-driven (a.k.a. template-based) and event-driven business process flow composition from existing Web services. It should be noted that the event here implies any kinds of events, which may come from an IT system (e.g., a server does not respond in two minutes), an application, a business (e.g., an annoucement is published), or a human being (e.g., a note is sent to a dash board). An effective services selection mechanism is needed to automatically construct an optimal, or near-optimal, business process using available Web services. An efficient tool is needed to support dynamic adaptations of Web services flow in regard to various modeling languages (e.g., BPEL). Finally, a step-by-step methodology is needed to guide through services-based business process composition and adaptation.

The goal of requirement modeling and search algorithms is to reduce search space. It is reasonable to imagine that a possible service space contains a large number of services, say 10,000. If one examines every item in this enormous service space for a possible service candidate, it is neither efficient nor practical. Therefore, business requirements should be represented in a consistent format (e.g., XML format) and be used to automatically generate search scripts to drive a service discovery engine for service candidates. After this first step, the big search space is intended to be largely reduced, say from 10,000 to 50 candidate services. Then the goal of the next steps is to explore a proper way to assemble the service candidates into a business process flow to satisfy business requirements. A global optimization algorithm[6] can be adopted to gradually find optimal business process. Example convergence criteria include delivery cost, delivery time, specific requirements, and preferred service provider. After these steps, a near-optimal business process could be obtained. Therefore, this technique is called a requirements-driven services composition.

9.2 Business Requirements Modeling

This section will introduce an information architectural model for capturing and representing comprehensive business requirements. This model could potentially benefit both business requirements composers and business service providers, as it provides guidance on what kinds of perspectives could be considered when designing requirements or services, respectively.

As shown in Fig. 9.1, business requirements typically cover four perspectives:

target components and surrounding environment, asset lifecycle management, project management, and finance management.

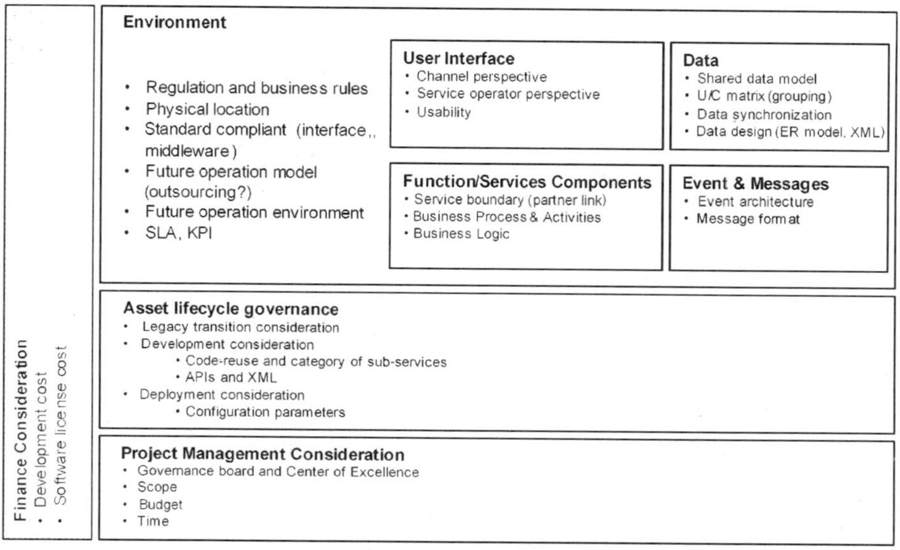

Figure 9.1 Requirements modeling framework

9.2.1 Target Components and Environment

The first and main part of the information architectural model intends to model the requirements on target components and surrounding environment. Requirements on target components can be in turn divided into the following four categories: user interfaces, functions, data models, and events and messages.

User Interfaces

Requirements on user interfaces may cover three perspectives of Human Computer Interaction (HCI) design, either through Graphical User Interface (GUI) or through programs: channel perspective, service operator perspective, and usability. First, a business service may provide multiple channels for users to access, e.g., desktop, Personal Data Assistants (PDAs), wireless phones, or other access facilities such as kiosk machines and ATM machines. Integration, sharing, and synchronization strategies between channels should be established and stay transparent to end users. Second, a business service should take into account user experiences from not only end users, but also service operators such as people at call centers or at service operation and support centers. Third, service usability should be taken into consideration early in the design stage between service providers and potential service consumers. A prototype is usually helpful to allow the users understand what the final user interface would be like and collect their feedbacks as early as possible. Early changes will have much lower cost compared with those happening at later stages.

Functions

Requirements on functions may cover three perspectives: business logic, business process and activity, and service boundary and partner link. First, business logic defines domain-specific logic that needs to be implemented by a business service. Second, business process and activity specifies a collection of structured activities that fulfill specific business logic of a business service. Third, nowadays, it is becoming more common that a business service requires collaborations from multiple business partners and needs to be conducted in heterogeneous environment, which is why SOA comes into the scene. In other words, requirements on services should also clearly define service boundaries and related partners and their relationships.

Data Models

Requirements on data models may cover four perspectives: shared data model, User/Creator (U/C) matrix, data synchronization, and data design and implementation. First, a shared uniform data model within an enterprise is critical for different business units to effectively and efficiently share the business artifacts and cooperate. An example of such a shared data model standard is eTOM's Shared Information Data Model (SID)[7]. Second, a U/C matrix method is often used to precisely define the relationships and usage patterns between data creators and data users. Third, since a modern business service typically exploits distributed data resources from different data sources, data synchronization needs to be ensured. Fourth, information management is migrating toward a convergence of structured (e.g., XML), unstructured (e.g., plain text), and other Entity Relationship (ER)[8] models embodied in traditional Database Management System (DBMS). In summary, all these different data models should be considered and the integrated data model should support evolutionary changes.

Events and Messages

Requirements on events and messages may cover two perspectives: event architecture and message format. Under the SOA environment, events and messages play critical roles to connect together loosely coupled systems. First, event architecture defines a framework of modeling an event and event hierarchy, such as event names, event queue numbers, event conditions, event actions, and so on. Second, message format defines a valid data structure of a message communicating between business services, such as message title, message body, message signature, and so on.

Environment

Requirements on an environment surrounding a business service may cover five perspectives: regulation and business rules, physical location, compliance with standards, operational model, and service agreements. First, regulation and business rules define the policies that need to be enforced during service execution. Second, physical location defines the specific physical environment of the execution environment for a business service. Third, compliance with standards defines the specific standards that need to be enforced, e.g., interface and middleware. Fourth, operational model defines how a business service should be invoked, e.g., using outsourcing model, hosted by third parties, or adopting an in-source model. Fifth, service agreements define service-level contracts between service providers and service consumers, such as Service Level Agreements (SLAs) and Key Performance Indicators (KPIs).

9.2.2 Asset Lifecycle Management

The second part of the information architectural model is to model the requirements on asset lifecycle management. An SOA-based software development process has been evolving from a labor-intensive development process to an asset-based development process to obtain acceptable profit margin and lower project risks. Requirements on asset lifecycle management can be in turn divided into the following three categories: legacy transition consideration, development consideration, and deployment consideration.

Legacy transition consideration defines whether some legacy systems will be integrated into the final system, and how they can be transited into the final service. For example, a COBOL-based system at a back-end server may need to be supported. Development consideration defines how to reuse existing programming segments, e.g., code, sub-services, and commonly shared APIs and XML schema. Deployment time consideration defines how to reuse and reconfigure existing assets to be used in runtime environment such as an application server.

9.2.3 Project Management

The third part of the information architectural model is to model the requirements on project management. Requirements on project management can be in turn divided into the following five categories: scope, time, budget, resource, and governance. Scope defines the boundary of business requirements of a project. Time defines the time frame for a project. Budget defines the sum of money allocated for a specific project. Resource covers the required physical resources (e.g., machine) and non-physical resources (e.g., people resources). Besides the above five often-mentioned key elements of project management, SOA-based project management needs to consider the governance board and center of excellence to enable propagation of best practices.

9.2.4 Finance Management

The fourth part yet maybe an even more important part of the information architectural model intends to model the requirements on finance management. Few people may argue that a successful project could only be fulfilled under strict financial management. Without well-planned finance management strategy, service providers may find themselves face high project risks, fail to react to customers' changing requirements, even lose their competitive advantages. The cost structure, such as development cost and software license cost, need to be well controlled within the budget of the service consumers and the service providers. Typically cost is closely related to resource and time.

9.2.5 Representation of Business Requirements Modeling

After business requirements are modeled and captured using the introduced information architectural model, they should be refined and expressed in a uniform and standard manner. As an example, Business Process Outsourcing Language (BPOL)[6] is an XML-based annotation language coined for representing a sub-set of business requirements for services composition. It focuses on specifications of service flow rules, customer preferences, and business rules, which can be used for effective service discovery and selection. The data structure of BPOL is summarized in Fig. 9.2, which describes the contained tags and their relationships with each other.

BPOL is composed of two major parts, namely flow rules and composition requirements. Flow rules refer to control flow rules for either parallel services or sequential services requested by customers. If parallel services are desired, the flow rules specify parallel numbers and parallel tasks. If sequential services are desired, the flow rules specify sequential numbers and sequential tasks. After a control flow is defined, each task in the flow can be realized by different service providers.

Composition requirements refer to data or data flow-related requirements and rules regarding businesses, preferences, and events. For example, one may prefer one particular service provider (e.g., taking one Airline instead of another) or one particular service (e.g., by air instead of by train). A business rule can be represented in different ways, such as policies, behaviors, conditions (e.g., QoS and benefits), related services, or relationships to other rules.

As shown in Fig. 9.2, the BPOL annotation language contains five major aspects to define and specify services composition requirements: *service name*, *preference*, *business rules binding*, *service relationship* (RelationLink), and *event* (for binding as well).

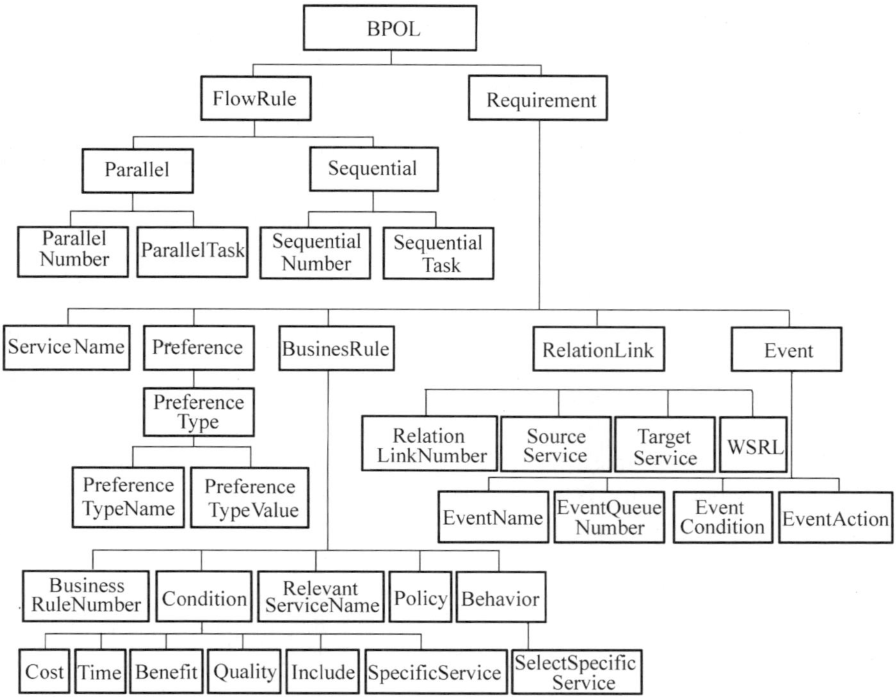

Figure 9.2 BPOL data structure

Service names specify a set of particular services to be used in a business process. Preferences include a set of name and value pairs, such as the preferred UDDI registry name and its location link. Business rules specify how various steps of a business process can be encoded in the form of reaction rules. More specifically, business rules govern the selection of Web services for optimal business processes. In more detail, a business rule is defined as a pentuple <business rule number, relevant service name, policy, condition, behavior>. The element of condition predefines cost, time, benefit or service bonus, quality of service, and specific or preferred services. The element of behavior specifies under which circumstances a specific service should be selected.

Preferences define whether some specific services or service providers are preferred.

Service relationships describe the business relationships between service providers. Detailed discussions on service relationships can be found in Chapter 6. A relationship is defined as a quadruple (relationship number, source service, target service, and WSRL definition of the relationship). An SOA-RML specification document can be embedded into a BPOL document via a link tag. As shown in Fig. 9.2, the *RelationLink* element of BPOL represents relationship information between service providers and services.

A business process may include multiple operations that conform to a certain invocation-sequencing rule. The event list defined in BPOL is used to capture the Event-Condition-Action (ECA) mapping for event-driven business process composition. A binding event associated with these operations in a Web service triggers an event action to be performed for evaluating the service selection. An event is defined as a quadruple <event name, event queue number, event condition, event action>. It captures the purpose of an event, the sequence that the event follows, the conditions to which the event conform, and the actions that the event takes. It should be noted that if an event-driven architectural reference document is already defined, one only needs to add an event reference link to the original document.

As shown in Fig. 9.2, the extensible structure of BPOL enables the import of existing XML files, such as FlowXML file, BusinessRuleXML file, PreferenceXML file, ECA-XML for business flow, business rules, preferences, and event-action mappings. In other words, BPOL not only acts as a container for existing XML formats, but also carries the annotation information among the objects listed in different XML files.

As mentioned, BPOL is an example that represents a sub-set of comprehensive business requirements illustrated in Fig. 9.1. BPOL can be extended to cover more or the whole set of requirement modeling.

9.3 Requirements Driven Services Discovery

Services composition requirements modeling provides guidance to the process of discovering appropriate business services from services repositories (i.e., registries). Search keywords can be extracted from corresponding business requirements specification documents and then be used to created search scripts.

In Chapter 4, the UDDI Search Markup Language (USML)[6] is introduced as an XML-based search script language aiming at representing search requests, including multiple queries, key words, UDDI sources, WSIL files, and aggregation operators. In order to facilitate automatic service discovery, it is important to translate business requirements specification documents into USML queries, so that search queries in USML documents derive from business needs and preferences. The relationships between multiple search queries can also be obtained from the parallel or sequential relationships defined between business services. In short, the business rules defined in information architectural model can help generate more precise USML scripts to retrieve qualified business services.

Figure 9.3 and Fig. 9.4 show an example of how a BPOL document in Fig. 9.3, as an example implementation of the information architectural model, is translated into a USML document in Fig. 9.4. The BPOL document specifies two parallel tasks: *MatchSelection* and *FoodReservation*. The task *FoodReservation* is further defined as a list of sequential tasks: *Start*, *RestaurantComparison*, *RestaurantBooking, Food,* and *End.*

```
<?xml version="1.0"?>
<BPOL xmlns="http://www.servicescomputing.org"
  xmlns:xsi="http://www.w3.org/2001/XMLSchema-instance"
  xsi:schemaLocation="http://www.servicescomputing.org/BPOL.xsd">

<BPOL>
  <FlowRule>
    <Parallel>
        <ParallelNumber>0</ParallelNumber>
        <ParallelTask>MatchSelection</ParallelTask>
        <ParallelTask>FoodReservation</ParallelTask>
    </Parallel>
  ...
    <Sequential>
        <SequentialNumber>5</SequentialNumber>
        <SequentialTask>Start</SequentialTask>
        <SequentialTask>RestaurantComparison</SequentialTask>
        <SequentialTask>RestaurantBooking</SequentialTask>
        <SequentialTask>Food</SequentialTask>
        <SequentialTask>End</SequentialTask>
    </Sequential>
  ...
  </FlowRule>
  ...
</BPOL>
```

Figure 9.3 A sample BPOL document

Based on the flow rules in the BPOL document, the categories derived from the task names, in conjunction with preference files and keywords, are used for generating USML search scripts. For example, in Fig. 9.4 task of *Food* with preference of *sit-down dinner* maps into the NAICS category of *Full-Service Restaurants* or 72211; a task of *Match* maps to the NAICS category of *Spectator Sports* or 71121; a task of *RestaurantComparison* maps to the NAICS category of *telecommunications* or 5133. The numbers represent the predefined category numbers in UDDI. In addition, the preference file also indicates which UDDI registry locations to search for Web services, i.e., the private *eMarket A* located at a particular URL (i.e., http://registry/services/uddi/inquiryAPI) or the public UDDI registry located at another URL (i.e., http://registry/services/uddi/inquiryAPI).

The generated USML script shown in Fig. 9.4 contains a process id (ProcessID) "0001", which is used for a search engine to uniquely identify the running instance and track its search status. The generated USML script contains three Query sections. The first Query section specifies the type of the search source

```
<?xml version="1.0"?>
<UDDISearch xmlns="http://www.servicescomputing.org"
  xmlns:xsi="http://www.w3.org/2001/XMLSchema-instance"
  xsi:schemaLocation="http://www.servicescomputing.org/UDDISearch.xsd">

<Search>
  <ProcessID>0001</ProcessID>
  <Query>
    <Source>Public UDDI</Source>
    <SourceURL>http://registry/services/uddi/inquiryAPI</SourceURL>
    <BusinessName>%</BusinessName>
    <Category type="NAICS">72211</Category>
    <FindBy>Business</FindBy>
  </Query>

  <Query>
     <Source>Private UDDI</Source>
     <SourceURL>http://registry/services/uddi/inquiryAPI</SourceURL>
     <BusinessName>%</BusinessName>
     <Category type="NAICS">71121</Category>
     <FindBy>Business</FindBy>
   </Query>

   <Query>
     <Source>Public UDDI</Source>
     <SourceURL>http://registry/services/uddi/inquiryAPI</SourceURL>
     <BusinessName>%</BusinessName>
     <Category type="NAICS">5133</Category>
     <FindBy>Business</FindBy>
   </Query>

   <AggOperation>OR</AggOperation>
 </Search>
```

Figure 9.4 A sample USML scripts generated from the BPOL document in Fig. 9.3

(Public UDDI) and the URL (http://registry/services/uddi/inquiryAPI). It tends to search for any business names (specified by "%") in the category of restaurant service (specified by 72211). The second Query section specifies the type of the search source (Private UDDI) and the URL (http://registry/services/uddi/ inquiryAPI). It tends to search for any business names (specified by "%") in the category of sports-related service (specified by 71121). The third Query section specifies the type of the search source (Public UDDI) and the URL (http://registry/services/uddi/inquiryAPI). It tends to search for any business names (specified by "%") in the category of telecommunication service (specified by 5133). In short, the three queries intend to search for three different categories of business entities. Afterwards, the USML script aggregates the three separate search results via an aggregation operator *OR* from all three searches, each denoted with the pair of

<Search> and </Search> tags, and returns the results to the caller all at once in a final list.

9.4 Optimization for Business Services Composition

The selection technique on USML script may discover a list of candidate services. The next task is to find the optimal services composition. In order to automate the optimization process, services composition has to be formalized first.

9.4.1 Formalization of Business Services Composition

A concept of service cluster[6] is introduced as a conceptual business service. As shown in Fig. 9.5, not referring to any real or concrete service, a service cluster represents a collection of available services provided by multiple service providers to perform a specific common function. For example, *Service Cluster* 1 may represent a Human Resources (HR) service; *Service Cluster* 2 may represent a payment service; ...; *Service Cluster n* may represent a shipping service. For each service cluster, there are multiple candidate services provided by multiple service providers.

The services in a service cluster differentiate with each other by specific features. For example, a shipping service may be provided by *Shipping Company A, Shipping Company B*, or *Shipping Company C*. As shown in Fig. 9.5, a service provider may provide multiple services. For example, *Shipping Company A* service offers overnight delivery service, second-day delivery service, three-day delivery service, five-day delivery service, and international delivery service. As shown by *Service z* provided by *Service Provider o* in Fig. 9.5, a specific service contains a set of features (a.k.a. attributes), which can be used to identify and select a particular service. Finally, relationships between service clusters and service providers caught in SOA-RML can also help in selecting appropriate services.

At the end of a services selection and business services composition process, a concrete or real service will be selected from a service cluster. A service cluster can be denoted as follows:

$$SC=\{s_1,s_2,\cdots,s_i\},\quad 1\leqslant i\leqslant M \tag{9.1}$$

where SC denotes a service cluster, $s_1,\cdots,s_M$ represent M services that all implement the same specific function of the service cluster SC. In the domain of the introduced Information Architecture model, Equation (9.1) means that the advanced services search engine (e.g., the Advanced Service Discovery Engine introduced in Chapter 4) may find a list of services for a specific service cluster, each being published by a corresponding service provider.

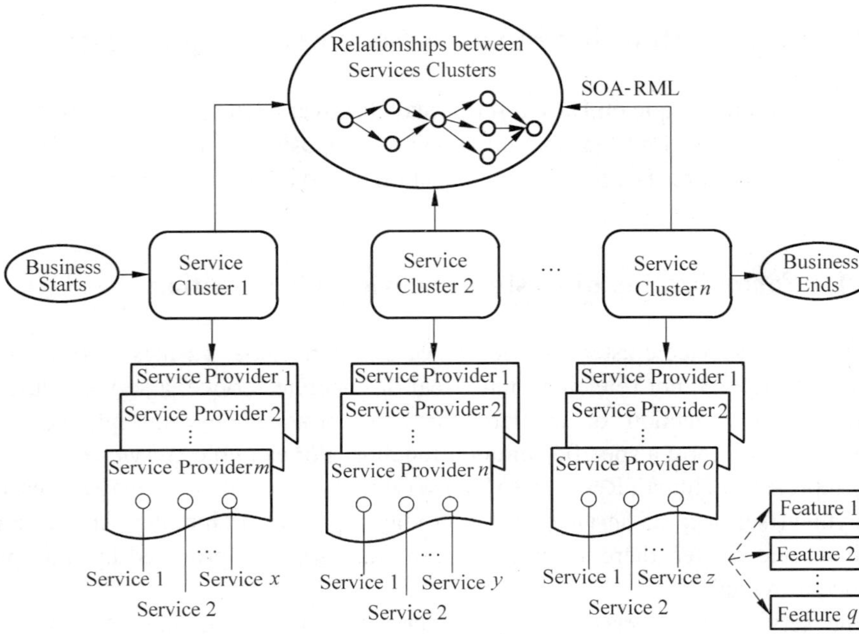

Figure 9.5 Concept of service cluster

A business process only cares about the level of service clusters, instead of individual services. The reason is apparent. A selected service may become unavailable at invocation time; therefore, it should be replaced by another available service in the same service cluster without being known by the users of the corresponding business process. There may exist relationships between service clusters involved in a business process, which can be modeled and defined in SOA-RML.

Figure 9.5 also shows a typical business process flow, which is comprised of multiple service clusters, as well as a business start and a business end. As shown in the top oval of Fig. 9.5, each node in the business process flow represents a service cluster; such a business process represents a conceptual business process.

Therefore, a business process composition (i.e., business services composition) can be formalized as a function over multiple service clusters as follows:

$$BP = f(SC_1, SC_2, \cdots, SC_i), \quad 1 \leqslant i \leqslant M \tag{9.2}$$

where BP represents a business process; SC_i represents a service cluster; f represents a specific function that glues the collection of service clusters together into a pre-defined business process. Using the Information Architectural model,

Equation (9.2) means that the goal of the advanced services search engine is to find available services from services registries for each service cluster defined for a specific business process.

All of the related service clusters for a specific business process together form a *service set*, which is introduced to represent a collection of candidate services for a specific business process. In other words, the concept of *service set* represents the total set of service candidates for a specific business process obtained from the advanced service selection techniques. The concept of service set can be defined as follows:

$$S = \{s_{j(1)}, s_{j(2)}, \cdots, s_{j(i)}\}, \ 1 \leqslant j \leqslant M; 1 \leqslant j(i) \leqslant N \tag{9.3}$$

where S represents a service set for a specific business process BP; $s_{j(i)}$ represents business service #i in one service cluster SC_j.

As shown in Equation (9.3), the business process BP_i includes M service clusters, each containing multiple services. One of the services specified in one service cluster is configured to serve as a component in a business process. Note that it is possible that two identical services are defined in the same service cluster. Two functionally identical services published by different service providers are considered as different services in a service cluster. It is also possible that one service in one service cluster may serve as different components in one business process.

Thus, a business process can be formulated as a schema over its corresponding service set, as shown in the following:

$$BP = BP(S) = h(S) \tag{9.4}$$

where h represents a construction schema defined in business requirements documents for configuring a business process based on the service set S.

The service set contains multiple service clusters, each containing multiple service candidates. In other words, a business process is always a function (h) over a specific service set. For the rest of the chapter, BP and $BP(S)$ will be used interchangeably. The function (h) typically implies interconnecting the set of services using sequential and parallel approaches, together with certain data transformation based upon relationship documents in SOA-RML and business rules and preferences defined in BPEL.

Theoretically, if a service set contains multiple services, then these services can be integrated into different business processes under different composition methods with different business rules. Consider a most simplified example. Suppose there are six service clusters defined in a service set, each containing one service. If a business process requires all six service clusters without any order, the total number of possible business processes that can be composed is a factorial of six, i.e., with 720 potential combinations ($6! = 720$). In our model, the relationships between two services (either sequential or parallel) are used to define a specific business process. The above representation in Equation (9.3) means that a business process is constructed by *j(i)* services. The number of *j(i)* shown in Equation (9.3) depends on the business requirements, such as preferences, flow rules, etc. In other words, the same service set can produce different business processes, using different combination rules:

$$BP_i = f_i(S), \quad 1 \leqslant i \leqslant P \tag{9.5}$$

where BP_i represents one specific business process, composed under a specific composition ffunction f_i. With P types of composition functions, the same service set S can produce P different business processes.

For a specific service, e.g., s_j, only one choice is made: either selected or not-selected. Theoretically, each business process can be constructed by one to N services, as follows:

$$BP = h(\{s_1, s_2, \cdots, s_p\}) = h(f(s_1), f(s_2), \cdots, f(s_p)), \quad 1 \leqslant p \leqslant N \tag{9.6}$$

where $f(s_i) = [0,1]$, meaning that a service can be either selected (1) or not (0). Equation (9.6) means that a business process is actually a function over selected services in the corresponding service set. For example, a business process is constructed by the following service set:

$$S = \{0,1,0,1,1\}, \quad N = 5$$

where "1" denotes that the corresponding service is selected, and "0" otherwise. In this example, there are five services in the service set; only service #2, service #4, and service #5 are selected.

For a business process, its expected result R^* is described as follows:

$$R^* = g(BP) = gg(S) \tag{9.7}$$

R^* features the functions and capabilities of a business process. This measure can be used to compare with some Key Performance Indicators (KPIs) in the business requirements (e.g., cost and time) and try to ensure minimum differences. Equation (9.7) means that the result or output of a business process is a function over its contained service set. A functional relation $g(BP)$ or $gg(S)$ returns a measure of quality or fitness, associated with the business process composition model. As discussed earlier, driven by different composition rules, the same service set can produce different business processes. A constructed business process should satisfy the corresponding business requirements (e.g., cost or time) and be the best option over other possible business processes that could be generated:

$$BP_{\text{matched}} = Best\{BP_1, BP_2, \cdots, BP_M\}, \quad 1 \leqslant i \leqslant P \tag{9.8}$$

where BP_{matched} denotes the best-fit business process, among all possible business processes over a specific service set.

Therefore, the construction of a business process is equivalent to finding the most appropriate services from the available service list. Recall that the service selection procedures introduced earlier are meant to construct a business process by finding the optimized services, which can be dynamically created by the advanced services search engine. Apparently, the services selection criterion is the first step and a key issue when configuring a new business process. A sample optimal criterion of service selection procedure is defined below as the one that most closely matches business requirements, as measured by a total error function *f* that is described as follows:

$$f(S) = \sum_{i=1}^{P} E_i = \sum_{i=1}^{P} \left[\frac{1}{2} \left(R_i^d - R_i^* \right)^2 \right] \tag{9.9}$$

Assuming that a business process includes a set of variables as requirements, the function is defined as the sum of the total errors deviated from the original business requirements set. The number of the variables is determined by the business process flow template or the dynamic behaviors of the event-driven business process. So the following equation represents minimizing the *least squares fitting* problem.

$$\min\{f(S)\} = \min\left\{ \sum_{i=1}^{P} E_i \right\} = \min\left\{ \sum_{i=1}^{P} \left[\frac{1}{2} w_i \left(R_i^d - R_i^* \right)^2 \right] \right\} \tag{9.10}$$

Here $\forall S \in \{0,1\}^N, 0 < f(S) < \infty, 0 \leqslant w_i \leqslant 1$ and $f(S) \neq \text{const}$. P is the number of business requirement indicators; w_i the weight of the i-th business requirement indicator R_i; R_i^d is the target (desired) requirement indicator of the i-th requirement; and R_i^* the estimated value derived from the search engine. Note that both R_i^d and R_i^* are normalized for evaluating the quality of the constructed business process. To normalize R_i, it is necessary to find a standard to evaluate each R_i^d. In general, we can find the largest $R_{\max}$ from a particular service cluster for a particular R_i. Thus, set $R_i^d = R_i / R_{\max}$, which means that the value of $R_i / R_{\max}$ is the normalized target of the requirement R_i^d. Another approach is to select users' expected R_e as the standard to normalize R_i^*. In either way, if R_i^d is more than 1, it means that the service is not an appropriate one; we then enforce $R_i^d = 1$. A regular R_i^d needs to fall between 0 and 1 to indicate that the service is a possible candidate in fulfilling users' requirements.

The requirements validation process thus becomes an important process of a service composition model. In reality, the evaluation of a business process over a business requirement is measured by a Quality of Service (QoS) indicator, which comprises multiple aspects. Typically, execution time and cost are considered to be quality indicators of a constructed business process. Other parameters, such as availability and accessibility, are also used to specify the metrics of the quality of a constructed business process.

As discussed earlier, a business process is constructed by synergistically composing a collection of service clusters. Therefore, in reality, the measurement of the QoS of a business process is often conducted by measuring the QoS parameters over the contained service clusters. Typical QoS parameters over a service cluster are a set of common software QoS attributes, or so-called *ilities*, such as reliability, security, maintainability, testability, accessibility, safety, and fault tolerance.

9.4.2 Optimization Algorithms for Business Services Composition

In order to find a BP_{matched} discussed in Equation (9.8), a "pluggable" optimization framework can adopt any suitable optimization algorithm to perform process optimization. Genetic Algorithms are such an example. It should be noted that the problem of business services composition is a non-linear optimization problem. Genetic Algorithms are not the only kind of optimization methods. Other optimization methods such as Taboo Search[9] or Simulated Annealing[10] may also be relevant under different circumstances.

Genetic Algorithms

Derived from biological evolution, Genetic Algorithms (GAs) are a popular type of techniques widely used for global and adaptive optimization based on the mechanics of natural selection and natural genetics. Detailed information about GAs can be found in numerous references[11]. In short, the rationale of GAs is to find a convergence point as an optimal (or near optimal) solution by simulating biological evolution. In more detail, GAs simulate a list of steps, or so-called genetic operators, which are very similar to those contained in biological evolution. Typical steps are *selection*, *reproduction*, *crossover*, and *mutation*. Due to the operator of mutation, after certain steps, GAs may reach a point in the solution space with non-zero probability, or they may converge to the global optimum if the best solution of a generation is always maintained in the offspring.

When applying the concept of GAs to business process optimizations, the service selection turns to a process of finding the "point" in parameter space corresponding to the model that maximizes the fitness function. In detail, a chromosome can be used to represent a potential business process, which in turn represents a solution to the corresponding business requirements, as shown below:

$$Chromosome = [s_1 \,\&\, s_2 \,\&\cdots\&\, s_n] \tag{9.11}$$

Each gene contained in a chromosome represents a service candidate s_i with two possible values of 0 and 1. If the value of a gene is 1, it means that the service is selected. Otherwise, the service is not selected. The symbol "&" means that a chromosome is a combination of possible services. The combination of the genes thus forms a chromosome, which is a series of selected and un-selected services.

A chromosome contains a combination of service clusters, as shown in Equation (9.12) below:

$$Chromosome = [SC_1 \ \& \ SC_2 \ \& \cdots \& \ SC_n] \tag{9.12}$$

where SC_i represents a services cluster, the symbol "&" means that a chromosome is a combination of service clusters.

Since every service cluster may contain multiple services as candidates, Equation (9.12) can be rewritten into Equation (9.13) as binary strings shown bellow:

$$Chromosome = [S_{11}S_{12} \cdots S_{1i} \ \& \ S_{21}S_{22} \cdots S_{2j} \ \& \cdots \& \ S_{n1}S_{n2} \cdots S_{nk}] \tag{9.13}$$

where n is the number of service clusters; *i, j, and k* represent the number of potential services provided by one or multiple service providers for a specific service cluster. S_{nk} represents a specific service. Therefore, S_{nk} is equal to either 0 or 1, depending on whether it is finally selected or not. It should be noted that there are two differences between Equation (9.13) and Equation (9.11). One difference is that in Equation (9.13), services are grouped in service clusters; while in Equation (9.11), services are put together without any order. The other difference is that Equation (9.13) enforces that at most one service can be selected from one service cluster. The symbol "&" in Equation (9.13) actually represents a delimiter between services grouped by service clusters.

To apply GAs for business process optimization, two properties need to be defined, namely, *fitness* and *weight*. Fitness is a value assigned to an individual chromosome that reflects how well it solves the task. Designing a fitness function is essential to the successful use of Genetic Algorithms. A fitness function is used to map a chromosome to a fitness value. To obtain an appropriate fitness function, weights are also important. Weight is a value assigned to a particular gene that is used to represent its importance in a chromosome. They are typically designed based on users' preferences and common sense in practical business procedures. Users need to define a domain-specific fitness function.

Applying GAs

To better apply GAs for business process optimization, several assumptions should be made. First, all members of a population should be represented in the next generation. In order to realize this goal, each member of each generation is assigned one of the three GA operations: *mutation*, *crossover*, and *selection*. The sum of the probabilities of all three GA operations is kept at 1.

Second, the *repeat times of best values* can be used as the terminating flag. In detail, if the fitness of a chromosome is kept the same for more than a predefined *repeat times of best values*, the solution is considered as the optimum, and the GA is terminated. The *total generation* is set up as an unlimited value.

Third, a variant crossover point selection mechanism is introduced to ensure that the multiple genes for a service cluster can be grouped together. This new mechanism is called a *constrained crossover point selection mechanism*. Since individual service clusters are separated by the symbol "&" in Equation (9.13), the potential crossover point can only be chosen in the position of the separation sign "&".

Furthermore, there is a possibility that no best chromosomes can be found, even if the worse chromosomes are dropped according to the algorithm. The reason is that the *crossover* and *reproduction* operations may not bring enough new chromosomes to the next generation. In case this situation occurs, it is difficult to obtain an optimum result. Therefore, under this circumstance, the *mutation* operation should be used.

9.5 Service Integration Framework

In this section, a framework is introduced to enable and facilitate requirements-driven business service composition. As shown in Fig. 9.6, the framework implies two phases: the first is service composition and configuration; the second is service integration and invocation. Seven major components are identified: *Requirements Analyzer*, *SOA-RML Parser*, *Information Architecture Manager*, *Business Services Discovery Engine*, *Business Process Composer*, *Output Adapter*, and *Service Integration and Invocation Engine*. The user of the framework is service consumer, who can be either an enterprise or an individual user. The input to the framework is refined business requirements.

The Requirements Analyzer takes business requirements as input and parses them into intermediate specifications. The SOA-RML Parser translates the part of business party relationships written in SOA-RML into the intermediate business requirements document. The Requirements Modeling Manager is the central management unit of the framework and coordinates with all other units. The Business Services Discovery Engine takes BPOL documents, translates them into USML documents, and automatically searches services registries (e.g., public UDDI registries) to obtain a list of service candidates. The Business Process Composer takes service candidates and organized business requirements, optimizes the combination, selects the composition of the most appropriate services, and creates the final business process in the form of composite services. As an example, BPEL is a business process language that can be used to represent composite services. The formed composite services are returned to the Service

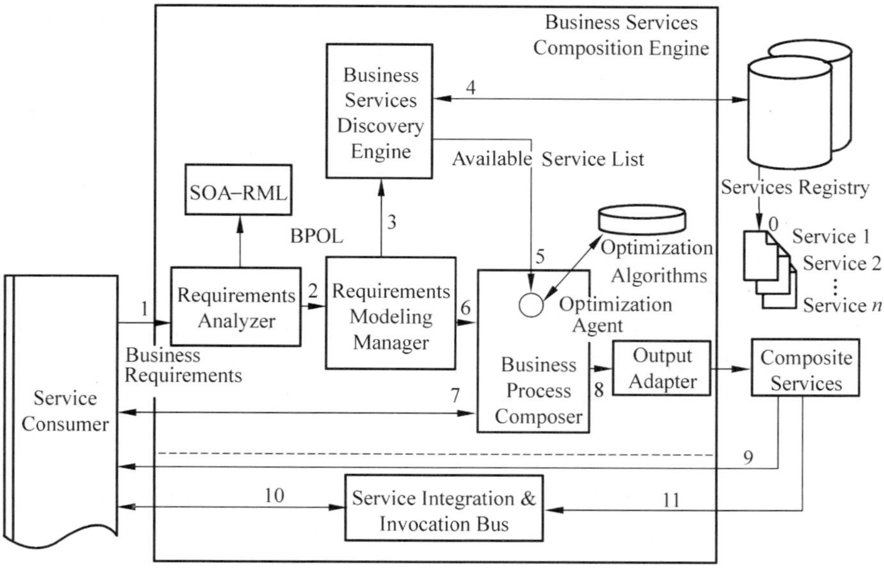

Figure 9.6 Business services composition framework

Consumer directly or the Service Integration and Invocation Bus for the Service Consumer. If business requirements are changed later on, this backward flow allows self-adaptation for process composition. Meanwhile, the service consumer can review the produced composite services for manual changes.

After the service consumer agrees upon the service composition, the Service Integration and Invocation Bus automatically executes a business process, by invoking corresponding predefined services. Enterprise Service Bus (ESB) is such an example of integration engine.

As shown in Fig. 9.6, these seven components together provide a two-level service selection mechanism. The first level takes business requirements as input, automatically generates USML search scripts, and utilizes the advanced service discovery mechanism (as discussed in Chapter 4) to find candidate services. The second level uses both business requirements and optimization algorithms to select the best suitable services from the initial candidate list created by the first level. It then optimizes the entire business process based on the business requirements. As an example implementation, the intermediate outputs of the framework are BPOL and USML documents; final outputs are BPEL documents that describe the process execution of selected services.

9.5.1 Services Integration Procedure

Figure 9.6 also implies a procedure of how to realize automatic business services composition.

Step 0: Business services are published to centralized services repositories, i.e., services registries.

Step 1: Business requirements are inputted, either in a user interactive way or in the form of XML documents, to the Requirement Analyzer. Flow rules, references, and business relationships are described in SOA-RML.

Step 2: The Requirement Analyzer creates business requirements documents based on the services composition requirements and SOA-RML annotations.

Step 3: The Requirements Modeling Manager parses the generated business requirements documents, automatically generates XML-based search scripts in USML, and passes the scripts to the Business Services Discovery Engine.

Step 4: The Business Services Discovery Engine conducts search processes across multiple services registries, based on the search criteria specified in the USML scripts created. The aggregated result is a list of available services that meet the search criteria.

Step 5: The available service list is passed to the Business Process Composer for service composition.

Step 6: The Optimization Agent in Business Process Composer uses SOA-RML documents as input to extract the business flow rules, and drafts a business process using the selected services from the candidate lists.

Step 7: Users can interact with the Business Process Composer via Web Browsers or GUIs to tune the service selection and composition process.

Step 8: The result of Business Process Composer is formatted in target composite services via the Output Adaptor.

Step 9: The resulting composite services are returned to the Service Consumer.

Step 10: When the users want to access and use the newly composed business process, a Service Integration and Invocation Bus dynamically invokes the respective services, which are part of the newly created business process.

Step 11: The Service Integration and Invocation Bus accesses composite services.

9.6 Discussions on Services Composition

At the time of writing, services composition is one of the most hyped and addressed issues in the field of Services Computing since the major goal of Services Computing is to effectively and efficiently reuse and compose existing services as components to build new business services. Toward this ultimate goal, four perspectives should be considered. First is how to precisely capture and formalize ever-changing business requirements; second is how to automatically translate formalized business requirements into services search scripts; third is how to formalize services composition problem; fourth is how to optimize services composition for constituting an optimal business process.

In order to provide a systematic approach to enable and facilitate requirements-driven services composition, this chapter addresses and focuses on the above four aspects. First, this chapter provides a hierarchical model for business requirements. BPOL is introduced as an example for formally recording and defining business requirements. Second, this chapter discusses how to translate business requirements written in formal languages (e.g., BPOL) to services search scripts (e.g., USML) to achieve automatic services discovery. Third, this chapter introduces the concept of service cluster and a formal model of services composition. Fourth, a Genetic Algorithm-based optimization method is introduced as an example. Finally, the chapter introduces a services composition framework associated with a step-by-step methodology for realizing automatic services composition.

This chapter provides basic ideas and methods toward automatic services composition. In order to accomplish feasible services composition in the real world, many research topics and issues are still waiting to be solved by researchers and practitioners. For example, business requirements are typically domain specific; how to capture and formalize domain-specific features and requirements yet keep awareness of generic business requirements remains challenging. In general, the following topics are open to be solved. First, the services space is enormously big and dynamic as new services become available on a daily basis. How to efficiently locate a reasonably small group of service candidates is challenging. Second, if there are multiple services that offer seemingly similar features with variations, how to find an appropriate one to better satisfy business requirements remains challenging. Third, how to generate services composition on the fly without human involvement based on constantly changing business requirements remains a challenge.

9.7 Summary

In this chapter, we focus on business requirements-driven services composition. We first introduced a business requirements modeling framework and an example modeling language BPOL. Then we discussed requirements-driven services discovery, by transforming business requirements into services discovery scripts such as USML. Afterwards, we introduced how to formalize services composition and how to optimize services composition using techniques such as Genetic Algorithm. Finally, we introduced a services integration framework as well as a step-by-step services integration procedure.

References

[1] IBM Rational Requisite Pro. http://www-306.ibm.com/software/awdtools/reqpro/

[2] Peltz C (2003) Web services orchestration and choreography. IEEE Computer 36: 46 – 52

[3] MDA (Model Driven Architecture). http://www.omg.org/mda/

[4] Business Process Execution Language for Web Services Version 1.1. http://www.ibm.com/developerworks/library/ws-bpel

[5] Web Service Choreography Interface. http://www.w3.org/TR/wsci/

[6] Zhang LJ, Li B (2004) Requirements driven dynamic business process composition for Web services solutions. Journal of Grid Computing 2: 121 – 140

[7] The Enhanced Telecom Operations Map (eTOM). http://www.tmforum.org/browse.aspx?catID = 1648

[8] Chen P (1976) The entity-relationship model-toward a unified view of data. ACM Transactions on Database Systems 1: 9 – 36

[9] Cvijovi D, Klinowski J (1995) Taboo search: an approach to the multiple minima problem. Science 267: 664 – 666

[10] Kirkpatrick S, Gelatt CD, Vecchi JMP (1983) Optimization by simulated annealing. Science 220: 671 – 680

[11] Goldberg DE (1989) Genetic algorithms in search, optimization, and machine learning. Addison-Wesley Professional

10 Services Value Chain Collaboration

10.1 Value Chain Collaboration

An enterprise in the twenty-first century can seldom stand alone any longer; instead, it usually needs to collaborate with its suppliers, partners, and customers on the value chain for a common goal. As the scales of enterprises grow larger and larger under the pressure of world-wide competition, the outsourcing model becomes an irrepressible trend. Instead of hiring people to do everything in house, an enterprise tends to outsource some tasks to other business entities to be more efficient, while performing the most competitive business services by itself. Meanwhile, instead of spending time to find end customers before starting a task, an enterprise also takes predefined tasks outsourced from other enterprises. Moreover, a modern business application is typically comprehensive enough to require broad specialties. While it is difficult for every single enterprise to possess a broad range of skill sets and products, it is more feasible that a set of enterprises each hold particular specialties (i.e., special services), while they together establish a virtual enterprise to provide high-quality products or services to the market sooner than what individual parties would have accomplished by their own. This kind of collaboration is different from traditional business collaboration, because it is usually project-based and service-based. As a result, not only does such a service-based value chain become more complex, but it is also usually formed dynamically instead of statically. On-demand business collaboration in a modern service-to-service value chain[1] thus requires a more structured yet flexible collaboration adaptability.

10.1.1 Example of Business Collaboration

Figure 10.1 shows a simple example of business collaboration using the outsourcing model. Assume that a laptop product company intends to design and develop a new model of its laptop series. Instead of conducting all the work by itself, it leverages some external services and available products. As shown in Fig. 10.1, it engages two Electronic Manufacturing Services (EMS) providers: one motherboard supplier and one monitor supplier. The product company itself designs some critical pieces, for example, an advanced chip that handles wireless connection and Bluetooth communication. The "partner" of the motherboard designer in turn engages another two partners down their value chains: one CPU supplier and one memory supplier. In short, this example shows that a modern enterprise requires comprehensive collaborations to achieve a business goal. Such a dynamically formed and adaptive partner network is called a design and supply "hyper-chain."

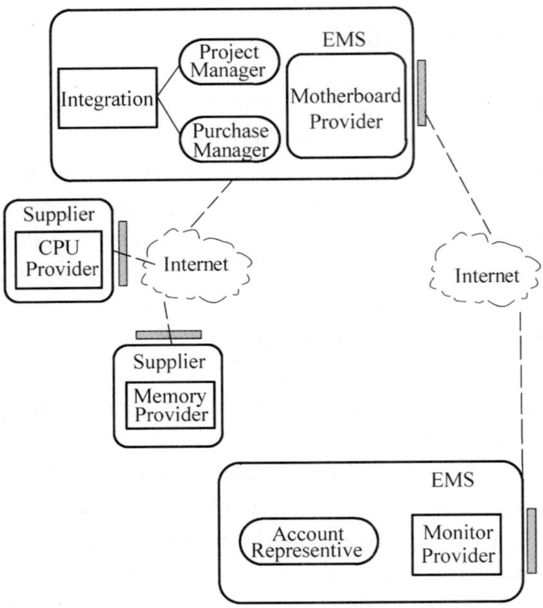

Figure 10.1 Business collaboration example of a new laptop design

The patterns of active connectivity and their durations in this *hyper-chain* are neither fixed nor static. This *hyper-chain* is apparently not a traditionally well-defined supply chain where all participants are fixed in advance. In a *hyper-chain,* each partner only knows and interacts with its immediate partners "on-demand"; while information is propagated up and down through the *hyper-chain*. In this setting, a business collaboration solution should support the observations and controls of related supply chain management and collaboration activities during the design and development of a product. Meanwhile, the desired business collaboration solution should manage the dynamics characterizing this environment, including the formation and disbanding of collaborating teams and other related effects. From the solution management point of view, the business collaboration solution needs to monitor the design process status and design data status at any granularities, across all design and development partners and across the individual participants. In cases of business exceptions or when quick decisions are required, the business collaboration solution intends to provide mechanisms to enable efficient escalation activation and timely problem resolution of issues that impact the design and development processes and schedules of a product as well as related business activities. In short, by bringing this product design and development into an ideal business collaboration, people move from *ad hoc* and transactional interactions to constructing, activating, tracking, and monitoring collaborative development and design processes of a product or solution involving multiple organizations.

10.1.2 Inter-and Intra-Enterprise Collaboration

Business collaboration happens not only between enterprises, but also within an enterprise among its business components. Figure 10.2 illustrates a simple scenario to describe the collaboration within and between two enterprises.

A modern enterprise is typically divided into departments with different focuses. Each department follows a common enterprise methodology to handle daily business processes. As shown in Fig. 10.2, each enterprise typically adopts a four-level model[1]: business model, execution model, solution architecture model, and IT infrastructure model. The business model layer decides business strategies; the execution model layer operates daily business activities; the solution architecture model focuses on high-level solution design; the implementation model realizes the solution design with proper IT infrastructures.

As shown in Fig. 10.2, *Enterprise M* has *Department A* and *Department B*, each following the four-layer model to conduct business. When these two departments collaborate, they cooperate at all of these four levels conceptually. At the business model level, they exchange high-level business strategies, for example, whether they want to form an alliance relationship to co-design a software product or solution. On the execution model level, they decide how they can achieve their business goals defined at the level of business model. In more detail, they need to define a list of detailed operational steps. On the solution architecture level, they need to create an IT environment and a high-level solution architectural design, for example, how to exchange documents, in which formats, how to store exchanged documents, who will make decisions, and so on. On the IT infrastructure level, they decide how to implement the solution architecture, for example, which platform to use, which programming language to use, and so on.

This layered collaboration can happen not only between various departments within one enterprise, but also between different enterprises. Traditional ways of using different teams for enterprise internal integration and external integration typically waste resources, since many of their integration mechanisms stay the same. As shown in Fig. 10.2, *Enterprise M* desires to do business with *Enterprise N*. Its high-level management teams draft a strategy-level agreement. The CEOs from both enterprises agree to collaborate to create an alliance for providing adaptive enterprise solutions. The decision is made after conducting all formal or informal communications at the business level.

Then both enterprises pass this strategic goal to the corresponding operation departments to sketch out some operation plans. One example of operation plan is

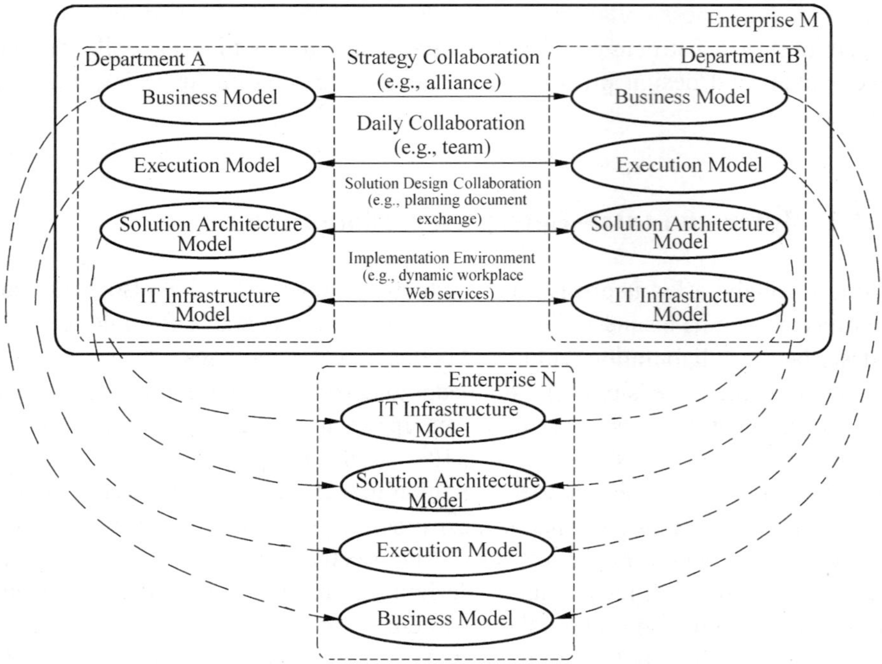

Figure 10.2 Example of business collaboration

to launch a joint design of a new product in a time frame of a few months. The communications and synchronizations at this operation level should have some patterns to follow. Afterwards, both enterprises put this operation plan into action. Lots of detailed execution plans should be coordinated between two enterprises, such as budget allocation plans, development plans, press release plans, and so forth.

At the solution architecture level, the project teams need to decide high-level solution models and architectures, so that it can be exchanged and synchronized between the two parties. This includes process flows, data formats, and data sources. Inside each enterprise, different platform-dependent implementation infrastructures may be used to run the collaborative product or solution development processes.

Finally, the project teams from both enterprises collaborate to implement the projects based upon predefined solution architectures.

Figure 10.2 shows that business interactions and collaborations are conducted frequently between different levels within enterprises, as well as across enterprise boundaries. In addition, human factor may also play a critical role in dealing with business exception handling and quick decision making. Human interactions with an application may be operated within one enterprise or across both enterprises. In order to facilitate both intra-enterprise and inter-enterprise interactions, a formalized collaboration model should be enforced.

10.1.3 Web Services Based Value Chain Collaboration

Several approaches have been proposed to represent business behaviors and a variety of "layered" models circulating in the business modeling domains. All models, independent of the number of layers identified, basically include a higher business layer and a lower Information Technology (IT) infrastructure layer. Typical business models include: Business-to-Customer (B2C), Application Service Provider (ASP), Application to Application (A2A), Enterprise Application Integration (EAI), and Business to Business (B2B). All of these "classic" business models strictly differentiate between intra-enterprise interactions and inter-enterprise interactions. In support of these enterprise-based interaction models, different interaction techniques (e.g., business portals, e-mail, and fax) and vertical industry standards (e.g., Electronic Data Interchange (EDI)[2], ebXML[3], and RosettaNet[4]) were emerged in the late 1990s, providing various levels of business interactions and connectivity deployments.

Leveraging emerging and evolving Web services standards is a key starting point to help address the aforementioned challenges and problems. As introduced in previous chapters, Web services are network-enabled reusable components that conform to interfaces with standard description formats and access protocols. The basic enabling infrastructure of Web services consists of UDDI registries, SOAP, WSDL, BPEL, WSIL, and so forth. In short, Web services provide a means to enable universal software integration in a standard way.

10.2 Extended Business Collaboration (eBC) Model

Extended Business Collaboration (eBC)[5] is a model aiming at dissolving or bypassing enterprise boundaries to facilitate business collaboration.

10.2.1 Introduction to Business Resources

By extending the concept of hyperlink from its common formats of HTML, text, image links to the domain of the whole value chain, a term of "business resource" is used to represent any entity, no matter whether it is a Web site, an organization, a project, a task, related requirement documents, annotation, or involved human resources such as people and role players. In other words, everything in a value chain collaboration is viewed as a business resource, so that they can be represented in a uniform way. As a result, information exchange between business resources can be unified and standardized; a value chain collaboration can be formalized.

Derived from the hyperlink concept, a business resource can be annotated with metadata, as shown in Fig. 10.3. For example, a business resource *Project Design*

Document can be annotated with the following information: the purpose of the document, the owner of the document, the change history of the document, the status of the document (e.g., pending or approved), the referenced documents, the policy such as who can access and who can modify the document, and so on. The actual Word document can be embedded as a hyperlink pointing to its URL, i.e., where the file is stored. Therefore, the sender of the *project design document* does not need to send the actual document; instead, a message can be sent including the annotated metadata. Upon receiving the message, the receiver can review the annotations and decide whether to move forward to download the actual design document based upon acting role(s) in the collaboration. For example, if the receiver is a senior executive, VP, or director, he/she may not be interested in the details of the design document, so there is no need for his/her to go through the link to download the document and save to his/her local machine. However, if the receiver is a project manager, he/she may be interested in downloading the design document and take a closer look. If the receiver is a design engineer, he/she may have to understand the detailed design specifications, so he/she can retrieve the document accordingly. Adopting such an annotation approach, one does not need to send a huge email containing a file of large-size. Instead, the original document can be stored at some accessible place (e.g., a Web server), and interested receivers can launch the document if necessary.

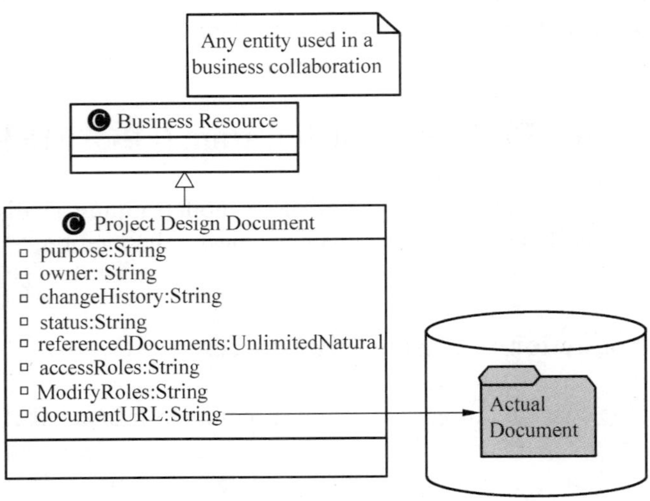

Figure 10.3 Business Resource and annotations

In short, the mechanism of metadata annotation hyperlinks associated with business resources allows collaborators to understand the structure of a business resource before retrieving detailed information. This message content driven business process integration mechanism can also facilitate dynamic value chain collaboration. A modern value chain collaboration typically requires dynamic involvement of new collaborators in the process of the collaboration. Thus, it is important to equip the new comers with the context of the collaboration. The information hyperlinks-based messages help the new comers in understanding the previous communications and discussions, without being overwhelmed by numerous documents.

10.2.2 Annotated Business HyperChain Technique

Based on the concept of business resource, the eBC technology proposes its Annotated Business HyperChain (ABH) technique. Extending the concept of hyperlinks to any business resources involved in a business collaboration chain, the ABH technique enables business collaboration in three steps: first is to express semantic relationships in an eBC ontology; second is to define communication rules in Collaborative Exchange Protocol (CxP); third is to manage information exchange using a HyperChain Manager to facilitate content-driven business process integration.

The eBC ontology provides the foundation for understanding and interpreting the information involved in a business collaboration process. It focuses on defining commonly shared knowledge regarding business semantics for information exchange during business collaborations. The eBC ontology enables a flexible and uniform annotation representation for information exchanges of various non-structured and *ad hoc* data without requiring predefined schemas.

Based on the eBC ontology, CxP defines a set of elementary or composite messages that may be exchanged between multiple parties engaged in collaborative business activities. CxP is a business goal-oriented protocol supporting a wide variety of business constructs and versatile message compositions that accommodate the needed variations in the lifecycle of a collaborative business process.

One driving force of the HyperChain Manager is to eliminate a large amount of data exchange. In detail, instead of sending all detailed data, senders only deliver schema-less HyperChain annotation data. Based on their roles or positions in the business chains, recipients then follow the HyperChains to fetch interested detailed information such as design files, design specifications, and bill of materials (BOM) files. These on-demand files and data transfer modes are enabled through self-retrieving or agent-based file transfer services. In the meantime, the model supports traceable information associated with any business resources, such as design files, design processes, and BOM files.

10.2.3 eBC to WS-Collab

The eBC technology provides a foundation and guidance to establish Web services-based value chain collaboration. To support service-centric business collaboration instead of generic business collaboration, eBC is extended into Web Services Collaboration (WS-Collab) technology.

10.3 Web Services Collaboration (WS-Collab) Resources

Given that the business collaboration requirements are often dynamically changing, product specifications with various formats and the status of projects may need to be passed back and forth from one enterprise to another. Due to the lack of commonly shared knowledge regarding the business semantics, correctly understanding of the exchanged information must involve many human-assisted methods (e.g., phone calls, emails, and meetings), which make the collaboration processes inefficient and non-cost-effective. In order to lower cost, reduce time-to-market, and streamline the collaboration processes, a flexible and uniform annotation representation of various non-structured and *ad hoc* information must be defined.

WS-Collab Resource specification extends eBC resource specification to provide a common semantic annotation model, by defining the Business Collaboration Ontology as an extensible common set of properties associated with relationships to describe intra- and inter-enterprise collaboration. As a realization example, it leverages the WSRF[6] to provide flexibility and versatility in supporting various data formats required in collaboration message flows and document exchanges. As discussed in previous chapters, the WS-Resource construct offers a means of expressing the relationship between stateful resources and Web services, as well as how the state of a WS-Resource is made accessible through a Web service interface.

Meanwhile, WS-Collab Resource extends WSRF in two ways. First, it uses WS-Resource as a realization example to model "virtual" business resources in addition to physical resources, such as organization, process, and task. Second, it adds relationships between business resources. In particular, it extends WS-ResourceProperties with relationships between different stateful resources. Thus, WS-Collab Resource carries more expressive power to model complex business scenarios.

10.3.1 WS-Collab Resources

An ontology or commonly shared knowledge provides a foundation for business collaboration, by defining the business semantics as information to be exchanged. Without such shared common knowledge, collaborators are not able to decipher the exchanged information. Figure 10.4 shows a high-level Business Collaboration Ontology or Meta-data Model for WS-Collab resources using Unified Modeling Language (UML) notations. Directed line with open arrowhead represents a heritage relationship, e.g., the relationship between "Status" and "ProjectStatus". Directed line with diamond represents an aggregation relationship, e.g., the relationship between "Requirement" and "Message". Directed line represents a dependency relationship, e.g., the relationship between "Project" and "Organization".

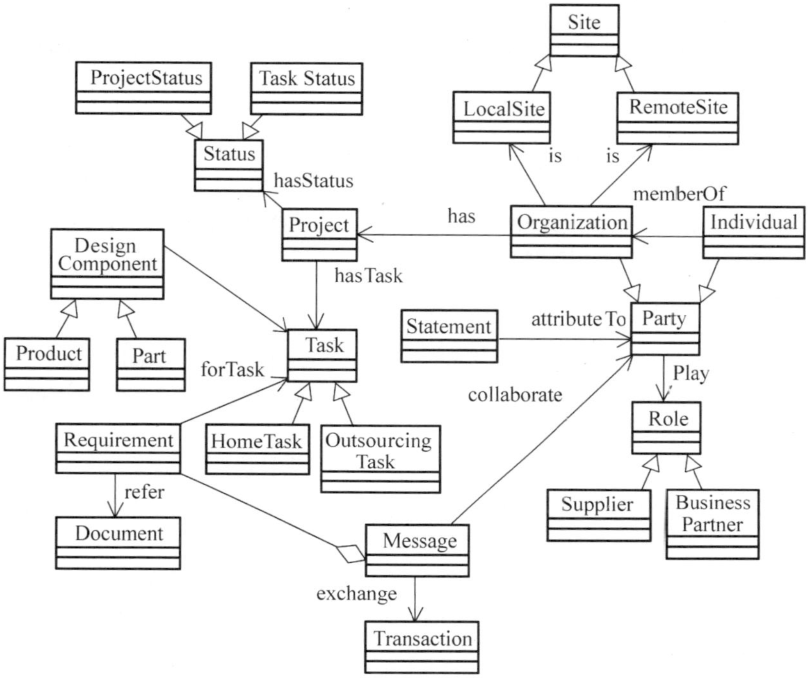

Figure 10.4 WS-Collab ontology for business resources

As shown in Fig. 10.4, a WS-Collab ontology, as a knowledge base, is centered on the concept of "project", since many modern enterprises are project-based businesses. In other words, many enterprises organize their routine tasks by projects. Therefore, a value chain collaboration is centered on clearly defined projects. A *project* belongs to *organizations*, each may offer either a local site or a remote site. An organization contains individuals as *members*. Both organizations and individuals are subclasses of the class *party*, which typically plays different roles as either suppliers or business partners under different circumstances. A party normally publishes statements about its business goals.

As shown in Fig. 10.4, a *project* is first defined. Underneath the project, *tasks* are identified, each being either in-house home task or outsourcing task. Each task is associated with clearly defined *requirements* recorded in documents. When a requirement is sent to a partner, it forms a *transaction* regulated by some *protocols*. Every transaction is associated with an *organization* (partner). It should be noted that multiple partners may be involved. As shown in Fig. 10.4, each requirement defines detailed information, such as specifications in various formats, design documents, outsourcing constraints, and access control.

WS-Collab ontology or Meta-data Model is extensible. Each collaborator could define customized ontology (or so-called Extended Ontology) and add additional annotations into the basic ontology for special needs. For instance, *fileName*, *fileSize*, and *format* can be used to annotate a specific design file. Obviously, these extended ontology or annotation definitions also need to be propagated to the corresponding business partners before business exchanges take place.

10.3.2 WS-Collab Resource Specifications

The following are two definition examples of WS-Collab ontology elements using WSRF: project and site. Other resources can be defined similarly.

Project

Figure 10.5 shows the representation of *Project* element in WSRF. Class Project contains data describing a project comprising multiple tasks to be completed either

```
<xsd:schema xmlns:xsd="http://www.w3.org/2001/XMLSchema"
      targetNamespace="http://WS-Collab-Resource.com/class"
      xmlns:tns="http://WS-Collab-Resource.com/class">
  <xsd:element name="Name" type="xsd:string"/>
  <xsd:element name="Owner" type="xsd:anyURI" default="http://WS-Collab-
    Resource.com/class#Organization"/>
  <xsd:element name="Manager" type="xsd:anyURI" default="http://WS-Collab-
    Resource.com/class#Individual"/>
  <xsd:element name="ForTask" type="xsd:anyURI" default="http://WS-Collab-
    Resource.com/class#Task"/>
  <xsd:element name="CreationTime" type="xsd:date"/>
  <!--HasTask Lists all the tasks belong to this project -->
  <xsd:simpleType name="HasTaskType">
    <xsd:list itemType="xsd:anyURI"/>
  </xsd:simpleType>
  <xsd:element name="HasTask" type="tns:HasTaskType" />
  <xsd:element name="Project">
    <xsd:annotation>
      <xsd:documentation> Projects are set up for completing a specific task by
        organizations, for example, designing a product </xsd:documentation>
      </xsd:annotation>
      <xsd:complexType>
        <xsd:sequence>
          <xsd:element ref="tns:Name"/>
            <xsd:element ref="tns:Owner"/>
            <xsd:element ref="tns:Manager"/>
            <xsd:element ref="tns:ForTask"/>
            <xsd:element ref="tns:CreationTime"/>
            <xsd:element ref="tns:HasTask"/>
          </xsd:sequence>
      </xsd:complexType>
  </xsd:element>
</xsd:schema>
```

Figure 10.5 Definition of Project using WSRF

in-house or outsourced to business partners. As shown in Fig. 10.5, a project contains the following elements: *Annotation*, *Name*, *Owner*, *Manager*, *ForTask*, *CreationTime*, and *HasTask*. *Name* defines the descriptive name of the project; *Owner* defines the project owner; *Manager* defines the project manager; *ForTask* defines the goal of the project; *CreationTime* defines the date when the project is created; *HasTask* lists all the tasks belonging to the project. The class *Project* has an owner that is a class *Organization*, and a manager that is a class *Individual* (i.e., each instance of the class *Project*). At least one organization owns the project; every project must have one individual who is the manager of the project.

As shown in Fig. 10.5, a project can be associated with annotations, which can in turn specify a verbose description of the project, as well as the high-level information of the project, such as name, owner, manager, goal, creation time, and whether there are tasks involved.

Site

Figure 10.6 shows the representation of a *Site* element in WSRF. A Site element contains data describing a collaboration site, in which one or more organizations reside. An organization collaborates with other organizations residing in the same or different sites. Class *Site* collects two types of sites: *LocalSite* and *RemoteSite*. *LocalSite* is with respect to a particular organization, and it is the owning site of the organization. By the same token, to this particular organization, any other organizations that do not belong to the same owning site are considered a *RemoteSite*. As shown in Fig. 10.6, a site contains several elements: *Annotation*, *Name*, *SubClassOf*, and *DisjointUnionOf*. *Name* defines the descriptive name of the site; *SubClassOf* defines whether the site is a sub-site of another site; *DisjointUnionOf* indicates whether the site needs to collaborate with others for a common goal. A site can be associated with a verbose annotation to describe its purpose.

Figure 10.7 shows a sample WSDL file for the business resource *Site* based on its WSRF definitions. A *portType* is defined with four operations and is associated with the corresponding WSRF definitions.

10.3.3 WS-Collab Ontology on Relationships Between Resources

Relationships between business resources are critical for modeling business collaboration scenarios. For example, given a specific task, one may want to know to which project this task belongs, who are involved in this task, and which documents are required in this task. In order to answer these questions, the relationships among task, project, people, and data must be clearly specified. Recall that Chapter 6 discusses relationships at the granularity of business level, business service level, Web service level, and operation level. WS-Collab intends to utilize WSRF to describe relationships at the granularity of any business resource level. However, WSRF, the embodiment of WS-Collab Resource, does

```
<xsd:schema xmlns:xsd="http://www.w3.org/2001/XMLSchema"
       targetNamespace="http://WS-Collab-Resource.com/class"
       xmlns:tns="http://WS-Collab-Resource.com/class">
  <xsd:element name="Name" type="xsd:string"/>
  <!--Disjoint Union of LocalSite & RemoteSite -->
  <xsd:simpleType name="DisjointUnionOfType">
    <xsd:list itemType="xsd:anyURI"/>
  </xsd:simpleType>
  <xsd:element name="DisjointUnionOf" type="tns:DisjointUnionOfType"/>
  <xsd:element name="SubClassOf" type="xsd:anyURI" default="http://WS-
      Collab-Resource.com/class#Resource"/>
  <xsd:element name="Site">
     <xsd:annotation>
     <xsd:documentation> A collaboration site where one or organizations reside,
       and an organization collaborates with other organizations residing in the
       same or different sites </xsd:documentation>
    </xsd:annotation>
    <xsd:complexType>
    <xsd:sequence>
      <xsd:element ref="tns:Name"/>
      <xsd:element ref="tns:SubClassOf"/>
      <xsd:element ref="tns:DisjointUnionOf"/>
    </xsd:sequence>
    </xsd:complexType>
  </xsd:element>
</xsd:schema>
```

Figure 10.6 Definition of Site using WSRF

```
<wsdl:definitions … xmlns:tns="http://WS-Collab-Resource.com/class#Site" …>
…
   <wsdl:types>
…
   </wsdl:types>
…
   <!-- Association of resource properties document to a portType -->
   <wsdl:portType name="GenericSite" wsrp:ResourceProperties="tns:Site">
      <operation name="add" …/>
      <operation name="remove" …/>
      <operation name="modify" …/>
      <operation name="getProperty" …/>
    </wsdl:portType>
…
</wsdl:definitions>
```

Figure 10.7 Sample WSDL for Site.

not directly support relationship modeling. Therefore, an extension to WSRF is needed, by using XML Schema's SimpleType and ComplexType to represent the relationships as SOA-RML recommends in Chapter 6.

Figure 10.8 defines a basic set of relationships that are frequently used in business collaborations. Four categories of relationships are identified: composition, aggregation, inheritance, and association. The definitions of the identified relationships conform to those of UML 2.0[7]. Association is the most generic relationships, meaning that two business resources have relationships with each other. Both composition and aggregation are special kinds of associations. Aggregation represents ownership or a whole/part relationship between two business resources; composition represents a stronger form of ownership implying coincident lifetime of part with the whole. In other words, the composition resource has responsibility for the disposition of its part resources in terms of creation and destruction. Inheritance represents an antecedent/descendant relationship between two business resources.

The four generic relationships can be further divided into sub-relationships. As shown in Fig. 10.8, aggregation relationship can be further divided into two sub-relationships: *DisJointUnionOf* and *JointUnionOf*; inheritance relationship can further derive into the *SubClassOf* relationship; association relationship can be further divided into *memberOf*, *Partner*, *AttributeTo*, and so on. *DisJointUnionOf* indicates a mutual exclusive aggregation relationship; *JointUnionOf* indicates a non-mutual exclusive aggregation relationship; *subClassOf* indicates a direct parent/child relationship; *memberOf* indicates a membership relationship; *partner* indicates that two resources form a partnership; *attributeTo* indicates that one resource is an attribute of another resource.

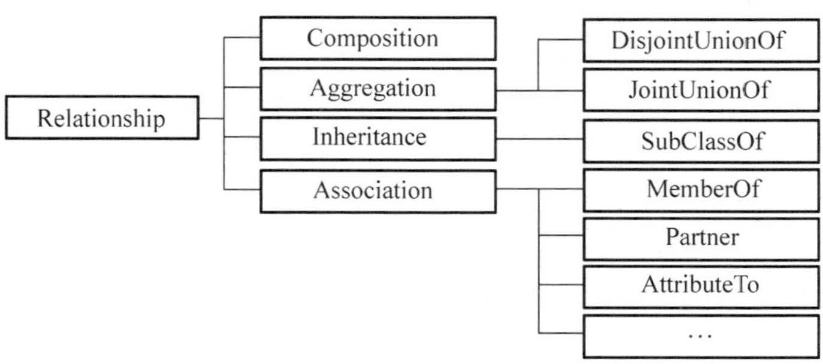

Figure 10.8 Business resource relationships

Table 10.1 summarizes the definitions of the identified business resource relationships and gives their code sample implementation in WSRF using the simpleType and complexType of XML Schemas. Composition relationship is represented by defining one element as the child of another element. As the example shown in Table 10.1, since *Name* composes *FirstName* and *LastName*, the *Name* element thus contains a complexType comprising a sequence with two child elements: *FirstName* and *LastName*.

Table 10.1 Business resource relationship definition

Category	Name	Description	CodeSample
Composition	All	Composition is represented by defining one element as the child of another element	<xsd:element name="Name"> <xsd:complexType> <xsd:sequence> <xsd:element name="FirstName" type="xsd:string"/> <xsd:element name="LastName" type="xsd:string"/> </xsd:sequence> </xsd:complexType> </xsd:element>
Aggregation	Disjoint-UnionOf	Mutual exclusive aggregation relationship	<xsd:simpleType name="DisjointUnionOfType"> <xsd:list itemType="xsd:anyURI"/> </xsd:simpleType> <xsd:element name="DisjointUnionOf" type="tns:DisjointUnionOfType"/>
	JointUnion Of	Non-mutual exclusive aggregation relationship	<xsd:simpleType name="JointUnionOfType"> <xsd:list itemType="xsd:anyURI"/> </xsd:simpleType> <xsd:element name="JointUnionOf" type="tns:JointUnionOfType"/>
Inheritance	SubClassOf	Class Inheritance relationship	<xsd:element name="SubClassOf" type="xsd:anyURI" de-fault="http://WS-Collab-Resource.com/class#Resource"/>
Association	All	Association is represented as a simpleType element	HasSubComponent Relationship: <xsd:simpleType name="HasSubComponentType"> <xsd:list itemType="xsd:anyURI"/> </xsd:simpleType> <xsd:element name="HasSubComponent" type="tns:HasSubComponentType"> AttributeTo Relaitionship from Statement or Party: <xsd:simpleType name="AttributeToType"> <xsd:list itemType="xsd:anyURI"/> </xsd:simpleType> <xsd:element name="AttributeTo" type="tns:AttributeToType"/>

Aggregation relationship is represented using simpleType. As shown in Table 10.1, both *DisjointUnionOf* and *JointUnionOf* aggregation relationships are defined as simpleType elements, which contain a list of component elements in the format of anyURI.

Since the inheritance relationship and its related SubClassOf relationship are both one-to-one relationship, their representation is simple as to use an XSD element with the name specified, whether it is a SubClassOf relationship for example.

As shown in Table 10.1, the association relationship is represented as a simpleType element, which contains a list of component elements in the format of anyURI.

The following is a list of identified association relationships between two business resources and their WSRF definitions: *HasTask, MemberOf, HasSubComponent, AttributeTo, Partner, Requestor, Responder, Reference*, and *Specification*.

HasTask

HasTask lists all the tasks belonging to a project. It is represented by a simpleType element as follows:

```
<xsd:simpleType name="HasTaskType">
  <xsd:list itemType="xsd:anyURI"/>
 </xsd:simpleType>
 <xsd:element name="HasTask" type="tns:HasTaskType"/>
```

MemberOf

MemberOf relates an individual resource to an Organization object, describing the individual as a member of the Organization. It is represented by a simpleType element as follows:

```
<xsd:simpleType name="MemberOfType">
<xsd:list itemType="xsd:anyURI"/>
</xsd:simpleType>
<xsd:element name="MemberOf" type="tns:MemberOfType" />
```

HasSubComponent

HasSubComponent indicates that one business resource contains sub-components. It is represented by a simpleType element as follows:

```
<xsd:simpleType name="HasSubComponentType">
<xsd:list itemType="xsd:anyURI"/>
</xsd:simpleType>
<xsd:element name="HasSubComponent" type="tns:HasSubComponentType" />
```

AttributeTo

AttributeTo indicates that one business resource is an attribute of another resource.

It is represented by a simpleType element as follows:

```
<xsd:simpleType name="AttributeToType">
  <xsd:list itemType="xsd:anyURI"/>
  </xsd:simpleType>
  <xsd:element name="AttributeTo" type="tns:AttributeToType" />
```

Partner

Partner relates two Organization resources together, describing their relationships as partners of each other in business collaborations. It is represented by a simpleType element as follows:

```
  <!--Partner from Organization to Organization -->
<xsd:simpleType name="PartnerType">
  <xsd:list itemType="xsd:anyURI"/>
  </xsd:simpleType>
<xsd:element name="Partner" type="tns:PartnerType"/>
```

Requester

Requester relates a Transaction resource to a Party object, where the Party refers to an Organization. It is represented by a simpleType element as follows:

```
<!--requester from party to transaction -->
<xsd:simpleType name="RequesterType">
  <xsd:list itemType="xsd:anyURI"/>
</xsd:simpleType>
<xsd:element name="Requester" type="tns:RequesterType" />
```

Responder

Responder relates a Transaction resource to a Party object, where the Party refers to an Organization. It is represented by a simpleType element as follows:

```
<!--responder from party to transaction -->
<xsd:simpleType name="ResponderType">
  <xsd:list itemType="xsd:anyURI"/>
</xsd:simpleType>
  <xsd:element name="Responder" type="tns:ResponderType" />
```

Reference

Reference indicates that one resource is a reference to another. It is represented by a simpleType element as follows:

```
<xsd:simpleType name="ReferenceType">
  <xsd:list itemType="xsd:anyURI"/>
  </xsd:simpleType>
<xsd:element name="Reference" type="tns:ReferenceType" />
```

Specification

Specification indicates that one resource is a specification to another. It is represented by a simpleType element as follows:

```
<xsd:simpleType name="SpecificationType">
  <xsd:list itemType="xsd:anyURI"/>
  </xsd:simpleType>
<xsd:element name="Specification" type="tns:SpecificationType"/>
```

10.4 Web Services Collaboration Message Primitives

Now that business ontology is defined, the next question is how to enable and facilitate communications between collaborators. In order to allow universal and reusable communications between any business participants, WS-Collab creates a uniform message-based communication format. Any business collaboration is conducted through exchange of collaboration information, such as adding new participants, requesting status update on task, and initiating collaboration task.

10.4.1 WS-Collab Primitive

After examining business collaboration scenarios, WS-Collab identifies a set of general-purpose, semi-structured, and extensible message primitives for collaboration activities. These message units can be used as fundamental message units for collaborators to interact with each other. A message typically contains a request requirement with specifications, references, and annotations. As shown in Table 10.2, WS-Collab defines two categories of basic types of message units: messages for request and messages for response.

Table 10.2 WS-Collab message primitives

Primitive type	Name	
Request	Request for Design (RFD)	RFD_RECEIPT_ACK
	Request for Quote (RFQ)	RFQ_RECEIPT_ACK
	Request for Information (RFI)	RFI_RECEIPT_ACK
	Request for Update (RFU)	RFU_RECEIPT_ACK
	Request for Opportunity (RFO)	RFO_RECEIPT_ACK
	Request for Sourcing (RFS)	RFS_RECEIPT_ACK
Response	Accept or Reject a request (A/R)	A/R_RECEIPT_ACK
	Design Submission (DS)	DS_RECEIPT_ACK
	Information Submission (IS)	IS_RECEIPT_ACK
	Update Submission (US)	US_RECEIPT_ACK

In the category of message for request, six primitives are identified: Request for Design (RFD), Request for Quote (RFQ), Request for Information (RFI), Request for Update (RFU), Request for Opportunity (RFO), and Request for Sourcing (RFS).

RFD is used when a business organization requests a design collaboration from suppliers or partners. RFQ is used when a business organization asks for a quote about a collaboration. RFI is used when a business organization queries information. RFU is used when a business organization checks progress or updates the status of a collaboration. RFO is used when a business organization pursues collaboration. RFS is used when a business organization asks for resources. Because business collaborations require reliable communication, each identified message primitive is associated with an acknowledgement message primitive, indicating that the receiver has received the requested message. For example, RFD is associated with an RFD_ RECEIPT_ACK; RFO is associated with an RFO_RECEIPT_ACK.

Taking the RFD primitive as an example, each collaborator uses the RFD primitive to request a partner to perform a design task. As illustrated in Fig. 10.9, an RFD primitive is comprised of three messages: an RFD message, an RFD_ RECEIPT_ACK message, and an RFD_ACCEPTANCE_ACK message.

Figure 10.9 also shows an asynchronous communication method. *Partner A* sends a business message of RFD to *Partner B*. Without sending back decision right away, *Partner B* only returns an acknowledgement of the receipt of the RFD message. Then *Partner B* starts an internal sub-process to review and evaluate the RFD proposal. After some time (e.g., a few days), *Partner B* sends back a final acceptance notice to *Partner A*. Only after these asynchronous message exchanges, a partner relationship can be finally formed. As a result, a new partner will be added into the corresponding value chain.

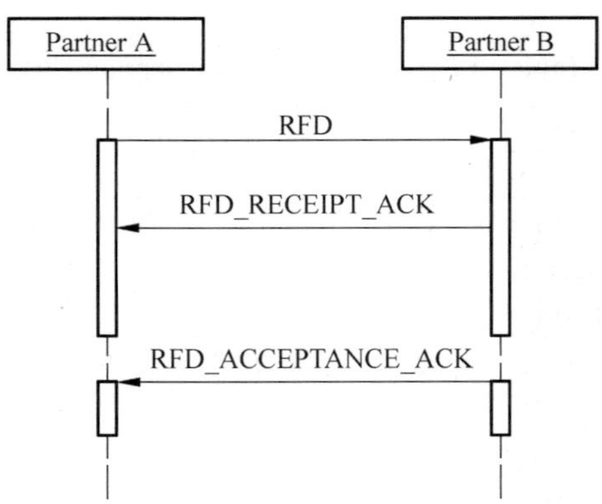

Figure 10.9 Message sequence diagram of RFD primitive

As shown in Table 10.2, in the category of message for response, four primitives are identified: Accept or Reject a request (A/R), Design Submission (DS), Information Submission (IS), and Update Submission (US).

A/R is used when an organization responds a collaboration request RFO. DS is used when an organization submits design documents in response to an RFD. IS is used when an organization submits information in response to an RFQ, RFI, or RFS. US is used when an organization updates collaboration status in response to an RFU. Similarly, each primitive is associated with an acknowledgement primitive, e.g., DS_RECEIPT_ACK and IS_RECEIPT_ACK.

10.4.2 WS-Collab Message Structure

In addition to the introduced basic message types, WS-Collab specifies a template for the structure of a message. In general, a message comprises of sections. Sections <transaction> and <task> are mandatory sections in every message; other sections are optional and are only present for particular messages.

Transaction

Figure 10.10 shows the schema of a transaction section. A transaction section can contain annotation, which describes verbose definitions for the specific transaction.

```
<xsd:schema xmlns:xsd="http://www.w3.org/2001/XMLSchema"
            targetNamespace="http://WS-Collab-Resource.com/class"
            xmlns:tns="http://WS-Collab-Resource.com/class">
   <xsd:element name="Name" type="xsd:string"/>
   <xsd:element name="SubClassOf" type="xsd:anyURI" default="http://WS-
Collab-Resource.com/class#Resource"/>
   <xsd:element name="ForTask" type="xsd:anyURI" default="http://WS-Collab-
Resource.com/class#Task"/>
   <xsd:element name="Transaction">
     <xsd:annotation>
        <xsd:documentation> A business transaction is the atomic unit of work
in a trading arrangement between two business partners </xsd:documentation>
       </xsd:annotation>
       <xsd:complexType>
          <xsd:sequence>
             <xsd:element ref="tns:Name"/>
             <xsd:element ref="tns:SubClassOf"/>
             <xsd:element ref="tns:ForTask"/>
          </xsd:sequence>
       </xsd:complexType>
   </xsd:element>
</xsd:schema>
```

Figure 10.10 Schema for a transaction section

In addition, a transaction contains three elements: *Name*, *SubClassOf*, and *ForTask*. *Name* defines the name of the transaction, *SubClassOf* defines the parent class of the transaction, and *ForTask* defines the task to which the transaction belongs.

Task

Figure 10.11 shows the representation of a *Task* element in WS-Collab. Class *Task* collects two types of tasks *HomeTask* and *OutsourcingTask*. An *OutsourcingTask* is a specialized task to be outsourced and completed by a business partner; a *HomeTask* refers to a task to be performed and completed in-house. As shown in Fig. 10.11, a task contains several elements: *Annotation*, *Name*, *Outsourcing*, *Performer*, and *ForProject*. *Name* defines the descriptive name of the task; *Outsourcing* defines whether the task is conducted through outsourcing or in-house; *Performer* defines the engineers; *ForProject* defines the project to which this task belongs.

```
<xsd:schema xmlns:xsd="http://www.w3.org/2001/XMLSchema"
         targetNamespace="http://WS-Collab-Resource.com/class"
         xmlns:tns="http://WS-Collab-Resource.com/class">
  <xsd:element name="Name" type="xsd:string"/>
  <!-- Outsourcing Task:True, Otherwise False-->
  <xsd:element name="Outsourcing" type="xsd:boolean"/>
  <xsd:element name="Performer" type="xsd:anyURI" default="http://WS-
   Collab-Resource.com/class#Party"/>
  <xsd:element name="ForProject" type="xsd:anyURI" default="http://WS-
   Collab-Resource.com/class#Project"/>
  <xsd:element name="Task">
    <xsd:annotation>
       <xsd:documentation> Task </xsd:documentation>
    </xsd:annotation>
    <xsd:complexType>
       <xsd:sequence>
          <xsd:element ref="tns:Name"/>
          <xsd:element ref="tns:Outsourcing"/>
          <xsd:element ref="tns:Performer"/>
          <xsd:element ref="tns:ForProject"/>
       </xsd:sequence>
      </xsd:complexType>
   </xsd:element>
</xsd:schema>
```

Figure 10.11 Definition of Task in WS-Collab

As shown in Fig. 10.11, a task can be associated with annotations, which can in turn specify a verbose description of the task, as well as the high-level information of the project, such as name, outsourcing status, performer, and the project name.

10.5 Web Services Collaboration Construct

Based on identified collaboration primitives, WS-Collab establishes business constructs. A business construct comprises a group of configured collaboration primitives for a specific business collaboration. In other words, a business construct is in a relatively fixed fashion to achieve a specific collaboration goal.

WS-Collab predefines five business constructs: RFD business construct, RFU business construct, RFI business construct, US business construct, and IS business construct. RFD business construct comprises RFD primitive and DS primitive; RFU business construct comprises RFU primitive and US primitive; RFI business construct comprises RFI primitive and IS primitive; US business construct mainly contains US primitive; IS business construct mainly contains US primitive.

Based on these basic business constructs, business collaborators can define more complex business scenarios. A business construct can be represented using a standard business process modeling language, such as BPEL. Figure 10.12 presents an RFD micro-flow in BPEL. As shown in Fig. 10.12, an RFD business construct contains one RFD collaboration primitive and one DS collaboration primitive. The *process* in Fig. 10.12 stands for "business process", which is a recommended way to describe a business process in BPEL.

```
<process name="RFDmicroflow"
   targetNamespace="urn:samples:BusinessConstructs"
   xmlns:tns="urn:samples:BusinessConstructs"
   xmlns="http://schemas.xmlsoap.org/ws/2003/03/business-process/">

   <partners>
      <partner name="RFDoriginator"
         serviceLinkType="tns:RFDoriginatingSLT"
         myRole="RFDoriginating"/>
      <partner name="RFDreceiver"
         serviceLinkType="tns:RFDreceivingSLT"
         myRole="RFDreceiving"/>
      <partner name="buyer"
         serviceLinkType="tns:buyingSLT"
         MyRole="buying"/>
   </partners>

   <variables>
     <variable name="RFDinvoke" messageType="tns:RFDinvoke"/>
     <variable name="RFDmsg" messageType="tns:RFDmsg"/>
     <variable name="RFD_Receipt_Ack" messageType="tns:RFD_Receipt_Ack"/>
     <variable name="Accept" messageType="tns:Accept"/>
     <variable name="DSinvoke" messageType="tns:DSinvoke"/>
     <variable name="DSmsg" messageType="tns:DSmsg"/>
     <variable name="DS_Receipt_Ack" messageType="tns:DS_Receipt_Ack"/>
   </variables>
```

Figure 10.12 An RFD business construct in BPEL

```
  <correlationSets>
    <correlationSet name="POIdentifier" properties="POIdentifier"/>
    <correlationSet name="RFDIdentifier" properties="RFDIdentifier"/>
  </correlationSets>

  <sequence>
    <receive partner="buyer" portType="tns:buyerPT"
      operation="purchase" variable="RFDinvoke"
      createInstance="yes" name="ReceivePurchase">

      <correlations>
         <correlation set="POIdentifier" initiate="yes"/>
      </correlations>
    </receive>

    <invoke name="invokeRFDoriginator"
      partner="RFDoriginator" portType="tns:RFDoriginatorPT"
      operation="sendRFD" inputVariable="RFDinvoke" outputVari-
able="RFDmsg">
    </invoke>

    <invoke name="invokeRFDreceiver"
       partner="RFDreceiver" portType="tns:RFDreceiverPT"
       operation="receiveRFD" inputVariable="RFDmsg" outputVari-
able="RFD_Receipt_Ack">
    </invoke>

    <invoke name="invokeRFD_Accept_Ack"
       partner="RFDreceiver" portType="tns:RFDreceiver"
       operation="sendRFD_Accept" inputVariable="RFDmsg" outputVari-
able="RFD_Accept_Ack">
    </invoke>

    <invoke name="invokeRFD_Accept_receive"
       partner="RFDoriginator" portType="tns:RFDoriginator"
       operation="receive_Accept" inputVariable="Accept">
    </invoke>

    <invoke name="invokeDS"
       partner="RFDreceiver" portType="tns:RFDreceiver"
       operation="submitDS" inputVariable="DSinvoke" outputVari-
able="DSmsg">
    </invoke>

    <invoke name="invokeDS_Receipt_Ack"
       partner="RFDoriginator" portType="tns:RFDoriginator"
       operation="receiveDS" inputVariable="DSmsg" outputVari-
able="DS_Receipt_Ack">
    </invoke>
  </sequence>
</process>
```

Figure 10.12 (Continued)

As shown in Fig. 10.12, the <process> section defines a WS-Collab message. In the <partners> section, each <partner name= > defines a partner with role in participating the business processes as specified by the WS-Collab message. In the <variables> section, each <variable name= > defines a message that constitutes the sequence of message exchanges. In the <links> section, each <link> expresses a synchronization dependency. The <sequence> section defines a sequence of activities contained in the business construct *RFD*. As shown in Fig. 10.12, six invocations need to be performed sequentially: *invokeRFDoriginator, invoke-RFDreceiver, invokeRFD_Accept_Ack, invokeRFD_Accept_receive, invokeDS, invokeDS_Receipt_Ack*.

Once represented by BPEL, multiple business constructs can form a comprehensive business scenario.

10.6 Web Services Collaborative Exchange Protocol

Based on the collaboration ontology, collaboration primitives, and collaboration construct, WS-Collab establishes a Collaborative Exchange Protocol (CxP) to annotate business collaboration processes. This technique is critical to allow peer-to-peer interactions between collaborative processes. As shown in Fig. 10.3, CxP bridges the IT transport layer and the business scenario layer. It builds on top of a set of standard protocols and adds the features needed for extended business collaboration processes. In other words, CxP can be used to transmit the semantic representation, control the information exchange flow, and monitor on-going activities in a dynamic fashion.

As shown in Fig. 10.3, in the IT transport layer, messages are considered as digital packages over standard transport protocols (e.g., SOAP over HTTP). In the CxP domain, collaboration primitives are selected and configured into collaboration

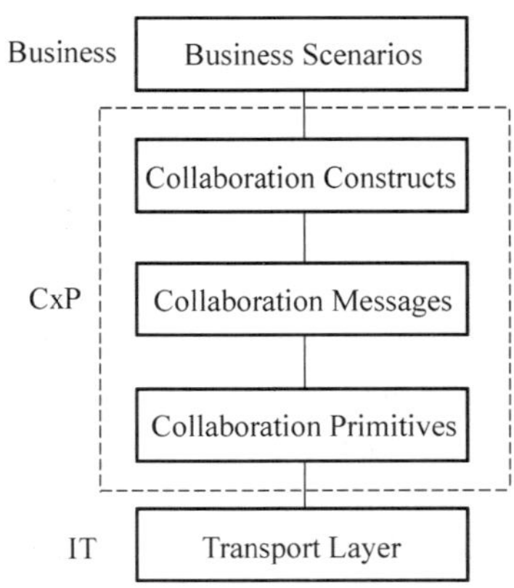

Figure 10.13 Collaborative Exchange Protocol (CxP) stack

messages; multiple collaboration messages are grouped based on specific collaboration requirements to form collaboration constructs. In the top business scenario layer, a combination of business constructs represents business scenarios with full semantic meanings. In other words, CxP bridges the gap between business and IT from constructing and configuring business goal-driven business protocols and process perspective. It should be noted that each component can be captured based on Web services standards. For example, the messages utilize XML-based WSRF schema; collaboration constructs use BPEL aggregations.

A business scenario typically serves a complex business goal, such as a design outsourcing scenario. Each business scenario typically comprises multiple business constructs depending on the corresponding business contexts. A business construct is a basic unit of a message exchange sequence that serves a single business goal. Figure 10.14 shows an example of exploiting a set of business constructs to establish a business process template. As shown in Fig. 10.14 on the left, a laptop design company sends RFDs to its three individual design partners for different designs. It asks design partner *A* for chip design, partner *B* for motherboard design, and partner *C* for memory design. Design partner *A* in turn sends RFDs to its two design partners to outsource part of the design work.

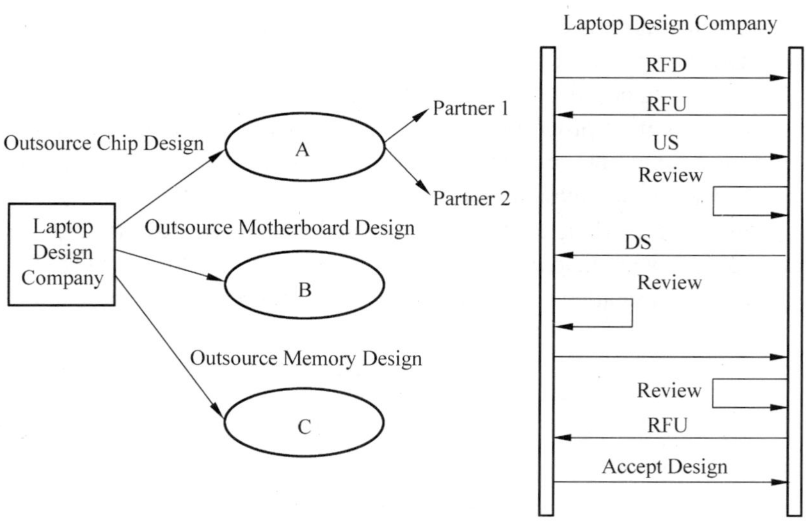

Figure 10.14 Example of a design process template

The right side of Fig. 10.14 shows a composition flow of business constructs. It illustrates how various messages flow between the two partners to fulfill a business scenario. The scenario starts from an RFD to the design partner. Upon accepting the RFD construct, the design partner sends an RFU back to the laptop design company, associated with an Accept primitive. If an RFD is accepted, eventually a design partner submits the design draft for an approval. The product company reviews the design draft. Messages come back and forth between the laptop design company and the design partner for zero to many rounds of revision, until the design draft is accepted by the laptop design company. Finally, an Accept notification is sent to the design partner to terminate the business scenario.

This sample design business process pattern illustrates the flexibility and versatility of the CxP to support message-content driven business process collaboration that requires various data formats in collaboration message flow and document exchanges.

10.7 WS-Collaboration Realization

The implementation of WS-Collab includes two steps. First is to construct an automatic process for annotation data generation; second is to set up an engine to capture and automate business collaboration interaction patterns based on the annotation data.

10.7.1 Annotation Data Generation Process

In order to enable business collaborations, a set of delivery policies is established to allow users to choose how contents are to be delivered on demand. Four basic levels of delivery models are identified: scheduled content delivery, on-demand content delivery, access control-based content delivery, and push-based content delivery.

To effectively annotate data for business collaborations, an extensible data structure is constructed based on WS-Collab ontology for data annotation, which describes collaboration processes and activities, such as requirements, references, specifications, and tools.

Scheduled Content Delivery

Information content is delivered to the intended recipients on a predetermined periodical schedule.

On-Demand Content Delivery

A part of information contents is delivered to users based on user requests. A user can follow HyperChain-specified links within the annotation data and download further information if needed. For example, in a typical collaboration scenario, a design file may be very large. Thus, a server-to-server file transfer mechanism may be needed to assist an on-demand content delivery.

Access Control-Based Content Delivery

Content is delivered depending on the role and authorization of a recipient and corresponding user credentials. Since a business collaboration generally involves multiple enterprises, the regular single-sign-on security mechanism needs to be enhanced. An annotated access control policy needs to be incorporated with business annotation data based on authorization. For example, an annotated access control policy specifies who can view a document or modify it and when a document should be sent back or forwarded to other collaboration participants.

Push-Based Content Delivery

Annotation data are delivered along with attachments. In general, this model is suitable for small-size file transfer.

10.7.2 HyperChain Manager

The HyperChain manager is the core processing engine responsible for creating, sending, receiving, and processing annotation messages. It implements the on-demand information exchange model and escalation process launch. In addition, the HyperChain manager provides an enabling platform for users to dynamically configure business constructs and guides the follow up interactions between collaborators. It also serves as a platform to provide an extendable data aggregation mechanism to integrate information from multiple partners' data sources for effective monitoring and visibility control. Figure 10.15 illustrates a HyperChain Manager serving as a CxP engine.

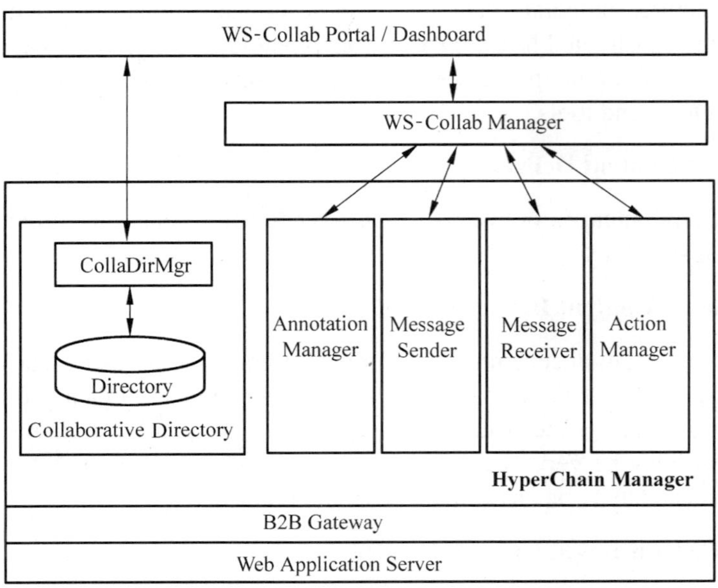

Figure 10.15 Internal structure of a HyperChain manager

The deployment architecture comprises an extended business collaboration portal/ dashboard, a WS-Collab manager, a HyperChain manager, and a B2B Gateway. The portal or dashboard includes applications that can access the HyperChain manager via the application programming interface (API) layer provided by the WS-Collab manager.

As shown in Fig. 10.15, the HyperChain manager is comprised of five components: a collaborative directory (including a directory manager and directory repository), an annotation manager, a message sender, a message receiver, and an action manager. The collaboration directory manager component manages the resources tracked by the HyperChain manager, such as organizations (partners), users, projects, and tasks. CxP messages are sent and received by the message sender and receiver components via SOAP messages or other protocol-based messages. The message sender and message receiver shown in Fig. 10.15 both have Web service interfaces.

The annotation manager processes the metadata or annotations created for the documents and information exchanged via CxP messages. Examples of annotations are file names, file types, version information, and author names. Annotations can also be used to specify "actions" to be performed on the documents. Examples of such actions may be "review" document, perform "RFTP" (reliable file transfer) and send actions to legacy applications like Enterprise Resource Planning (ERP) and Product Data Management (PDM).

The annotations in the received messages are forwarded to the Action Manager, which is an integration layer to back-end legacy applications and components like RFTP. The action manager invokes proper actions on the documents.

It should be noted again that the HyperChain manager is constructed based on and built for SOA. As shown in Fig. 10.15, each component is a Web service and communicates with others using standard protocols. Each component is enabled by Web services and bears its own API.

10.8 Relationships with Industry Standards

The relationship among CxP, RosettaNet, and BPEL can be summarized as follows. CxP identifies the primitives for the collaborative Partner Profile Processes (PIP) (in the RosettaNet sense) (RosettaNet)[4] as well as the extendable hyperlinked data descriptions. CxP is immediately compatible at a high level with the RosettaNet PIP model. As illustrated earlier, CxP can be restructured to become BPEL compatible. The CxP Message data are extensible in supporting hyperlinked document types, which can be used to compose collaborative business primitives such as the different variety of Request for Information (RFI) and Request for Updates (RFU).

One of the constraints of the HyperChain Manager discussed in this chapter is that it cannot directly process platform or channel specific information such as

Computer Aided Design (CAD) files, RosettaNet protocols, and ebXML protocols. However, the HyperChain Manager can route these activities to the right applications based on the business annotated data carried in the CxP messages. Therefore, CxP and its implementation, HyperChain Manager, provide an extensible platform to extend the current SOA foundation to build composite business applications that support content-driven business process integration and management.

10.9 Discussions on Service-Based Business Collaboration

This chapter shows how a systematic approach leveraging and extending SOA and Web services technologies can be applied to facilitate business collaboration through effective information management framework. A business collaboration-oriented ontology is introduced, followed by collaboration primitives, messages, constructs, and CxP protocols.

In general, the key goals of an effective and efficient business collaboration model are six-fold. First is to define a flexible format for annotation information representation; second is to deliver information in a formalized fashion; third is to interpret, process, and direct information exchanges upon an on-demand basis; fourth is to control information exchanges and flow dynamically; fifth is to monitor the status of process flows and document exchanges; and sixth is to secure all communication channels and information access. There are spaces for each aspect that needs researchers and practitioners to design more effective solutions.

10.10 Summary

In this chapter, we have introduced an on-demand business collaboration solution framework, WS-Collab, which supports a novel model of integration of a collaboration workplace with B2B collaborative process flow based on SOA. The Collaborative exchange Protocols (CxP) stack of WS-Collab supports elements of various granularities. The introduced WS-Collab ontology or Meta-data Model is the foundation for business collaboration; collaboration primitives provide reusable assets for constructing interaction messages; business constructs form communication patterns for specific business collaboration. This techniques are very helpful for building an open and flexible composite applications and service ecosystem.

References

[1] Zhang LJ, Jeckle M (2003) The Next Big Thing: Web Services Collaboration. Lecture Notes in Computer Science 2853: 1 – 10

[2] United Nations Centre for Trade facilitation and Electronic Business (UN/CEFACT). http://www.unece.org/cefact/
[3] ebXML. http://www.ebxml.org/
[4] RosettaNet. http://www.rosettanet.org/
[5] Sayah JY, Zhang LJ (2005) On-demand business collaboration enablement with web services. Decision Support Systems 40(1): 107 – 127
[6] (2004) Web Services Notification and Web Services Resource Framework (WSRF). http://www-106.ibm.com/developerworks/webservices/library/ws-resource
[7] OMG UML 2.0 superstructure and infrastructure. http://www.omg.org/technology/documents/formal/uml.htm

11 Business Process Management and Integration

11.1 Business Process Modeling

Business companies are typically driven by underlying business processes, each referring to a set of activities that are coordinated to achieve a certain business goal. Although there are various definitions for business processes, three keywords have been widely used: *tasks*, *flow*, and *business goal*. A business process always implies an integration of sub-processes, or so-called tasks, each being fulfilled by individual business entities or role players. These tasks are usually organized in an activity flow that specifies a specific integration order for the tasks, either parallel or sequential, guarded by particular conditions and rules. Above all, all tasks and the activity flows serve the same business goal for the entire business process. Summarizing these key points, we define a business process as a structured and measurable set of activities that consume certain resources and are designed to produce the specified output for a particular business requirement.

Nowadays, enterprise businesses build information systems to automate their business processes for higher efficiency. In order to stay competitive in the global market, enterprises have to constantly adapt and optimize their business processes in accordance with ever-changing business requirements and environments. Whenever changes happen to business processes, corresponding information systems have to undergo consequent changes to stay aligning with the business processes. It is known that without a systematic approach, changing and modifying an existing information system is a highly time-consuming and error-prone job. How to properly model business processes in an agile manner oriented to potential variations and changes is thus a key technique.

Business Process Management (BPM) refers to a procedure of exploiting a set of technologies and standards for the design, execution, administration, and monitoring of business processes[1,2]. Numerous methodologies have been proposed and widely used to facilitate business process modeling, including formatted text-based descriptions, graphical tool-supported business process modeling, and formal rule-based business process modeling and reasoning.

Over the last ten years, the scope of business processes and BPM has been largely broadened. Less than a decade ago, BPM referred to the groupware technology that assisted in managing human-oriented, paper-driven processes within a corporate department. Nowadays, BPM has become an enterprise management and integration technology complementing SOA and Enterprise Application Integration (EAI). It intends to handle large-scale, paperless processes within and across business boundaries. The contemporary BPM process orchestrates complex interactions among computerized workflow, and is itself a service capable of communicating and conversing with the processes across corporate boundaries according to well-defined technical contracts. For example, a travel booking management process handles the activity flow among a flight reservation service, a car reservation services, a hotel reservation service, and a credit card checking service.

11.2 SOA-Based Business Process Management

The emergence of the concept of Services Computing paves a new way for integration of heterogeneous applications into a business process based on SOA. In contrast with traditional business process management that focuses on merely understanding business flow and finding IT solutions, SOA-based business process modeling focuses on identifying potential services for constructing business processes, while paying specific attention to keeping high cohesion inside of services and low coupling between services to achieve high reusability of services.

As shown in Fig. 11.1, SOA-based business process management can be performed through two strategies: either through a top-down approach or through a bottom-up approach. The former focuses on decomposing a business process into tasks until finding proper existing service assets to fulfill the tasks or deciding to build software to fulfill the tasks; while the latter focuses on composing existing service assets into a business process to fulfill business requirements.

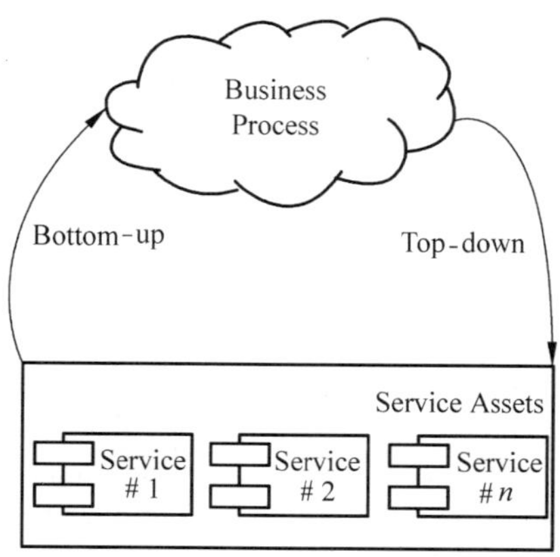

Figure 11.1 Business process management approaches

Recall that Chapter 5 introduces a nine-layer SOA Reference Architecture for an SOA solution. A dedicated layer is identified to handle business process management and integration. Underneath the Business Process layer, three layers are established to support both top-down and bottom-up business composition and decomposition.

11.2.1 Top-down Business Process Management

As shown in Fig. 11.2, the top-down business process management approach refers to the procedure of recursively decomposing a business process into sub-processes or tasks and decomposing a sub-process into smaller sub- subprocesses, until each task is manageable and can be realized by services, either existing services or services that can be developed. An existing service might have to be adapted and transformed to realize a specific business goal.

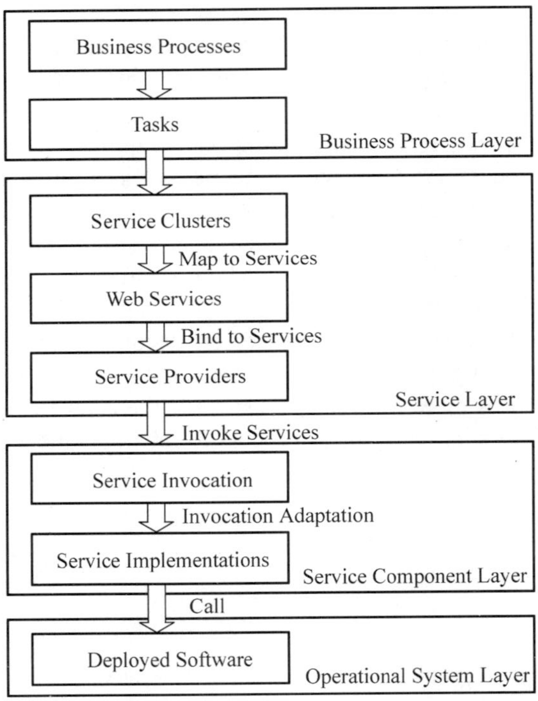

Figure 11.2 Business process management: top-down approach

As shown in Fig. 11.2, from the top-down direction, business processes can be either directly decomposed as business services in the Service layer or used to compose business services; business processes can also be used to compose new implementation components in the Service Component layer.

Figure 11.2 shows an example of realizing an SOA solution using the top-down approach. In the Business Process layer, a business process is decomposed into tasks and then mapped to conceptual service clusters (a.k.a. business services). Then each service cluster is mapped to actual Web services in the Service layer and bound to target service providers. Afterwards, the Service Component layer will invoke actual implementation of the found services, which may in turn call deployed software or legacy systems from the Operational System layer.

This strategy has two significant benefits. First, by focusing on business problems, it offers flexible support for abstraction and reusability. Second, this strategy can best align with business requirements. However, this strategy also faces significant challenge. Focusing on business process decomposition, service transformation may require significant efforts to fill the gap between business goals and existing services.

11.2.2 Bottom-up Business Process Management

As shown in Fig. 11.3, the bottom-up business process management approach refers to the procedure of configuring, mediating, transforming, adapting, and integrating existing services into a business process.

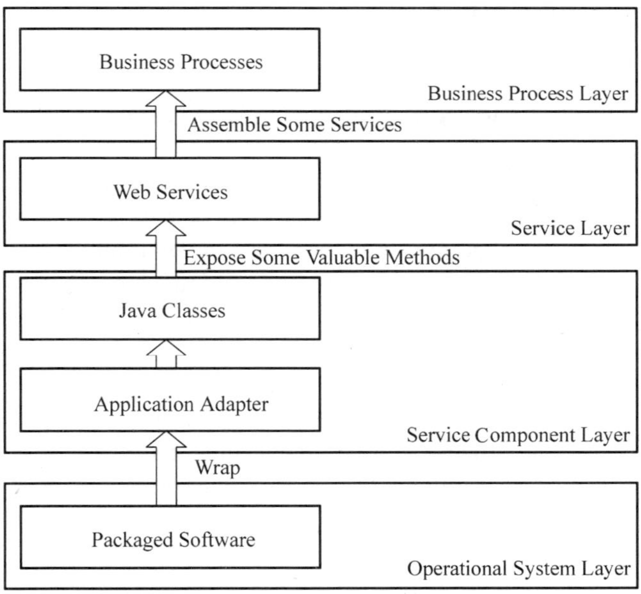

Figure 11.3 Business process management: bottom-up approach

As shown in Fig. 11.3, from the bottom-up direction, software components from the Operational System layer can be used to develop service components in the Service Component layer; service components can then be used to implement business services in the Service layer; business services can then be used to compose business processes or coordinate business processes in the Business Process layer.

Figure 11.3 shows an example of SOA-oriented solution composition using the bottom-up approach. Packaged software components from the Operational layer are wrapped by the Service Component layer and integrated into reusable software components in a specific programming language, such as Java classes. Some methods from generated Java classes can be exposed to the Service layer as Web services. Web services from the Service layer can be selected and assembled into business processes in the Business Process layer. A requirements-driven business process composition approach is introduced in Chapter 9.

This strategy has two significant benefits. First, by aggregating existing services into new business processes, this approach keeps existing investments through asset reuse. Second, the validation of such a business process development is relatively cheaper since theoretically, only integration test among services are needed. However, this bottom-up approach typically suffers from lacking an integrated view of the entire system with limited architectural styles.

11.3 Bridging Gap Between Business Modeling and IT Implementation

11.3.1 Business Process Modeling from Business Analysts

Business process modeling typically starts from business analysts who are domain experts and understand specific business process scenarios and requirements. A business analyst can utilize any modeling tool or environment to document a business process. The essential idea is to identify business tasks as well as their inter-relationships and record them in a formal and visual way. Afterwards these documents can be used to communicate with other business analysts or can be handed to IT architects for further reviews and discussions.

Figure 11.4 shows a simplified travel booking business process diagram. As shown in Fig. 11.4, the process starts by requesting credit card information from a user. After checking and verifying the credit card information, the travel booking agent searches and reserves flight, car, and hotel rooms before generating confirmation information.

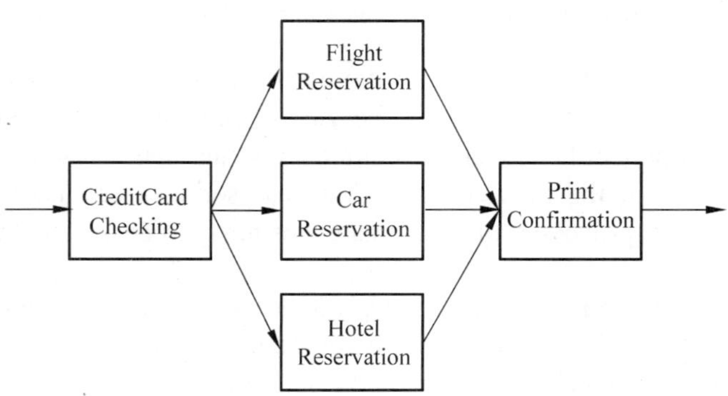

Figure 11.4 An example of business process modeling

11.3.2 Business Process Re-engineering in SOA

However, a good business process is not necessarily a good or even feasible SOA solution. There is a widely recognized gap between business models and IT development models. The business models normally cannot be directly used for development by software engineers. The reasons are apparent. The business models are designed by business analysts, who do not have much IT knowledge. For example, they may not be aware of the naming convention in programming languages. It should be noted that business analysts typically consider from business function's perspective instead of from IT implementation perspective. As a result, the provided models generally have to be refined and re-engineered by software architects. Considering SOA modeling particularly, business models might not even be easy to be used. Therefore, they are normally be used as a guideline of the modeling business process; services and services components are typically identified and proposed by IT architects.

Re-examining the travel booking example shown in Fig. 11.4, an IT architect typically will not strictly follow the business models created by business analysts. Instead, the architect may explore available services, keeping the business models in mind. After investigating existing services in the market, the IT architect decides to adopt three services: *flight reservation service, car reservation service,* and *hotel reservation service.* Meanwhile, the IT architect decides that a *travel booking service* needs to be developed in house for dispatching tasks to the three existing services and integrating results from three services. Furthermore, the IT architect finds that all three existing services include their own integrated credit card checking facility (assuming that the car reservation service, for example, has integrated procedures to take credit card information). As a result, the IT architect refines the business process as shown in Fig. 11.5.

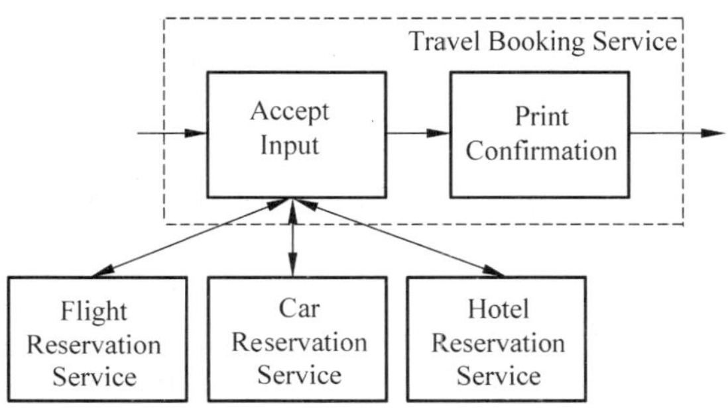

Figure 11.5 Refine business process modeling into service modeling

The refined business process starts from the *travel booking service* by accepting user requests including credit card information. The *travel booking service* dispatches the request to three existing services and then gathers results from them: *flight reservation service, car reservation service,* and *hotel reservation service,* respectively. Then the *travel booking service* integrates the results and print confirmation information to the user as a response.

11.3.3 Generic Guidance for Re-engineering Business Process Modeling in SOA

It has been shown that a reasonable business process may not lead to a good SOA solution. Thus, an IT architect needs to investigate existing service assets and transform a business process into an appropriate SOA solution. In general, SOA-based modeling not just requires functional decomposition for addressing both business and IT requirements; it may result in significant reengineering of business processes to reflect SOA requirements. The architect needs to keep in mind that one key value of SOA is flexibility achieved through separation of concerns, loose coupling, and late binding.

The following are three generic guidance principles for an SOA architect to reengineer a business process model into an SOA-based model: partition process, allocate service, and identify patterns.

The partition process means that an SOA architect should partition the business process by business functional areas to increase cohesion and reduce coupling, since eventually each task, or each group of tasks are to be realized by a service that should exhibit and favor reusability.

The allocate service means that an SOA architect should identify services to fulfill tasks. A business process might need to be refactored: a number of related business process tasks may be implemented by a single service, or a complicated business process may be implemented by a set of choreographed services.

The identify patterns means that an SOA architect should identify and summarize patterns from commonly recurring business processes. These patterns and corresponding services should be kept configurable and reconfigurable.

11.3.4 Methodology for Re-engineering Business Process Models in SOA

The essential element of re-engineering business process models in SOA is to find appropriate services to fulfill the tasks in the business processes. A step-by-step procedure is created to guide the business process identification and implementation: process decomposition, business service clustering, service selection through discovery, data modeling, service definition, business logic refinement based on interfaces, service implementation, service deployment on application servers, daily operation with monitoring and management, and service maintenance. This procedure also illustrates a lifecycle of business process management.

Process Decomposition

This phase intends to decompose a business process into controllable smaller tasks, so that it will be easier to find appropriate services to implement individual tasks. Complex business functions and processes are broken down into simpler activities. This top-down technique allows for greater precision in understanding and verifying business objectives. The degree of process decomposition depends on the purpose and scope of the project. It is important to identify proper point to stop. The level of decomposition that is coherent and has meaning to business must be determined.

Business Service Clustering

In this phase, business analysts and business architects examine the initial ideas of partitioning the business, and delineate functional areas (a.k.a. business domains) aggregating cohesive business functionalities that could be assigned to relatively independent services.

Meanwhile, business analysts specify business goals, including long-term strategic goals and short-term operational goals, with which the business can be planned and managed using Key Performance Indicators (KPIs) and metrics. The identified goals and KPIs provide the basis for measuring and ensuring business processes specifications and realizations. The results of this phase are a set of service clusters that are introduced in Chapter 9.

Service Selection

In this phase, SOA architects identify Web services that could potentially fulfill specific business processes. They should closely work with business analysts and business architects in this step. In more detail, they explore existing service assets that may be used to fulfill one or more business tasks. Differences between existing services and business requirements as well as adaptations needed are also identified and recorded. The identified candidate Web services may subject to additional refinements; however, these services form an initial set of candidate services.

Data Modeling

In this phase, data models and message formats are to be designed. Many services are actually data-centric services instead of process-centric services; thus, their development tends to focus more on data models. Specially, data models have to be developed from the existing applications, which can be used to identify coherent subsets that can be treated as autonomous elements.

Service Definition

This phase intends to analyze and design services that will be used to fulfill business processes from services' metadata perspective. SOA architects and IT designers typically work closely to accomplish the work. This phase in turn contains three key steps: identify commonality and variability, identify security patterns, and define service details.

First is to analyze metadata of identified services and specify which metadata elements are common to different business tasks, and which elements are vary in different tasks. Therefore, the variability can be factored out of the services while the commonality can be factored in toward a more robust, flexible, and highly reusable service design.

Second, security architects need to step in during this initial architectural modeling phase to identify and select key security patterns, in order to assure the proper level of security for the entire SOA solution. In more detail, a two-level security patterns need to be enforced. First, high-level security patterns should be identified to associate with architectural elements regarding security requirements and policies; second, these security patterns are then refined in accordance with specific technologies and platforms.

Third, for each metadata element associated with services, its design details are to be defined and modeled. This level of definition includes two aspects, one is its invocation interface, including operations as well as their input and output signatures; the other one is its internal operational flow. Dependencies and the communications between services are also defined.

Business Logic Refinement

In this phase, business logic of the defined services is refined iteratively based on interfaces and associated back to business goals and KPIs. Services and services components identified and defined earlier may need to be re-factored from the perspective of the entire system. New candidate services are also possible to be identified as supporting and utility services during this process. The essential goal of this step is to re-factor the system architecture for higher reusability.

Service Implementation

This phase intends to address how to transform business process models into IT implementation models. While the business process models and IT models in the previous phases are generally technology and platform independent, the implementation models in this phase are typically technology and platform dependent. Actual code is also generated in this phase. In more detail, specified services are used to generate corresponding data schemas, WSDL files, BPEL processes, and other implementation artifacts based upon predefined rules. These generated artifacts can be then imported into final implementation platforms for IT engineers to realize the SOA solutions.

Service Deployment

In this phase, implemented services are deployed on application servers to become runnable services. This step ties the services to specific deployment platforms. However, underlying deployment platforms should not change the ways the services are to be invoked. In other words, service users should not need to be aware of the hosting platforms. A comprehensive procedure of testing is required before the services become discoverable from public services registries.

Monitoring and Management

In this phase, daily operation of monitoring and management is performed on deployed services to ensure their proper functioning. Typical operations intend to monitor the Quality of Service (QoS) features of the services such as their availability, security, safety, fault tolerance, and reliability. These monitoring operations are usually conducted on the usage basis and are accumulated for statistical analysis, which can be used as a basis for service maintenance.

Service Maintenance

In this phase, necessary maintenance work is conducted to existing functioning services. Maintenance requirements may come from either previous service monitoring and management phase or from service user requirements. For example, the execution of existing services may report certain bugs under certain circumstances that need to be fixed in a timely manner. For another example, service users may propose new business requirements to be implemented in existing services. For yet another example, one running service may have to undergo upgrading efforts to support a higher volume of concurrent users. One typical yet critical requirement of this phase is that service maintenance should remain a minimum down time of the services, meaning that the corresponding service users should be able to continue to use the services without knowing the underlying changes.

It is noted that Service Oriented Modeling and Architecture (SOMA)[3] is a consulting-oriented services development method. SOMA consulting practice can be conducted along with this SOA-based process reengineering method introduced in this chapter. SOMA includes "services identification, services specification, and services realization." Readers may find that the three-phase procedure is analogous to the three-phase traditional Object-Oriented design procedure for objects: identify objects, specify identified objects, and implement defined objects. The major difference is that, instead of oriented to objects, the procedure is oriented to services. In the first phase, instead of identifying objects to mimic real-world self-contained entities, the procedure intends to identify existing services. In the second phase, instead of specifying attributes and operations of an identified object, the procedure intends to specify the interfaces of an identified service. In the third phase, instead of implementing the specified object in a specific object-oriented programming language on a specific platform, the procedure intends to set up an invocation mechanism for the specified service on the target platform.

11.4 Flexible Business Process Integration in SOA

One easy way to integrating existing legacy applications is to wrap them with Web service interfaces, so that they can directly interact with each other toward a common business goal. However, this *wrapper* design pattern-based business integration technique has limitations. One of the key obstacles is that the integration between applications has to be generally predefined and effectively hard-wired. Changing business requirements may cause re-development as well as extensive integration testing and re-deployment efforts. Many programs may have to be rewritten to incorporate changes specific to each application integration; interfaces between components may have to be adjusted also. As a result, reusability of applications becomes restricted. Furthermore, there are many approaches in the field of business process integration. In order to integrate an existing application into a business process, a dedicated adaptor is typically required to be developed to assure the application's proper interactions with other services in the process. Moreover, corresponding middle tiers often have to be adjusted accordingly. In summary, this customized one-of-a-kind integration approach not only is labor intensive but also usually suffers from severe limitations in terms of scalability of functions.

In order to facilitate adaptive business process integration, this section will introduce an approach to minimize the efforts needed to integrate new applications into an existing business process infrastructure. A concept of Integration Activity Chain ontology[3] is coined to capture the activities in the business process, as well as the integration requirements including adaptation behaviors, action properties, business rules, and access control policy references. By enabling adaptive business process/application integration in a "plug-and-play" fashion, the introduced mechanisms and framework provide an alternative to the costly and labor-intensive single-point application integration.

11.4.1 Integration Ontology

One essential challenge of adaptive business process integration is how to precisely and properly capture business process integration requirements. A business process-oriented integration ontology is introduced as a dynamic vehicle providing flexibility towards integrating applications into existing environments. Effectively capturing the relationship mappings of the services to be integrated, this integration ontology is able to precisely describe business process flow as well as application properties, parameters, conditions, and access control policy preferences.

It has been widely acknowledged that ontology can be used to share common understanding of the structure of information among people or software components. It can also enable reuse and analysis of domain knowledge that may be separated from operational knowledge. Ontology can thus be applied to facilitate business process integration. If captured in terms of ontology, high-level business process integration knowledge can be separated from the "operational" hard code; thus, the knowledge can be reused among different services. Furthermore, if business process integration conditions can be captured explicitly by ontology, automatic monitoring and self-management become feasible. The integration ontology is therefore coined as a dedicated instance of ontology or metadata model in the domain of business process integration.

The integration ontology can be equipped into the lifecycle of business process management. In the definition phase, the integration ontology can be used to define business process flow; in the development phase, it can be used to describe the parameters needed for an adaptation, while shielding integration engineers from the details of the applications to be integrated; in the execution phase, it can be used by integration engineers to ensure the proper invocation of applications as defined.

Note that integration ontology is domain specific, centered on a generalized notation *activity*. Every task involved in an integration scenario is modeled as an activity annotation, represented as a reference link in the high-level annotated business annotation data. Thus, an activity annotation can be specified at any granularity. Meanwhile, since an activity annotation can be retrieved on an on-demand basis to invoke the integration action at runtime, activity annotations together form a dynamic business process flow. Flexible linkages can be used to capture conditions between individual integration ontology.

An Example of Integration Ontology

The logical architecture of an example integration ontology is shown in Fig. 11.6. The top-level entity is an abstract class *Activity*, which contains two properties: one *DataTypeProperty* "securityHandler" and one *ObjectProperty* "actname." The *ObjectProperty* "actname" implies a range that is represented by a Class "Actname," which is a collection enumerating six elements: *GridFTP*, *FTP*, *HTTP*, *Inv-service*, *Inv-Appl* and *Search-Annot*.

The abstract class *Activity* has two predefined subclasses: *GridFTP* and *FTP*. According to the DARPA Agent Markup Language + DAML + OIL[4] syntax, a subclass is specified as a collection that inherits the super class with some restrictions on certain properties. For example, the subclass *GridFTP* is a collection that inherits the class *Activity* with two *DataTypeProperty* restrictions: a *source* and a *destination*. Similarly, the subclass *FTP* is a collection that inherits the class *Activity* with another two *DataTypeProperty* restrictions: a *getFrom* and a *sendTo*.

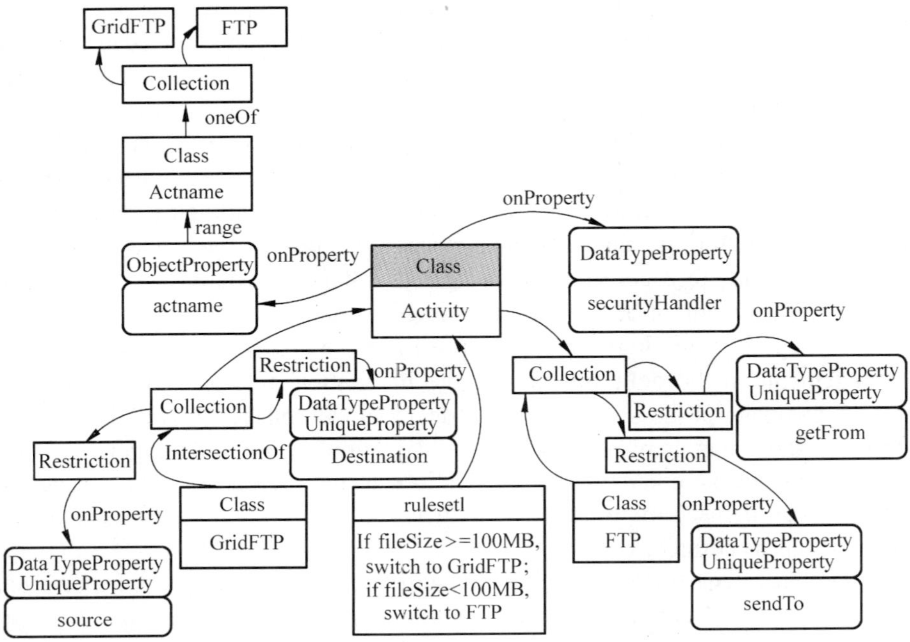

Figure 11.6 An example integration ontology for business process integration

GridFTP and *FTP* exhibit the same function as conducting file transfer. *GridFTP* is more efficient yet more complex than *FTP*. Different mechanisms can be used to express this comparison. For example, one can use Simple Rule Markup Language (SRML)[5] to specify the rule of competing relationships between *GridFTP* and *FTP*. Other rule languages can also be used.

Integration Ontology Representation

Integration ontology can be presented by various formats. As an example, Fig. 11.7 illustrates how to use Resource Definition Framework (RDF)[6] schema to represent the element *GridFTP* in the integration ontology in Fig. 11.6. As shown in Fig. 11.7, *GridFTP* is represented as an activity, with its *source* and *destination* defined as two annotations.

The integration ontology defines terms and conditions in a design process integration scenario, thus providing a flexible enabling infrastructure to support extensible business process integration in any other domain. For example, as shown in Fig. 11.8, we use *ruleset*1 to specify the competition condition between *GridFTP* and *FTP* as follows:

If FileToTransfer.fileSize < 100MB, switch to FTP.

```
<daml:Class rdf:ID="GridFTP">
    <daml:intersectionOf rdf:parseType="daml:collection">
        <daml:Class rdf:about="#Activity"/>
            <daml:Restriction>
                <daml:onProperty rdf:resource="#source"/>
            </daml:Restriction>

            <daml:Restriction>
                <daml:onProperty rdf:resource="#destination"/>
            </daml:Restriction>
        </daml:Class>
    </daml:intersectionOf>
</daml:Class>

<daml:DatatypeProperty rdf:ID="source">
    <rdfs:comment>This is the source for GridFTP </rdfs:comment>
    <rdfs:type
rdf:resource="http://www.w3.org/2001/10/daml+oil#UniqueProperty" />
    <rdfs:range rdf:resource="http://www.w3.org/2001/XMLSchema#anyURI ">
<daml:DatatypeProperty>

<daml:DatatypeProperty rdf:ID="destination">
    <rdfs:comment>This is the destination for GridFTP </rdfs:comment>
    <rdfs:type
rdf:resource="http://www.w3.org/2001/10/daml+oil#UniqueProperty" />
    <rdfs:range rdf:resource="http://www.w3.org/2001/XMLSchema#anyURI ">
<daml:DatatypeProperty>
```

Figure 11.7 An example of Activity Chain ontology representation

When *fileSize* is less than 100MB, *FTP* will be used. Figure 11.8 illustrates how to use flexible linkages to provide constraints to the relationships between individual activities.

```
<rdf:RDF  xmlns:rdf="http://www.w3.org/1999/02/22-rdf-syntax-ns#"
  xmlns:RDFNsId2="http://www.servicescomputing.org/dc/directory/ruleset#">
<RDFNsId2:ruleset rdf:ID= "ruleset1">

   <rule name= "switchToFTP">
   <conditionPart>
     <simpleCondition className="FileToTransfer" objectVariable="s">
         <binaryExp operator="lt">
         <field name="fileSize"/>
         <constant type="float" value="100" unit= "MB"/>
         </binaryExp>
     </simpleCondition>
  </conditionPart>
```

Figure 11.8 An example of Flexible linkage between individual activities

```
   <actionPart>
     <modify>
       <variable name="s"/>
       <assignment>
        <field name="actname"/>
        <constant type="String" value="FTP"/>
      </assignment>
     </modify>
    </actionPart>
    </rule>
   </RDFNsId2:ruleset>
</rdf:RDF>
```

Figure 11.8 (Continued)

11.4.2 Integration Manager

An Integration Manager is developed to provide a "Plug-and-Play" mechanism for dynamically integrating applications into a business process infrastructure by leveraging the integration ontology[7]. As shown in Fig. 11.9, an Integration Manager contains seven major components: an *Activity Parser*, a *Controller*, an *Event Capturer*, an *Access Control Utility*, an *Exception Handler*, *Adaptation Layers*, and *Ontology Stores*.

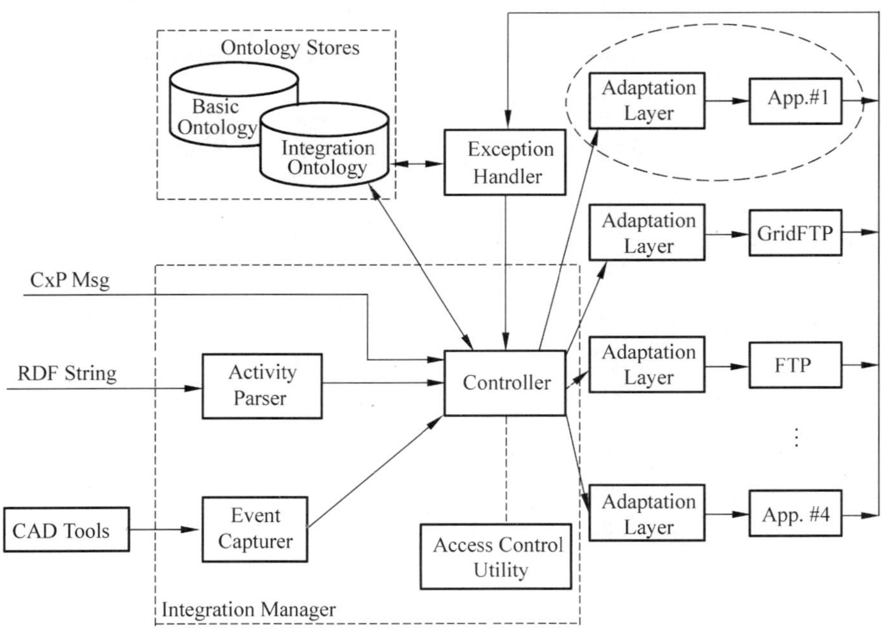

Figure 11.9 Components of an Integration Manager

The central component of an Integration Manager is *Controller*, whose major task is to accept integration actions parsed by *Activity Parser* and to invoke the corresponding activities based on the activity names. The Integration Manager also handles internal activities for *Event Capturer* to catch internal behaviors. Another important function of *Controller* is to react with actions when some exception occurs during activity executions. The function of *Activity Parser* is to retrieve the integration activity name from an input parameter, such as an RDF string or an annotation of a message. Before the actual invocation of a corresponding activity, by consulting Integration Ontology for the valid parameter requirements and the conditions between activities, *Access Control Utility* checks to ensure that the invocation will be within valid scope of the security domain. *Event Capturer* catches predefined events, such as when a designer finishes a CAD design document. The caught event may later trigger an activity, which is to notify the design partner that the design document is done. *Access Control Utility* checks and ensures the authorization of all access to the resources/application integrated. *Exception Handler* monitors all activities at runtime. When an exception occurs, *Exception Handler* makes decisions based on the specifications in the Integration ontology and triggers *Controller* to take appropriate actions. An *Adaptation Layer* realizes the "adaptive" feature of an Integration Manager. It is an integration layer that isolates an Integration Manager from individual applications to be integrated. As an example, the right-hand side of Fig. 11.9 shows four applications: *App.* #1, *Grid FTP*, *FTP*, and *App.* #4. Each application requires a dedicated *Adaptation Layer* before it can be integrated with the left-hand side complex system. Finally, an Integration Manager also contains *Ontology Stores*, which include Basic Ontology store (for domain-specific generic ontologies) and *Integration Ontology store*.

11.4.3 Lifecycle of an Integration Activity

The lifecycle of an integration activity managed by Integration Manager contains three steps. The first step is to capture the new activity in the Integration Ontology, which will be used later by *Controller* and *Exception Handler* in Integration Manager, e.g., Integration Ontology for integrating FTP File Transfer in Fig. 11.8. The second step is to either use a GUI tool or manually add an extended part shown in Fig. 11.8 into the existing Integration *Ontology Store*. The third step is to develop *Adaptation Layer* for this activity by implementing the predefined interface known to Integration Manager.

The implementation of the adaptation layer can be realized by a Web service, which in this example is created by a JavaBean. Its interface is defined first, and then implemented in Java, for example. The Web service accepts an XML string as the input parameter matching the Integration Ontology. The implementation class is responsible for constructing the input parameters as needed and performing the actual invocation. Finally, WSDL files can be generated from the JavaBean class to publish it as a Web service (e.g., *FTPAdaptor-service.wsdl* and *FTPAdaptor-binding.wsdl*). In *FTPAdaptor-service.wsdl*, a service called *FTPAdaptorService* is defined, including the binding information and SOAP address. Note that the message is the same XML string, only the service name for each adaptor is different. Typically, a service name reflects an actname defined in the Integration Ontology.

11.4.4 Business Process Monitoring

In order to prove a modeling of a business process integration is deadlock free, formal verification techniques (e.g., Petri nets) can be exploited. Equipped with a powerful mathematical tool with graphical interfaces, Petri nets have been widely used to formally model various systems, such as manufacturing systems and business processes. Due to their ability to model systems of distributed, concurrent, and asynchronous control, Petri nets are used as an example to model the adaptive activity management systems.

Using Petri nets, an Integration Manager can be modeled as follows:

Place: Each Activity has two states: *done* or *fail*. An Action Manager has two states: *ready* or *ToDispatch*. A place is represented by a circle in a Petri net graph.

Transition: Each Activity itself is an operation, so it can be modeled as a transition. An activity can also embed a Petri nets representation, thus constructing a hierarchical Petri net. A transition is represented by a rectangle in a Petri net graph.

Token: Activity Annotation (Message).

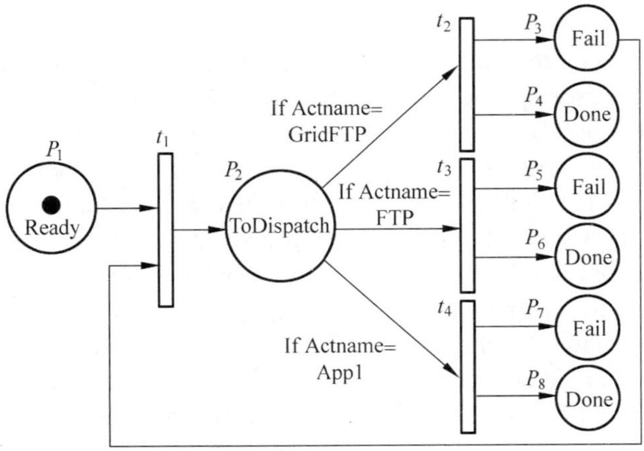

Figure 11.10 Petri net representation of an Integration Manager

Figure 11.10 shows the Petri net representation of an Integration Manager. Transition t_2, t_3, t_4 are corresponding to *GridFTP, FTP*, and *App1* in an Integration Manager as shown in Fig. 11.9, respectively. Places, $p_3, p_4, p_5, p_6, p_7, p_8$ represent the status "*Fail*" or "*Done*" for *GridFTP, FTP*, and *App*1. Transition t_1 can be viewed as Activity Parser + Controller in Fig. 11.9.

As shown in Fig. 11.10, after an Integration Manager accepts an input message, a token is moved from p_1 : *Ready* to p_2 : *ToDispatch*. The token is then passed to either t_2 or t_3 or t_4 according to the *Actname*. The result may be either *Fail* or *Done*. If *GridFTP* is failed, it may request the Integration Manager to restart.

Each individual activity transition can be modeled as follows:

- *Place*: All the properties defined in the Integration ontology can be represented by a set of places including a place called *Ack* (i.e., Acknowledgement).
- *Transition*: The operation primitive can be a transition.
- *Token*: Activity Annotation (Message).

In summary, with the aid of the key features of Petri nets that enable simulation, analysis, and validation, some important properties of the actual system may be revealed, such as deadlock-free, and safeness.

11.5 Discussions on Business Process Management and Integration

There are a wealth of techniques and methodologies in the field of business process management and integration. This chapter focuses on SOA-based business process management and integration. In more detail, this chapter introduces both top-down and bottom-up approaches to transform business processes into services, and then introduces ontology-based business process integration based on services.

Transforming business process integration and management into SOA solutions can be tedious and error prone without an automatic tool support. Such a toolkit should support end-to-end SOA solution-level design and development in a systematic manner. Specific solution-level SOA-oriented facilities for business process management and implementation are needed as plug-ins to existing tooling environments.

In order to facilitate adaptive business process integration, three fundamental issues need to be resolved. The first is a uniform representation to capture detailed and appropriate requirements of each application integration activity, such as method names, input and output parameter formats, and so on. This information should not be represented in a hard-wired manner. The second is adaptability of recruiting applications into business process integration. A new integration activity should not require a significant amount of programming efforts on the middleware infrastructure. The third is a flexible mechanism to express business rules or conditions governing integration activities during a business process. For example, an integration policy may require that, above a certain threshold, one integration activity *A* is to be invoked; otherwise, another integration activity *B* is to be used as a replacement.

11.6 Summary

In this chapter, we first introduced SOA-based business process management and how to bridge the gap between business process management and application integration. Then we introduced ontology-based business process integration based on SOA. An enabling infrastructure that includes the integration ontology and Integration Manager was introduced to provide a uniform way to integrate business applications or processes within one enterprise or across multiple enterprises.

References

[1] Malone TW, Crowston K, Herman GA (2003) Organizing Business Knowledge: The MIT Process Handbook. MIT Press
[2] Havey M (2005) Essential Business Process Modeling. 1st edn. O'Reilly Media
[3] SOMA. http://www-128.ibm.com/developerworks/webservices/library/ws-soa-design1/
[4] (2002) DAML-S: Semantic Markup For Web Services. http://www.daml.org/services/daml-s/2001/10/daml-s.html
[5] Simple Rule Markup Language (SRML). http://xml.coverpages.org/srml.html
[6] Resource Description Framework (RDF). http://www.w3.org/RDF/
[7] Zhang LJ, Long Y, Chao T, Chang H, Sayah J (2004) Adaptive integration activity management for on demand business process collaboration. Information Systems and E-Business Management 2: 149 – 166

12 Business Grid

12.1 Grid Computing

When most people think of a Grid, a picture comes to mind as an interconnected system for the distribution and sharing of electricity, supported by a network of high-tension cables and power stations. Around 1995, this concept of electronic grid was applied to the field of distributed computing and parallel computing to facilitate sharing of computing power and storage resources over computers on a network. An example definition for Grid and Grid Computing is as follows[1]:

> *"A Grid is a collection of distributed computing resources available over a local or wide area network that appears to an end user or application as one large virtual computing system. The vision is to create virtual dynamic organizations through secure, coordinated resource sharing among individuals, institutions, and resources. Grid computing is an approach to distributed computing that spans not only locations, but also organizations, machine architectures, and software boundaries to provide unlimited power, collaboration, and information access to everyone connected to a Grid."*

Nowadays, when an organization builds an internal solution, it typically requires standard ways to share and access applications across multiple locations—a common practice that becomes more significant as the organization grows. Moreover, in the modern society, an organization can no longer be isolated. Instead, it is typical that it needs to communicate with other organizations for collaboration. Such internal and external structures and interdependencies demand standard and scalable ways to share various computing resources (including data, applications, and devices) in a distributed environment within and across organizational boundaries effectively and efficiently. Grid and Grid computing are such promising candidate enabling infrastructures.

To date, the Grid computing technology has been used in a variety of areas, such as finance, defense, medical discovery, decision-making, and collaborative design. A Grid helps people from different organizations and distributed locations to work together to solve a common problem, such as design collaboration that is a typical scenario requiring dynamic resource sharing and information exchange. A Grid computing platform allows resource discovery, resource sharing, and collaboration in a distributed environment.

Recently, Grid computing is moving from sharing computing power and storage resources to sharing business resources, including any abstract business entities and resources. This new trend remains a big challenge, since these universal business resources typically do not belong to the same level. Describing them is already difficult; describing them in a unified way is even more difficult[2]. Therefore, Grid computing has started to leverage the Web services technology, its infrastructure and standard approaches, to define standard interfaces for inter-Grid resource communications and interactions.

Existing Grid computing paradigm uses localized Grid solutions, which hold individual software programs typically installed behind corresponding firewalls. These localized Grid applications not only are platform dependent, but also may have incompatible communication protocols. In addition, they usually offer few integration mechanisms for communicating with other localized Grids. Moreover, it is hard to add new applications from different vendors to the existing localized Grids due to their proprietary interfaces, which restrict business expansion and increases operating costs. In short, the present Grid solutions generally lack a way to quickly and easily interact and integrate with external business processes and services provided by different localized Grids using a secure, affordable, and manageable approach. The emerging Web services model offers a solution to standardize the Grid computing technology to realize actual interoperability and resource sharing.

12.2 Open Grid Services Architecture (OGSA)

A major driving force behind the latest standardization of the Grid computing technology was the Global Grid Forum (GGF)[3]. GGF and the Enterprise Grid Alliance (EGA) have merged to "Open Grid Forum (OGF)" to drive standardization for Grid community[3]. The Open Grid Service Interface Working Group of the GGF defines the Open Grid Services Architecture (OGSA)[4] based on the emerging Web services standards.

OGSA is a distributed interaction and computing architecture oriented to Grid services, which are represented by WSRF[5]. Its major goal is to assure interoperability on heterogeneous environments, so that different types of systems can communicate and share resources with each other. It utilizes the Web services technology to move the traditional Grid computing toward services-oriented architecture. In detail, the most central idea of OGSA is to leverage the concept of Web services to describe Grid services.

As a result, a Grid can be organized into three levels, as shown in Fig. 12.1: service level (Service Grid), partner (Partner Grid), and enterprise (Enterprise Grid). The lowest level is the Service Grid, which interacts with the underlying Web services platform to provide a standard communication channel supporting the higher-level Grids. A Service Grid typically includes a set of Grid services within an enterprise and handles their interactions and collaborations. The middle level is the Partner Grid, which composes and orchestrates available Grid services from multiple Service Grids to provide larger-scale value chain-oriented Grid services. The highest level is the enterprise Grid, which integrates Grid services from multiple Partner Grids to solve real business problems involving business processes, business functions, and business resources.

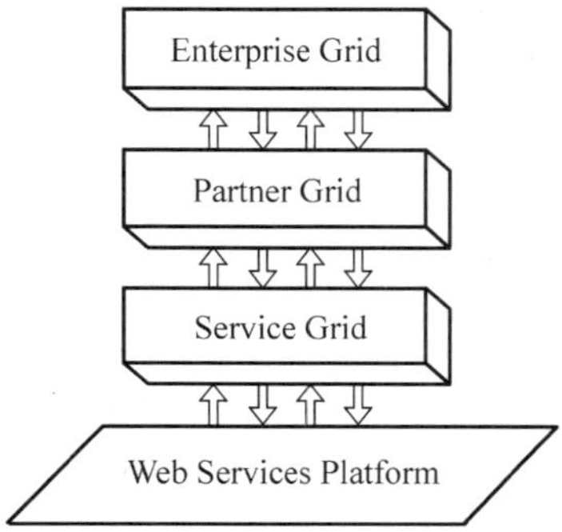

Figure 12.1 Grid computing layers

Several critical components in the OGSA specifications are still in the early stages of development: *Factory, Registry, Discovery, Lifecycle, Query service data, Notification,* and *Reliable invocation.*

12.2.1 Distributed Resource Sharing Using OGSA

OGSA describes and defines a Web services-based Grid architecture to facilitate distributed resource sharing and accessing in heterogeneous environments. OGSA relies on the definition of Grid services in WSDL and WSRF[6], which defines method names, parameters, and types for Grid service accesses. Figure 12.2 illustrates a typical OGSA architecture.

The fundamental concept behind OGSA is that it is a Web services-oriented Grid architecture powered by Grid services. As shown in Fig. 12.2, OGSA is composed of a set of Grid services, each being represented by a standard interface. Such Grid services can be deployed on different hosting environments—even different operating systems such as Unix, Linux, and Windows. As long as a standard interface is defined, these Grid services can interact with each other by exchanging messages delivered by the SOAP protocol.

Figure 12.2 also shows that a Grid service can be implemented in different programming languages on different platforms. For example, on a Windows platform, Java, Visual Basic, or C# can be used to implement a Grid service; on a Unix platform, C or Java can be used. Meanwhile, OGSA provides a Grid security mechanism to secure all communication among services.

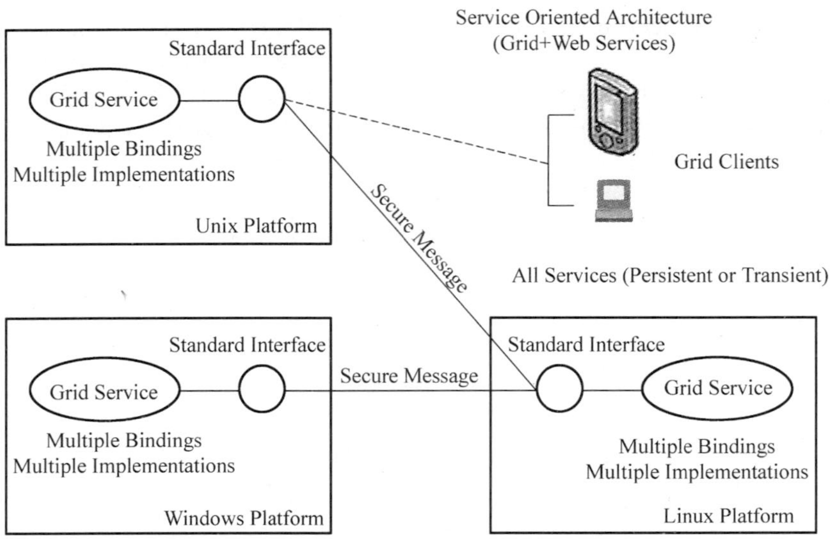

Figure 12.2 OGSA deployment

As shown in Fig. 12.2, OGSA architecture also covers Grid computing devices, such as a cell phone or a computer system. They can act as Grid computing clients to access resources and invoke applications from a Grid computing environment via SOAP. It should be noted that a Grid service may exist in one of the two states: persistent or transient. In other words, a Grid environment consists of dynamic Grid services. In summary, the foundation of OGSA is a binary tuple <Grid structure, Web services>.

OGSA defines the semantics of a Grid service instance, including its service capability, service versioning and upgrading, soft state management, Grid service deployment and publishing, and Grid service creation and invocation. For a Grid service, each invocation from a Grid client leads to the creation of an individual service instance at run time. Therefore, at some point, a Grid service may have many running instances, each containing specific state information. In general, the creation of a new Grid service instance involves the creation of a new process in the hosting environment, whose primary responsibility is to ensure that its supporting services adhere to the defined Grid service semantics. From the time a service instance is created to the time it is destroyed, its lifetime management issues also need to be captured. Furthermore, the communication protocols between Grid service instances need to be defined.

Service capability refers to what a Grid service can offer and how it can be shared by others. For example, a shipping service might have the service capability of delivering packages in two days for less than $10. A Grid service is characterized by its offered capabilities.

The compatibility between Grid services can be managed in OGSA based on versioning information. A Grid service can be independently upgraded based on the versioning information.

Soft-State Management

Grid services can maintain internal states, which distinguish one running instance from another. An interaction between service instances through message exchange triggers an event that may alter the state of an involving service instance. For a transient stateful service, OGSA provides a mechanism to capture the state information associated with any failed operations. If an operation fails, the service instance changes the value of its attribute *keepalive* to *false* to prevent service clients from invoking it any longer. The instance then automatically times out and frees the computing resources associated with it.

Grid Service Deployment and Publishing

The deployment and publishing of a Grid service is nothing different from that of a common Web service. WSRF (Web services property) document(s) may be attached to Web services to capture the stateful information of Grid services. Figure 12.3 illustrates an example. Assuming that an application is developed as a J2EE Enterprise JavaBean (EJB) class in Java, the EJB class can be first deployed to an application server, as long as it provides a SOAP support engine. Regarding Java, a SOAP servlet is needed to support SOAP handling and invocation. Using any OGSA tool to generate WSDL documents, the application can be wrapped into a Grid service, which can be then published to a UDDI registry, or to a Web server as a WSIL document, or to any other services registries. As discussed in Chapter 4, there are two types of UDDI registries: *private* and *public*. A Grid service can be published either to a public UDDI registry operated by known organizations or to a private UDDI registry for internal use. Meanwhile, for testing purposes or small-scale integration, Grid services can also be published to WSIL documents.

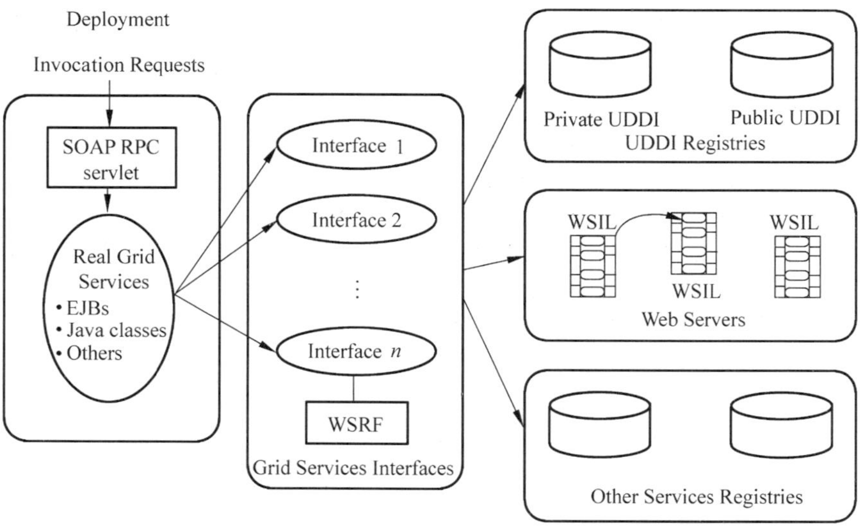

Figure 12.3 An example of Grid service deployment and publishing

12.3 Business Grid

A Grid solution enables applications to efficiently share data and computing resources within and across organizational boundaries. Existing Grid computing technologies take advantage of unused computing capacities to solve business problems and provide an IT-level infrastructure to support business applications. The SOA model offers a solution to quickly and easily integrate business processes and services that are provided by different local Grids in a secure, affordable, and manageable manner. In other words, Services Computing has been impacting and transforming the traditional Grid computing into a Business Grid, which refers to an application of Grid computing oriented to services-based business enterprises.

12.3.1 Enhancing OGSA with Advanced Web Services Technologies

The convergence of Web services and Grid computing provides an unprecedented and powerful technique to support resource sharing. As Grid computing is moving from sharing computing power and storage resources to sharing business resources, many advanced Web services works can be shaped to the Grid computing space to help business-level resource sharing. These techniques include: adaptive Web services invocation mechanism, the advanced Web services discovery technique, SOA Relationship Modeling Language (SOA-RML), and Web services composition.

Adaptive Web service invocation mechanism can be used to enhance OGSA to perform reliable and dynamic invocations of a Grid service. It is able to perform method signature adaptation (including input and output) automatically for dynamic services invocation. As discussed in Chapter 5, MetaWSDL[7] can be used as a universal XML representation to carry the semantic information of WSDL, such as the information for describing and quantifying the input and output parameters. Such information is critical when conversions between parties are required. By supplying metadata and describing them in MetaWSDL, OGSA can be correctly and automatically adapted for Grid service invocation without human intervention. Output parameters can be adapted as well. Detailed information of the adaptive service invocation mechanism can be found in Chapter 5.

The technology of advanced Web services discovery technique can be used to enhance OGSA to discover Grid services. It provides an efficient method and uniform interface to discover Grid services using the UDDI Search Markup Language (USML) script rather than accessing the low-level programming APIs. The detailed information of advanced Web services discovery technique can be found in Chapter 4.

SOA Relationship Modeling Language (SOA-RML) can be used to enhance OGSA to define complicated relationships among Grid services. Basic Grid services information can be described in WSDL. However, an important part of the data about Grid services is the relationships among business entities, business services, Web services, and operations. These relationships are keys to composing and executing dynamic business processes. In addition, SOA-RML captures service relationships at different granularities, which can be important facilitators in selecting and composing the right set of services that meet customer requirements. The detailed information of SOA-RML can be found in Chapter 6.

Requirements-driven Web services composition technology can be used to enhance OGSA to compose a new business process using the existing Grid services, based on some optimal service selection mechanisms and composition schema. The detailed information of the technique and composition methodology can be found in Chapter 9.

12.3.2 Concept of Business Grid

The core idea of a Business Grid is to apply the utility model of Grid computing to provide a virtualized infrastructure that supports the transparent use and sharing of business services on demand in an orchestrated manner. A Business Grid aims to provide supporting services for charging users on a pay-per-use basis, similar as a utility company charges for electricity. In this way, the vendor takes the responsibility for application maintenance and upgrade. However, how to build a SOA-based Grid solution leveraging remote application systems on different platforms remains a challenge. Six categories of issues need to be solved: comprehensive administration, resource provisioning, application integration, data sharing and access, activity monitoring, and policy-based Grid management mechanisms.

We need to build a comprehensive administration system that enables a solution creator and administrator to register a new Grid service and manage other Grids' profiles easily. Administrators or service providers decide when to make specific computing resources visible to a Grid solution. From the developers' perspective, this process is referred to as *resource provisioning*. Grid solutions apply corresponding entitlement mechanisms to make resources secure and accessible for specific requesters, which can be an application, a long-running business process, or another Grid solution. Grid solutions allocate sensitive data, private applications, and confidential information in a virtually private place (e.g., a private UDDI registry), which serves special types of applications. The universal data access mechanism is needed for application requestors to share and access data and applications. In addition, a Grid solution should provide a policy-based resource explorer to enable accessing resources located on different Grids.

In short, Business Grid intends to move Grid computing from traditional computing power sharing and resource sharing toward business resource sharing and application sharing. It thus demands a flexible solution architecture to enable business resource sharing among collaborators in a secure and manageable fashion.

12.3.3 Business Grid Solution Framework

As shown in Fig. 12.4, an SOA-based Business Grid foundation framework utilizes a layered Grid structure to realize business resource and application sharing[8]. Such a framework can be envisioned as a Business Grid solution sphere that consists of two layers of Grids: one physical Grid and one logical Grid[9].

A physical Grid refers to computer power and other hardware resources that can be shared by users over a distributed network. Each specific task possesses its predefined configuration for a corresponding physical Grid. Theoretically, Grid solution developers use a physical Grid as a component Grid, which can be used by multiple logical Grids that provide different functionalities. A typical physical Grid is the computer-power sharing infrastructure.

A logical Grid refers to software and application sharing infrastructure, as well as higher-level business process sharing platform. Grid solution developers can create a logical Grid by using multiple physical Grids that work together to perform a specific task, such as weather forecasting or financial analysis. In general, a logical Grid can be dynamically configured based on customer requirements. Data Grid is an example of such a logical Grid to leverage multiple existing physical Grids if necessary. A possible infrastructure of a logic Grid will be discussed in the next section.

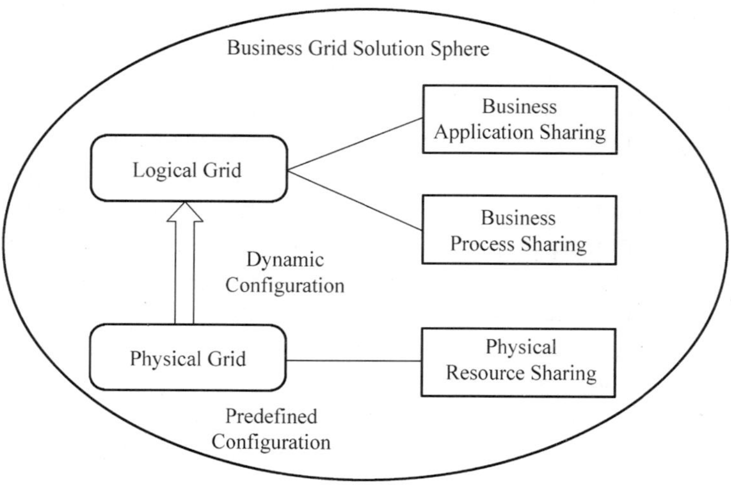

Figure 12.4 Business Grid framework

In the Business Grid framework shown in Fig. 12.4, administrators are allowed to control access to Grid resources and enable users or applications to access Grid resources. OGSA can be used to build the solution, which addresses issues of security, information infrastructure, resource management, communication, fault detection, and portability.

12.4 Logical Grid Infrastructure

As shown in Fig. 12.5, from the implementation perspective, a Logical Grid relies on three synergistically-related techniques to realize its ultimate goal: Packaged Application Grid (PAG), Business Grid Middleware (BGM), and Business Process Grid (BPG). The PAG technique organizes and leverages existing application services and wraps them into Grid services to support new business processes; the BGM technique provides an IT-level infrastructure to provide support facilities; the BPG technique provides business process provisioning and outsourcing, integration, collaboration, monitoring, and management infrastructure.

12.4.1 Packaged Application Grid

As shown in Fig. 12.5, the major goal of a Packaged Application Grid (PAG) is to hide the complexity of various existing applications and provide a unified layer of Grid services. A PAG uses the existing Grid computing technologies to knit together various existing application services, which are either legacy applications or application packages provided by Independent Software Vendors (ISVs). In order for these applications to be shared by other business processes, they need to be first wrapped as Web services. As shown in Fig. 12.5, one packaged applications may be wrapped into different Grid services with different interfaces. For example, *Packaged Application* 1 is exposed as two Grid services: *Service* 1.1 and *Service* 1.2.

In order to organize available applications as Grid resources, the control of a PAG can be centralized, although its computations and storages are usually geographically distributed. One machine typically takes charge of all synchronization and coordination tasks. Applications participating in a PAG are usually interdependent on each other.

The PAG paradigm may be attractive to businesses whose applications are not associated with a Grid, since they can be plugged into a PAG and collaborate with the applications contained in the PAG. A successful example is when a financial bank joins in a PAG to utilize other application resources provided by other banks in the PAG. By utilizing existing application services wrapped as Grid services, the bank avoids constructing everything from scratch. Another example comes

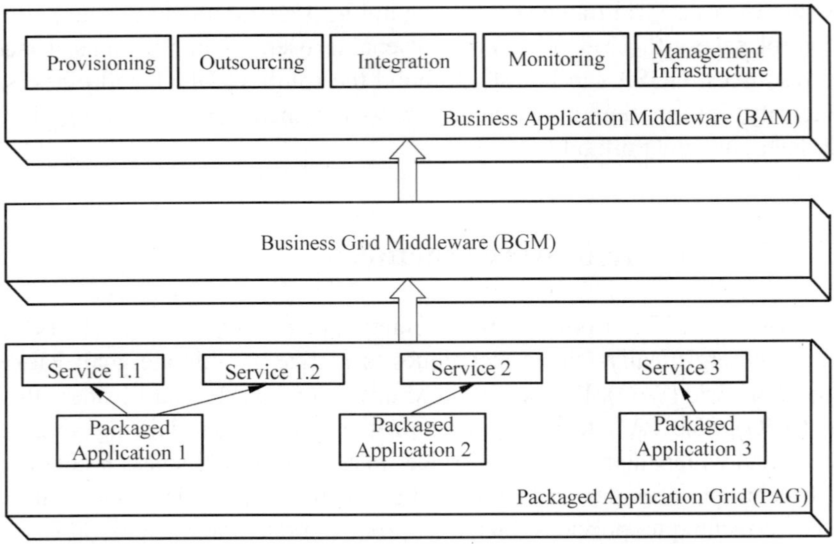

Figure 12.5 Logical Grid infrastructure

from the highly competitive petroleum business, whose companies are under pressure to reduce their IT costs. The petroleum exploration and production consume significant computer power. Moreover, the amount of data gathered during the exploration and production has grown dramatically over the past few years. Utilizing the PAG model and exploiting existing applications, the development cycle of a management software system for a gas company can be reduced from months or years to days or weeks.

However, a PAG may not work well on business processes requiring significant coordination work. For example, design collaborations among multiple organizations across country boundaries may not be easily solved by using PAGs alone.

12.4.2 Business Grid Middleware

Business Grid Middleware (BGM) aims to provide an IT-level infrastructure to support business applications. By IT-level, it means that the infrastructure provides component services to support the composition, submission, deployment, and management of business applications. Note that the infrastructure of BGM does not include the component services that implement concrete business functions, such as a credit card checking service and a shipping handling service.

A BGM typically needs to provide the following five key technologies: generic job support, job portability support, automatic deployment support, policy-based management, and interoperability. Generic job support provides a mechanism to enable a diversity of applications to run on the same Business Grid, such as interactive Web applications, traditional computational batch jobs, and legacy applications. Job portability support provides a standard archive format for job descriptions and utilizations. Automatic deployment support enables program and user data to be automatically deployed and configured. Policy-based management support provides self-healing and self-optimization management based on configurable policies. Interoperability support offers a mechanism to integrate a software component with existing middleware for commercial system management. Typically, a BGM can utilize the Open Grid Services Architecture (OGSA) to define standard interfaces for business application software.

12.4.3 Business Process Grid

The scope of a Business Process Grid (BPG) covers the business process provisioning and outsourcing, integration, collaboration, monitoring, and management infrastructure. Current research and work in this area stays at the business process level rather than at the IT level. In the near future, Business Process Grids will become the backbone for the next generation of business applications. In our view, Grids could potentially enhance the performance of systems for enterprise resource planning. They might also support systems that manage customer relationships, supply chains, partner relationships, and product lifecycles. Figure 12.5 shows the components and evolution of a Business Process Grid.

Example Business Process Grid

To better understand the concept of a Business Process Grid, let us consider the following scenario involving a chip manufacturer. The designers for the manufacturer intend to create a layout design in the headquarters, while the data design will come from its outsourced company #1. Meanwhile, the hardware testing will take place in its outsourced company #2, the simulations in its outsourced company #3; and finally the manufacturing in its outsourced company #4. In this scenario, each task is an integral part of a business process of the electronic chip design. Without the concept of Grid-enabled design collaboration, today's design team may have to synchronize its design versions by phone, e-mail, or instant messaging.

A BPG can step in and facilitate in automating the collaboration. The basic idea is to treat each design task as a Web service in a Grid environment and use a service flow description language, e.g., Business Process Execution Language (BPEL), to model the flow among different design tasks. WSDL and BPEL can be combined to create customized data entities, collaboration protocols, and dynamic scenario configurations. Grid Services Flow Language (GSFL)[10,11] is another option to model the business process flow in a Grid environment.

Workflow in a Business Process Grid

Workflow technology is a promising candidate for supporting a Grid services flow. However, traditional workflow is typically static, thus unable to exploit dynamic information from a Grid. In a Grid environment, it is thus necessary to develop a flow technology capable of adapting to dynamic Grid environments and ever-changing requirements of Grid applications.

Most existing work in this area is implementation specific and typically tailored to a particular Grid application. One evidence is that almost every existing major Grid project or Grid system creates its own flow language. GSF provides a standard platform-independent way to specify the flow of Grid services. Grid Service Flow Language (GSFL)[10] is an attempt to integrate efforts from the Grid computing, Web services, and workflow areas. Currently, it consists of four components: service providers, activity, composition, and lifecycle models.

With the introduction of the Web Service Resource Framework (WSRF)[5], the integration of Grid computing and Web services has reached an unprecedented level. WSRF has been considered as the foundation for the next generation of Grid services implementations. As a result, much of the work in Web services flow will greatly influence Grid services flow and the Business Process Grid. Eventually, Grid computing and SOA community will create one single services flow standard.

12.5 Business Grid Service Development and Invocation

Having discussed a Business Grid solution architecture, it is ready to discuss how to write a Business Grid service that is pluggable into the solution architecture. An example of a stock quote Grid service is used to facilitate discussions. As shown in Fig. 12.6, the original stock quote application is developed on a legacy

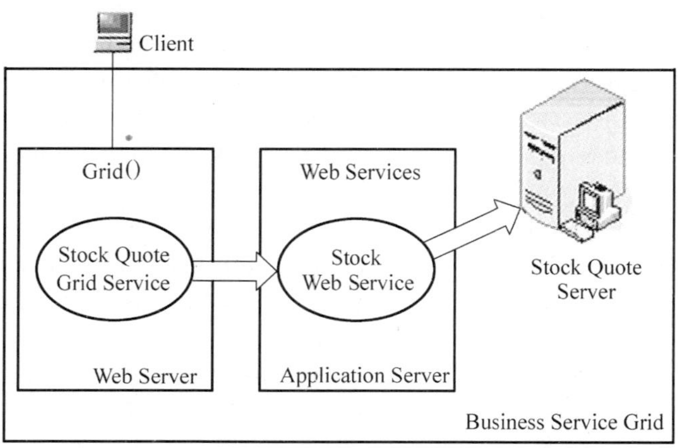

Figure 12.6 Business Grid development

server. It is then wrapped as a Web service and is deployed on an application server as a *stock Web service*. The Web service is then wrapped into a Grid service *stock quote Grid service* on a Web server where a client can access. As shown in Fig. 12.6, the business Grid hides the complexity of accessing a business Grid service.

12.6 Discussions on Business Grid

Grid computing provides a framework and deployment platform that enables resource sharing, accessing, aggregation, and management in a distributed computing environment based on system performance, QoS, as well as emerging open standards such as Web services. Existing Grid computing technologies take advantage of underused computing capacities to solve business problems and provide an IT-level infrastructure to support business applications. Business Grid relies on a solution architecture to enable resource sharing among collaborators in a secure and manageable fashion, based on both physical Grid and logical Grid.

12.7 Summary

In this chapter, we introduced the concept of Business Grid and the potential enhancement or directions for Grid computing. We also discussed one way to construct an infrastructure of a logical Grid, which relies on three techniques: Packaged Application Grid (PAG), Business Grid Middleware (BGM), and Business Process Grid (BPG).

References

[1] Zhang, LJ, Chung, JY, Zhou Q (2005) Developing Grid computing applications, part 1. http://www-128.ibm.com/developerworks/library/gr-grid1/

[2] Luo Z, Zhang J, Badia RM (2007) Service grid for business computing. In: Grid computational methods, WIT Press

[3] Open Grid Forum. http://www.ogf.org/

[4] Globus: OGSA —The Open Grid Services Architecture. http://www.globus.org/ogsa/

[5] (2004) Web Services Notification and Web Services Resource Framework (WSRF). http: //www-106.ibm.com/developerworks/webservices/library/ws-resource/

[6] http://www.ggf.org/documents/GFD.72.pdf

[7] Zhang LJ, Chao T, Chang H, Chung JY (2002) Automatic Method Signature Adaptation Framework for Dynamic Web Service Invocation. In: 6th World Multi Conference on Systemics, Cybernetics and Informatics (SCI 2002), pp 541 – 546

[8] Zhang LJ, Li H, Lam H (2004) Toward a Business Process Grid for Utility Computing. IT Professional 6: 62 – 64

[9] Zhang LJ, Zhou Q, Chung JY (2003) Develop grid computing applications: Introducing an architecture and toolkit for building Grid solutions. IBM DeveloperWorks Journal 10 – 15

[10] Krishnan S, Wagstrom P, von Laszewski G (2002) GSFL: A workflow framework for Grid Services, Technical Report, The Globus Project. http://www-unix.globus.org/cog/projects/workflow/gsfl-paper.pdf

[11] GSFL: a workflow framework for Grid services. http://www-unix.globus.org/cog/projects/workflow/

Part 3 Service Delivery and Services Engineering

13 Enterprise Modeling

13.1 Introduction

Why enterprise models are important? In general, there are two major reasons: the dynamics nature of service ecosystem that makes the modern business more sophisticated and the requirements from decision makers who ask for better internal communication.

13.1.1 Dynamics of Services Ecosystem

Nowadays the global business environment is under rapid change. For example, a lot of IT services have been outsourced from US to developing countries. An enterprise is not standalone anymore, it needs to collaborate with its partners, suppliers, and end users in the value chain environment. For example, in a typical IT service project, collaboration is needed from multiple service providers, such as hardware providers, middleware providers, Project Management Office (PMO) providers, and system integration providers.

There are lots of successful enterprises who have built very flexible and extensible IT platforms to support changing business models. In this section, Amazon.com is taken as an example.

Amazon.com[1], previously a recognized online book seller, has evolved its business model from an online retailer to a service provider for the retail industry-enabled by SOA and Web services technology. Its marketplace partner model is highly successful, with tens of thousands of subscribers to its Web services-enabled back-end interfaces. Now Amazon.com is providing end-to-end services to other retailers, running their entire on-line operations (including Web site, orders, and fulfillment). Amazon's three typical business models are summarized in Fig. 13.1.

Amazon's core platform is built for adapting changes of its business models. There are three major partnering business models: Transaction Partner, Marketplace Partner, and Platform Partner. Amazon's ecosystem includes these Amazon Partners (APs) supported by the Amazon platform. The following 4 types of role players are the active users of Amazon's platform:

Buyers—There are over 39 million active customer accounts;

Sellers—They are merchants who sell on the Amazon's platform. There are over 600,000 active seller accounts;

Web Site Owners (Associates) —They are people who own their Web sites and link to Amazon with referral fees. There are hundreds of thousands of associates;

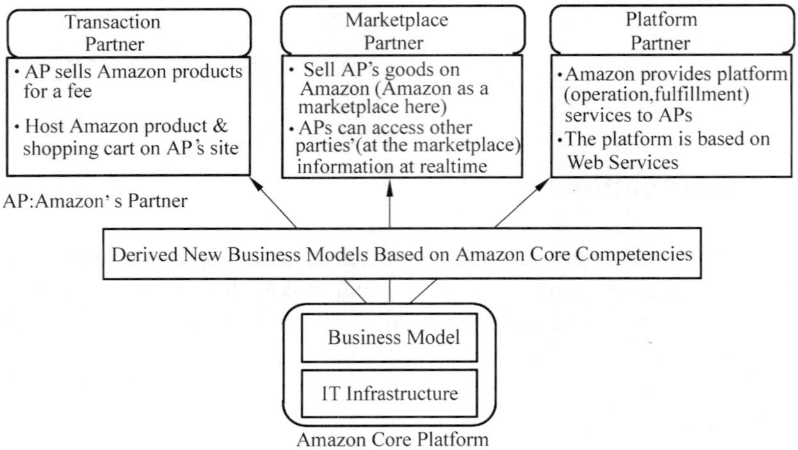

Figure 13.1 Business models of Amazon

Developers—They are people who use Amazon Web Services (AWS) to create applications and tools. There are over 50,000 registered developers.

AWS can be incorporated in an e-Commerce Web site at different levels:

- First is plugging-in a standard Amazon "mall." APs can earn commissions on selling standard Amazon product offerings.
- Second is customizing the Amazon "mall." APs support for co-branding, embedded search results, remote shopping, and customization of look- and-feel.
- Third is building a customized store. APs bundle their product offerings with Amazon's product offerings.
- Fourth is embedding Amazon product listings into APs' stores by conducting fine-grain integration in Web sites with support for automatic product categorization, addition, and update. For example, Web 2.0 and Really Simple Syndication (RSS) technology can be used to automatically update Amazon's product lists on APs' Web site.
- Fifth is flexible merchandising. Product content can be integrated into the look and design of APs' Web sites.
- Sixth is product search by enabling APs' visitors to conduct product searches within or across major product categories available at Amazon.com. Product search results can be embedded directly into APs' Web sites.
- Seventh is remote shopping cart by enabling APs' visitors to add products into the Amazon shopping cart while they shop on the APs' Web sites.

This flexible enablement platform for introducing new business models has demonstrated the value of SOA and Web services technology in building an adaptive service ecosystem for Amazon.com.

13.1.2 Requirements from Decision Makers

As shown in Fig. 13.2, there are different stakeholders in an enterprise. C-level management team (CEO/CIO/CFO) needs to be well communicated to better leverage resources and achieve business goals. Only with a common model can they communicate and do the impact analysis and then take actions. So the visibility control mechanism should be enabled for the C-level team to monitor and manage business operations in near real-time.

Different role players in an enterprise may wear colored glass or have biased thinking towards their own needs. Without an enterprise model, it is hardly to let the management team agree on how to execute the business strategy.

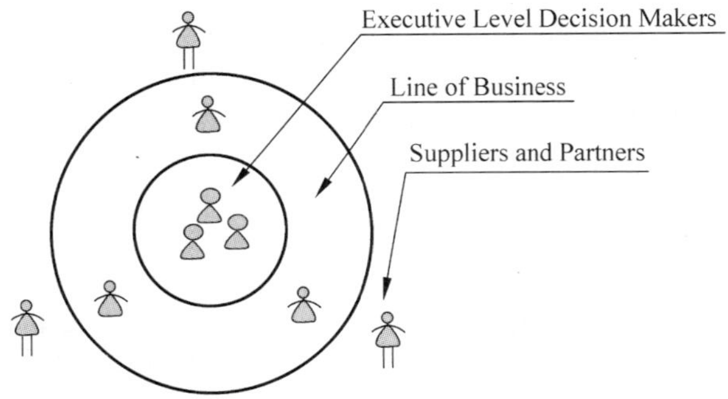

Figure 13.2 Complexity of decision making process in a service system

The C-level executives (e.g., CEO, CFO, CIO) within the first circle are a group of core decision makers. Their concerns include business strategy and plan, strategic partnership, IT strategy, enterprise management functions like human resource management, and adoption of new technology.

Most of the people within the second circle in an enterprise belong to a line of business. Their concerns include service delivery and operation and how to lead their businesses in the market.

Outside of second circle, there are suppliers and partners of the enterprise. Their concerns may include cost, delivery cycle, and Account Payable, Account Receivable (AP/AR). During their routine operations, these people seldom care other people's concern. There usually exists gaps between different business units (BUs). Enterprise modeling methodologies could facilitate better communication among different BUs and provide coherent business and IT governance. In this way, service resources could be best leveraged to meet the strategic business needs.

13.2 Methodologies for Enterprise Modeling

13.2.1 Balanced Scorecard and Strategy Map

Balanced Scorecard (BSC)

The original Balanced Scorecard (BSC) concept comes from Kaplan & Norton's book "*The Balanced Scorecard: Transforming Strategy into Actions*"[2] published in 1997. Then they further evolved their work into "Strategy Map" published in their book "*Strategy Maps*: *Converting Intangible Assets into Tangible Outcomes*".[3]

BSC was originally designed as a communication tool within an enterprise. Its purpose is to allow different group of people collaborate to work on different aspects of an enterprise, not only the financial aspect. It covers the balance of finance and non-finance factors, balance of near term and long term, as well as balance of tangible and intangible assets.

Specifically, BSC covers the following four perspectives: finance, customer, process, and innovation and growth. There are four items associated with each perspective: objectives, measurement, target, and initiatives. During the execution of a BSC, current status can be measured and compared with the target value.

Besides a communication tool, the execution of BSC is also a continuous improvement process. As shown in Fig. 13.3, the decision makers could study perspectives including finance, then customer, then process, and lastly innovation and growth. They can then adjust their assumptions and targets and run the whole process again, with possibly more people involved. BSC is a useful tool for business design in an iterative manner.

Items / Perspectives	Objectives	Measurement	Target	Initiatives
Finance				
Customer				
Process				
Innovation & Growth				

Figure 13.3 Balanced Scorecard model

Strategy Map

From their practices of using BSC in enterprises, Kaplan and Norton further improved their BSC method and reached a new version of BSC, which they call Strategy Map. It has two meanings. First, it is a map that has vertices and edges. Second, the map represents strategic level concerns. In a Strategy Map, a vertex represents an index of a concern in four perspectives, a directed edge (link) represents a link from influencing index (e.g., "Customer Satisfaction" in "Customer & Product" Perspective of Fig. 13.4) to impacted index (e.g., "Cost" in "Finance" Perspective of Fig. 13.4).

The Strategy Map in Fig. 13.4 has four perspectives namely Finance, Customer and Product, Process, and Innovation and Growth. They have the same meaning as in a Balanced Scorecard. What's different with those in a Balanced Scorecard is that a Causal Link (the line with an arrow) pointing from one index in a low level perspective to another index in a higher perspective clearly shows the cause of improving a Key Performance Indicator (KPI) of a component in a higher level. For example, in Fig. 13.4, we could understand that in order to improve performance of a "Call Center" business index, the company needs to improve the "Adopt New Technology" index and "Training" index. Similarly, in order to improve the performance of a "Product Portfolio" component, the company needs to improve "Front Desk" component and "Back Office" index. Further, in order to improve the performance of "Cost" index, meaning lower cost, the company needs to improve "Product Portfolio" index and "Customer Satisfaction" index.

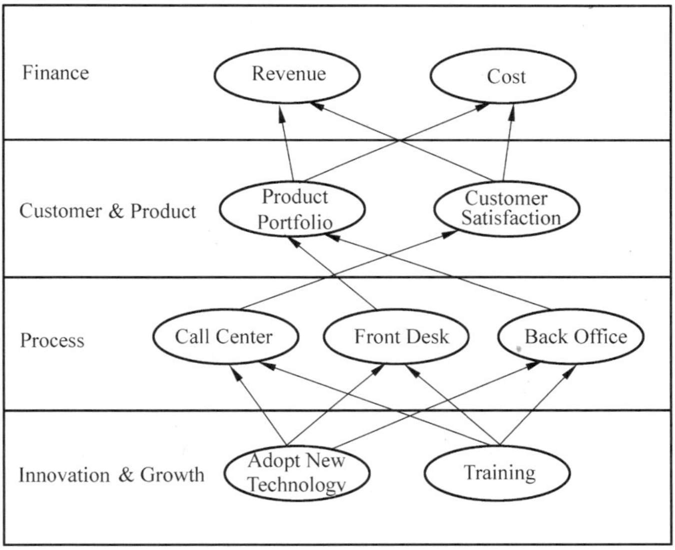

Figure 13.4 An example of Strategy Map

Align Operation with Business Design

Model-Driven Architecture (MDA)[4] is a useful approach in operation-level design methodology aiming at aligning IT modules with business initiatives. In Fig. 13.5, we show how to use MDA approach to model business contents in a strategy map. Since it is model-driven, the contents can be reused at operation level, even at implementation level.

As shown in Fig. 13.5, a strategy map may have several (usually four) "perspectives". The default perspectives are "Finance", "Customer & Product", "Process", and "Innovation & Growth". A perspective may consist of several "Scores" that have four attributes: "Objective", "Measurement", "Target", and "Initiative".

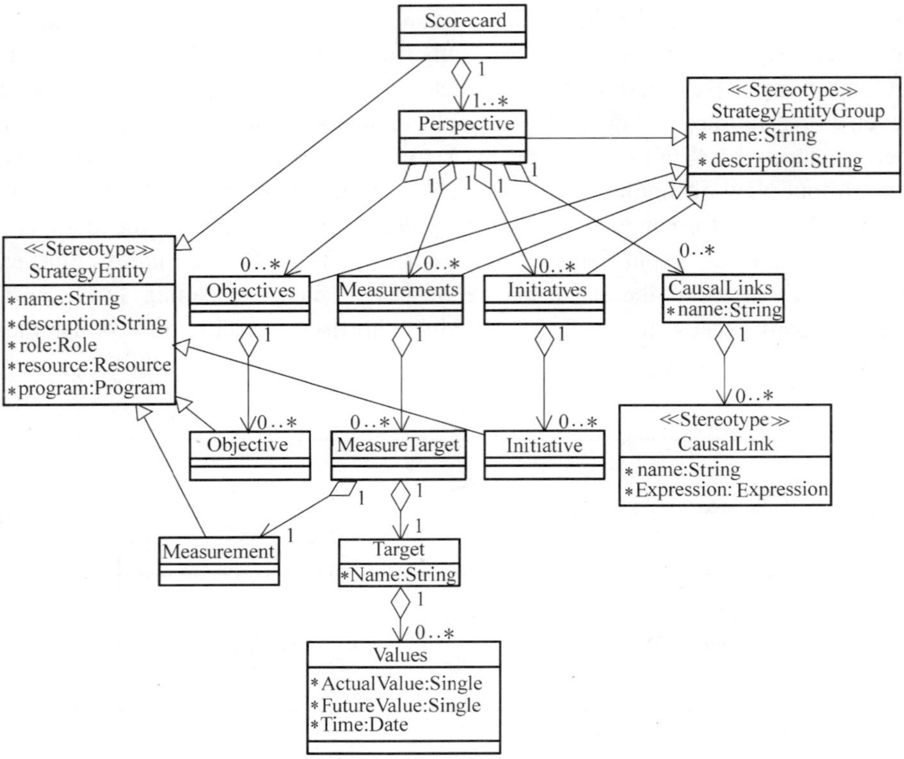

Figure 13.5 Strategy management metamodel for facilitating IT implementation and monitoring

"Objective" means the business goal of the Score to be measured. "Measurement" means the method of measuring the Score. A Measurement is typically associated with a predefined "Target", which should be realistic and workable. The "Target" is often associated with a predefined "Value". Lastly, a "Score" has its associated "Initiatives". "Initiatives" refer to possible actions or programs, which if executed are expected to improve the "Score". It is also reflected that BSC can be used as a method of "Transforming Strategy into Actions".

13.2.2 Component Business Modeling Circle

The Component Business Modeling Circle (CBMC) Method

The CBMC method is based on and extended from IBM Component Business Modeling (CBM) methodology[5−7] ,which is a consulting methodology invented by PwCC and now owned by IBM. The goals of CBM are three-fold. First is to keep people acting in different roles on the same page. From this perspective,

CBM is a communication tool among executives and LOB managers. Second, as a consulting tool, CBM could be used for gap analysis by providing insights for different components, such as which component is weak or which component should be improved. Third, the CBM (map) could be used as a starting point for analyzing how to align IT infrastructure and components with business components.

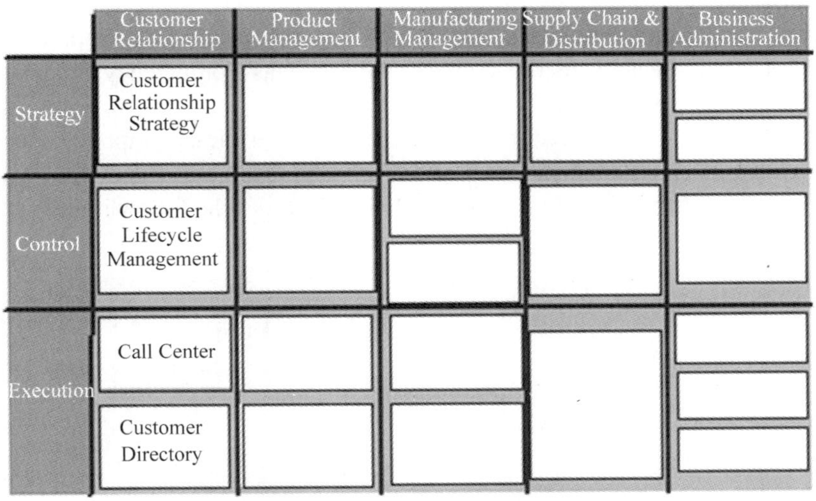

Figure 13.6 Component Business Model

As shown in Fig. 13.6, CBM is a method that captures the business components of an enterprise in a two-dimension map. There are three fixed rows in the map, namely "Strategy", "Control", and "Execution", respectively. They are actually three key phases in a service's life cycle. In addition, there could be different numbers of columns representing different groups of business functions. In the first column of the above example, under the umbrella of "Customer Relationship", three types of components deserve special attention.

First is the "Customer Relationship Strategy" component in the "Strategy" row. This component is a strategy-level function. It is usually a planning type of work executed by senior executives, who are experts of CRM and have experience of defining the roadmap and strategy of CRM.

Second is the "Customer Lifecycle Management" component in the "Control" row. This component is a control-level function. It is usually a control, monitoring, or managing type of work executed by specific roles, who are experts in controlling the results of execution of CRM (in the "Execution" row). They are responsible for ensuring that the execution is aligned with the defined plan or strategy.

Third are the "Call Center" and the "Customer Directory" components. These are operation-level components executed by operation-level roles. For example, a

"Call Center" component can be executed by Call Center operators, and a "Customer Directory" component is executed by people who are responsible for managing (adding/deleting/merging) customer directory.

The value of CBM is to create many predefined CBM maps for different industries. For decision makers of an enterprise or for an individual consultant, the CBM map can be customized to fit the needs of business design of that enterprise.

After the components are grouped into the two-dimension map, there are different ways to analyze the components, such as competency analysis and value/cost analysis, as shown in Fig. 13.7.

CBMC method introduced in this book takes the business components as input to perform business analysis and produce high-level constructs for business services. As shown in Fig. 13.7, CBMC Method includes the following five steps.

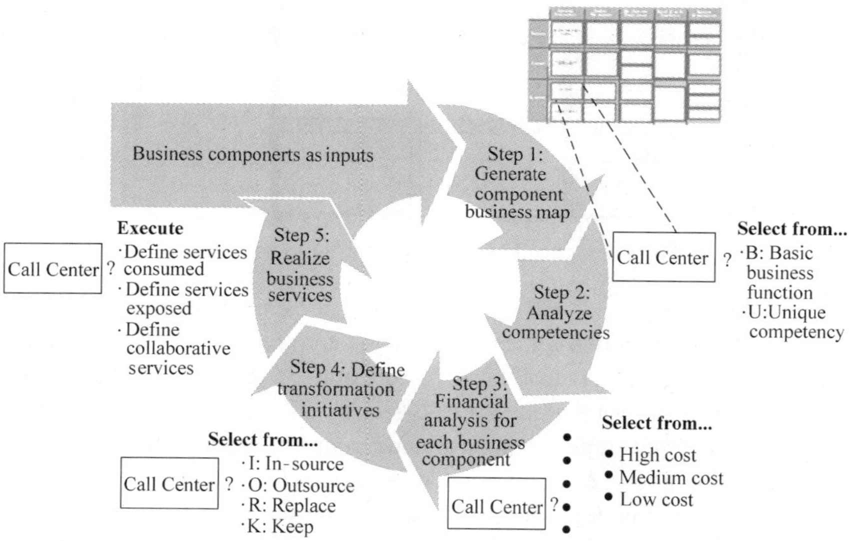

Figure 13.7 Component Business Model Circle (CBMC)

Step 1: Generate Component Business Map

In this step, all information related to the business components is collected and grouped into table-like categories, based on the Component Business Model (CBM) or other enterprise componentization techniques.

Step 2: Analyze Competencies

In this step, an analysis of an enterprise's core competency is performed, as shown in Fig. 13.7. The components are categorized into two types: *basic competency* and *unique competency*. A basic type of component means that the enterprise's capability of the component is below the average of industry standard. A unique type of component means that the enterprise's capability of the component is above average of the industry standard and has competitive capability. With the fast evolving service ecosystem, there's no need, if not impossible, for an enterprise to own all capabilities of functions of an enterprise. Instead, they usually partner with other parties to provide the best services to their customers in an integrated manner.

Step 3: Conduct Financial Analysis for Each Business Component

In this step, financial analysis is carried out. Besides capability analysis for the business components, cost/value analysis is also useful. Every component is executed by some human resources leveraging physical resources which may trigger cost changes. Capital/Cost analysis in Fig. 13.7 is such a method that intends to identify the business components that introduce high capital or high cost. Then actions could be taken to optimize the capital/cost structure of an enterprise to make the overall service system efficient.

Step 4: Define Transformation Initiatives

In this step, transformation decisions are made on the business initiatives. This step takes a transformation view to identify business components that are critical for optimizing the service system and need to be transformed. There are four transformation options: *outsource*, *in-source*, *replace*, and *keep*. *Outsource* means that the component is not highly critical; thus, it could be outsourced to some third parties with the same or lower cost. *In-source* means that the component is running quite efficient and could be scaled out to support more volumes of transactions or operations. *Replace* means that the component cannot meet business needs; thus, it should be replaced with some new functions, e.g., by leveraging innovative IT infrastructure. *Keep* means that the original business component should be kept unchanged in a certain time frame.

Step 5: Realize Business Services

Business services should be considered to implement business components. In this step, potential services to be collaborated or consumed should be identified. Then the service interfaces for the business service should be defined. The low-level message specification and linkage with IT-enabled services can be further explored by leveraging Web services technology.

CBMC Maturity Model

Besides the CBMC method, a maturity model is created to describe the current and future maturities of business components. As shown in Fig. 13.8, it is a visual approach to quickly understand the current status of the enterprise and to which direction it should go.

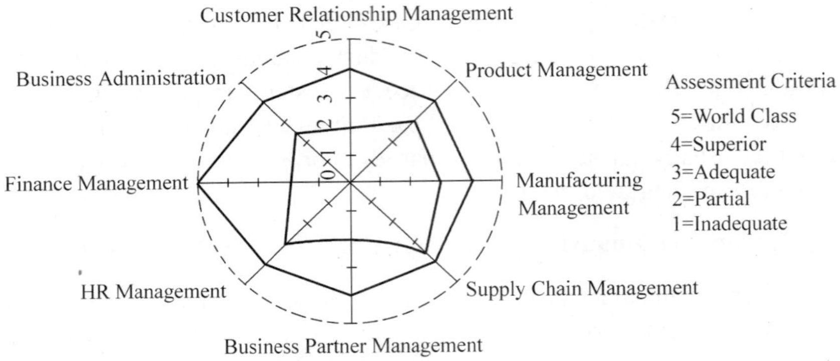

Figure 13.8 CBMC maturity model

As could be seen in Fig. 13.8, the inner polygon in the dashed circle represents current (As Is) maturity levels of different business functions, while the outer polygon represents future (To Be) maturity levels of different business functions. The maturity levels will be rated from "1" (meaning lowest, or inadequate) to "5" (meaning highest, or World Class). This representation could help the decision makers to understand where the biggest gaps lie and the direction of future improvements.

Componentization Roadmap

In a real-life scenario, customers should adopt relevant entries according to the enterprise's maturity, which we call componentization roadmap[8].

As shown in Fig. 13.9, a customer should take a relevant entry point based on its status and needs. There are 4 stages of service-oriented transformation for an enterprise: individual Web services implementation, service-oriented business integration, enterprise wide transformation, and value-chain level collaboration. The detailed stages are described below.

Stage 1: An enterprise may decide to migrate parts of its service to the SOA infrastructure, starting from individual business components that are more independent. Through this step, the enterprise could accumulate experiences for the next step.

Stage 2: This step concentrates on the integration of services enabled in Stage 1. More services are moved to the SOA architecture to enable the integration of business functions.

Stage 3: All initiatives should be aligned with real business priorities. The enterprise has well-defined enterprise architecture in an SOA environment. There is seldom any silo within the enterprise. The enterprise becomes more adaptive and customer-oriented.

Stage 4: The service-oriented integration and collaboration now extends to third parties who have business partnership with the enterprise. This makes the enterprise more flexible in the service chain, and become more adaptable for business dynamics.

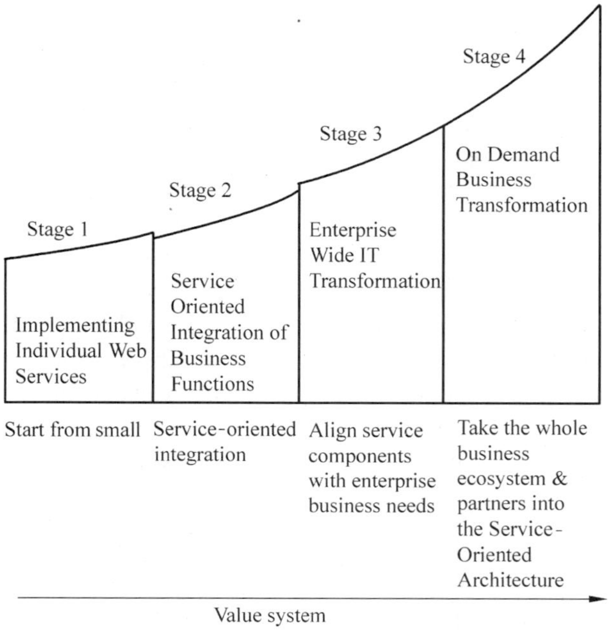

Figure 13.9 Service transformation maturity reference model

The purpose of this book is to provide an insight on how to align IT innovations and technologies with business dynamics. Too often are IT people focus only on IT itself. CBM and Componentization Roadmap could provide an insight on the current status and the future trends of business components, business services, and their current maturity stage. Actually, from business point of view, not all business components are necessarily to be developed in-house. As could be seen from Amazon's expandable business models, some of the business components could be realized by integrating software services into the overall SOA-based enterprise solutions. In addition, some of the business components can be outsourced.

CBM, together with Componentization Roadmap and CBMC, could be leveraged to help communication among business executives and CIOs, so that they could define a proper agenda towards SOA and adaptive business.

13.2.3 Enterprise Architecture

Enterprise Architecture Method

In this section, we will discuss another important enterprise modeling tool: Enterprise Architecture (EA)[9]. Conceptually, EA can be envisioned as an analog to a city plan that consists of five key elements: the principles of how to use the lands, the layout of the roads, the design of utility infrastructure, the rules of dividing the zones, and the governance through hierarchical commissions and elected officials. Without such a plan, a city cannot be constructed as expected if not in a mass.

Similarly, without a well-defined architecture, integrating services may cause them unworkable. Without a well-defined architecture, any, even little, future change may bring about significant cost and may influence other parts of a service system that is unexpected. EA is a method that ensures IT-based business solutions to be compliant with business strategies generated from CBM.

EA has been well leveraged in a lot of large-scale projects and programs management and transition process. A successful example of application of EA is the Federal Enterprise Architecture (FEA)[10], an extension of the core EA concept in the e-Government area. Another example of using and extending the EA concept is US Treasury Enterprise Architecture Framework (TEAF)[11]. A high-level flow of execution of EA in Telecommunication Industry is shown in Fig. 13.10.

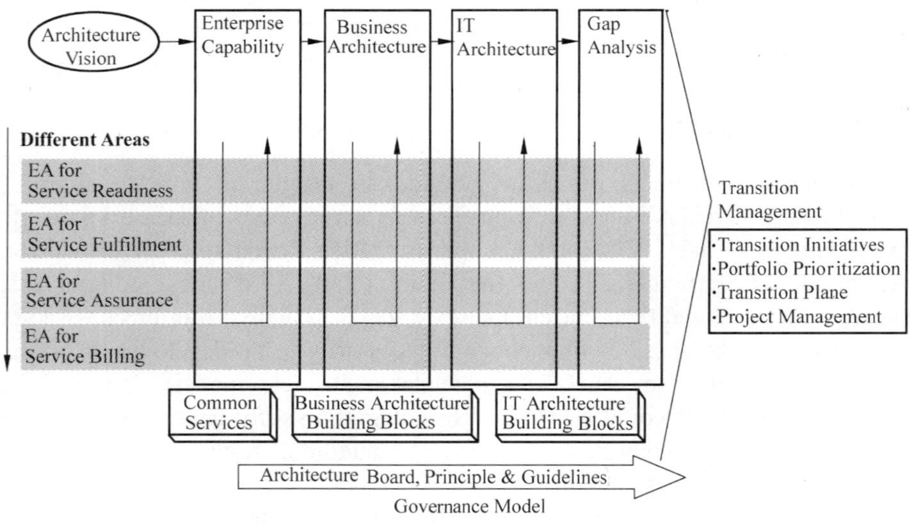

Figure 13.10 Enterprise Architecture methodology

This is a modified EA based on Open Group Architecture Framework[12] and eTOM[13]. EA method is represented in a two-dimension chart. The horizontal dimension represents EA design phases with a governance model supervising all phases. The vertical dimension represents important areas in the business of an enterprise which are customer facing, e.g., Service Fulfillment, Service Assurance, and Service Billing. Within each step of the EA process, multiple iterations may be needed, taking various areas into consideration.

As shown in Fig. 13.10, EA methodology covers three perspectives: architecture, governance, and transition. In the architecture phase, both business architecture and IT architecture should be well designed and balanced. In the governance phase, a steering committee and a governance board (i.e., with enough authority) should be formed to monitor and manage the overall execution of EA methodology. Overall design or change needs to be agreed upon by a certain number of stakeholders. In the transition phase, transformation initiatives should be identified after the EA activities have been finished.

In detail, EA could be realized in the following six steps.

In Step 1, the architecture vision (i.e., which direction the enterprise should go to) should be defined.

In Step 2, the "Enterprise Capability" should be identified, which includes agreed vision, core competencies of the enterprise, and competency enabler. The outcome of this step is a set of common services.

In Step 3, the "Business Architecture" should be defined, which includes business roles, business processes, enterprise information, and process/data usage. The outcome of this step is a set of business architecture building blocks.

In Step 4, the "IT Architecture" should be defined, which includes application functions (or application packages/components), data stores, user groups, and technology framework. The outcome of this step is a set of IT architecture building blocks.

In Step 5, with analysis results from the previous steps, gap analysis should be conducted, which includes business gap analysis, IT gap analysis, and architecture assessment.

Within each of these steps, one needs to completely cover different service areas of the business, e.g., Service Readiness, Service Fulfillment, Service Assurance, and Service Billing. All the steps may involve different roles to keep a consistent view and reach real common building blocks in each phase of EA. Therefore, a common agreed-upon governance model is important to ensure that end-to-end EA could be executed. After Step 5, one should obtain a business architecture and IT architecture, together with common building blocks and gaps.

In Step 6, the transformation initiatives should be derived and "transition management" should be conducted. The activities within transition management include: identifying transition initiatives, prioritizing portfolio, defining transition plan, and managing projects.

After the six steps, the mission of EA is completed. Then one can start project-phase activities.

The Trend: Service-Oriented Enterprise Architecture

The integration of EA and SOA is not a fad but rather a foundation. Although EA has been developed for quite some time while Web services and SOA are emerging open standards, the core of EA is to define architectural models of an enterprise to meet requirements of future changes in the most efficient and planned manner. Therefore, governance models, principles, and building blocks are the most visible concepts in EA. Meanwhile, SOA represents the latest evolution of open standards and technology in terms of interoperability. SOA has potential to complement and improve EA from the following five perspectives.

First, open standards of SOA could enable interoperability of applications from different service providers. Second, the architecture in SOA could enable EA business and IT architectures, by providing SOA patterns and industry best practices. As a result, the enterprises could speed up their paces of migrating to service-oriented enterprises. Third, SOA-compliant service building blocks could be reused or easily selected or bought from third parties who could provide better or the most relevant service components. SOA-compliant feature enables these building blocks to be easily plugged into the overall SOA architecture of an enterprise. Fourth, SOA provides a unified foundation for migration from legacy systems to a consistent service-oriented framework. Fifth, the common data format and metadata schemas could provide the basis for the EA data architecture.

The goal of using SOA to enable EA is to make EA more executable, while EA makes SOA more manageable and organized.

13.2.4 Relationships Between Enterprise Models and Business Process Transformation Model

Business and IT componentization can facilitate in reaching the snapshot of an enterprise and the understanding of their current status. However, components without interaction could only show *static* views. In any business, it is people who run the business and provide services by leveraging IT innovations. Typically, the services are provided through some business processes aggregated by usable services. Therefore, these relationships form a *dynamic* view, which contains interactions among different role players.

For an enterprise under business transformation, the next step after reaching enterprise models is to analyze its business process transformation models. The decision makers could capture their current "AsIs" business processes, compare with industry best practices, and analyze where the bottlenecks are. Then they could depict the vision of future or ideal business processes "ToBe" to perform gap analysis, and then find the roadmap to future status.

With the evolution of SOA, these tasks do not have to be done from scratch. Instead, the dynamic views of the enterprises (e.g., the business processes) could now be described using a process flow language such as Business Process Execution Language (BPEL) to quickly create a version. This change allows ideas from business people to be quickly transferred to IT people. IT people could, in turn, transfer these ideas as requirements to third-party service providers, who may use different process tools but adopt process representation standards such as BPEL.

Besides the benefits of dynamics and model-based capturing of business process, business process transformation models (e.g., using BPEL) also provide a possibility to conduct simulation before a business process is actually implemented. This feature further lowers the risk of business transformation.

13.3 Discussions on Enterprise Modeling

In the past several years, SOA was usually viewed interchangeably with Web services that is technology oriented; IT investment was often initiated from a specific department without a complete view of the strategies of the entire enterprise. At present, more and more people have recognized that the key objective of SOA is how to enable new business models under open environment using IT innovations. SOA should be business driven instead of IT driven. Meanwhile, SOA implementation typically requires collaboration from different stakeholders. Enterprise modeling has thus become a highly practical and important step of business design before making any large IT investment. Enterprise modeling methods can help business executives and business analysts face these challenges, by improving communication among stakeholders through showing different perspectives of the business for different people.

Enterprise modeling has been evolving from intangible approaches to more tangible approaches. Enterprise modeling methods are currently leveraging service-oriented and component-based concepts. Challenges will remain, e.g., how to reuse knowledge of subject matter experts of enterprise modeling in new projects instead of building everything from scratch. Moreover, the current practices of enterprise modeling are still document based. In the future, we expect to see more structured representation of business knowledge and structured representation of enterprise modeling in software tools.

13.4 Summary

Enterprise Modeling methods are important in the filed of Services Computing, because they are the initial steps to make IT investment align with business evolution through service-oriented componentization. There are many examples showing that huge investments on IT projects may not necessarily bring expected business impacts. The reason often comes from a lack of alignment between IT investment and business needs. Enterprise Modeling methods are key methods to enable a complete view on all perspectives of an enterprise using business-driven approach.

The evolution of enterprise modeling methods, together with evolution of SOA modeling and design methods, could enable modeling and designing from perspectives of business and IT componentization. In this way, business people and IT people could have clear and common understanding of the "AsIs" and

"ToBe" status of the enterprise, and be aware of the roadmap toward SOA-compliant architecture.

References

[1] Amazon Web Services. http://www.amazon.com/webservices/

[2] Kaplan RS, Norton DP (1996) The balanced scorecard: translating strategy into action. Harvard Business School Press

[3] Kaplan RS, Norton DP (2004) Strategy maps: converting intangible assets into tangible outcomes. 1st edn. Harvard Business School Press

[4] MDA (Model Driven Architecture). http://www.omg.org/mda/

[5] Cherbakov L, Galambos G, Harishankar R, Kalyana S, Rackham G (2005) Impact of service orientation at the business level. IBM System Journal 44: 653 – 668

[6] Hernandez, Hector (2004) Service Oriented Architecture enables On Demand (CBM method). http://www.websphere.org/docs/presentations/SOA_Overview-Principles72404.ppt

[7] Giangarra P (2004) Practical experiences with SOA. http://www.softwaresummit.com/2004/speakers/GiangarraPracticalSOA.pdf

[8] IGS Component Business Model (CBM). http://www.seasim.org/archive/sim05b2005.pdf

[9] Alexander G, Vincent K, Oleksiak A (2005) Transformational techniques in the journey toward shared IT services. http://www.showcaseontario.com/2005/Presentations/Sept20_FW34_Trans%20Techniques.pdf

[10] Federal Enterprise Architecture. http://www.whitehouse.gov/omb/egov/a-1-fea.html

[11] (2000) Treasury Enterprise Architecture Framework. http://www.eaframeworks.com/TEAF/teaf.doc

[12] The Open Group Architecture Framework (TOGAF). http://www.opengroup.org/togaf/

[13] The Enhanced Telecom Operations Map (eTOM). http://www.tmforum.org/browse.aspx?catID = 1648

14 Project Based Enterprise Performance Management

14.1 Changes of Enterprise Operational Views

According to Goyette and Lamar[1], "an enterprise involves an amalgamation of interdependent resources (including people, processes, facilities, and technologies) organized to obtain a strategic advantage in support of mission or business objectives." One can see that the operational model of a modern enterprise has become significantly different than that of a traditional enterprise. The major cause is that enterprises have to survive unprecedented challenges, such as fluctuating market environments, world-wide competition, ever-changing customer requirements, increasingly demanded collaborations across enterprise boundaries, and disruptive technologies.

Figure 14.1 illustrates the organizational view of a traditional large enterprise, which comprises multiple functional departments, such as *Human Resource Department*, *Marketing Department*, and *Business Development Department*. Each of these departments runs its own business processes for its daily operations. For example, the *Business Development Department* uses five business processes (*new product development, customer relationship management, industry solutions, supply chain management,* and *IT support*); the *Marketing Department* uses three business processes (*customer relationship management, industry solutions,* and *IT support*). These business processes do not share with each other. As shown in Fig. 14.1, all four departments have their own business process *IT support*, meaning that they hire their own dedicated IT personnel. These IT people only work for the corresponding departments, no matter whether there are projects at a moment. In addition, the interactions and collaborations between these individual business processes are light. In other words, a traditional large enterprise adopts a single-dimensional operational model, which apparently bears low reusability, efficiency, and flexibility.

A modern enterprise typically adopts a two-dimension operational infrastructure. As shown in Fig. 14.2, a well-functioning, comprehensive enterprise is organized along two dimensions: a vertical (or physical or organization) dimension and a horizontal (or conceptual or business process) dimension.

Along the vertical dimension, an enterprise is divided into multiple physical divisions or departments, such as *Business Development Department*, *Marketing Department*, *Development Department*, and *Human Resource Department*. Each department acts as an individual entity in the boundary of the enterprise and

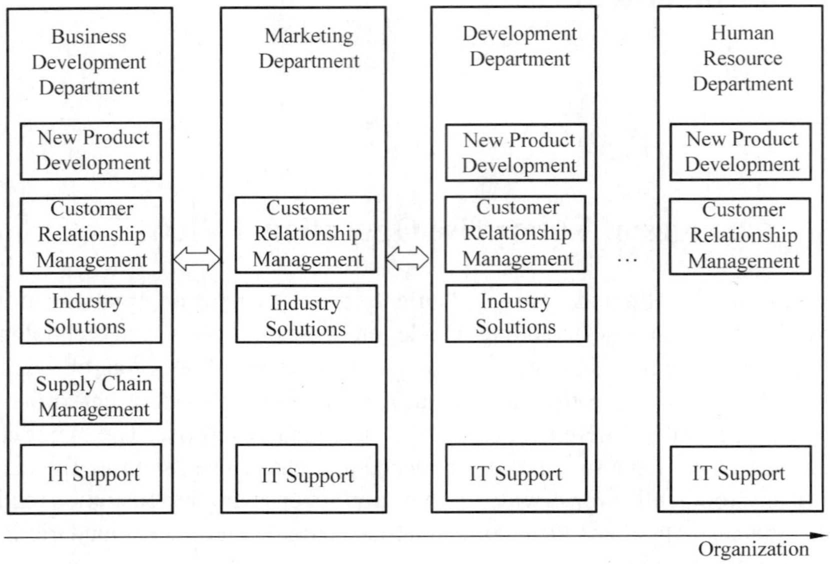

Figure 14.1 Single-dimensional organizations of a traditional enterprise

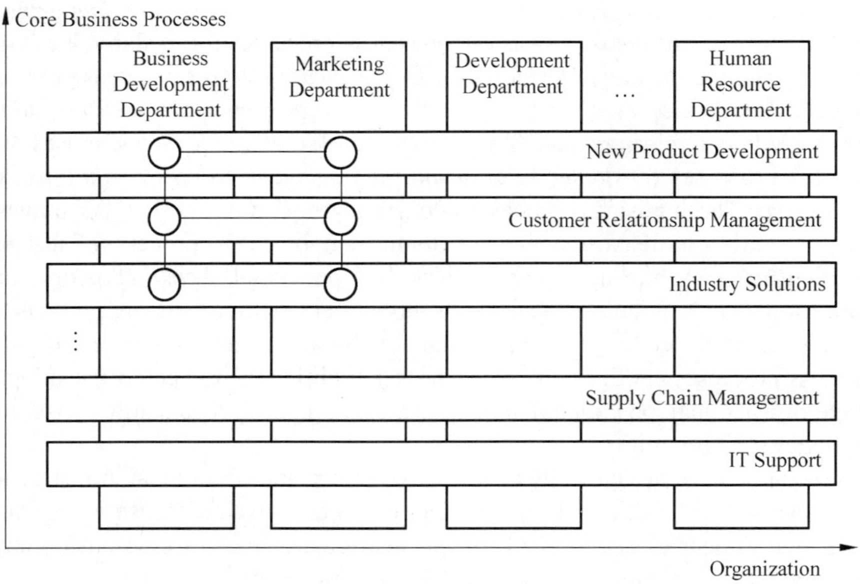

Figure 14.2 Business value network in a modern enterprise

interacts with other entities. It should be noted that in a modern enterprise, different business departments may reside at different physical locations. In addition, one department may in turn be divided into sub-departments and span cross multiple locations.

Along the conceptual dimension, various business solutions and business processes are identified to embody concrete business values. Typical business processes are *New Product Development*, *Customer Relationship Management* (*CRM*), *Industry Solutions*, *Supply Chain Management* (*SCM*), and so forth. As shown in Fig. 14.2, unlike in a traditional large enterprise, these core business processes are normally executed and shared across multiple departments within the enterprise as well as outside of the enterprise. For example, as illustrated in Fig. 14.2, the previously department-oriented IT teams are integrated as an integrated IT supporting team working for the whole enterprise. When departments submit requests for a project, high-level analysis and assessment are conducted to prioritize the projects and assign IT resources to them accordingly.

In addition, different departments may require interactions between them. For example, in order to better plan marketing strategies, the *Marketing Department* needs to keep track of the latest product information from the *Development Department*. These interactions are carried out by corresponding business processes. In summary, a business process may involve multiple business departments, and an individual department may be involved in multiple business processes. As a result, business departments and business processes synergistically intermingle together to form a business value network as shown in Fig. 14.2. Such a network exhibits a stable, flexible, and extensible structure that often undergoes dynamic environmental changes.

14.2 Overview of Project Management

As shown in Fig. 14.2, a modern enterprise is comprised of a comprehensive operational view, which requires effective and efficient management. Among other essential perspectives, project management occupies a critical position in the establishment and operation of a business value network. The reason is that any business activity and process is carried out through ongoing projects, and the implementation and realization of an enterprise-level IT project has to be supervised and conveyed by project management methodologies to achieve strategic alignment. By clearly planning and precisely tracking projects, businesses can respond with greater agility to the demands of an ever-changing business environment. As a result, project management has been widely considered as an imperative function in any business organization. It has been successfully applied in various domains and industries, such as aircraft design, software development, services delivery, solution development, and government programs. Project management covers the entire lifecycle of an IT project, including initialization, planning, execution, monitoring and controlling, and closing.

It should be noted that this chapter focuses on project management from IT perspective. Project management can also be examined from business perspective, where two handbooks are well known: "*A Guide to the Project Management Body of Knowledge* (*PMBOK Guide*)" by US Project Management Institution (PMI)[2] and "*PRINCE, Projects in Controlled Environments*"[3] from UK Office of Government Commerce (OGC).

There are multiple frameworks to enable project management by guiding project team and minimizing project risk, such as Rational Unified Process (RUP)[4]. Created by the Rational Software Corporation that is now a division of IBM, RUP defines a stepwise, formal, and iterative software development process oriented to large-scale projects.

According to RUP, a software development lifecycle is comprised of iterative development cycles, which is in turn divided into four phases delimited by corresponding milestones (i.e., deliverables): *inception phase*, *elaboration phase*, *construction phase*, and *transition phase*. The goal of an inception phase is to establish business cases, including business contexts, success factors, and financial forecasts. The goal of an elaboration phase is to complete problem domain analyses and obtain an undeveloped form of the project architecture. The goal of a construction phase is to develop required software components and features through construction iterations. The goal of the transition phase is to deliver the products to end users, train the end users on how to use the products, and validate the products against the quality requirements set in the inception phase.

RUP identifies a set of roles in the lifecycle of a software project development, such as *software architect*, *business process analyst*, *systems analyst*, *integrator*, *test manager*, *test designer*, and *project manager*. Each role is associated with a list of clearly defined behaviors and responsibilities in the phases of a software development lifecycle.

RUP is considered as a unified methodology, mainly because it fully incorporates with a formal standard designing and modeling language: *Unified Modeling Language* (*UML*)[5]. UML defines a set of diagrams: *use case diagram, class diagram, sequence diagram, activity diagram, interaction diagram, deployment diagram, package diagram, and collaboration diagram.* These diagrams enable visual modeling of a software system from different perspectives in a standard manner.

There exist many project management software and service providers, such as Microsoft Office Project[1] and Rational Portfolio Manager[1]. A major goal of Project Management software or online service is to help project managers and members in developing plans, assigning resources, monitoring progresses, managing budgets, and analyzing workloads. Resource management is emphasized in the lifecycle of a project; these resources include people resources (e.g., developers), hardware resources (e.g., devices), and abstract resources (e.g., time, calendar). Most of the Project Management software and online services adopt role-based access control strategy on resources.

14.3 Enterprise Performance Management (EPM)

In the context of a modern project that may comprise a variety of data, resources, and protocols within and across organizational boundaries, traditional project management (PM) is facing new challenges. How to integrate business requirement data, project data, project progress, and resources information into one single managed environment, while allowing decision makers to monitor the progress in real time to adjust decisions dynamically with visibility control? Furthermore, as shown in Fig. 14.2, in order to exploit limited resources to the largest extent, modern enterprises widely adopt business value networks, which demand unprecedented interaction and collaboration among company-wide projects. In other words, a new methodology is needed to coordinate and handle a set of projects in the context of an enterprise for the best performance. In addition, most of the enterprises are project-based businesses. The overall performance of an enterprise is measured by the results of involved projects. Therefore, the term *Enterprise Performance Management* (*EPM*) was coined to address the management of project-based businesses.

14.3.1 Concept of EPM

The major concerns about the EPM are "the integration of planning, strategy, resource allocation, and architecture management to achieve the best value to the enterprise." EPM clearly opens a new market[6,7].

14.3.2 EPM Framework

Figure 14.3 illustrates a typical EPM framework. It shows how an EPM framework assists an enterprise in originating and fulfilling its business goals to the largest extent. As shown in Fig. 14.3, the EPM framework depicts the execution procedure of an EPM process: from the formation of an idea, to the origination of initiatives, to the realization by the IT department. The left-hand side illustrates the different roles involved in an EPM process, while the right-hand side illustrates each role's core actions and responsibilities. As shown in Fig. 14.3, an enterprise-level project is comprised of four phases. A project starts from its C-level executives (e.g., CEO or CTO), who define the missions and business objectives. This first phase stays at a strategy level. Then the C-level executives pass the project to Line of Business (LOB) managers (e.g., division manager, IT manager, and policy makers), who are typically domain experts. In this phase, the LOB managers transform the business strategies into business initiatives and submit them to some specific committees. The business initiatives are then transformed into IT requirements and passed to the IT department, which assesses and prioritizes the requirements, creates a project if necessary, and assigns project managers to manage the project. A group of projects form a project portfolio. A project management office (PMO) is created to coordinate among projects. Therefore, it is project managers and PMO's responsibilities to create, manage, and balance project portfolios in the third phase. In this phase, PMO also needs to fully utilize and well organize enterprise-wide available IT resources, including analysts, developers, and testers. In the last phase or realization phase, IT engineers develop software to fulfill the requirements of the projects.

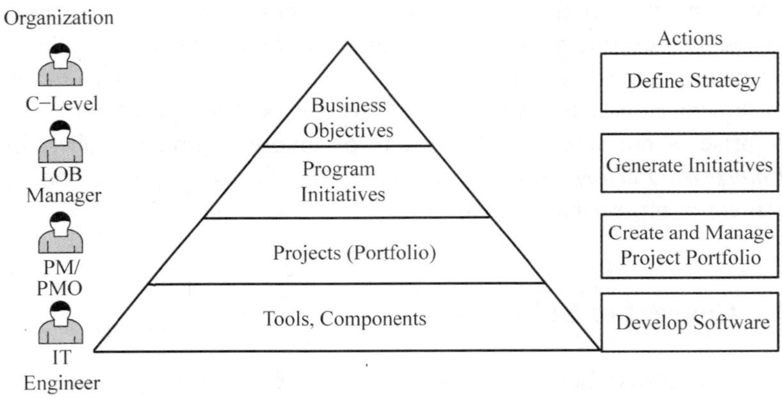

Figure 14. 3 EPM framework (business view)

As shown in Fig. 14.3, an EPM process forms a pyramidal structure, meaning that the ultimate goal of EPM is to realize the business objectives of the enterprise. In other words, an EPM process intends to fulfill these objectives through business-level strategy management, program management, and project management. In addition, the pyramidal structure of an EPM process implies the increase of the number of resources (i.e., people) involved in different phases. The top-down execution model also refers to a process from a strategy level to a detailed implementation level; different roles interactively perform EPM actions.

14.3.3 From Project Management to Enterprise Portfolio Management

As shown in Fig. 14.3, EPM differentiates from the traditional PM in many perspectives. The traditional project management contains only part of the third layer and the fourth (lowest) layer of the pyramidal EPM layers. PM focuses on individual projects: their management and development. EPM needs to consider all enterprise-wide projects. In other words, PM stands at project level, while

EPM stands at enterprise or project portfolio level.

In addition, traditional PM starts after a to-go decision has been made for a project; it refers to a process to ensure the realization of the project, from its conceptual modeling to its implementation and development. On the other hand, EPM starts from a high-level proposal, which needs to be assessed and may or may not lead to one or more projects. In other words, PM addresses an isolated project; EPM addresses projects in the context of an enterprise, which involves many more concerns such as resource coordination between projects.

Furthermore, EPM focuses on business strategies and decision making process, while PM focuses on the planning and tracking of tasks. Traditional project management aims at fulfilling project objectives; EPM aims at fulfilling enterprise objectives.

Moreover, unlike traditional project management being originated by project managers, EPM is originated by C-level executives of an enterprise. Traditional PM typically involves project managers and engineers only; EPM involves C-level executives and LOB managers in addition to project managers and engineers.

In summary, PM can be considered as part of the last step of EPM. After a project is formed, PM can be plugged in and handle IT and workflow-related tasks. In order to allow enterprises manage company-wide projects, traditional PM tools have been extended into EPM tools, including RUP and some project management tools in the market.

14.4 Service-Oriented Enterprise Project Management

14.4.1 EPM toward SOA

As shown in Fig. 14.3, an effective and efficient EPM framework is required to apply the pyramidal EPM layers to the business value network of an enterprise. In order to capture the profound activities crossing different layers of EPM and seamlessly communicate with all components in the value chain network, it is necessary to integrate businesses with IT properties.

Due to the diverse nature of business enterprises, there is apparently no uniform way to capture the capabilities of each internal business department, summarize business requirements of each core business process, composed business processes or activities, and formalize policies in a business value network. Instead, in the lifecycle of an EPM process, all related resources will be dynamically allocated based on the corresponding project goals, budgets, schedules, statuses, and exceptions. Meanwhile, each formed project typically is associated with a specific internal business organization, which is located at a specific geographical site. A project may contain one or more tasks that can be assigned to internal organizations or outsourced to other organizations in other enterprises. Thus,

EPM further requires coordination between internal or external organizations either collocated or not. In short, how to dynamically manage and coordinate a diverse variety of resources in EPM is a critical challenge.

These new challenges to EPM pose new requirements of integrating business with IT properties. By proposing a standard-based interface description language and communication protocol, the emerging paradigm of Services Computing has become the most promising technology to address the IT interoperability issue in heterogeneous environments, including different platforms and programming languages. This concept sheds a light on EPM by treating all components including resources, both at the business level or IT level, as “services”. Therefore, all activities can be captured and operated in a standard way.

In order to pursue flexibility, extensibility, and re-configurability, the EPM methodologies and tools need to move toward SOA. The EPM framework shown in Fig. 14.3 is thus turned into Fig. 14.4. The difference is on the right-hand action side. SOA enables all EPM-related activities, from low-level software development, to project and portfolio management, to high-level enterprise initiatives and strategies establishment. This SOA enablement leads to a systematic engineering methodology as *SOA engineering*.

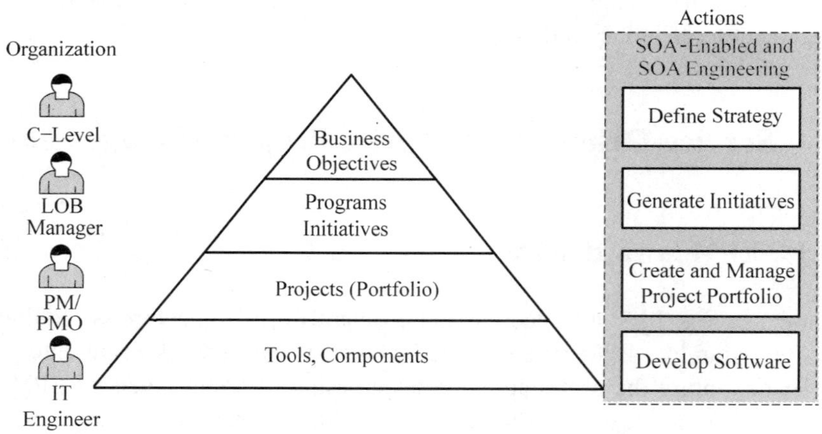

Figure 14.4 SOA-enabled EPM framework

The rest of this chapter will introduce a service-oriented EPM framework, which is implemented in Web services, as an example to illustrate how an SOA-enablement enhances an EPM framework.

14.4.2 WS-EPM Framework

WS-EPM stands for Web Services-based Enterprise Performance Management. As the most appropriate implementation technology for realizing an SOA, Web services is used to enable EPM. It shows how to move the current SOA standards to the business level from the perspective of enterprise performance management. In detail, WS-EPM exploits the concept of SOA to formalize and enable an EPM process[8], which is shown in Fig. 14.5. EPM is a continuous process, and is executed periodically and interactively. Five major stages are identified: *initialization*, *planning*, *executing*, *monitoring and controlling*, and *closing*. In the initialization phase, high-level project objectives are created. In the planning phase, detailed plans are shaped. In the executing phase, the project is implemented under supervision. In the monitoring and controlling phase, appropriate management operations are conducted in parallel to the project process, to ensure that the project is realized during the specified time line and abides by the predefined criteria. In the closing phase, the project is well documented and concluded prior to the delivery of the project.

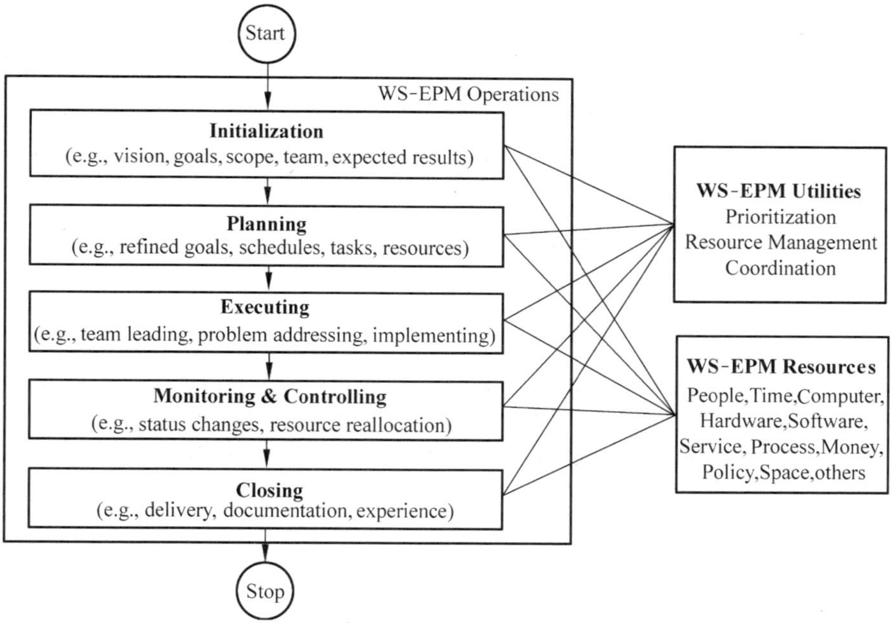

Figure 14.5 Web services-based WS-EPM framework

As shown in Fig. 14.5, the WS-EPM process is supported by a set of *WS-EPM utilities* and a centralized *WS-EPM resource management facility*. These utilities and facility can be shared by all projects in a portfolio. The WS-EPM utilities provide a set of predefined system utilities to facilitate portfolio prioritization, resource management, and portfolio coordination if conflicts exist. This set of utility tools is available to all five phases in the lifecycle of an EPM procedure.

As shown in the figure, WS-EPM provides a centralized management facility over all resources involved, including both physical and conceptual resources such as computers, hardware, software, people, time, services, processes, spaces, and others. All resources are captured in a standard format, such as WS-Resource[1].

14.4.3 WS-EPM Operations

WS-EPM defines a set of operations for all five phases of the EPM process: initialization, planning, executing, monitoring and controlling, and closing. Each individual project may have its own specific activities in each phase. Taking a product development project as an example, several processes (activities) can be identified, such as assessment, requirement definition, macro design, micro design, development, change management, and auditing.

Activities within a project typically have some inherent dependencies. These dependencies can be sequential relationships when one activity must follow another activity, resource sharing relationships when an activity must wait until another activity releases a resource instance, or other dependencies. Activity dependencies can be further categorized into different types, such as finish to start, start to start, finish to finish, and start to finish[9]. Figure 14.5 also illustrates typical operations for each phase.

It should be noted that all operations are encapsulated as Web service processes; thus, they can interoperate with each other in a standardized manner. Furthermore, all operations or flows can be captured and formalized in BPEL[1,2], so they can be reused and formally verified.

Initialization Phase

In the initialization phase, processes are used to set the initial vision, goals, teams, expected results and scope for every project. Typical initialization operations include: establishing project vision, setting up goals, delimiting project scope, forming project teams, and documenting expected results.

Planning Phase

In the planning stage, the project goals and scope are refined. A set of specific tasks or activities associated with each project are outlined. The initial schedule and budget allocation are also planned. Typical planning operations include: refining project goals, laying out project schedules, identifying tasks, and allocating resources.

Executing Phase

In the executing stage, the most important goal is to achieve project portfolio success by working with development teams. Along with this long-running process, problem solving (e.g., creating innovative technology to address a key solution problem) and project implementation are two major activities.

Monitoring and Controlling Phase

In this phase, a monitoring and controlling process monitors project portfolio progress and adjusts actions. Typical monitoring and controlling operations include: checking project status, monitoring changes, and performing dynamic resource allocation.

Closing Phase

The last step in an EPM lifecycle is the closing process, which focuses on the final product or service delivery. At the same time, preparing documents and releasing allocated resources are important activities for closing a project successfully. Typical closing operations include: delivering projects, properly documenting projects, and closing experiences and lessons learned from the projects.

14.4.4 Formalization of WS-EPM Methodology

As shown in Fig. 14.5, WS-EPM presents a step-by-step methodology for enterprise portfolio management. Figure 14.6 formalizes the highest level of EPM flows in BPEL. As shown in the figure, the high-level flow of EPM *productDevProcess* contains a sequence of five processes. Triggered by receiving a customer request with business requirements, the EPM flow starts from *InitializationPT, PlanningPT*, then moves to *ExecutingPT*, followed by *Monitoring-ControllingPT*, and ends with *ClosingPT*. Each process provides an invocation interface denoted by the tag "operation": The process *InitializationPT* exposes operation *requestInitialization*; the process *PlanningPT* exposes operation *requestPlanning*; the process *ExecutingPT* exposes operation *requestExecuting*; the process *Monitoring-ControllingPT* exposes operation *requestMonitoring-Controlling*; the process *ClosingPT* exposes operation *requestClosing*. Upon finishing the process, a reply is sent back to the customer with the original business requirements as attachments.

The BPEL snippet shown in Fig. 14.6 models the high-level operations of WS-EPM as an automated system, which takes business requirements as input and generates new products or services as response to the received business requirements. The sequential operations or services are performed accordingly. As mentioned earlier, what's shown in Fig. 14.6 is a highly simplified model of a WS-EPM process. In a real process, many roles may be identified and interact with each other; processes may not be sequentially followed, overlaps and iterations may exist, and so on.

In the domain of WS-EPM, a Web service process can also be treated as a special type of resource, so it can be organized and managed in the same way as other general-purpose resources. The next section will discuss how, in WS-EPM, a process can be defined as a resource in the format of WS-Resource as an example.

```
    <process name="productDevProcess"
        targetNamespace="http://ws-epm.com/ws-bp/ws-epm"
        xmlns="http://schemas.xmlsoap.org/ws/2003/03/business-process/"
        xmlns:lns="http://ws-epm.org/wsdl/ws-epm">
      <receive partnerLink="Customers"
          portType="lns:ws-epmPT"
          operation="sendBusinessRequirements"
          variable="BusinessRequirements">
      </receive>

      <flow>
        <sequence>
          <invoke  portType="lns:InitializationPT"
               operation="requestInitialization"
          </invoke>
          <invoke  portType="lns:PlanningPT"
               operation="requestPlanning"
          </invoke>
          <invoke  portType="lns:ExecutingPT"
               operation="requestExecuting"
          </invoke>
          <invoke  portType="lns:Monitoring-ControllingPT"
               operation="requestMonitoring-Controlling"
          </invoke>
          <invoke  portType="lns:ClosingPT"
               operation="requestClosing"
          </invoke>
         </sequence>
      </flow>

      <reply partnerLink="Customers"
          portType="lns:ws-epmPT"
          operation="sendBusinessRequirements" />

  </process>
```

Figure 14.6 Example high-level EPM flow in BPEL

14.5 WS-EPM Common Services

As shown in Fig. 14.5, WS-EPM contains two categories of common services to facilitate enterprise portfolio management: WS-EPM resource management facility and three EPM utilities.

14.5.1 WS-EPM Resource Management Facility

As discussed earlier, WS-EPM-related resources include both physical and non-physical resources, such as people, time, computers, other hardware and software, services, money, and spaces. Some resources can be considered as stateless (i.e., transient) resources to be consumed upon request. For example, a device may be allocated and consumed upon a request. Other resources need to stay stateful in part or in the entire lifecycle of corresponding projects. For example, a human resource assigned as a project manager in charge of a specific project may stay stateful in the whole lifecycle of the project.

Instead of creating another new resource description method, WS-EPM applies and extends the Web Services Resource Framework (WSRF)[10] to define stateful resources in the domain of enterprises. As introduced in the previous chapters, WSRF defines a set of specifications for managing and accessing stateful resources using Web services. It also supports dynamic creation of resource properties and associated values.

WS-EPM extends the usage of WSRF from IT computing resource descriptions to business-level resource descriptions. Applying the concept of WSRF to WS-EPM pursues different objectives, which is different from its original purpose of modeling Grid resources. A resources in a WS-EPM context are more diverse than those in a Grid context. Resources in a Grid are typically physical computing resources, such as memory, CPU, and storage. Resources in an EPM environment, however, include not only physical resources but also non-physical resources such as people, money, and time. Therefore, resource allocation and management not only is constrained by resource conflict, but also needs to be governed by business strategy, i.e., priority of different business objectives.

With WSRF, stateful resources in WS-EPM can be represented in Web Services Resource Property language and then registered into a WS-EPM-associated services repository according to corresponding skill sets. In an enterprise environment, three types of factors deserve further investigation: business components, business policies, and non-functional requirements.

- **Business components:** A business component refers to a specific kind of service in the operational environment of an enterprise, for example, customer service, product manufacturing process, and auditing and management process. Under a business transformation, people from an enterprise may find that some existing business components cannot provide necessary functions (which causes a business gap) or they are redundant with other components (which causes business overlap). People may also find the necessity of identifying or defining completely new business components. No matter under which circumstance, a business component is required to be improved as a business initiative. Consequently, a project will be established with a goal to achieve some outcomes to influence one or multiple related business components. It is the features of business components (e.g., whether it is urgent to be improved) that lead to final decision of the sequence of projects within a project portfolio, and how related resources (e.g., people and budget) are allocated to the projects.

- **Business policies:** A business policy refers to a set of business rules aiming at facilitating a project or certain actions needed to be taken in order to be compliant with existing regulations.
- **Non-functional requirements:** Compared with "What" a business component can do, non-functional requirements cover other concerns such as user interface, project duration, budget allocation, and skill sets requirement that are "How Good" a business component can do. Non-functional requirements are usually directly linked with business strategies. Key Performance Indicators (KPIs) are part of the business level non-functional requirements.

Figure 14.7 illustrates how to use WSRF to define a business resource "Product Development Process" in a WS-EPM environment with its properties. The tag <wsdl:definitions> is used to delimit the definition of the business component. As shown in Fig. 14.7, six simple XML data types are defined. Four of them are strings: *NameofProduct, ProductManager, StartTime,* and *ReleaseTime*; two of them are integers: *NumberOfTeam* and *TeamSize*. One complex XML data type *GenericProductDevBPProperties* is defined as an unbounded array, each element being a list of the six simple data types: *NameofProduct*, *NumberOfTeam*, *TeamSize*, *ProductManager*, *StartTime*, and *ReleaseTime*. The association of the resource properties document *GenericProductDevBPProperties* with the portType *GenericProductDevBP* defines the type of the WS-Resource.

```
<wsdl:definitions xmlns:tns="http://ws-epm.com/productDevBP" ...>
...
   <wsdl:types>
     <xsd:schema targetNamespace="http://ws-epm.com/productDevBP" ... >
     <!-- Resource property element declarations -->
        <xsd:element name="NameofProduct" type="xsd:string"/>
        <xsd:element name="NumberOfTeam" type="xsd:integer"/>
        <xsd:element name="TeamSize" type="xsd:integer" />
        <xsd:element name="ProductManager" type="xsd:string" />
        <xsd:element name="StartTime" type="xsd:string" />
        <xsd:element name="ReleaseTime" type="xsd:string" />

        <!-- Resource properties document declaration -->
        <xsd:element name="GenericProductDevBPProperties">
           <xsd:complexType>
              <xsd:sequence>
                 <xsd:element ref="tns:NameofProduct"/>
                 <xsd:element ref="tns:NumberOfTeam"/>
                 <xsd:element ref="tns:TeamSize"/>
                 <xsd:element ref="tns:ProductManager"/>
                 <xsd:element ref="tns:StartTime"/>
                 <xsd:element ref="tns:ReleaseTime"/>
                 <xsd:any minOccurs="0" maxOccurs="unbounded"/>
              </xsd:sequence>
```

Figure 14.7 Example WSDL Using WS-Resource for defining WS-EPM resources

```
            </xsd:complexType>
            </xsd:element>
...
      </xsd:schema>
    </wsdl:types>
...
    <!-- Association of resource properties document to a portType -->
     <wsdl:portType name="GenericProductDevBP"
      wsrp:ResourceProperties="tns:GenericProductDevBPProperties">
      <operation name="start"/>
      <operation name="monitor" .../>
      <operation name="reschedule" .../>
      <operation name="change-management" .../>
      <operation name="stop" .../>
...
    </wsdl:portType>
...
</wsdl:definitions>
```

Figure 14.7 (Continued)

Since creating WS-Resource-compatible WSDL files is not the main focus, this chapter focuses on identifying, requesting, and retrieving resources in the context of WS-EPM. In WS-EPM, a Web service call is used to discover all resources related to EPM and the properties of the resources. For example, one can retrieve all the information about a resource such as Product Development Business Process (ProductDevBP). The example in Fig. 14.8 illustrates how to retrieve three resource property elements: *NameofProduct*, *ProductManager*, and *ReleaseTime* from the WS-Resource that implements the portType *Generic-ProductDevBP*.

```
...
<wsrp:GetMultipleResourceProperties xmlns:tns="http://ws-
epm.com/productdev" ...>
   <wsrp:ResourceProperty>tns:NameofProduct</wsrp:ResourceProperty>
   <wsrp:ResourceProperty>tns:ProductManager</wsrp:ResourceProperty>
   <wsrp:ResourceProperty>tns:ReleaseTime</wsrp:ResourceProperty>
</wsrp:GetMultipleResourceProperties>
...
```

Figure 14.8 Request of accessing WS-EPM resource properties

The corresponding response about the product development business process is shown in Fig. 14.9. The value of the property *NameofProduct* is *WS-EPM Sphere*; the value of the property *ProductManager* is *John Smith*; the value of the property *ReleaseTime* is *06/01/2006*.

```
...
<wsrp:GetMultipleResourcePropertiesResponse xmlns:ns1="http://ws-
epm.com/productdev" ...>
  <ns1:NameofProduct>WS-EPM Sphere</ns1:NameofProduct>
  <ns1:ProductManager>John Smith</ns1:ProductManager>
  <ns1:ReleaseTime>06/01/2006</ns1:ReleaseTime>
</wsrp:GetMultipleResourcePropertiesResponse>
...
```

Figure 14.9 Response of accessing WS-EPM resource properties

Both WS-Resource requests and responses are encoded in SOAP messages. It is also easy to set properties for WS-EPM resources by using SOAP encoding-based communication mechanisms.

WS-Resource defines a set of operations to monitor and manage the lifetime of stateful resources. WS-EPM directly utilizes these operations to set, update, and monitor WS-EPM Resources. Typical actions are: *GetResourceProperty, GetResourcePropertyResponse, GetMultipleResourceProperties, SetResourceProperties,* and *QueryResourceProperties*.

14.5.2 WS-EPM Utilities

In order to facilitate EPM coordination, WS-EPM defines three types of system-level utilities: *portfolio prioritization*, *resource management*, and *portfolio coordination*. The portfolio prioritization utility supports C-Level manager to prioritize projects in the context of portfolios. The resource management utility supports administrators for low-level detailed resource allocation and assignment. The portfolio coordination utility supports PMOs to schedule and coordinate related projects and portfolios to avoid potential conflicts of resource usage.

Portfolio Prioritization Utility

The priority of a project depends on many factors, such as its tangible values (e.g., revenue), intangible values (e.g., brand), category, scope, required time to market, and other factors deciding whether the project is suitable to be developed inside or outside of an enterprise (e.g., outsourcing). Deciding the priority of a project in the context of a portfolio is critical since the result can serve as a criterion to guide the coordination of different projects. The C-Level executives or similar-level committees use this utility to assess individual initiatives and rank a proposed project before assigning it to PMOs.

Figure 14.10 illustrates a simplified example of how to prioritize projects based upon the corporate strategy decided by the C-Level executives. A tree-like structure is created representing the criteria of selecting projects. Various methods can be used to decide the project scores (priorities) from the generated tree structure, such as the Analytical Hierarchy Process (AHP) method[11].

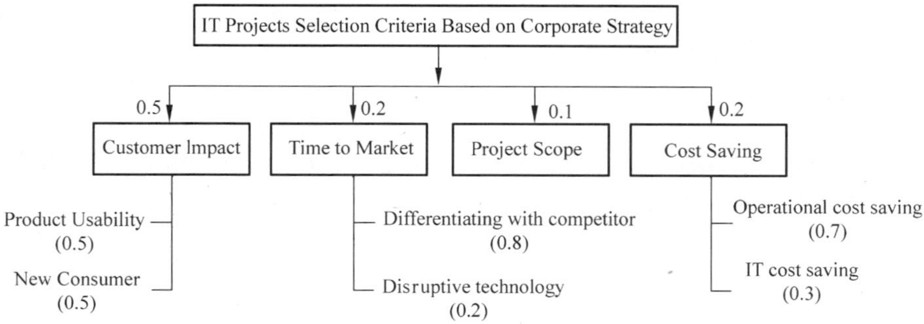

Figure 14.10 Project prioritization based on business strategy

As shown in Fig. 14.10, each criterion is assigned a weight representing its importance in the decision making process. For the example enterprise as shown in Fig. 14.10, four high-level criteria are identified: *customer impact*, *time to market*, *project scope*, and *cost saving*. The weights for scoring the priorities for them are 0.5, 0.2, 0.1, and 0.2, respectively. Each criterion is in turn divided into sub-criteria associated with priorities. The priorities for the criterion of *customer impact* is equally divided between *product usability* and attraction to *new customers* (i.e., 0.5 each). The priority of *time to market* is divided between *differentiating with competitors* (0.8) and *disruptive technology* (0.2). For the aspect of cost saving, *operational cost saving* has a higher priority (0.7) compared with *IT cost saving* (0.3). It should be noted that the sum of the weights assigned on every horizontal layer and vertical layer should be 1.0. For example, the sum of the weights of the four highest-level criteria is equal to 1.0 (0.5+0.2+0.1+0.2=1.0); the sum of the weights of the left-most line of *customer impact* is also equal to 1.0 (0.5+0.5=1.0).

Resource Management Utility

With the fixed amount of resources in an enterprise, how to balance the resources for a specific project to achieve an overall best performance is a critical topic. In order to facilitate management of diverse resources involved, WS-EPM divides resources into two categories: internal resources and external resources. Internal resources are developed internally, while external resources are outsourced. Internal resources are organized into a large resource pool, so that the whole enterprise can enjoy the cost saving brought by shared services. Attributes of a resource may also be changed. This utility provides tools for administrators to view, monitor, and allocate various types of resources.

Portfolio Coordination Utility

Since resources are usually limited and shared among different business projects and portfolios, it is common that at a certain time, different project activities require the same kind of resources, which leads to a resource conflict. A key factor influencing resource conflict is resource dependencies among different project activities. WS-EPM provides three ways to produce possible solutions to resource conflicts among project portfolios according to their priorities. The final decision is up to PMOs.

In order to facilitate describing the basic algorithms of the utility, a portfolio (i.e., the projects supporting the same line of business) can be denoted as PP, and the number of projects in PP as N. Apparently $\text{PP} = \{P_1, P_2, \cdots, P_N\}$. The projects in the PP can be further sorted by their priorities in a descending order, so that P_1 has the highest priority and P_N has the lowest priority, assuming that P_1 uses M resource types $(R_1, R_2, \cdots, R_M)$ and is involved in a resource conflict.

In order to perform portfolio coordination, three Web services, namely *ConflictTransferWS, RelaxResourceWS*, and *SearchResourceWS*, are constructed to realize the following three approaches, respectively: *ConflictTransferWS*, *RelaxResourceWS*, and *SearchResourceWS*. Approach 1 (ConflictTransferWS) is to identify the conflicted resources in P_1, transfer these conflicts directly to other projects in PP. Approach 2 (RelaxResourceWS) is to relax the resources' requirements in P_1, e.g., by changing the project duration or Full Time Equivalent (FTE) and verify if the conflicts diminish. Approach 3 (SearchResourceWS) is to go back to resource allocation operation and search for substitute resources.

14.6 WS-EPM Workspace

In order for users to perform EPM effectively and efficiently, it is important to provide an integrated WS-EPM workspace to model resources, perform project prioritization, and facilitate resources management. Since various roles of people are involved in an EPM process with different privileges and responsibilities, such a workspace should be able to be personalized according to an individual's role. Figure 14.11 shows a sample workspace for PMOs.

In its basic form, a WS-EPM workspace should include several key modules for a PMO: *project prioritization*, *project scheduling and re-scheduling*, *resource allocation and re-allocation*, and *project confliction management*. A PMO officer can register into the workspace and manage projects and resource information at run time. The project prioritization module allows PMO Officer to organize and prioritize various criteria to decide a rank for each project. The project scheduling and re-scheduling module allows PMO Officer to schedule projects and time lines based on available resources and priorities. The resource allocation and re-allocation module is used to allocate a resource based upon availability, requirements, and status. The project conflict management module is created to monitor existing resources and resolve potential resource conflicts at run time.

An EPM Workspace for PMO

Project Prioritization

Name	Time	Prio.	Size	Rank
P1	10	1	M	1
P2	20	2	L	2
P3	5	3	S	3
P4	15	3	M	3
P5	12	2	M	3
...				

Projecl (Re)-Scheduling

Name	Skills	#Co.	Prio.	Date
P1	Java,C#	1	H	5/1/06
P2	Java	2	M	5/2/06
P3	Java,C#	1	H	4/3/06
P4	C#	3	H	6/1/06
P5	C++	1	H	7/1/06
...				

Resource (Re)-Allocation

Name	Skills	Status	Cl.	Avai
Co.1	Java	P1	Cl.1	5/1/06
Co.2	C#	–		4/6/06
Co.3	Java,C#	P2	Cl.2	7/1/06
Co.4	C++	P3	Cl.2	5/2/06
Co.5	Java	P4	Cl.3	5/5/06
...				

Project Conflict Management

Name	Skills	#Co.	Prio.	Date
Cl.1	Java,C#	1	H	5/1/06
Cl.2	Java	2	M	5/2/06
Cl.3	Java,C#	1	H	4/3/06
Cl.4	C#	3	H	6/1/06
Cl.5	C++	1	H	7/1/06

Figure 14.11 Project portfolio prioritization workbench

It is worth noting that underneath the workspace some higher-level APIs on top of the predefined WS-EPM operations can be created to facilitate complex operations. For example, an operation named *WS-EPM-ProductDev-Operation* can be created to read and write property values of the *ProductDev*-related resources. The newly created operation hides the complexity of calling multiple regular WS-Resource operations. Meanwhile, it provides a customized solution for WS-EPM by using the underlying WS-Resource framework.

A detailed operation procedure is illustrated as follows. During the designing phase, projects are registered according to their impacts on various business components, as well as their characteristics represented by WS-EPM resources. During the executing phase, project activities and their interdependencies are captured and monitored using a formalized business process representation such as BPEL4WS.

The WS-EPM tool set and workspace can be applied in various project management domains, such as the banking industry and electronics industry. The concept of WS-EPM can be introduced into business processes and solution development activities, which can be adjusted accordingly to enhance business performance efficiency driven by projects. A variety of successful business cases have proven that through EPM, customers could achieve IT alignment with business strategies, cost saving through enterprise-wide coordination, efficient use of resources and budget, shortened time to market, and visibility control.

14.7 Discussions on SOA-Based EPM

When talking about project management, it is easy for people to think about various project management methodologies and tools. In order to better utilize limited company-wide resources, traditional project management has to be extended and enhanced toward EPM direction, where enterprise-wide projects need to be managed synergistically. This chapter introduces an SOA-based project management technique, which standardizes an EPM process and facilitates comprehensive resource sharing and management.

WS-EPM integrates business processes, resources (either physical or conceptual), and project management within an enterprise or across value chain networks. As a realization approach, it melts Web services infrastructure into critical EPM processes and improves working efficiency. In short, WS-EPM can be leveraged to better manage limited resources and improve ROI of IT investments.

Towards a future business management standard, we envision that WS-EPM can be expanded in the following five directions. First, one should explore integrating WS-EPM with the current ERP or CRM systems. Second, one can examine cross enterprise collaboration (including Business Process Outsourcing) in a WS-EPM environment. Third, one can perform deep business value/cost analysis for WS-EPM. Fourth, one can conduct boundary analysis of business components using WS-EPM for future improvement. Fifth, this chapter focuses on how to enable the EPM framework from the perspective of an SOA infrastructure. How SOA could enable business strategy and initiative management remains challenging. All these potential topics and issues are open to researchers and practitioners.

14.8 Discussions on Enterprise Portfolio Management

Realization of business initiatives is often project based. A large business entity typically has many ongoing projects simultaneously, which usually cause resource competition. In order to achieve the maximum output from a portfolio of IT projects, an organization and people are responsible for supervising and controlling the execution of those projects. Enterprise portfolio management is such a kind of methodology. In the era of SOA, we should not only adopt EPM but also adapt EPM toward SOA. EPM and SOA could be interweaved, meaning that the concept of resource sharing could be used in EPM and EPM could be used in SOA business initiatives.

Most of the current practices of EPM are more like paper work. In the future, we expect to see tools of EPM seamlessly integrated with SOA infrastructure of the enterprise so that EPM could be executed and monitored in a continuous manner.

14.9 Summary

In this chapter, we first introduced the history of project management and the concept of SOA-based Enterprise Performance Management (EPM), then we introduced WS-EPM, an realization of the SOA-based framework for project-driven EPM. We showed that SOA technologies such as BPEL and WSRF can enable EPM, while EPM as a methodology can guide SOA solutions and services development in a large enterprise.

References

[1] Goyette E, Lamar B (2003) A new Era of Enterprise Portfolio Management. http://www.mitre.org/news/the_edge/fall_03/goyette.html
[2] Institute PM (2000) A guide to the Project Management Body of Knowledge (PMBOK Guide). Project Management Institute
[3] PRINCE, Projects in Controlled Environments. http://www.prince2.com/
[4] Rational Unified Process. http://www.rational.com/products/rup/
[5] OMG. Unified Modeling Language. http://www.uml.org
[6] Light M (2003) Project portfolio management: within reach? In: Proceedings of Project Portfolio Management, San Francisco, CA, USA, pp 13 – 15
[7] Murphy P, Visitacion M (2002) Forrester research: application and project portfolio management - making the most of existing applications. http://www.forrester.com/research/legacyIT/Except/0,7208,27324,00.html
[8] Zhang LJ, Cai H, Chung JY, Chang H (2004) WS-EPM: Web services for enterprise project management. In: Proceedings of 2004 IEEE International Conference on Services Computing (SCC 2004), pp 177 – 185
[9] Microsoft Project. http://office.microsoft.com/project
[10] (2004) Web Services Notification and Web Services Resource Framework (WSRF). http://www-106.ibm.com/developerworks/webservices/library/ws-resource/
[11] Liberatore MJ (1987) An extension of the analytical hierarchy process for industrial R&D project selection and resource allocation. IEEE Transactions on Engineering Management 34: 12 – 18

15 Service-Oriented Business Consulting Methodology

15.1 Vision of Services System

With the development of global economy, the business components in enterprises are becoming more complex. At early stage of a business entity, the boundary between business components could be quite clear and simple. However, when the enterprise grows and become large-scale, some of the business components may become overlapped with others, as shown in Fig. 15.1.

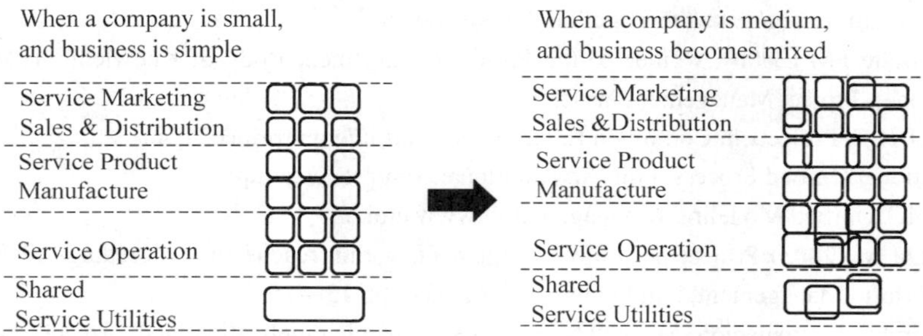

Figure 15.1 Business components become complex when a company grows

When an enterprise becomes even more complex, e.g., when it partners with suppliers in a value chain or when it goes for Initial Public Offering (IPO), even small modifications on a business component may become a hard mission if not impossible. Therefore, as shown in Fig. 15.2, the enterprise needs to be more adaptive and have clear boundary between business components. Furthermore,

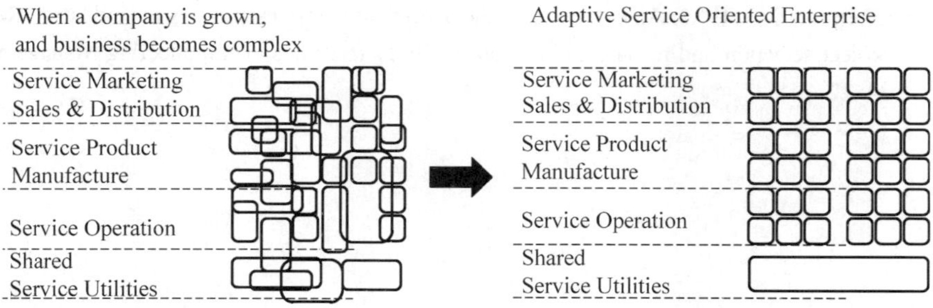

Figure 15.2 Business components need to be adaptive and dynamic in a value chain

the IT application and infrastructure also need to be componentized and become adaptive to catch up with continuous business transformation.

In reality, the alignment between IT components and business components could be difficult; therefore, a systematic approach is needed to take into consideration changes in a services system. Typical service-oriented business-IT alignment methods can be divided into three layers: enterprise level, process level, and IT infrastructure level.

Enterprise level

At the enterprise level, three methods introduced in Chapter 13 stand out: Balanced Scorecard[1], Component Business Modeling[2], and Enterprise Architecture[3]. Balanced Scorecard method takes actions from perspectives of finance, customer, process, innovation, growth, and so on. The Component Business Modeling method is a consulting method created by IBM. It categorizes the business components in an enterprise into different dimensions to obtain a full view of an enterprise. The Enterprise Architecture refers to a method of designing proper architecture for an enterprise before the transition phase to avoid waste of investment and to pave a way for sustainable business and IT evolution. One successful example of application in government sector is Federal Enterprise Architecture.

Process level

At this level, there are many well-known modeling methods and standards for Business Process Integration and Management, e.g., IBM WebSphere Business Modeler[4], computer integrated manufacturing open system architecture (CIMOSA)[5] developed by ESPRIT-AMICE, ARIS by Professor Scheer of Gemany[6], and so on. It has been proven that communication of flow of business logic and activities is useful and could be leveraged to identify bottlenecks in an enterprise. Meanwhile, it could be leveraged before IT implementation.

IT Infrastructure level

The well-known methods in this level include the famous IT Infrastructure Library (ITIL) and the IT Service Management framework from OGC of UK[7].

All methods in these three areas have made significant progress and are becoming more mature. However, it is worth noting that the progress on SOA may have significant influences on the methods. The traditional usage of SOA is mainly in IT through Web services standards; however, the ideas and concepts are becoming absorbed in business area as well. All these progress in enterprise modeling and SOA make it possible to have better alignment between business services and IT services. In this chapter, we mainly focus on business-driven alignment using the enterprise modeling methods introduced in Chapter 13. Readers can refer to the resources listed at the end of this chapter for the methods in the other two areas.

15.2 The Traditional Business Consulting Methods

15.2.1 Traditional Consulting Method for Strategic Change

Traditional business consulting methods for strategic changes typically include the following aspects.

The strategy of a business will be defined first. The strategy of a business often includes its vision that represents its business leaders' views for its future, its strategic position in the market, its strategy of working with its business partners and forming of alliance in the market.

Then a governance model and proper organizational hierarchy (including board members and responsible managers) are defined. The reason is obvious: every strategy must be executed by a team.

In addition, suggestions for improving business processes are recommended to match goals of the organization and the business.

Typical deliverables of the traditional methods often include: white papers that define the strategy of the business or its position in the market, analysis of its current status and future status or gap with benchmarking data, and a financial report of the business.

15.2.2 Traditional Consulting Method for IT Strategic Plan

After a business strategy is defined, IT Strategic Plan[8] can be formed in three phases as shown in Fig. 15.3.

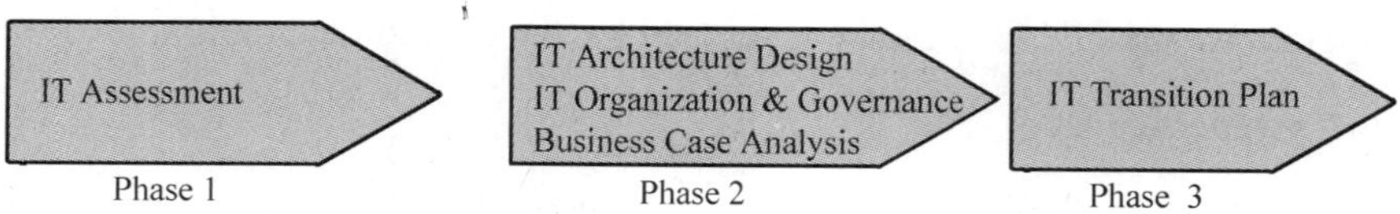

Figure 15.3 Phases of an IT Strategic Plan

Phase 1 is the assessment phase. The objectives of this phase are to:

- Understand business priority, organization, and external environment;
- Assess the IT organization, governance, and architecture;
- Collect the global benchmark and best practice;
- Perform gap analysis and maturity assessment;
- Establish the overall IT strategy and organization for the enterprise;
- Lower risk by leveraging clear and measurable business cases. The deliverables of this phase often include analysis of the current status of the enterprise and the key issues, case studies of leading companies, IT strategy

and principle of the company, the overall IT architecture and organization, and key IT initiatives.

Phase 2 is the phase of defining the governance model and candidate business transformation initiatives. The objectives of this phase are to:

- Give suggestions to IT organization;
- Generate detailed IT architecture;
- Define initial IT projects and ROI of key projects;
- Determine detailed IT budget and an approval process. The deliverables of this phase often include: detailed IT organization and IT Governance, detailed IT architecture, detailed IT budget and an approval process.

Phase 3 is the phase of defining an IT transition plan. The objectives of this phase are to:

- Prioritize key projects;
- Define Statement of Work (SOW) for the key projects;
- Create a migration path;
- Prepare a multi-year IT implementation plan with key milestones;
- Define a project management framework. The deliverables of this phase often include: analysis results of project dependency and priority, Return on Investment (ROI) of key projects, descriptions for projects with high priority, a migration plan, main schedules of implementation, and a project management framework.

15.2.3 Shortcomings of Traditional Methods

Consulting methods for Business / IT alignment usually require systematic approaches (or system-level engineering methods). Decision makers would care about progresses of IT technologies as well as overall business needs and the trend of business transformations.

In the traditional methods, most of the functions/components are included in boundary within the enterprise. Meanwhile, the traditional methods often overlook the possibility of reusing assets and leveraging the open service ecosystem.

Therefore, this chapter will introduce a consulting method aiming at business evolutions by leveraging the concepts of Services Computing.

15.3 Modeling of Services Ecosystem

The services ecosystem is becoming more diverse and collaborative. Within the services ecosystem (or value chain), four typical types of roles are identified: service customers (clients) who pay the money, various business partners who understand the clients and have trust with them, service component providers who focus on specific (common) service components reusable in different customer cases or even cross industries, and often-time PMO (Project Management Office)—a business unit providing the overall coordination for the service delivery processes.

All the roles mentioned above often collaborate closely to provide integrated services to the service customer. The trend is that the division of work (the boundary) among different roles becomes more and more vague. This kind of organization is the natural evolution of complex business environments (as shown in Fig. 15.4) and could meet the need for more complex business transformations.

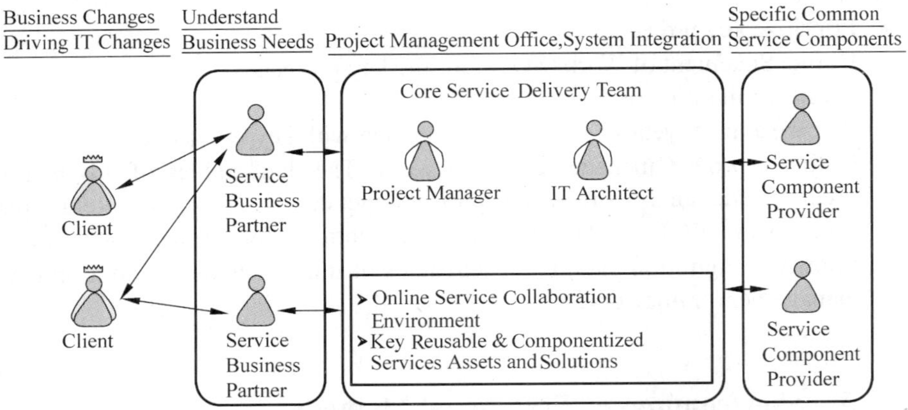

Figure 15.4 Evolution of dynamic service ecosystems

As shown in Figure 15.4, in a modern services ecosystem, service consumers, or "*Clients*", no longer directly face the service providers because technologies evolve very fast, it is very difficult for them to follow up with all the latest technologies or solutions. On the contrary, they select to face *Service Business Partners* who understand their business needs very well because of long term relationship and trust, but may not have technologies ready in their hand. So those *Service Business Partners* may further approach vendors who provide *project management* services, *IT architect* services, and then *enterprise application integration* services. These vendors are sometimes called contractors. As described in Chapter 14, modern services business are often project based, the success of services business often lie on success of projects. Besides project management and IT architect competencies, those contractors provide online service collaboration environments for carrying out the projects and manage service componentization and asset reuse to improve quality of project delivery. The contractor could further discover and compose services components provided by *Service Component Providers* who can provide best of breed high quality services components.

Meanwhile, many innovative service business models emerge as technology evolve (e.g., Web 2.0 and SOA). Among others, typical new models are: Application Hosting Service (e.g., Salesforce), Open Development Platform (e.g., Google Map), Business Process Outsourcing, Data Center Outsourcing, and Software as Service.

By recognizing the evolution of both open technologies and open value chain, the service providers and service consumers could grasp the benefits, such as decoupled business services and decoupled IT services, alignment of IT service components with business service components, collaboration between the service ecosystems through open standards, open source initiatives, open community, and flexible and innovative service delivery or hosting models.

15.4 Service-Oriented Business Consulting Method

The Service-Oriented Business Consulting Method (SO-BCM) introduced in this chapter contains seven key steps: gap analysis over SOA, initiatives identification, value chain analysis, business case analysis, portfolio analysis and transition planning, service-oriented project management and collaboration, and IT services management. To make this method easily understood and executable, we will show four elements for each step: objectives, involved roles, activities, and deliverables.

15.4.1 Gap Analysis over SOA

Similar to every consulting method, SO-BCM provides a route from an "AsIs" status of an enterprise to a "ToBe" status. In order to accomplish this objective, the first step is to analyze the gap between the *AsIs* and the *ToBe* status.

Contrasted with the traditional consulting methods, SO-BCM is built on the basis of an assumption about surrounding business environments. In SO-BCM, we assume that we view the gap from the perspective of business and IT service components, instead of *ad hoc* services or traditional components.

Typically, two types of roles are involved in this phase: first are business executives of the customer (e.g., CEO or Vice Presidents) who understand both the overall current status and the direction the business leads to; second are business analysts who understand business analysis methods.

The following major activities are typically executed in this step (often between the consulting company and the customer):

- Analyzing the goals of business services and information models (enterprise modeling methods);
- Analyzing business services exposed from the business components, e.g., using Component Business Modeling method;

- Analyzing Enterprise Architecture to ensure that any change is aligned with the overall architecture to avoid contradiction.

After or even during the execution of these activities, the customer is expected to gather the results (deliverables) from the consulting company. This step typically produces various types of deliverables, for example:

- Strategy, e.g., represented in a balanced scorecard;
- Business component maps and business services maps;
- Enterprise architectures;
- Gaps between business components and business services;
- Gaps in enterprise architectures.

Figure 15.5 shows an example of part of a deliverable.

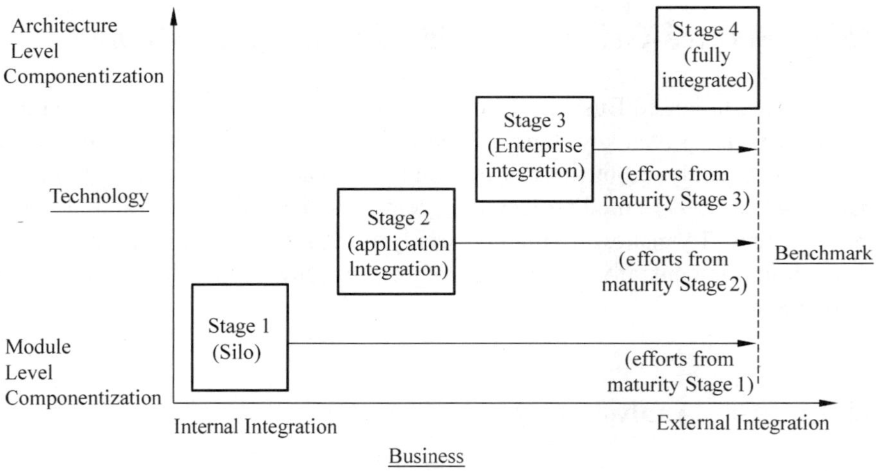

Figure 15.5 "AsIs" and "ToBe" analysis taking into consideration business and IT componentization

The deliverable shown in Fig. 15.5 is a roadmap towards more mature service componentization. The IT consultants could provide values to the service consumers because they own both methodologies and data. For example, as shown in Fig. 15.5, the methodology corresponds to the definition of four maturity stages. The silo stage means the applications in the business unit are not clearly designed and are not scalable; they do not connect and share with each other. The application integration stage means the applications in the business unit are selected to be componentized and integrated. The enterprise integration stage means most of the applications are well designed under service-oriented architecture and are well connected within the scope of the business unit. Fully integrated stage means the service-oriented concept is also applied to integration with the business entity's partners in the value chain. Even more important to an IT service consultant and its service consumer is data, which actually means benchmark data the IT service consultant owns based on its past practices. It gives a very important foundation for the service consumer to understand its position in the industry and its distance from industry leaders.

In this phase, it is natural for the enterprise to seek help from other third-party consulting companies, which have industry best practices and benchmarking data. These third-party companies could help the enterprise to decide which maturity stage the enterprise resides at, before an appropriate strategy being defined for the enterprise to promote itself to the next stage.

15.4.2 Identification of Transformation Initiatives

The objective of this step is to identify business initiatives through reasonable analysis steps. According to the company's strategy, several methods should be used, e.g., B/C/D (Basic/Competitive/Differentiative) analysis, capital/cost analysis, transformational view analysis in CBM method, and architecture assessment in Enterprise Architecture method. The result is a list of service transformation initiatives that aim at achieving the following goals.

- Leading the business to target defined in the strategy;
- Aligning with the overall architecture of the enterprise;
- Illustrating how it could enhance specific business components and how it may benefit the architecture or future service transformation.

Typical roles involved in this phase include: Line of Business (LOB) managers, business analysts, and CIOs. A set of activities should be executed in this step: Analyze the business components using Component Business Modeling (CBM) method; Analyze the Enterprise Architecture; Analyze and determine different kinds of relevant changes mode, e.g., redesign, integration and composition, decomposition and re-configuration, and design mediation.

Major deliverables produced in this step include: a list of service transformation initiatives; a linkage from these initiatives to a business strategy.

Figure 15.6 shows an example of a transition plan for business initiatives.

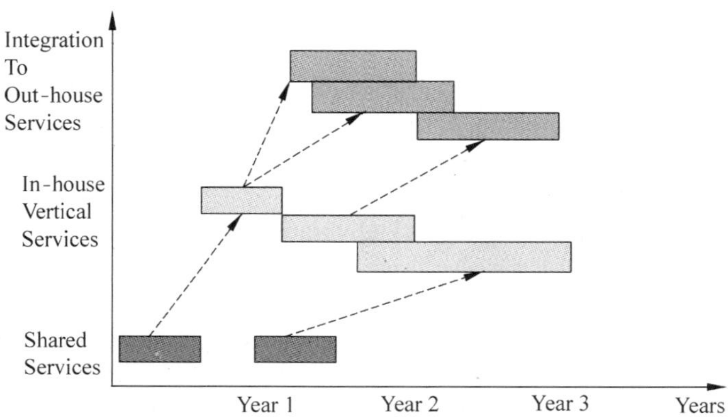

Figure 15.6 Define the transition plan for business initiatives

As shown in Fig. 15.6, there're 9 initiatives (projects) identified, falling into 3 categories, namely "shared services", "in-house vertical service," and "integration with out-house service". Figure 15.6 clearly shows the dependency among the services. For example, some in-house services may depend on shared services, so these shared services should be built first. Then some out-house services may depend on some in-house services, so these in-house services should be built before out-house services. Based on business judgments, initiatives within the same category may have different priorities; those with higher priority should be planned first. In short, the transition plan should be business-driven.

Different lines of businesses and business executives may create different business/IT initiatives. With limited resources, it is impossible to execute all these initiatives at the same time. The enterprise needs to have a detailed plan for coordinating these initiatives, taking into consideration the possible risks and the dependencies between the initiatives.

15.4.3 Value Chain Analysis

The objective of this step is to analyze and manage business partners and component providers in a distributed service environment. As discussed earlier, a service transformation initiative could hardly be accomplished completely when it is isolated from other initiatives. Therefore, it is necessary to analyze the relationship (closeness) between business partners and service customers. It is also necessary to analyze the maturity of the service components that could be leveraged. Success story of using those components in the past are helpful in this step.

Typical roles involved in this phase include: Business Development team, CIO, and CRM Manager. The following major activities are executed in this step: communicate customer needs with business partners; select vendors; perform high-level use case analysis. The deliverables from this step normally include the following items:

- A structured description of customer needs;
- Stakeholder analysis;
- Profiles of service component providers;
- Flexibility of service composition and configuration;
- Risk analysis of partnership with business partners and service component providers.

Figure 15.7 shows an example of a deliverable of vendor selection based on a Harvey-Ball table.

A Harvey-Ball table is a known consulting method to compare the strength and weakness between different candidates or factors. As shown in Fig. 15.7, different vendors (e.g., Service Component Provider SCP1, SCP2, SCP3, SCP4, and SCP5) may have different competencies valid for different types of work during certain periods of time when the partnership relationships exist. A few

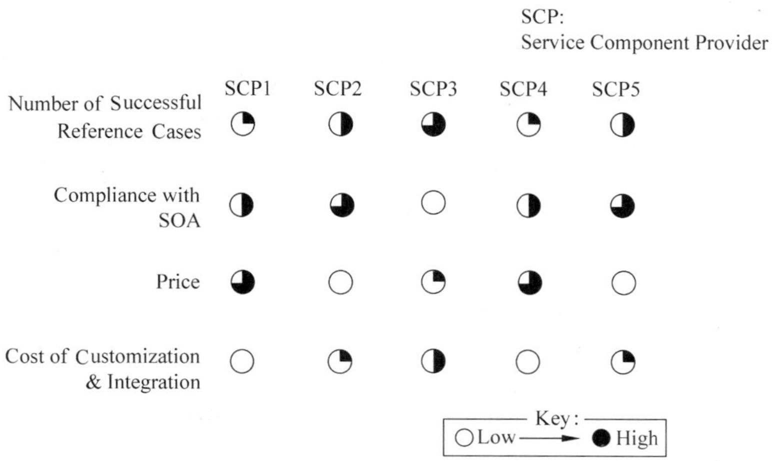

Figure 15.7 Vendor selection based on a Harvey-Ball table

example competencies, such as number of successful reference cases, compliance with SOA, price, cost of customization & integration, are used to evaluate the Service Component Providers. In order to lower risk, the enterprise should compare the vendors from competencies perspectives and select the one that best fits the sub-services in a service's life cycle.

15.4.4 Business Case Analysis

The objective of this step is to estimate the business benefits from an IT investment. Logically, a critical business initiative should be implemented first. In reality, however, there are typically too many business initiatives while the resource/money is always limited. As a result, when decision makers decide the roadmap for a transformation, they must calculate the value/cost of initiatives (ROI analysis) and carry out a risk analysis.

The roles involved in this phase typically include: market intelligence people who understand the market value and finance people. Activities executed in this step include: project into a figure the investment and the benefit from the initiatives (normally based on yearly estimation); calculate the data of investment and benefits for each year. Typical deliverables of this step are the results of business case studies, such as the example shown in Fig. 15.8. It illustrates the earned money based on years.

Similar to any business initiatives, an IT initiative must deserve the investment at the beginning. A business normally will not invest on a new technology unless it can benefit the business. In this case, a Return on Investment analysis or business case analysis should be carried out, which illustrates how the IT investment could benefit the business in the future.

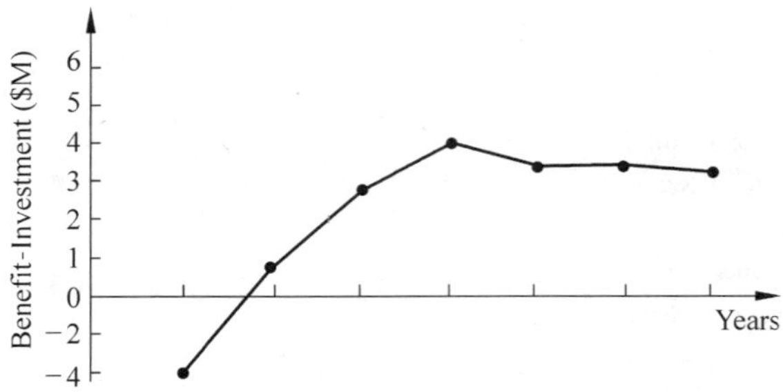

Figure 15.8 Business case analysis

15.4.5 Portfolio Analysis and Transition Planning

It is common that many initiatives are proposed by different business units during a certain time period, each competing for higher priority. The objective of this step is to prioritize the list of initiatives based on benefit, project scale, coverage or influence power to other initiatives, and so on. Typical roles involved in this phase include: business analyst, finance people, and marketing people. The following major types of activities are executed in this step:

- List all projects and conduct a committee meeting to communicate the factors to be considered;
- Calculate the scores of each initiative (based on business case analysis) and to perform portfolio analysis;
- Analyze dependences between services;
- Prioritize the initiatives;
- Communicate with different levels of business executives.

The deliverable of this step is typically an optimized portfolio diagram, as shown in Fig. 15.9.

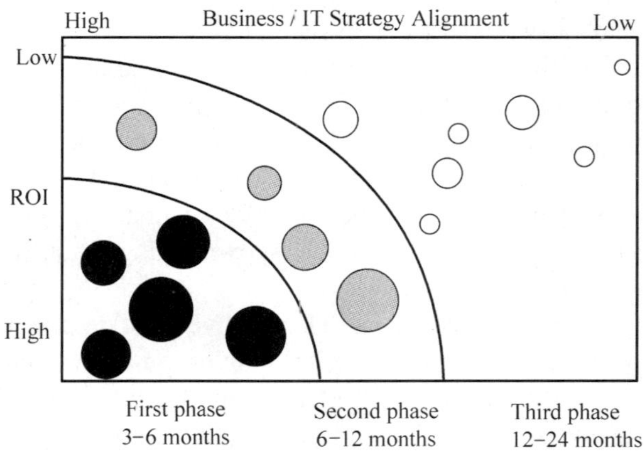

Figure 15.9 Enterprise project portfolio analysis

As shown in Fig. 15.9, the candidate projects in an enterprise form a project portfolio and are shown visually in a so called "bubble diagram" to facilitate decision making processes. Each "bubble" in the diagram represents one candidate project. The diameter of a bubble represents the scope (or investment) of the project. Different colors/shades represent different clusters. The most important clusters are those projects that could potentially be accomplished in short term (e.g., 3 months), have high expected ROIs, and could be served as basis for other initiatives, which mean low risk (as shown in lower left corner of the diagram). The least important clusters are those projects with high risks which mean low expected ROIs, long expected duration, e.g., 12 – 24 months, and are often standard alone projects (in higher right corner of the diagram).

After this diagram is obtained, it is ready to create the prioritized roadmap of project portfolio that leads to this enterprise's future stage.

15.4.6 Service-Oriented Project Management and Collaboration

The objective of this step is to clarify roles and responsibilities of parties involved in the overall services business transformation (e.g., PMO, business partners (BP), and service component providers). In general, the following types of activities are executed at this step:

- Determine scope, budget, and schedule;
- Clarify capability and responsibility of different roles;
- Break down working items;
- Define SOW.

The deliverable of this step is often a SOW for different parties involved.

15.4.7 IT Service Management

The objective of this step is to ensure that after the service is delivered to the service customer, the service operations could satisfy the predefined Service Level Agreements (SLAs). The roles involved in this phase usually include: call center staff, outsourcers, data center operators, and IT specialists. In general, the following activities are executed in this step:

- Set up the call center and incident management routines;
- Set up the change and problem management processes;
- Set up the release management processes;
- Set up the configuration management processes;
- Set up IT continuity management processes;
- Produces deliverables such as daily monitoring results, incidence resolution results, configuration update results, and service-level change or violation results.

15.5 Discussion on SO-BCM

Business consulting methodologies have long been kept as a secret within the boundary of a small group of business consultants. We believe that by understanding the conducting steps and the rationale of business consulting, service providers and service customers could sit together and make more reasonable decisions. Consulting work is often a work of multi-discipline however; thus, the challenges always exist.

As shown from Section 15.4.1 to 15.4.7, many different potential research and development topics exist. For example, for business gap analysis, extensive case studies and benchmarking work are needed; for initiatives identification, financial analysis and management accounting should be of help; for portfolio analysis and transition planning, Operations Research could play a key role.

15.6 Summary

In this chapter, we discussed Service-Oriented Business Consulting Method (SO-BCM). This method derives from the existing consulting methods, such as Component Business Modeling and Enterprise Architecture. Meanwhile, it takes a valuable insight from SOA.

Closely coupled system is hard to adapt to changes. Componentization and modularization offer more options with more value. In order to adapt to fast changes of service ecosystems, business and IT infrastructure need to be componentized. The purpose of this method is to align IT components with business components through a systematic approach. In this way, we reach a business-driven method that guides the design of IT project portfolios over an SOA-based infrastructure. This approach leads to some principles of SOA system design. It also paves a way for future evolution of enterprises to meet ever-changing business dynamics.

References

[1] Kaplan RS, Norton DP (1996) The Balanced Scorecard: Translating Strategy into Action. Harvard Business School Press

[2] A component-based approach to strategic change. http://www-935.ibm.com/services/us/igs/cbm/html/bizmodel.html

[3] Enterprise Architecture Tools. http://www.enterprise-architecture.info/EA_Tools.htm

[4] IBM WebSphere Business Modeler. http://www.ibm.com/software/integration/wbimodeler/

[5] ESPRIT Consortium AMICE(1993) CIMOSA: Open System Architecture for CIM. Springer
[6] ARIS. http://www.ids-scheer.com/
[7] Commerce OOG (2000) ITIL Complete Library (Book Format) (OGC Best Practice Series). The Stationery Office
[8] IT Strategic Planning. http://www.ucsf.edu/itplan/

16 End-to-End Services Delivery Platform and Methodology

16.1 Introduction to Services Delivery

Services delivery is not a simple activity, nor is it the duty of a single role. It is the lifecycle of a service provider delivering services to a service customer as committed in a previously signed contract to satisfy the customer. The goal here is to deliver the services in an efficient way with high quality, and secure the service provider's profit. During the services delivery lifecycle, a service provider would organize relevant resources such as people with necessary skills, using relevant software tools. It goes far more beyond project management by including setting up the IT governance before hand so that the services delivery team could follow a common principle. Common good practices covered by the governance includes asset reuse and compliant with service-oriented architecture (SOA). The lifecycle comprises of services delivery readiness phase, services delivery creation phase and services delivery operation phase.

Services delivery is not a new topic, but with the proliferation of business environment and with the advancement of information technologies, there come the new challenges and new opportunities for the service providers and service customers. First, the business models greatly changed because of IT innovations (e.g., Google model[1], Amazon model[2], and Salesforce model[3]). Second, the service customer may have different scales, meaning the service provider needs to adjust their services delivery processes that are suitable for the customer, although the services delivery methodology may be the same. Third, a service provider is usually not alone; it may partner with other parties to finally delivery the necessary services, so it should take the services ecosystem into consideration. Fourth, technologies evolve very fast; a service provider should pick up the relevant (not necessarily latest) tools.

16.2 Changes of Services Delivery Mechanisms

The world is flattened[4] and Internet technologies have brought people and enterprises closer together than ever before. The business services are becoming componentized, e.g., an enterprise's billing service may be provided by company A, its marketing service by company B, and call center service by company C. In some circumstances, a Human Resource (HR) business process may be outsourced, while in another scenario its IT infrastructure and development work may be outsourced to an IT company. None of these can be successfully accomplished without the help of advanced IT services delivery technologies, especially if the customers are knowledge workers, because all services mentioned above heavily involve exchange of domain information and knowledge. IT services delivery technologies give knowledge workers very efficient tools so that different players could leverage their own unique competencies to add value in the service value chain.

Within recent years, we also observe the change of partnership among the service providers. Traditionally, there are mainly one service provider and one service customer involved in a services delivery process. The service provider builds almost everything for the service customer. When the project is completed, the service customer owns the assets and will be responsible for operating the IT system physically on its own site. But now, industries are becoming more and more specialized. For example, there exist companies only focused on express goods delivery, companies specialized on marketing and communication, companies specialized on recruiting, companies specialized on software development, companies specialized on IT service management, etc. So we could expect different flexible services delivery mechanisms, such as software as service. The trend is every company works on specific tasks that it is good at and contributes to the whole service value chain.

Furthermore, with the advancement of technologies IT infrastructure is becoming more and more powerful and complex. Servers and storages become more powerful, and best practices and software tools make some companies more competitive at managing the IT services than other companies. On one hand, with the advancement of Web services and then service-oriented architecture (SOA), business services could now be packaged as service components with standard interfaces. The services now have much better interoperability. Technologies enable loose coupled services that are reconfigurable. The traditional programming models are replaced with loosely couple mechanisms with message-oriented features and mediation (like that in Enterprise Service Bus) as one important mechanism. On the other hand, with the advancement of business process integration and management technologies such as Model Driven Architecture[5], changes of business processes become more visualized and traceable. All the advancement of technologies bring new opportunities to service providers and service consumers to deliver services in a standardized, manageable, remote, and online approach.

To summarize, new ways are needed to address the challenges in this new era. Some topics are listed as follows:

(1) Leveraging the best breed of services;

(2) Quick service integration, not building everything from zero;

(3) Establishing the IT governance especially under the sophisticated business and IT environment;

(4) Being compliant with open standards so that the business is not locked by a specific technology or product vendor.

In remaining parts of this chapter, we will show how a well designed services delivery platform could address these topics.

16.3 An SOA-Based Services Delivery Platform

The described services delivery platform (SDP) below comes from the authors' practices (e-Hub)[6,7] and industry best practices. In this section, we will show two views of the platform: a layered structured view showing different levels of concerns, and a collaboration view showing how different components collaborate to accomplish services delivery task.

16.3.1 Layered View of the Services Delivery Platform

The requirements of modern services delivery platform come from:

(1) The need of a platform to adapt to business dynamics, such as change of business services, changes of business roles, composition of business services, etc.

(2) The need of a platform to reuse the assets available in the service customer or from service partners as much as possible to minimize the risk and lower the cost.

(3) The need of separation of business services from IT infrastructure services, so that for some service customers, e.g., Small and Medium Business (SMB) or some industries that have little IT skills, they could mainly focus on their core business functions and outsource their IT infrastructure to others or remotely subscribe to the services.

The layered view of the services delivery platform is shown in Fig. 16.1. It's very useful for separation of concerns and definition of loosely coupled interfaces between layers with different functions.

We will go through the details of the services delivery platform below.

At the bottom is the *Core Infrastructure Services* layer. It provides fundamental support for all other layers in the platform. In this layer, there are extensive services for managing physical IT resources. The layer consists of hardware such as server, storage, network, etc. The layer is also supported by software like operating system, database management system, etc.

The *IT Service Management* layer sits on top of the *Core Infrastructure Services* to help manage the IT infrastructure efficiently. The industry best practices of IT Service Management have been merged into ITIL (IT Infrastructure Library)[8]. It is a collection of guidelines and high level processes collected for operating the IT resources. It gives guidelines such as how to work on call center, incident

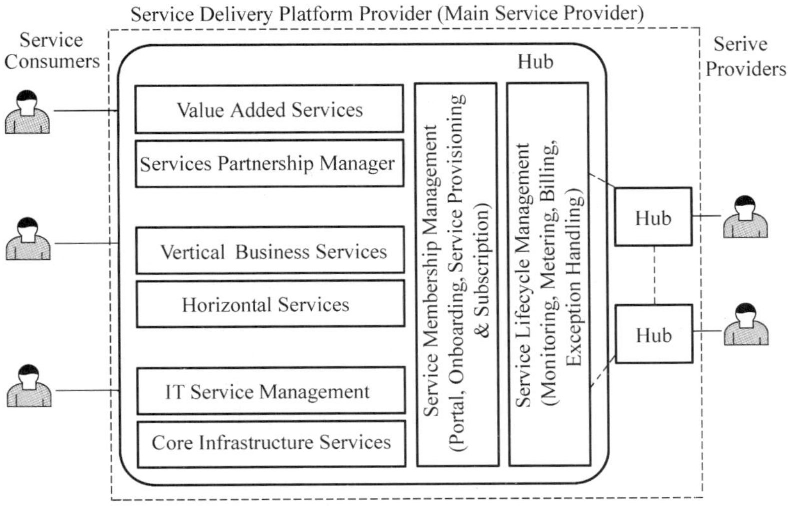

Figure 16.1 Layered view of a services delivery platform

management, change and problem management, release management, configuration management, availability management, IT continuity management, security management, etc.

The *Horizontal Services* layer supports common IT services like Web application services, calendar services, collaboration services, etc. It also supports common business services including human resources services, logistic services, etc.

The *Vertical Business Services* layer organizes and maintains applications that can be used to implement a specific business process or a solution for a specific industry. Some sample vertical services are loan services for the banking industry and claim services for the insurance industry.

The *Services Partnership Manager* is a featured function module within the services delivery platform to manage the relationships of the available service assets. It enables customers to dynamically configure a business process based on incoming requirements and precious solution expertise. It can also be used by internal applications to build new value-added services using existing services hosted by the platform. In order to achieve this, it should provide a mechanism of service configuration and re-configuration so that a service can be realized and deployed with minimum effort without changing the codes.

At the top level is the *Value Added Services* layer. This layer organizes and manages services integration based on *horizontal business services* and *vertical industry applications by leveraging Services Partnership Manager*. It provides services that are customized to a specific customer's need. It could also provide the customer with services delivery dashboard if needed, so that the information related to the services delivery lifecycle is always available to the customer. For instance, with a services delivery dashboard, a service customer could know the overall transaction in the past month, plan for capacity expansion, be aware of shipping information when the platform has other 3rd party service providers connected to it. The customer does not need to own his/her own IT assets in this scenario.

Besides the six horizontal layers mentioned above, the platform should also have two vertical layers for management purpose. These two layers are: *Service Membership Management* function that is responsible for the enablement of portal access, business entity on-boarding, service provisioning and subscription; *Service Lifecycle Management* function that is responsible for monitoring, metering, billing, and exception handling.

The services delivery platform should be built upon industry standards such as SOA for achieving flexibility and extensibility. Service partners connected to this platform should agree upon each party's service level agreements.

16.3.2 Collaboration View of the Services Delivery Platform

Besides the simple layered view, we also give a more detailed collaboration view of the services delivery platform in Fig. 16.2 to illustrate how different roles collaborate to delivery services. It is based on the e-Hub concept, but extends its functions. We will call a services delivery platform below as an e-Hub, because the center of a services delivery platform is a hub like structure that has the capability of managing the whole services delivery lifecycle. Since it's a collaboration

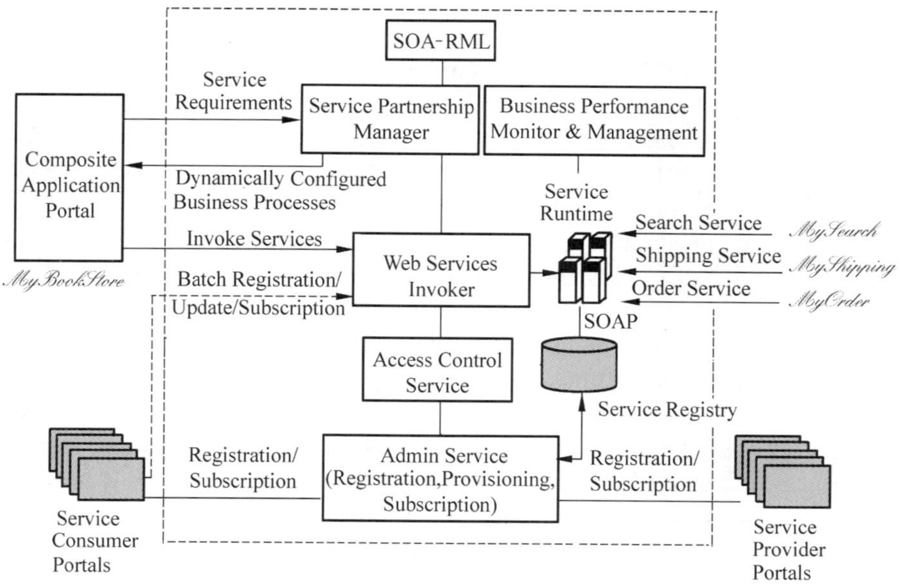

Figure 16.2 Services delivery platform: collaboration view

view from business capabilities perspective, we omit the bottom two layers (infrastructure services) in the layered view, namely "*Core Infrastructure Services*" and "*IT Service Management*" respectively.

As shown in Fig. 16.2, a Managed e-Hub is composed of those major components to facilitate integrating services: *SOA-RML* (SOA Relationship Modeling Language) introduced in Chapter 6, *Web services Invoker Service, Service Partnership Manager*, *Access Control Service,* and *Admin Service.*

We organize the components in a manner below so that they could be mapped to the top four layers in Fig. 16.1.

Value Added Services

The *SOA-RML* in Fig. 16.2 provides the taxonomy for describing the relationship between entities involved in the overall services delivery processes.

In addition, the Managed e-Hub provides *value added services* that provide collaboration and knowledge sharing capability. For example, an Intelligent Shipping Agent service looks up the e-Hub service registry, and dynamically constructs an appropriate shipping service provider list based on the information of the selected purchase order, e.g., dispatch country, shipping address, shipping price, etc.

Services Membership Management

The Admin Service in Fig. 16.2 enables service customers to subscribe and unsubscribe to the services provisioned by service providers. The *Admin Service* allows different service parties to register and remove business entities, users, and services with the e-Hub. In other words, this interface provides an administration / membership portal to manage the profiles of outsourcing businesses and users. For registered businesses and users, e-Hub supports a variety of utilities, such as Web services publishing by constructing an XML script-based request; Web services syndicator which enables legacy applications to be easily migrated to Web services; Data mapping services through meta-data infrastructure.

Service Partnership Manager

The *Service Partnership Manager* is responsible for taking business requirements from the service customers and compose business services or business applications that satisfy customers' requirements. The requirements include preferences, business rules, and some constraints. This is enabled by an engine that supports rule management, dynamic service configuration, etc. An example way of creating composite business applications based on business process management techniques was introduced in Chapter 9. Since all of the remote invocations regarding service integration are performed by the *Web Service Invoker*, this mechanism facilitates remote invocations in a unified manner.

Services Lifecycle Management

To monitor the transactions and trace communications across the e-Hub, a *Business Performance Manager* is established to trace the interactions among business entities, users, and services. In addition, the behaviors of the running business processes need to be monitored and controlled based on the Service Level Agreement (SLA) or other performance indicators. The control actions can be taken from one of the following activities: stopping a currently running business process, starting a new business process, changing a property file to dynamically affect a work flow, etc. The SLA can be created to monitor the interactions between a business and a service as well as the interactions between two services.

Vertical Business Services

The vertical business services include category of services that can help the service customer quickly own a specific service competency, e.g., e-procurement services or purchase order (PO) services, CRM services, account receivable/payable (AP/AR) services, productivity services for knowledge workers (calendar services, market intelligence services), etc. In this chapter, the following three examples are given: search service (a service by a fictitious company called "MySearch"), shipping service (a service by a fictitious company called "MyShipping"), order service (a service by a fictitious company called "MyOrder").

Horizontal Services

The Service Partnership Manager module takes information from Service Requirements and partnership relationship with SOA-RML, it then finds service components using Advanced Web services discovery engine. The *Advanced Web services discovery engine* in Fig. 16.2 provides a Web services-based service discovery mechanism so that other services could find and bind to the relevant service at runtime. This could avoid the high cost of rewriting various search codes in a service system.

The centralized *Web services invoker* makes it possible to construct a SOAP call using Remote Procedure Call (RPC) and Web services Invocation Framework (WSIF)[9]. Any application can use this generic *Web services invocation broker* to invoke any Web services in an easy way. The only input information is the location of the WSDL document, the method name, as well as the input parameters.

The e-Hub addresses the security issues of virtual private e-Hub, where the hub supports virtual communities of businesses that share private collaborative business processes via the hub. A two-level security mechanism is used to ensure security of all communications through the e-Hub. The first level of security is assured by a secured communication infrastructure, such as HTTPS or SSL. The second level of security is assured by access control. In more details, this level of security is ensured by two-layered authentication and authorization. First, the *Access Control Service* grants Web services based access control. Second, the *membership portal* grants Web browser-based access control to relevant parties.

The *Access Control Service* shown in Fig. 16.2 provides the foundation for the Web services access layer of e-Hub's two-level security model. It is the central access point for the Web services based authentication and authorization. In addition, *Access Control Service* also handles requests such as obtaining quotes on available services and generating responses.

In summary, the Managed e-Hub is a typical instance of the services delivery platform that centers around the *Value Added Services* and *Service Partnership Manager* to dynamically compose business processes. The whole structure realizes the service model for composite business application on-demand where a central portal of *Business Performance Monitoring and Management* monitors and manages composed business services in the services delivery environment.

Next, we will examine several critical components in details: advanced Web services discovery engine, central membership portal, and Service Partnership Manager. Those are examples of how we can leverage research results introduced in previous chapters to create industry-leading services delivery platform.

16.3.3 Key Services Needed in the Services Delivery Platform

Advanced Web Services Discovery Engine

Service providers can publish their services as Web services at service registries such as UDDI registries, so that the services can be reused by other service requesters (i.e., users). On the other hand, service requesters can also explore service registries for appropriate outsourcing applications, so that they can save the budget of hiring outsourcing providers to develop a new application from scratch. So creating Search Service in the services delivery platform is key to effective discovery of a proper published service in service registries.

As we discussed in the previous chapters, the current Web services search technologies provide two ways to search UDDI registries: program clients as search requesters and Web browser-based search tools. Examples of the former include the one provided by UDDI registry operators, examples of the latter include some Web sites[10]. Searching a UDDI registry using program clients requires developers to write significant amount of code, in order to obtain specific information needed for target Web services via the use of APIs such as UDDI for Java (UDDI4J). Searching a UDDI registry with Web browser-based tools also has issues, in the sense that the search result could either yield too much information or no result at all unless one can provide some specific information about the businesses or services, such as partial business name or service type, or know which specific categories that data are registered with. Both types of search technologies have their limitations. First, only one registry can be specified per request and multiple sequential searches must be performed if multiple registries are involved. Second, no advanced search capabilities are provided to perform result aggregation, i.e., to union or intersect multiple search results returned by UDDI registries.

Therefore, in the e-Hub, the Advanced Web services Discovery Engine utilizes the technology of the Business Explorer for Web services (BE4WS)[11], which is discussed in detail in Chapter 3, to provide advanced search capabilities for outsourcing management. BE4WS provides an XML-based UDDI "exploring engine," which presents to developers with a standard set of interfaces to carry out complex searches in multiple UDDI directories with one single request. It also accumulates results from multiple UDDI queries and then processes aggregation before returning the final result to service requesters.

Figure 16.3 illustrates a sample BE4WS search script with two search queries. Each query is specified between a tag pair of <Query> and </Query>. The first query intends to search the "Private UDDI Registry 1" with the URL value specified between the tag pair of <SourceURL> and </SourceURL>. The value between the tag pair of <BusinessName> and </BusinessName> specifies the search criteria of business names, i.e., starting with "Video". The value between the tag pair of <FindBy> and </FindBy> specifies a data type, which specifies a specific business entity. Similar constructs exist for the second query, which searches a different UDDI registry "Private UDDI Registry 2" for business names including the word "Processing".

```
<?xml version="1.0"?>
<Search>
<Query>
<Source>Private UDDI Registry 1</Source>
<SourceURL>http://USearch.com/services/uddi/inquiryAPI</SourceURL>
<BusinessName>Video</BusinessName>
<FindBy>Business</FindBy>
</Query>
<Query>
  <Source>Private UDDI Registry 2</Source>
  <SourceURL>http://TSearch.com/services/uddi/servlet/uddi</SourceURL>
  <BusinessName>Processing</BusinessName>
  <FindBy>Business</FindBy>
</Query>
<AggOperator>OR</AggOperator>
</Search>
```

Figure 16.3 Sample BE4WS-based search script

Central Membership Portal

The Central Membership Portal provides a virtual environment with the involved outsourcing business entities and users. It also manages service provision and service subscription. In other words, the Central Membership Portal includes two major functions: membership management and a rapid on-boarding suite.

The membership management functions beneath the portal allow the involved outsourcing parties to register on the e-Hub with different types of memberships.

For each business entity, the Central Membership Portal captures the information of the business, the users of the business. It requires a business administrator (executing the approval processes and other system administrations), a service provision manager (if provisioning services is needed), and a subscription manager (if subscription to services is needed). For a business entity that provides services, it needs to register a service provision manager to expose its services to the e-Hub. For a business entity that consumes services, it needs to register a subscription manager to subscribe to services.

Figure 16.4 describes in detail the process of registration, provision, and subscription. The left hand side of Fig. 16.4 illustrates a provisioning process.

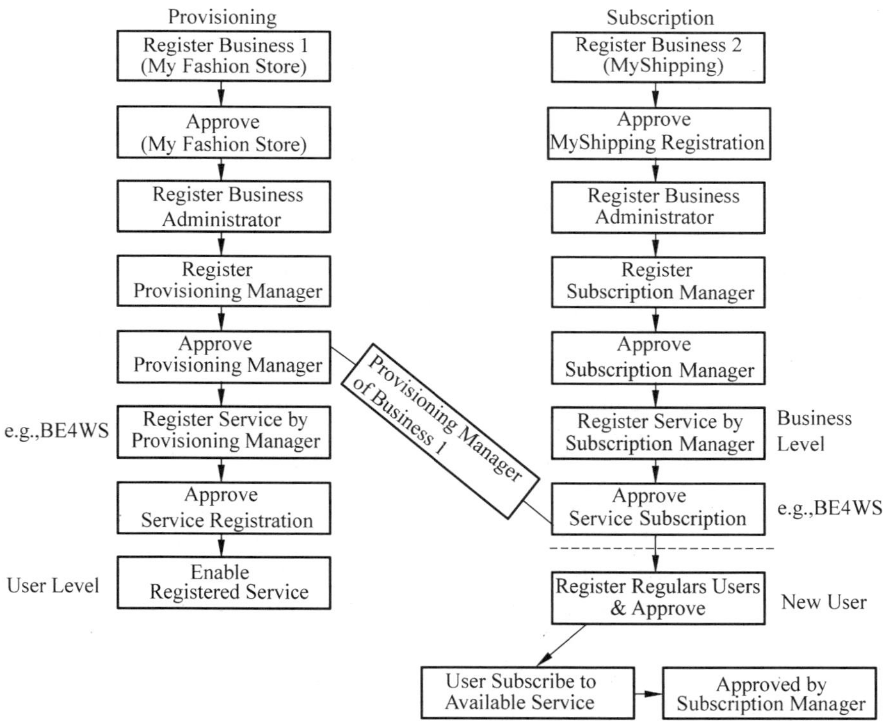

Figure 16.4 Registration/Provisioning/Subscription process flow

The right hand side of the Fig. 16.4 illustrates a subscription process. Similarly, the process starts with the registration of an outsourcing business party (e.g., MyFashion Store) first. After the business party registration is approved by the e-Hub administration, it can register a business administrator who can in turn register involving users within its organization. Then the business registers a service subscription manager. Upon approval by the e-Hub administrator, the service subscription manager can subscribe to services previously provisioned and enabled on the e-Hub.

As shown in Fig. 16.4, the e-Hub forwards the subscription request from the right hand side to the corresponding service provision manager on the left hand side. If the service provision manager approves the subscription request, the corresponding business administrator of the outsourcing business party (i.e., on the right hand side) then registers regular users for the service. In order to add another level of control (e.g., due to service usage fees upon per-usage basis), whenever a registered regular user wants to use the service, a request need to be sent to the subscription manager in that business entity for approval before the service could be launched.

Note that a service can be provisioned but not enabled. A provisioned service can be searched in the domain of the corresponding e-Hub. However, a service needs to be enabled before outsourcing users can subscribe and use it. In addition, subscription to services can be conducted at two levels, namely business entity level and user level. A subscription at the business entity level refers that the corresponding service subscription submits the subscription request for the whole outsourcing business party. A subscription at the user level refers that an individual user subscribes to an enabled outsourcing server for usage. A subscription can be performed at one level or both levels. However, in order for a user to subscribe to a certain service, the service must have already been subscribed at the business entity level. In addition, a user subscription request must be approved by the corresponding subscription manager.

In addition to a Web browser based membership management portal, a rapid on-boarding suite provides a set of APIs supporting Web services for registration and updates of the membership information, thus enabling rapid on-boarding process of business entities, users, as well as provisioning and subscription to services. A configuration XML file is used to incrementally update business registry information. The configuration file can be customized for individual business entity.

From the data synchronization perspective, the e-Hub provides the capability to synchronize the data in its business registries with that in UDDI registries for the corresponding businesses and services information. That is to say, after a business entity is registered with an e-Hub, the information can be published to UDDI registry automatically by the e-Hub. On the other hand, an e-Hub can also fetch the information about the business entity, if it already exists in a UDDI registry, and store the information in its local business registry.

Service Partnership Manager

The Service Partnership Manager enables outsourcing customers to dynamically configure a new business process based on incoming requirements. It can also be used to build a new value-added service using existing services hosted by the e-Hub, such as the purchase order management business process described in the next section.

However, composing individual Web services described in WSDL documents into a business process is not a trivial task, let alone the fact that the current technologies lack corresponding supportive mechanisms in many aspects. As a result, the integration process normally requires a number of manual steps, which are not only time-consuming but also error-prone. As discussed in Chapter 9, these tasks typically involve the following steps: (1) gather subjective requirements, (2) translate the requirements into service search criteria, (3) perform search(s) to obtain a list of candidate Web services that meet the criteria, (4) filter and select the ones that best fit based upon customer preferences, (5) repeat the steps (3) and (4) to collect a set of Web services that satisfy the functions required in the business process, (6) select the optimal combination of Web services in the end-to-end process, and (7) monitor and tune the service composition at runtime or design time.

In order to illustrate how the Service Partnership Manager facilitates automatic and dynamic composition of a business process using existing outsourcing services, let us consider a simple example of establishing a small Web store named "Fashion Gift". Customers could view, select and buy fashion gift on line. The owner of the store knows very well the preferences of a segment of customers; however, the owner doesn't intend to own a lot of IT assets, nor to build the Web site and non-core services such as shipping service or ordering service from scratch. What the owner can do is to build a fashion Web site for marketing, by leveraging four business services below.

- Search Service: from MySearch, so that customers could easily find the products they want;
- Ordering Service: from MyOrder, so that customers could easily pay by credit card or a online payment agency such as PayPal;
- Shipping Services: from MyShipping, so that the owner of the store will provide ordered, shipping address and then the remaining part will be handled by MyShipping company;
- Platform Service: from a platform owner. Through the services delivery platform, the owner of the Web store could monitor the performance of all the Web services and know the status of each transaction.

All of the four tasks are realized by outsourcing services. The customer first enters above requirements of price, timeframe, type of services needed, and the sequence of tasks to be performed via a menu-driven Graphic User Interface provided by the e-Hub, with the requirements captured as XML-based specifications. Preferences, process flow rules, constraints, and business logic can also be captured. Based on these specifications, the Service Partnership Manager automatically creates search scripts to look up the private UDDI registry for available outsourcing Web services of each type that is required, e.g., payment services, shipping companies, and phone services. The Web services discovery is performed by the Advanced Web services Discovery Engine. Based on the customer preferences together with the relationships between the service providers, the Service Partnership Manager selects the best service of each type that meets the combined requirements for a composed business process, and generates the process specification according to the sequence of tasks to be performed. The owner of the Web store could switch a services from search service, ordering service, or shipping services, if he finds sometime later that the service level agreement is not met. Or he could use this to negotiate with the service providers.

It should be noted that a single-sign-on (SSO) mechanism is necessary to allow a registered and logged-in user to have access to the subsequent processes. This is a basic and important service provided by the services delivery platform.

16.4 The End-to-End Services Delivery Methodology

Besides the functions of services delivery platform described in previous sections, a systematic methodology is critical in carrying out a services delivery process, since there're many different roles involved in a services delivery lifecycle.

Figure 16.5 is a two dimensional view of the end-to-end services delivery methodology. The horizontal dimension represents the services delivery lifecycle which comprises several phases. The end-to-end services delivery methodology covers three phases of services delivery processes, namely "Services Delivery Readiness", "Services Delivery Creation", "Services Delivery Operation". The vertical dimension represents the relationship among business services, roles, technologies, and overall governance within each phase.

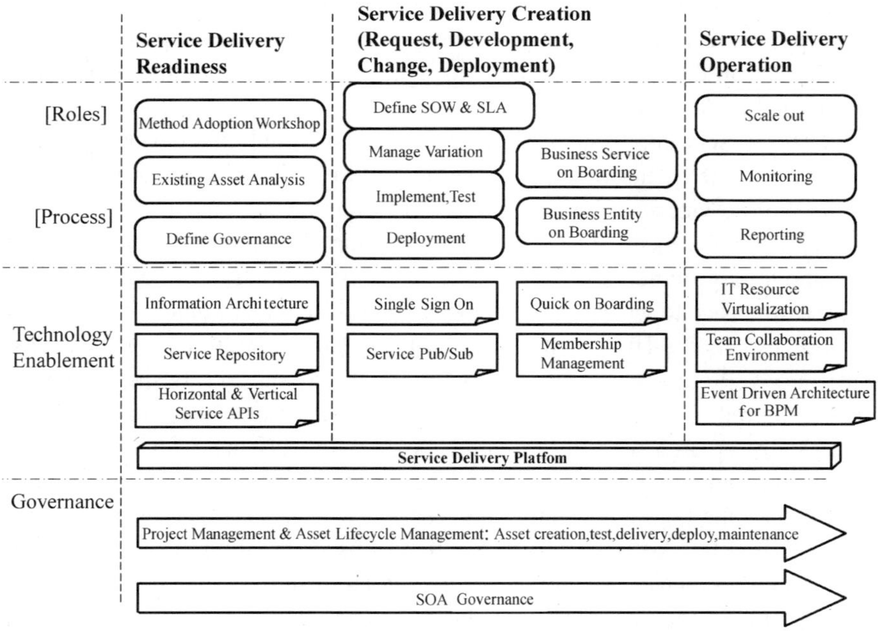

Figure 16.5 A two dimensional view of the end to end services delivery methodology

We will explain the key activities and technologies involved in those phases below in details. But first, we should notice that Project Management and Asset Lifecycle Management cover all the phases, and IT governance that is SOA compliant should be established before the services delivery process and should be used to guide the overall processes.

16.4.1 Services Delivery Readiness Phase

Notice that a services delivery process is not done by a service provider alone, rather there're rich interactions between a service customer and service providers. As shown in Fig. 16.6, in the Services Delivery Readiness phase, a service provider is engaged with a service customer through a service method adoption workshop. During the workshop, the customer will discuss with the service provider and agree on future services delivery contents and methods. Then the service provider may help the service customer do the existing asset analysis to better leverage the assets. The service provider will leverage the best practices and help the customer define the services delivery governance, which covers organizations, services delivery principles that are far more important than technology alone.

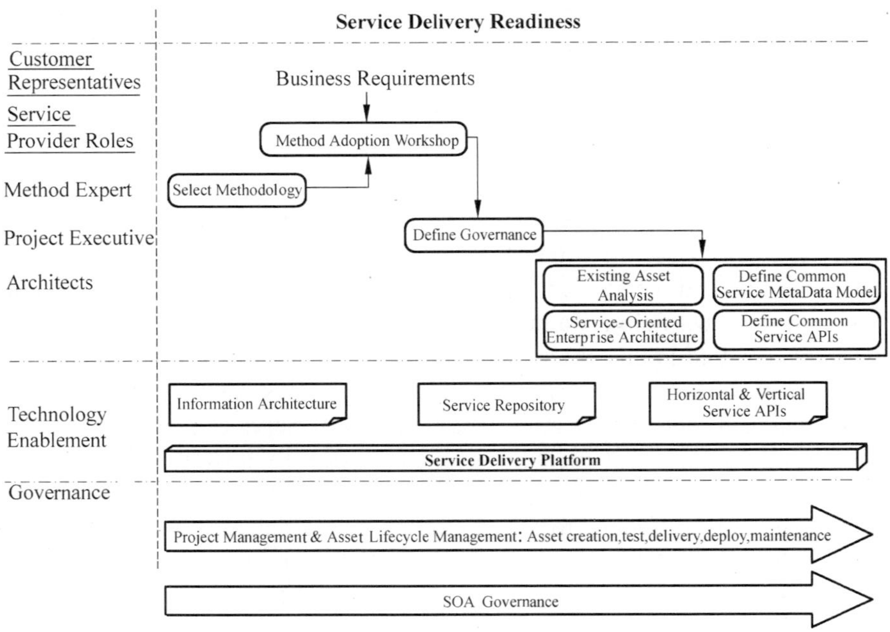

Figure 16.6 Key business processes in Services Delivery Readiness phase

The main roles involved in this phase from the service provider side include Project Executive, Senior IT Architect, and Method Expert. From the customer side, there should be representatives from CIO office, Project Management Office, etc.

There are several important business services provided during this phase, e.g., a service for analyzing the existing assets. In this phase, the framework of the services delivery platform will be established, including the service metadata model, common service APIs, information architecture, services repository for unified service registration and management, etc.

Within this phase, the service provider could leverage the best practices and help the service customer establish the customized Information Architecture, Service Repository and Service APIs for future work. The preparation work during the Services delivery Readiness phase is critical to ensure that the overall activities by different roles who follow the same principle and the IT investment could be best leveraged. It also promises that every role within the services delivery lifecycle understand his/her responsibility and know how to collaborate with other roles and how to select proper tools. Efficient communication is expected during this phase.

In order to make the services delivery platform ready, the service provider should undergo these activities. First, the service provider may organize a method adoption workshop, and include IT architect and IT experts to select the methodology and IT governance for managing the services delivery platform. After establishing the principles, the service provider could then create the framework as described above, including common data models and common services APIs.

16.4.2 Services Delivery Creation Phase

Once the services delivery preparation work is ready, the next phase is Services delivery Creation phase. Its contents include communication process between the service provider and the service customer, and finally reach an agreement on the scope of the services delivery and service levels shown in Fig. 16.7.

Contents covered in this phase include managing service variation; implement, test and deploy the service by leveraging the services delivery platform and technologies and tools. Other important elements of Services Delivery Creation phase shown in Fig. 16.7 include business service on boarding and business entity on boarding. These two pieces make our end to end services delivery methodology very different from traditional services delivery method in which case there is usually only one service provider delivering the service to only one service customer. While in our case, we assume there are different partners working together in a dynamic services ecosystem. A specific party may have its own, unique competency that makes it relied by other parties. Examples of such competencies may include low cost services development, highly-skilled expertise in some service components and in services deployment, a mature service component, deep understanding of the industry, etc.

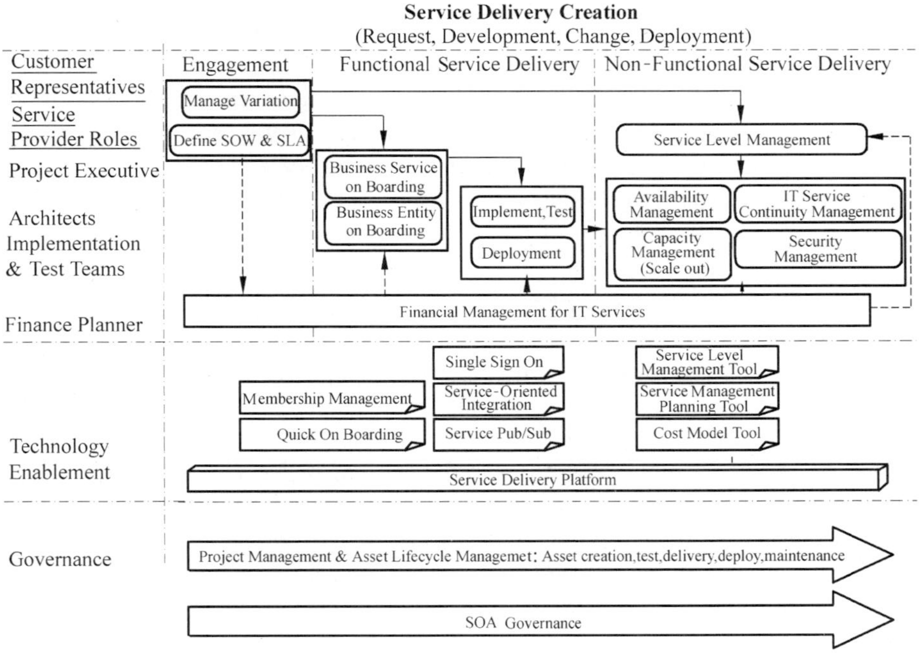

Figure 16.7 Business processes for Services Delivery Creation

The business service on boarding process could help a business service be plugged into the services delivery platform to satisfy predefined criteria. The Business Entity on Boarding process could help a specific service provider quickly connect to the Services Delivery Platform following standard interfaces.

The important roles involved within this phase include project managers, IT architects, sub-contract service providers who outsource part of the jobs, such as development, IT experts who have unique knowledge within the whole service creation lifecycle (e.g., system configuration, services deployment, change management).

During this phase, it is very important to select proper partners/teams, technologies & standards/interfaces, tools and a services delivery platform to secure the collaboration between different parties. It is not a simple work- break-down structure like in the traditional project management activities, but rather every party involved in the collaboration should understand its commitment/ responsibilities, benefit and the approach of delivering its own part of the service piece. The other part of this phase may still follow the traditional project management activities which include defining the scope of work, understanding the service level agreement, breaking the work into pieces, defining the schedule and estimating the cost, etc.

Services delivery platform at this phase provides several important Platform Services, e.g., SOW & SLA management, solution creation, test, deployment, release management, service membership management, service on boarding management, Single Sign On, service provisioning and service subscription management, etc.

For every business, there're not only functional requirements, but also non-functional requirements, e.g., scale out, availability of services, ability to recover from operation failure, security constraints, etc. The non-functional requirements should also be considered seriously during service design and creation phase.

16.4.3 Services Delivery Operation Phase

After implementing, testing and deploying the services successfully, the relationship between the service provider and the service customer changes to Services Delivery Operation. This phase is the steady state in which the service operation team will monitor and report the state of the service system produced from the previous phase. This phase mainly interfaces with previous phase through clearly defined service level agreement. It is inevitable that a service system may encounter some incidents or small changes. It's the service operation team's duty to continuously monitor the service system and bring the system back to steady state if the system shows unexpected behaviors.

As shown in Fig. 16.8, there are several important business services provided at this phase, such as incident management, change and problem management, release management, and configuration management.

The main roles at this phase are responsible for operating the service system in steady state. There's designer for service operation environment to make sure that the services system could be scaled out in large amount of transactions environments; monitoring role's job is to keep his/her eyes closely on the screen and see if all the IT resources operate normally; change and problem management role is responsible for any change; reporting role is very clear about Service Level Agreement so understand how the system is performed relative to predefined SLA.

With the advancement of technologies, we can leverage IT resource virtualization tools such as VMWare[2], IBM's Dynamic logical partitioning (LPAR)[3], team collaboration tools (such as a Web based portal that aggregates all the relevant information for a specific role within the operation team). Besides those, now we can leverage the flexible event-driven architecture for business performance management. This makes sure that different tools or software components from different vendors could be interoperable with each other and accomplish the predefined tasks.

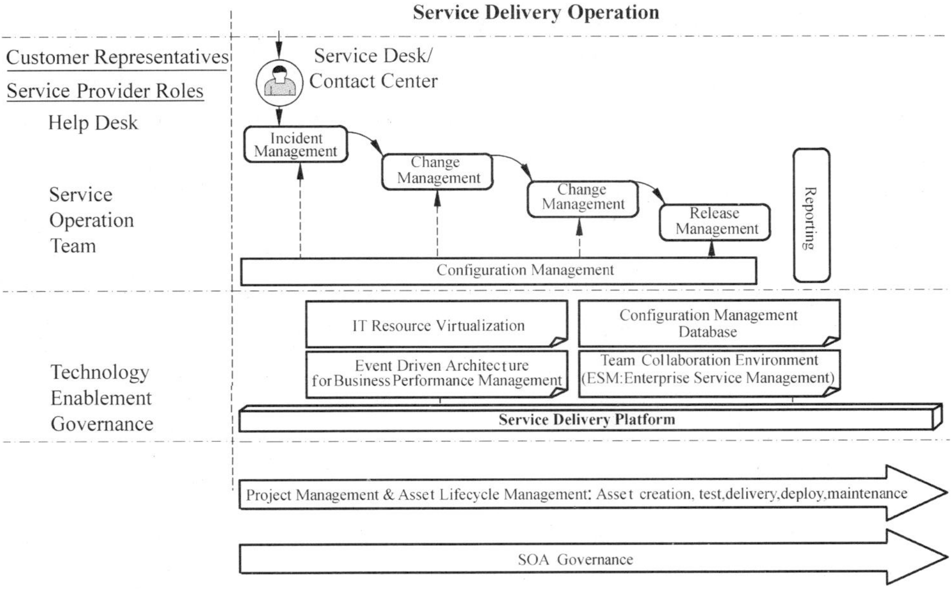

Figure 16.8 Business processes for Services Delivery Operation

Crossing all these phases, there could be focal points from the service provider side and from the customer side in order to improve mutual communication between the two parties. In a loosely coupled services delivery environment, the traditional project management methods are not enough to secure the execution of the project. The collaborative teams should follow the same principle: Service-Oriented Architecture, it's not simply an IT architecture but should cover business architecture, information architecture, IT operational architectures, etc.

Services delivery platform in this phase provides several important platform services, e.g., capacity planning services for service scale out, helpdesk, IT service management processes (like those covered by ITIL). These are enabled with IT resource virtualization technologies, service management collaboration tools, event-driven architecture for business performance management, etc.

16.5 Discussions on the Services Delivery Methodology and Platform

Services delivery is a key phase in the whole service lifecycle. It goes beyond software development, system integration, or even projects. Modern services delivery processes often rely on efficient infrastructures and tools. As shown in this chapter, an efficient services delivery platform could greatly facilitate innovation of business services, by composing distributed business services and IT services. However, since both the business environment and the IT technologies are evolving, new challenges are keeping on arising.

For example, different businesses may require different preferences, while the mission of a services delivery platform intends to solve common problems and provide common services delivery methods. As a result, a way is needed to quickly generate customized service solutions for different customers. Beyond that, a services delivery platform should not only fulfill functional requirements but also non-functional requirements—different Service Level Agreements (SLAs). Moreover, since a services delivery process covers design, delivery, and operation, a common model of the customer's service business may be helpful to track the variations from any of the three phases and analyze their impacts on other phases.

16.6 Summary

In this chapter, we introduced an end-to-end services delivery platform and a formalized service deivery. It is noted that a services delivery platform may interact with other services delivery platforms based on needs. A way of implementing services delivery platform is Hub-type of deployment environment. The collaboration among Hubs is another reflection of service-ecosystem from delivery perspective. The realization example consists of centralized membership portal with services registry synchronization for rapid registration, subscription, and provisioning of business services, as well as central connection and control security model for participating businesses and users to access services. In addition, as an business process outsourcing platform, the Managed e-Hub enables users to dynamically configure a business process based on incoming requirements using the Hub-hosted services or registered services provided by other outsourcing service providers.

The case study of establishing an online fashion store demonstrates the following services delivery and integration features of using the services delivery platform: (1) rapid on-boarding of businesses, users and services, (2) business process management, (3) dynamic business process composition, (4) advanced discovery and invocation of business services published in services registries, (5) service access control.

References

[1] Google. http://www.google.com
[2] Amazon.com. http://www.amazon.com
[3] Salesforce. http://www.salesforce.com/

[4] Friedman TL (2006) The World Is Flat: A Brief History of the Twenty-first Century. Farrar Straus Giroux

[5] Model Driven Architecture. http://www.mda.org

[6] Zhang LJ, Chang H, Chao T, Chung JY, Tian Z, Xu J, Zuo Y, Yang S (2002) A manageable Web services hub framework and enabling technologies for e-sourcing. In: 2002 IEEE International Conference on Systems, Man and Cybernetics, pp 6 – 9

[7] Xu JM, Zuo YN, Yang SX, Tian Z, Chang H, Zhang LJ (2003) Membership portal and service provisioning system for an infrastructure of Hubs: Managed e-Hub. In: 2003 International Conference on Enterprise Information Systems, pp 143 – 150

[8] Commerce OOG (2000) ITIL Complete Library (Book Format) (OGC Best Practice Series). The Stationery Office

[9] Duftler MJ, Mukhi NK, Slominski A, Weerawarana S (2001) Web Services Invocation Framework (WSIF). http://www.research.ibm.com/people/b/bth/OOWS2001/duftler.pdf

[10] SOAPClient.http://soapclient.com

[11] Zhang LJ, Chao T (2001) Business Explorer for Web Services (BE4WS). http://www.alphaworks.ibm.com/tech/be4ws

[12] VMWare. http://www.vmware.com/

[13] Dynamic logical partitioning (LPAR). http://www-03.ibm.com/servers/eserver/iseries/lpar/

17 Software as Services and Services as Software

17.1 Software as Services

Over the last several decades, software has become an integral part of all government, military, and business systems. After enabled by SOA and Web services, software systems have become more flexible, extensible, and scalable. When such an SOA-enabled software system is deployed on the Web, any users who have access to the Internet can access the software system and consume the provided services from the Internet. Such a typical scenario represents a rapidly emerging computing and business model: *Software as Services*.

In short, Software as Services represents a model that supports services delivery without buying stand alone software packages. The key idea of the model is to expose software solutions, including features and capabilities, to users over either Internet or Intranet. One of the successful examples of realizing the model of Software as Services is Salesforce.com[1].

Salesforce was originated as an online Customer Relationship Management (CRM) software provider. Starting from 2005, Salesforce has been heading toward a Software as Services provider by offering "*AppExchange*", which is an online development platform with a comprehensive set of Web services-based interfaces for open community members to quickly develop new services.

In many ways, *AppExchange* is a significant contribution of software industry, as it can be viewed as equivalents to the next generation of several present dominant software products and platforms: Operating Systems, database management systems (DBMS), and software development platforms. Similar to an Operating System, *AppExchange* offers facilities to manage resources and provides Human Computer Interfaces (HCI). Similar to a DBMS, *AppExchange* provides a standard API to manage databases. Similar to a software development platform, *AppExchange* provides an integrated development environment (IDE) carrying a comprehensive set of templates for engineers to quickly develop applications without starting everything from scratch. Salesforce's vision is that all applications will be delivered and used online through the Internet. This is Google's vision[2] as well.

One key success factor of Software as Services is how to effectively and efficiently deliver software systems as services. To date, the realization of Software as Services has gone through two phases. The first phase is to use Web technologies to transform a software system into a Web application, which can be accessed by individuals from the Internet or Intranet. Typical examples are Google searching services, Amazon.com shopping services, and PayPal online payment services. The second phase is to leverage SOA and Web services technologies to transform existing software systems into Web services, which can be accessed by programs and integrated into other business processes. In addition, new Web services can be quickly established by leveraging multiple existing software systems or services from different sources. Recently, traditional service providers have been working on delivering Web services, in addition to their Web applications. For example, Google, Amzaon.com, and PayPal all have announced their Web services interfaces, so that their searching, shopping, and payment services can also be reached by programs without going through Web pages.

The services delivery platform introduced in Chapter 16 provides an example of suitable platform and a systematic approach to enable and facilitate the delivery of SOA-based services from software components. In recent years, a new technique called Web 2.0 is emerging to provide an open, collaborative platform to deliver software as services.

17.1.1 Next Generation of Internet: Web 2.0

Web 2.0 represents a collection of the next-generation technologies over the Internet. In contrast with other services delivery methods, the tenet of Web 2.0 is "complete openness." In detail, its openness is four-fold. First, Web 2.0 introduces a concept of "open community": users and partners can participant in Web 2.0 to collaborate in a loosely regulated manner for a common business goal. Second, feedbacks and improvements all go through online approaches and become available to participants instantaneously. Third, Web 2.0 encourages people to leverage open-source software components. Fourth, Web 2.0 is mainly built on open standards. With such an open framework, Web 2.0 intends to greatly save the cost and time needed for services delivery and services development[3].

Figure 17.1 illustrates the key ideas of Web 2.0. Aiming at providing an open platform for open community users to collaborate on, Web 2.0 relies on open standards and technologies as foundations. Web 2.0 is enabled by its core *enabling platform* that comprises six major components: *business requirements repository*, *shared context*, *value-added manager*, *relationship manager*, *collaborators*, and *collaboration space*. For a specific business purpose, a shared context is formed based on particular business requirements. As shown in Fig. 17.1, Web 2.0 is managed by two key control components: a value-added manager and a relationship manager, each interacting with the shared context to be aware of specific business requirements. The value-added manager evaluates and assesses included software components or service components to ensure that they add values to the ultimate service to be delivered. The relationship manager handles the relationships between composed software components and service components to ensure that they comply with some predefined rules and policies.

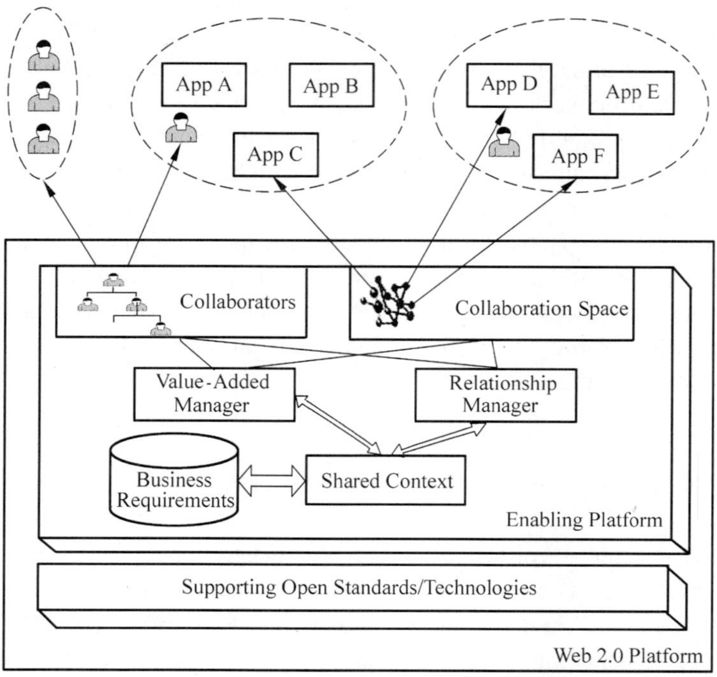

Figure 17.1 Basic concepts of Web 2.0

As shown in Fig. 17.1, Web 2.0 is oriented to open community; collaborators may come from different communities and organizations. Meanwhile, software components used in Web 2.0 may be produced and published by various organizations or communities. They can be either open-source or associated with fees. Web 2.0 allows various collaborators to participate in the collaboration, while organizes them with an internal hierarchy tree for proper management. With collaborators organized, Web 2.0 provides a collaboration space to enable collaborators to cooperate on a shared work product to be delivered as an ultimate service. As shown in Fig. 17.1, the components of the service product may be software components or service components coming from various communities or organizations.

As shown in Fig. 17.1, Web 2.0 is an SOA-based services delivery model that eliminates risks for both service providers and service consumers. From the service provider's perspective, a Web 2.0-based services delivery process can be rapidly conducted by composing existing software and service components with a comprehensive set of tools on a standard development platform. Therefore, risks on development and testing are largely reduced. From the service consumer's perspective, a Web 2.0-based service is accessed and consumed remotely without installing and testing on local environments. Therefore, risks on installation and testing are largely reduced.

In summary, Web 2.0-based Software as Services delivery features the following four patterns: *the long tail, rich information architecture, user-involved value creation process*, and *open collaboration*.

The long tail means that with open technologies and open communities, the "small applications" that used to be too small to be developed by large companies but too big for individuals can now be developed by Web 2.0 open community. Figure 17.2 shows the importance for supporting long-tail applications. The long-tail applications typically serve more targeted audiences that cannot afford distribution or infrastructure. As shown in Fig. 17.2, the number of long-tail applications largely exceeds the number of other applications, including mass-market applications that occupy a large number of users, as well as niche applications that bear low cost or provide added functionality to appeal to specific audiences.

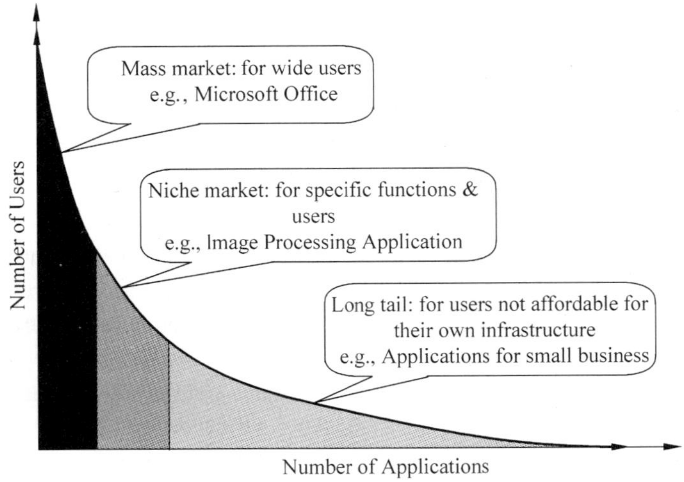

Figure 17.2 Importance for supporting long-tail applications

Rich information architecture means that Web 2.0-based services are typically composed of a set of services encapsulating comprehensive data and associated data management facilities. For example, the open service "Google House" is constructed based on the Google Map data using the so-called "Mash-up" technology, which seamlessly integrates Google data with house information and leads to a completely new type of service. It should be noted that Google data are handled by Google Map; Google House merely use the data without any control over them.

User-involved value creation process means that participants do not just passively accept what they get; instead, they can actively participate in the design and development process. For example, each participant can "tag" the contents (i.e., a kind of self-categorization process) and associate the contents with their defined semantics.

Open collaboration implies weak control over collaboration (at least theoretically). Since Web 2.0 is built upon open community, the services and development process should be regulated in a loose manner. The open community works in a way of cooperation.

17.1.2 A Case Study of Web 2.0 Service Model—Service Mash-up

This section shows an example of leveraging Web 2.0 to quickly deliver software as services. Wikipedia[4], the largest reference Web site in the world, provides a free encyclopedia that anyone can edit. Wikipedia provides a set of simple *wiki* commands for users to compose services or software components, as well as client code. This Web 2.0-based service composition process is called a "mash-up." Wikipedia defines a "mash-up" as follows:

> *"A mash-up is a website or Web application that uses content from more than one source to create a completely new service. Content used in mashups is typically sourced from a third party via a public interface or API. Other methods of sourcing content for mashups include Web feeds (e.g., RSS or Atom) and JavaScript."*

Figure 17.3 shows an example of a mashed-up application[4] that seamlessly integrates multiple Web services, software applications, and client code. At the top is a list of stores owned by a franchise. The application leverages two live Web services: a Google map service and a NOAA weather service. The new application utilizes Really Simple Syndication (RSS) feeds to obtain top-selling items from the stores shown on the top of Fig. 17.3. An SAP order application shows order progress. All these components are mashed-up using simple wiki commands.

As shown in Fig. 17.3, the mash-up of software applications results in aggregated services not quite envisioned when the individual applications were written. Before aggregation, these applications may be provided by different service providers, with different business models, technologies, and different user experiences. This requires that the users switch between different user interfaces in a complex way to complete a service. With the Web 2.0 mash-up technology, users can now only visit one portal, which seamlessly integrates the pieces of services from different providers, without knowing where the services come from. The service is thus fulfilled in a consistent manner.

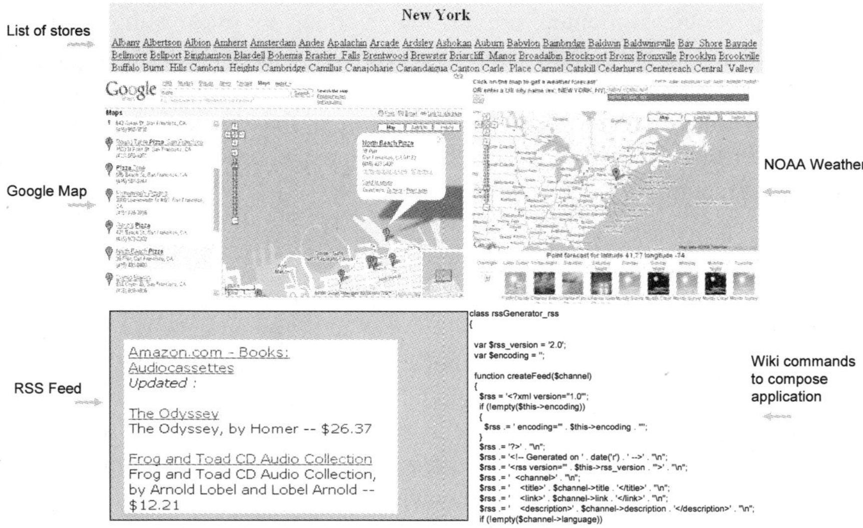

Figure 17.3 Service mash-up enabled by Web 2.0 technologies

17.1.3 New Business Models Through Software as Services

As shown in Fig. 17.2, the model Software as Services has big advantages and potential to enter the long-tail application business, which can hardly be covered by the traditional service model that is propriety, labor-based, and heavy- weighted.

As introduced earlier, Salesforce.com is a good example of exploring one niche market: CRM service. To date, CRM service is still the main competency of Salesforce.com. In recent years, with *AppExchange*, and its associated ecosystems (i.e., the open development community and the Small and Media business), Salesforce.com enters a variety of other Software as Services application markets, such as Human Resource Management (HRM), Enterprise Resource Planning (ERP), Finance and Accounting (F&A), and Office Automation (OA). With the support of their services, users in these markets no longer need to purchase software products and run them on physical machines. Instead, the users can "subscribe" to Salesforce.com services by paying monthly fees.

In addition, users can utilize and integrate the services provided to start their new small businesses. Salesforce.com provides a special payment business model for small business owners. When a business is small, its owner pays for a small number of subscribers, say 5 subscribers. Later on, when the business grows, the owner can increase the number of subscribers to be supported and pay more. In short, Salesforce.com allows scalable IT investment. This business model is highly welcomed by small businesses, and that is one of the reasons why Salesforce.com model is successful today.

Based on their success, Salesforce.com intends to become the next "eBay" in

Software as Services-oriented application market, by motivating individual buyers and sellers to participate in the marketplace to play. Recall that Chapter 1 introduces a business model adopted by Amazon.com, which is also a marketplace model based on Amazon.com Web services and the Amazon.com platform. Comparing to that model, Salesforce.com adopts the "open community" base, which may attract many more developers and users.

17.1.4 Tips for Software as Services Model

The model of Software as Services is nevertheless not a silver bullet. In order to well exploit the model, the following guidelines should be kept in mind.

- A Web 2.0 platform owner needs to protect the IP rights of involved developers. Since the platform intends to support open community, it is possible that some participants may wish to protect their privacy.
- A Software as Services project needs to be well managed about its route to market and corresponding channels. Like any new business model, Software as Services is still a new type of service that demands a proper way to market.
- There is need for more killer applications. To date, CRM is still the most dominant Software as Services application that attracts most users. In order for it to be adopted by more users, the model Software as Services needs to take into consideration business requirements from various potential service requestors.

17.2 Services as Software

Currently, there is another rapidly emerging trend aiming to transform services into software. The concept refers to transforming the current consulting experiences into software products, which can be shared by others. Assume that an experienced consultant, who has three critical cases at hand, has to take a week of sick days off. Her absence may directly cause delay of services to the three critical clients. If a new employee is hired to temporarily take over the consultant's position when she is unavailable, the problem is that the new colleague may need months of training before being able to face clients independently. This example illustrates one big issue as how to modernize consulting services or generic services delivery from knowledge sharing and transfer perspective.

Conceptually, the solution to this issue is not that complicated. One can incorporate the experiences and knowledge of the professionals and experts into software, and leverage the software to help realize and manage consulting (or in general, business) flow. Thus, a consulting process turns into a consulting service based on computer software. Such a new form of service industry has a library of software components encapsulating knowledge and expertise of business consultants. These software components can be reused and integrated together into new reusable components. By rapidly constructing a services delivery process using the re-configurable and reusable software components, the consulting services can be greatly facilitated. In this way, the original labor-based service industries can be transformed into asset-based service businesses.

Figure 17.4 illustrates a two-phase "Services as Software" model, which includes services software development phase and services software delivery phase.

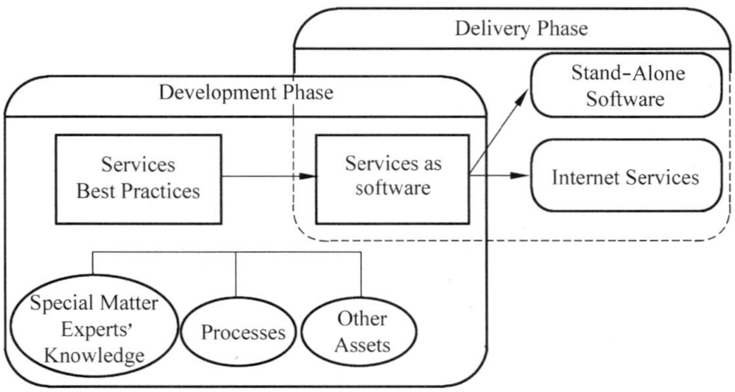

Figure 17.4 Two phases of Services as Software Model

In the development phase, services software models and implements the information architecture and processes extracted from the best services practices, which include special matter experts' knowledge, services governance processes, as well as other useful assets such as architectures, design documents, services delivery materials, training courses, and sales materials. Once the services software is developed, the delivery phase starts. Services software is shipped as a stand-alone software toolkit or delivered as an Internet service.

17.3 Successful Business Cases

Transforming services into software can not only make the services more easily grasped by novices, but also expedite the service processes. As shown in Fig. 17.5, Efutong.com (http://www.efutong.com), a leading Services as Software service provider in China, integrates their years of consulting experiences, especially on Enterprise Performance Management services, into software, so as to deliver enterprise transformation and process improvement services more quickly. Some work that originally took one month to finish now can now be completed in days. It is worth noting that the consultants using the software do not have to be top-level consultants with dozens of years' experience. An example Enterprise

Performance Management Services platform is shown below. Dynamic business process configuration capability of its Enterprise Performance Management Service shown in Fig. 17.5 enables the seamless integration of project management and enterprise performance metrics.

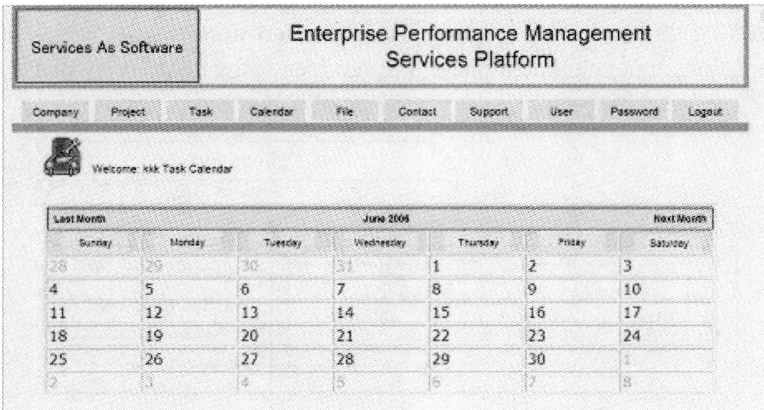

Figure 17.5 EPMS Portal Example

Services as Software and *Software as Services* are emerging in every industry. It is transforming not just individual companies, but also entire industries themselves. Typical examples are the insurance industry and the finance industry.

In the insurance industry, an insurance company tracks customer driving information in real-time. Software integrates telematics data with its collected services delivery excellences to create premiums based on individual driving behavior. In the finance industry, a financial trading house manages complex global risk in real-time based on finance services experience.

The following sub-sections will illustrate several additional successful business cases representing Services as Software and Software as Services: healthcare under transformation, future store, personalized insurance premiums, and business performance transformation services.

17.3.1 Healthcare Under Transformation

Reform has a high demand in the healthcare industry. According to a 2005 survey, most patients still need to fill out paper forms when they visit doctors; sharing test results among a patient's multiple doctors is still mostly through a manual process; medical mistakes (e.g., incorrect diagnosis and prescription) are still identified as the eighth leading cause of death. All of these medical inefficiencies put a huge financial burden on consumers, physicians, insurers, and the entire healthcare industry.

Taking innovative steps, healthcare organizations collaborate with software corporations to build ecosystems towards an adaptive health information infrastructure, which improves patient care and reduces medical error and costs while protecting patient privacy. Figure 17.6 illustrates a typical medical ecosystem. The greatest medical minds are joined to treat illnesses and cure diseases. These ecosystems typically focus on the realm of patient histories. Supported by an adaptive business solution, medical organizations integrate their millions of patient records into a unified system with robust security and privacy. Such a system increases exponentially its ability to sift through demographics, diagnostics, and laboratory results from its vast data warehouse. Searches that once took months are completed in a matter of minutes. Adopting new techniques, these systems further enhance their abilities to analyze patient records to improve diagnoses, deep computing power to model diseases to find cures, and new information access devices to transform how patients and physicians interact. As a result, doctors can quickly obtain patients' historical information; provide appropriate prescriptions, so as to cure patients quickly. In one word, medicine can thus become less about the science of trial-and-error but more about the art of healing.

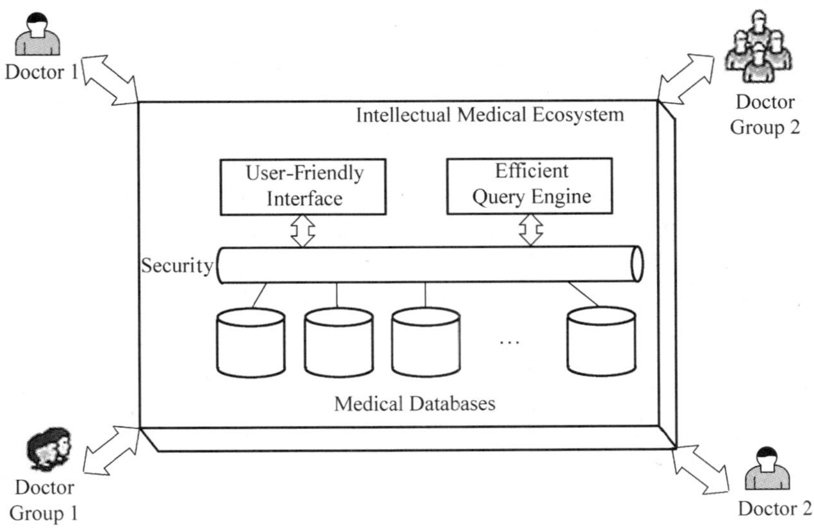

Figure 17.6 A typical medical ecosystem

This transformation solution is a typical "Software as Services" play from delivery perspective because the solution is mainly created to provide information access services for the partners in the ecosystem. On the other hand, the development of this adaptive medical solution can be categorized into "Services as Software" because it incorporates lots of doctor's expertise.

17.3.2 Innovative Store

A new business model emerges for the retail industry. Radio Frequency Identification (RFID) technology[5] is exploited to enhance the shopping experience and sales. Real-time inventory monitoring can largely raise customer satisfaction.

Large retailers partner with software corporations on innovative technologies and integration for their innovative store initiative, which is a model of the "sense and respond" enterprise. Figure 17.7 illustrates a typical RFID-based intelligent store. New technologies are explored to introduce new services, control in-stock availability, increase per-transaction revenue, improve supply chain processes, and enhance the overall customer experience.

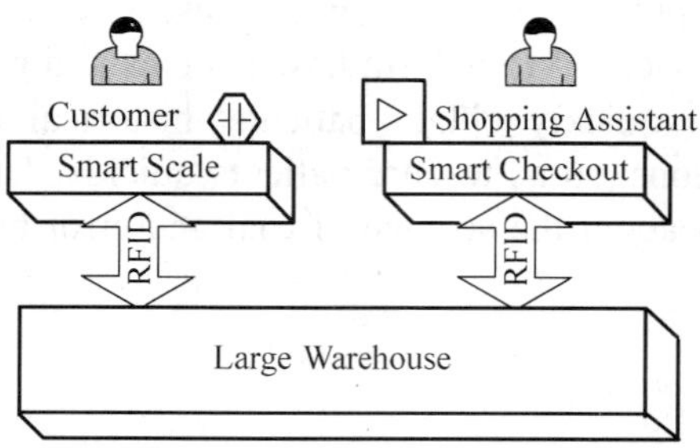

Figure 17.7 RFID-based intelligent store

RFID technology is typically rolling throughout the entire supply chain[6]. A camera-equipped "intelligent scale" can recognize fruits and vegetables being weighed; a "Smartshelves" system tracks items in real time from warehouse to stock room, to shelf, and to checkout; a Personal Shopping Assistant recalls past shopping lists and prompts based on shopping history; shoppers have several check-out options: their Personal Shopping Assistant, a self-checkout kiosk, or a traditional register.

This solution is a typical "Services as Software" play because the solution is mainly used by the retail stores. If the services are delivered to the Internet users, then it becomes "Software as Services" model.

17.3.3 Personalized Insurance Premiums

In the insurance industry, gaining real-time information on customer driving patterns provides the basis for a more informed, more profitable pricing strategy. Everybody knows about the importance and necessity of automobile insurance.

Traditionally, in the US and in almost all other countries, an individual insurance policy is mainly based on four categories of information: a person's personal information, the status of the automobile to be insured, the prediction of automobile usage patterns, and the residual environment. A person's personal information includes driving records, age, marriage status, the number of children to support, household income, occupation, employer, and the number of years of the driver's license obtainment. The status of an automobile includes its make, model, year, mileages used, and years used. A driving pattern of an automobile includes predicted daily mileage, yearly mileage, and so on. Residual environment information refers to the neighborhood environment, whether it is in a suburb or in a city or in a distant countryside.

Based on this information, an insurance agent provides an initial evaluation, and the person pays monthly insurance fees, such as $100. This monthly fee never changes until some above criteria change, for example, the person gets married or moves to another neighborhood. Even though the person will not use the automobile in one month at all because of a business trip, he/she still has to pay the monthly auto insurance.

The new model uses a dynamic model instead of the traditional static model, as shown in Fig. 17.8. A person's insurance payment stays at zero if the automobile is not used. The actual payment is based on a person's driving patterns, such as the number of mileage of driving distance and road conditions. This model is obviously suitable for most people. Of course, it may not be very suitable to youngsters since they might like to drive long distance that leads to high insurance payments. This novel Internet-based business model in the insurance industry has been attracting significant attentions.

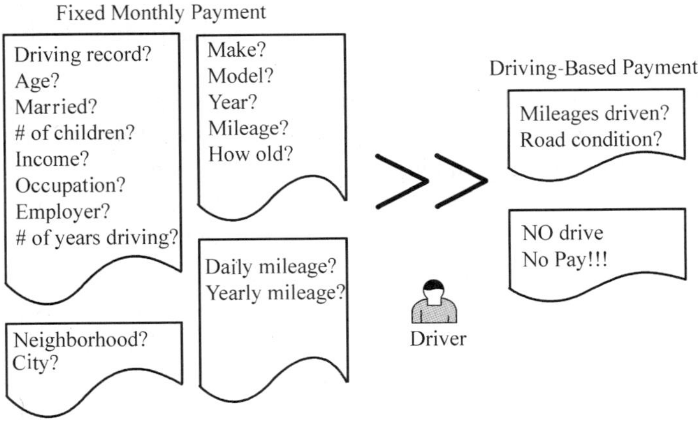

Figure 17.8 New driving-based insurance model

Some insurance organizations have been cooperating with IT corporations to replace their original "broad-brush" pricing strategies with personalized, user-driven pricing by gaining real-time information on customer driving patterns. This new technology provides actuaries with a wealth of data on which to base their premiums, in addition to their traditional focus merely on the model of the vehicle, and the age, location and driving record of the policyholder. A black box, combining small computing devices with Global Positioning System (GPS) and wireless technology, is installed in vehicles to transmit data back and forth with vehicles in motion. The information gathering is based on when, where, and how a car is driven, instead of the make and model or the address where the car is registered. Obtained data depict how a car is actually used, as well as which factors can be used to form the basis for "pay as you drive" rates. Case studies have proven that the new insurance model attracts more customers and leads to higher profits. This is a typical win-win case: policy holders enjoy flexible rates, and insurance companies use this technology to offer additional services to drive revenues and retain customers.

This solution is a typical "Services as Software" play because the pricing solution is mainly used by the insurance companies or agents. If the pricing services are delivered to the Internet users, then it becomes "Software as Services" model.

17.3.4 Business Performance Transformation Services

On-Demand Business acts as a catalyst to an expansion of the traditional IT industry. Driven by open standards, pervasive technology, and innovative business models merged with advanced IT and research capabilities, many traditional businesses are under transformation by leveraging "economies of expertise". As shown in Fig. 17.9, in general, these enterprises adopt the following three strategies: optimize the enterprise by transforming business processes, leverage the in-depth skills of professional services, and enable the infrastructure with innovative technologies.

All of these three strategies are deeply rooted in the Services Computing technology. Businesses develop new services and capabilities in very different ways than in the past, by taking advantages of available services, either self-developed or obtained from the Internet. Business processes that were once vertical are moving to a far more integrated level of enterprise-wide change. This integrated, enterprise-level performance is required for businesses and governments to deal with volatile new markets and competitive and economic realities. Meanwhile, clients are fundamentally shifting the ways they allocate their budgets. Money spent internally today will be spent externally in the future. This is happening across many industries.

Based on the Services Computing-supported strategies, various industries have been collaborating with IT corporations to rewrite or transform their legacy systems for higher customer satisfaction and lower IT costs. For example, a corporation can exploit Services Computing technology to revise their entire customer care operations, including people, processes, and technology. For another example, a corporation can streamline its human resources processes by reusing many of its legacy systems to build new business processes.

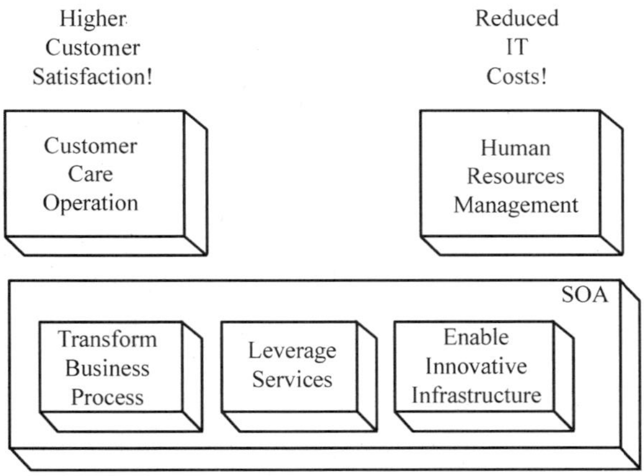

Figure 17.9 SOA-supported business transformation

This business performance transformation capability is enabled by *Services as Software* model. The services are delivered through "Software as Services" model.

17.4 Summary

In this chapter we introduced two innovative business models: Software as Services and Services as Software. Web 2.0 was introduced to illustrate the services aggregation from various sources using software technology. Then we introduced Services as Software that captures services best practices into software. A two-phase model of Services as Software was briefly introduced. Various successful examples from different industries illustrate the effectiveness and efficiency of the two business models.

References

[1] Salesforce. http://www.salesforce.com/
[2] Google Web Services. http://www.google.com/apis/
[3] Zhang LJ, Allam A, Gonzales CA (2006) Service-oriented order-to-cash solution with business RSS information exchange framework. In: IEEE International Conference on Web Services (ICWS 2006), Chicago, IL, USA, pp 841 – 848
[4] Wikipedia. http://en.wikipedia.org
[5] http://en.wikipedia.org/wiki/RFID
[6] Li H, Hung PCK, Zhang J, Ahn D (2006) Privacy issues of applying RFID in retail industry. International Journal of Cases on Electronic Commerce, 2(3): 33 – 52

Index